Tongue of Water, Teeth of Stones

Northern Irish Poetry and Social Violence

Jonathan Hufstader

THE UNIVERSITY
PRESS OF
KENTUCKY

Publication of this volume was made possible in part
by a grant from the National Endowment for the Humanities.

Scholarly publisher for the Commonwealth,
serving Bellarmine College, Berea College, Centre
College of Kentucky, Eastern Kentucky University,
The Filson Club Historical Society, Georgetown College,
Kentucky Historical Society, Kentucky State University,
Morehead State University, Murray State University,
Northern Kentucky University, Transylvania University,
University of Kentucky, University of Louisville,
and Western Kentucky University.

Editorial and Sales Offices: The University Press of Kentucky
663 South Limestone Street, Lexington, Kentucky 40508-4008

03 02 01 00 99   5 4 3 2 1

Library of Congress Cataloging-in-Publication Data

Hufstader, Jonathan, 1939-
    Tongue of water, teeth of stones : Northern Irish poetry and
social violence / Jonathan Hufstader.
        p.   cm.—(Irish literature, history, and culture)
    Includes bibliographical references (p.   ) and index.
    ISBN 0-8131-2106-X (alk. paper)
    1. English poetry—Northern Ireland—History and
criticism. 2. Literature and society—Northern Ireland—
History—20th century. 3. English poetry—Irish authors—
History and criticism. 4. Northern Ireland—In literature.
5. Social problems in literature. 6. Violence in literature.
I. Title. II. Series.
PR8761.H84   1999
821´.914099416—dc21   99-13689

For Janis,
 Becky,
 and
 Susannah

CONTENTS

ACKNOWLEDGMENTS

I owe a large debt of thanks to Helen Vendler of Harvard University for helping me start this book, and to Jonathan Allison of the University of Kentucky for helping me to finish it. Lee Jacobus and J.D. O'Hara, my colleagues at the University of Connecticut, read parts of the manuscript and made helpful comments. Thanks to the "Wednesday group" of the University of Connecticut English Department for listening patiently to early segments of the book and for offering unexpected and rewarding insights. Thanks to Robert Cardish, who introduced me to the writings of Heinz Kohut. Thanks to Ellen O'Brien, who helped me to learn about McGuckian, and to all my other fellow students of poetry and friends who have encouraged and assisted me. Joanna Juzwik McDonald brought her unerring eye and unfailing good judgment to the editorial process. Greatest thanks of all to the three to whom this book is dedicated; without them, these pages would still be blank.

Citations from Gerald Dawe, *The Rest is History* (Dublin: The Abbey Press, 1998), are made with permission of the author.

Citations from Seamus Heaney, "Death of a Naturalist," "The Tollund Man," "The Grauballe Man," "Strange Fruit," "Kinship," "Whatever You Say Say Nothing," "Casualty," "Station Island," "Clearance," "The Mud Vision," "Weighing In," "The Flight Path,"

"Mycenae Lookout," "Tollund," and *Crediting Poetry: The Nobel Lecture* (Copyright © 1995 by The Nobel Foundation) are reprinted by permission of Farrar, Straus & Giroux, Inc. Aforementioned poems appear in *Selected Poems 1966-1987* (Copyright © 1990 by Seamus Heaney) and *The Spirit Level* (Copyright © 1996 by Seamus Heaney). Citations from "Cauled," "Sweet William," and "The Discharged Soldier" are made with permission of Ulsterman Publications and with the kind permission of the author. Citations from *Stations* are made with the kind permission of the author.

Citations from Michael Longley, "Fleance," "Wounds," "The Linen Workers," "Edward Thomas's War Diary," "The War Poets," epigraph to *An Exploded View,* "Argos," "Ceasefire," are made with the permission of the Wake Forest University Press and the author. "Argos" appears in *Gorse Fires,* "Ceasefire" appears in *Ghost Orchid,* and all the others appear in *Poems, 1963-1983,* published by Wake Forest University Press. Citations from Michael Longley, *Tupenny Stung,* are made with permission of the author.

Citations from Derek Mahon, "Ecclesiastes," "Afterlives," "The Snow Party," "A Disused Shed in Co. Wexford," "Autobiographies," are from Derek Mahon, *Selected Poems,* (1991), by permission of Oxford University Press. Citations from "The Hunt by Night" and "Courtyards in Delft" from *The Hunt by Night*; from "An Bonnan Bui" and "Death in Bangor" from *The Yellow Book,* with the permission of Wake Forest University Press.

Citations from Paul Muldoon, "October, 1950," "Cuba," "Something of a Departure," "Anseo," "Immram," "Why Brownlee Left" from *Why Brownlee Left*; "Clonfeacle," "Lunch with Pancho Villa," "The Mixed Marriage" are taken from *Mules and Other Poems*; "A Trifle," "Quoof," "The More a Man Has the More a Man Wants," "The Frog" from *Quoof*; "October, 1950," "Cuba," "Something of a

Departure," "Anseo," "Immram," "Why Brownlee Left" from *Why Brownlee Left*; "Meeting the British," "Sushi," "The Soap-Pig," "7, Middagh Street" from *Meeting the British,* with permission of Wake Forest University Press. Citations from *The Prince of the Quotidian* are with permission of Wake Forest University Press. Citations from Paul Muldoon, "The Birth," "Sonogram" (*The Annals of Chile,* Copyright © 1994 by Paul Muldoon) are reprinted by permission of Farrar, Straus & Giroux, Inc.

Citations from Tom Paulin, "The Caravans on Lüneburg Heath," "In the Lost Province," "Before History," "The Strange Museum," "The Book of Juniper," "Presbyterian Study," "Desertmartin," "Father of History," "Politik," "Of Difference Does it Make," "Now for the Orange Card," "Fivemiletown," "L," are from Tom Paulin, *Selected Poems 1972–1990,* and are made with permission of Faber and Faber, Ltd.

Citations from C.K. Williams, "My Mother's Lips" (*Selected Poems,* Copyright © 1994 by C.K. Williams), are reprinted by permission of Farrar, Straus, & Giroux, Inc.

Citations from Ciarán Carson, "Belfast Confetti," "Slate Street School," from *The Irish for No*; from "Queen's Gambit," "Last Orders," "Jawbox," "Question Time" from *Belfast Confetti*; from "Two to Tango," "The Ballad of HMS Belfast," "Ovid: *Metamorphoses*, XIII, 576-619" from *First Language*; from "Zulu" from *Opera et Cetera,* with the permission of Wake Forest University Press.

Citations from Medbh McGuckian, "Venus and the Rain" from *Venus and the Rain*; from "Captain Lavender," "The Appropriate Moment," "Field Heart," "Elegy for an Irish Speaker," "The Aisling Hat," "Flirting with Saviours," "The Colour Shop," "Dividing the Political Temperature" from *Captain Lavender,* with the permission of Wake Forest University Press.

1

INTRODUCTION

In "Clonfeacle," an early poem published in 1973, Paul Muldoon writes of a river where Saint Patrick is said to have washed: "A tongue of water passing / Between teeth of stones."[1] Over half a century earlier, Yeats had also written of streams and stones:

> Hearts with one purpose alone
> Through summer and winter seem
> Enchanted to a stone
> To trouble the living stream.[2]

In Yeats's poem, the stream stood for the vibrant, changing life of nature and art; the stone represented the fixed ideology of those bent on violence to achieve their ends, a menace of fixity and death lurking at the bottom of the stream. Muldoon's lines, although drawn from a poem concerned with religion and sexuality rather than political issues, provide a sense of the language in which Northern Irish poets since 1966 have responded to the social chaos and violence euphemistically referred to as the Troubles. Yeats saw the stream and said the stone was hidden; in the poem about 1916, social violence still only lurked as a threat to civility and the natural course of life. Muldoon sees stones everywhere and just a tongue of water passing over them. There is no longer anything hidden about rigid ideologies of violence. The living stream of poetic speech now takes the form of a tongue which depends for its utterance on the surrounding teeth of stones.

In the late sixties and early seventies, two widely different sets of events occurred in Northern Ireland: an outbreak of social violence and a flowering of fine poetry. Both violence and poetry have continued on their divergent but chronologically parallel courses through the seventies and eighties. One can only hope to see the former die out and the latter continue to prosper by the century's end. No one that I know supposes a causal connection of violence to poetry (still less the other way around); either one could have developed without the other. Yet no one would deny the effect that the Troubles have had on Northern Irish poetry. The problem is to determine exactly what that effect has been, or rather to determine how poetry has most effectively dealt with violence within its artistic domain.

This problem has provoked considerable debate in the last decade. The school of thought associated with Seamus Deane and Field Day views poetry as part of a larger body of discourse, including political prose, to be interpreted in the perspectives of post-colonial theory. One thinks also, despite their differences from Deane, of David Lloyd and Clair Wills. This view denies poetry's traditional claim to a separate, nonhistorical status with its own aesthetic rules of interpretation and its privileging of subjectivity. That Arnoldian idea of art, it is argued, was just another product of a repressive colonial politics. Post-colonial criticism largely rejects Heaney's idea of poetry as a humanistic defense or redress of the civilized self against barbaric violence.

Another school of thought, sometimes calling itself revisionist and including Edna Longley, Peter McDonald and Gerald Dawe among its champions, opposes the work of those who read poetry in search of some coherent theoretical narrative, be it Marxist, nationalist or post-colonial. Revisionist critics, in their turn, read poetry in search of deconstructive styles which dismantle theoretical narratives and return to the intractability of poetic details. For them the best Northern Irish poetry demonstrates "a distrust of the tendencies towards coherence which narrative generates" (for "narrative," read "Marxist or post-colonial theory").[3]

It is not my intention to enter these debates. The respective merits of unionist and nationalist positions, whatever they may be, go unjudged in these pages. Theoretical approaches that read poetry as either embodying or deconstructing some form of political statement provide us with much illuminating commentary, but they limit our awareness of what poetry, as poetry, can do. No good poem, not even a good political poem, succeeds by making statements, however obliquely. In this book I offer an alternative approach to contemporary Northern Irish poetry by examining its artistic enactments of inner conflicts provoked by political forces. By redirecting our attention to the lyric voice, my focus on a speaking self runs counter to the postmodern method of considering texts as collections of language unconnected to any coherent personal sources. By listening more acutely to poetry, instead of analyzing it for concealed content, we can better understand its real significance and vigor within the context of a politically troubled culture.

According to Seamus Heaney in his Grasmere lecture of 1984, the earliest works that he and his contemporaries produced, several years before the killings began, were written in response to political conditions:

> The fact that a literary action was afoot was itself a new political condition, and the poets did not feel the need to address themselves to the specifics of politics because they assumed that the tolerances and subtleties of their art were precisely what they had to set against the repetitive intolerance of public life. When Derek Mahon, Michael Longley, James Simmons and myself were having our first book published, Paisley was already in full sectarian cry and Northern Ireland's cabinet ministers regularly massaged the atavisms of Orangemen on the twelfth of July. Hair-raising bigotries were propounded and reported in the press as a matter of course and not a matter for comment.

Later in the lecture, he gives the thought a more personal coloring: "The idea of poetry was itself that higher ideal to which the poets unconsciously had turned in order to survive in the demeaning conditions, demeaned by resentment in the case of the Nationalist, by embarrassment at least and guilt at best in the case of the Unionists."[4] Had violence been the hidden stone, one would have had to point it out, but since stones were everywhere, nothing needed to be said about them. Poetry's best defense against stones was to write of, to be, the stream, thus providing some alternative language to the rhetoric of intolerance. Writing in such a world, says Heaney, lyric poets would become political poets, not so much by writing about politics as by being faithful to their lyric craft.[5]

Half concealed in this statement of poetic ideals—ideals which Heaney has maintained consistently and as recently as his Nobel Lecture—lies a statement of personal needs. By mentioning resentment, embarrassment, or guilt, and his unconscious personal attempts to resist them, Heaney lifts the curtain on the drama of contemporary Northern Irish poetry, a poetry in which the speaking persona undertakes self-fashioning in order to survive demeaning circumstances. Heaney, by his own account, has found such survival in the very fact of writing pure lyric, of countering agit-prop with art, of opposing transcendent to sectarian values, and of replacing atavistic rage with "the timeless formal pleasure" of the poem.[6] To say only this, however, is not to allow for more urgent personal needs, for the more deeply unconscious work of a lyric self beset by social violence. It is the critic's task, in reading the works of Northern Irish poets, to question their voices, asking what strategies they are developing for emotional survival, and how they represent these strategies in the formal techniques of lyric.

In *The Breaking of Style,* making specific reference to Heaney, Helen Vendler argues that changes of style constitute "an act of violence, so to speak, on the self."[7] My interest is in the stylistic ways in which seven poets seek to construct a self, one which will be responsive to political violence and yet be free from the self-destroying social atmospheres that generate such violence. When one examines the early work of almost all these poets, one does not see the cryptic mappings of political position which much criticism purports to discover, but rather the effort of a poetic persona to work free from the constraints of history. (The exception is the early McGuckian, who keeps her back turned on history until later in her career.) Having found such a poetic persona, they then initiate a breaking of style somewhere in mid-career, as various forces, whether objective (the intermittent cease-fires of the late nineties) or subjective (emigration, aging), raise new artistic problems and stimulate new, often brilliant solutions. In many cases, a writer's recent poems (those published since 1990) call into question and reinterpret that same writer's achievement in earlier, much anthologized work. It will be necessary, then, to examine the contours of each poet's artistic career, situating poetry along the trajectory of a changing poetic self.

Catholic Heaney and Protestants Longley and Mahon, the first two born in 1939 and the last in 1941, published their earliest works just prior to the first shootings and bombings: Heaney's *Death of a Naturalist* (1966) and *Door into the Dark* (1969); Longley's *No Continuing City* (1969); Mahon's *Night Crossing* (1968). With the outbreak of civic violence, punctuated by the Derry riots of 1969, the arrival of British troops, and the events of Bloody Sunday in January, 1972 (that year was to exceed all previous ones in bloodiness, with 10,628 shootings, 1,853 bombs planted, and 467 deaths), poetry began to deal more explicitly with those shocks to human sensibility which were occurring regularly in Northern Ireland.[8] Heaney's *Wintering Out* (1972) seeks survival strategies for a time of crisis, as its title implies, while Mahon's *Lives* (1972) explores imaginative alternatives to dreadful realities.

In the mid–seventies, Northern Irish poets began most explicitly to respond to the events of the province. 1974 was the year of the Sunningdale Agreement, the scheme for power–sharing among all rival factions in the governance of Northern Ireland which is widely thought to have been the single best hope for a settlement to the fighting prior to 1998, but which was soon sabotaged by loyalist strikes. Longley's *An Exploded View* had already appeared in 1973 when, in 1975, Heaney published both *Stations* and *North*, and Mahon published *The Snow Party*. In these works, the writers betray a sense of siege; they are striving to come to terms with crisis. It is the mid-point of their struggle.

I once considered arranging the chapters of this book not by authors, but as a chronology of style, showing how the various works of poetry published in 1972–73 served as prelude to those published in 1975–77—how, that is, poets were developing their responses to social chaos as the events of the seventies took their course. Although I rejected this plan as being unduly deterministic (and ever open to the rival claims of biography), I do still think that Heaney's progress from *Wintering Out* to *North* largely parallels Mahon's development from *Lives* to *The Snow Party*, and that both writers show another parallel development in the late seventies and early eighties. The appearances of Heaney's *Field Work* in 1979 and *Station Island* in 1984 correspond in some ways to Mahon's *Courtyards in Delft* (1981) and *The Hunt by Night* (1982). Both writers, having wrestled with violence in the mid–seventies, are now seeking to remove themselves from it. By 1987, Heaney in *The Haw Lantern* will view civic unrest from an even more distant perspective. With the prospect, if not the reality, of peace in Ulster in the mid–nineties, we see Heaney (in *The Spirit Level*) and Longley (in *The Ghost Orchid*) returning once again to issues of social chaos, trying once more to strike the right personal and poetic note.

In their early poetry, Catholic Muldoon (born 1955) and Protestant Paulin (born 1949) trace a curve of engagement with violence which partially follows that of Heaney and Mahon, except that it comes about five years later and exhibits very different contours. (Muldoon, the youngest but also the most precocious of these poets, published *New Weather* in 1973 at the age of 18; it is the collection in which "Clonfeacle" appeared.) *Mules* (1977) presents Muldoon's first sustained representations of violence, as does Paulin's first collection, *State of Justice* (1977). Both poets then develop their points of view in the early eighties, in works which explicitly deal with politics: Muldoon's *Why Brownlee Left* (1980) and *Quoof* (1983); Paulin's *Strange Museum* (1980), *Book of Juniper* (1982) and *Liberty Tree* (1983). By 1987, when Muldoon's *Meeting the British* and Paulin's *Fivemiletown* appear, both writers have consolidated their responses to violence and are moving in other directions. Here again, though, as in the cases of Heaney and Longley, Muldoon and Paulin will write new kinds of political poetry in the nineties—Muldoon, after *Madoc,* in *The Annals of Chile* and *The Prince of the Quotidian;* Paulin in *Walking a Line.*

The work of Ciarán Carson (born 1948) and Medbh McGuckian (born 1950) follows a still more recent chronology, in that they come to the poetry of social violence at a slightly later age. Carson's first collection, *The New Estate,* was published in 1976, but had no sequel for a period of eleven years, during which time Carson, as Traditional Arts Officer for the Arts Council of Northern Ireland, became an authority on traditional Irish music. In 1987 *The Irish for No* appeared, to be followed by *Belfast Confetti* in 1989. Since Carson is the most urban of these seven writers and his city is Belfast, one might expect his poems to present the

most vivid, on-the-street images of current events, and at first read-
ing this is what they seem to do. Perhaps because he is so close to
chaos, though, Carson in his poetry looks for ways to avoid being
a part of what he sees, using his well-known maps of Belfast war
zones and his long-lined, rambling pub talk as buffers, as ways of
distancing his self from his world.

Although McGuckian's first poems began to appear in the early
eighties, it is only in her fifth volume, *Captain Lavender* (1995),
that she turns to political poetry. Until then her poems were do-
mestic, intimate, erotic. Writing in *Captain Lavender* of the death
of her father and of her experiences teaching prisoners at Long
Kesh, McGuckian brings her unique voice—unique in Ulster for
being a major female poetic voice, unique also in her seemingly
self-absorbed style—into the larger chorus of poets dealing with
violence.

Not the least interesting matter to occupy us will be the marked
differences between the ways that members of the two generations
express artistic solutions to the problems of self-formation. Whereas
Heaney, Longley, and Mahon reflect the mentality of liberal mod-
ernism with its assumption of a unified consciousness, Muldoon,
Paulin, Carson, and McGuckian live in the philosophical and sty-
listic world of postmodernism, where selves and ideals, objects and
regions, traditions and discourses, are disintegrated into many frag-
ments. This is not to say that the latter four writers are any less
intent on self-formation than the former three or less concerned to
deal with violence as a threat to the self. It does, however, mean
that they approach these tasks with different assumptions and ex-
pectations, and accomplish them in different ways. It will therefore
be necessary to evaluate the functions of modern and postmodern
visions and voices as the differing means by which artists find ways
to forge identities in the midst of chaos.

As I was writing in late 1997, Northern Ireland had experi-
enced some temporary "exhaustions nominated peace" (the phrase
is Heaney's). Cease-fires had been announced, had prevailed for
some time, had been broken, and had been renewed, as rival fac-
tions jockeyed, or refused to jockey for position around a still hy-
pothetical peace table. Random sectarian murders occurred less
regularly in Ulster's cities and towns. Yet, as I finished the book in
the summer of 1998, the era of political killings had not ended.

"Even now there are places where a thought might grow": all of the poets studied here (with the exception of Mahon, who wrote the line just cited) have recently engaged themselves with social violence in new ways, have once again passed their tongues between teeth of stones.

The best Northern Irish political poems of the last thirty years confront politics without turning poetry into political statement. Instead they achieve lyric greatness without attempting to deny the political. As an illustration, let us consider two texts about daytime bomb alerts in Belfast. The first is "A Trifle," a sonnet by Muldoon published in 1983:

> I had been meaning to work through lunch
> the day before yesterday.
> Our office block is the tallest in Belfast;
> when the Tannoy sounds
>
> another bomb alert
> we take four or five minutes to run down
> the thirty-odd flights of steps
> to street level.
>
> I had been trying to get past
> a woman who held, at arm's length, a tray,
> and on the tray the remains of her dessert—
>
> a plate of blue-pink trifle
> or jelly sponge,
> with a dollop of whipped cream on top.[9]

The second is a prose passage by Gerald Dawe, first published in 1986. Dawe recounts a similar lunch-hour evacuation:

> We stood, almost humbly, on our lunch hour, waiting, perhaps silenced, under instructions, irrespective of political leanings, religious inclinations, loyalties or whatever, depersonalised like a group of prisoners until finally the bomb exploded, a mass of shattering glass spilling on

the ground, sundered brick sliding across the street to the squeals of women. Hesitantly at first, and then with more fluency, we went our separate ways. But just as the bomb went off, momentarily caught in the waves that plumbed the street, I saw a care-worn oldish woman, dressed in the usual sturdy, frayed overcoat and the workaday handbag, suddenly wince as if drowning in the sound of the explosion. Torn by its invisible pressure, she turned in a gasp into an image of pain like that in Munch's *The Scream*. I grasped then how oppression works its way right through our very bodies and buries in our souls a physical terror that debilitates and makes acceptable the imposition of any final order.[10]

These two texts, both written in the first person, recount a personal experience, whether fictive or reported, and both seek an image from a female bystander—Muldoon's trifle, Dawe's scream—in order to make sense of a threateningly absurd situation. Like the more journalistic prose passage, the poem makes sense only if we suppose the speaker to be a person who fears instant death. Although no bombs go off in the poem, the poet is in greater danger (Dawe is receiving instructions from a policeman); Muldoon's image therefore brings him to more graphic ideas about massacred bodies (jelly sponge, a dollop of whipped cream). Both texts recognize—the poem implicitly and the prose explicitly—that violence penetrates the person who experiences it and that the person must therefore find strategies for withstanding that penetration—even strategies that, like Muldoon's, exhibit their ineffectiveness in the face of those inescapable terrors which were a part of everyday Belfast life in the eighties.

Muldoon and his contemporaries address social forces in a lyric mode by their representations of a poetic persona or self. Because they are engaged in the poetic task of constructing a self—a complex of thoughts and feelings which may be inferred as the human origin of what is said—Northern Irish poets are implicitly engaged in politics. It is the "troubled self" which serves to unify the aesthetic virtuosity of Northern Irish poetry and the political concerns which pervade it. I propose to read the poems of Heaney, Longley, Mahon, Muldoon, Paulin, Carson, and McGuckian as exercises in soul-making, carried out under the pressures of sectarian conflict.

How do poems successfully represent social conflict without explicitly discussing it in the manner of prose? This question may be taken as a question about poetry, that is, of style, or as a question about social conflict, that is, of theory. Since we will be largely concerned with questions of style in the chapters ahead, I want to ask the more theoretical question here: what is it about social conflict that makes it a fit subject for lyric poetry?

In his structuralist analysis of religious sacrifice, René Girard begins with the assumption that social violence is endemic to social groups. Not originally imposed on people from an external enemy, it is rather a potent force urging itself upon us from within. This theory, one imagines, does not sit well with violent people, or with those who include violence within a theoretical "narrative," according to which violent actions are provoked by someone else. Northern nationalists, presumably, would prefer to trace the current bloodshed in Ulster to an old Irish conflict with English colonists than to an even older conflict amongst the Irish themselves, one which was going on in the days of the *Táin*.[11] "Men," writes Girard, "cannot confront the naked truth of their own violence without the risk of abandoning themselves to it entirely."[12] Such violence manifests itself in what Girard calls "mimetic desire": my neighbor desires what I desire not because it is desirable, but because I desire it. Imitating each other, we come to blows. "Thus, mimesis coupled with desire leads automatically to conflict."[13] For Girard original violence exists not so much in Freudian aggression between father and sons as it does in competition between siblings. My antagonist and I act as doubles or twins; it is our mutual imitation, not the object of desire, that pits us against each other. Although we think of each other in categories of opposition and difference, the causes of our hostility are to be found in sameness. "From within the system, only differences are perceived; from without, the antagonists seem all alike. From inside, sameness is not visible; from outside, differences cannot be seen."[14]

When violence breaks out, it perpetuates itself; violence cannot stop violence. Hence the ancient system of religious sacrifice which "serve[s] to polarize the community's aggressive impulses and redirect them towards victims that . . . are always incapable of propagating further vengeance."[15] This ritual—the punishment of a scapegoat—serves to draw off and render harmless the violent tendencies of people who would otherwise mutually destroy themselves. Sacrifice must be regularly repeated. The most familiar version of such a repeated ritual is war against a common enemy— "in the spring of the year, the time when kings go forth to battle."[16] If such a ritual victim is not available, a sacrificial crisis occurs and a surrogate victim, a scapegoat from within the community, must be found. (Such a scapegoat, in Girard's analysis, is Oedipus, who must assume the guilt for everyone else's wish to murder father and possess mother.) If the surrogate victim resembles the sacrificers too closely, however, violence will escape from its prescribed channels and the original chaos will return. "As soon as they are installed on a reservation, members of a group tend to turn against one another."[17]

This grim reminder is enough to inspire some reflections on the applicability of Girard's theories to the six counties of Northern Ireland, a confining political identity created in 1921, a place of "great hatred, little room" where antagonists resemble each other.[18] (The Northern Irish bleakly joke about "telling" Catholics from Protestants: "Norman, Ken and Sidney signalled Prod / And Seamus (call me Sean) was sure-fire Pape."[19]) The historical reasons for this mutual distrust are well-known. Some of them can no longer be rectified (dispossession of land), while others can, and either have been or are being addressed (political voice, housing conditions, employment).

Then there is religion. According to Girard, the divinity is the greatest of all causes of violence.[20] What is most desired by the pious—salvation—engenders the greatest mimetic fascination, the greatest sense of a prize to be competed for. When Beckett's famous duo believe (erroneously) that salvation may be near at hand, they instantly sense that, as in the famous case of the two thieves crucified with Jesus, one and one only can have the coveted prize:

> ESTRAGON: *(stopping, brandishing his fists, at the top of his voice)*. God have pity on me!
> VLADIMIR: *(vexed)*. And me?
> ESTRAGON: On me! On me! Pity! On me![21]

The structural phenomenon of sectarian rivalry remains, in Ed Cairns's words, that of "one group attaining a sense of superiority at the other group's expense,"[22] and seems unlikely to change as long as children of the two loyalties are educated in almost total separation from each other.

So much for the hatred. As for the room, one is reminded of Sartre's economical notion that people in hell, closeted in one room, can act as each other's torturers. Confined to a province where historical circumstances have engendered high amounts of social antagonism, the Northern Irish have been deprived of any foe but each other. The IRA rhetoric of "Brits out" does not convince anyone who reflects that the soldiers came, and have stayed, only to prevent the two factions from killing each other. Heaney's image of "that holmgang / Where two berserks club each other to death / For honour's sake"[23] all too accurately represents a scene of mutual scapegoating in which two sets of people fatally attempt to relieve their hostility on each other. The scapegoat, Girard reminds us, must always be incapable of propagating further violence (either because he is a defeated "other," such as an alien soldier, or because he has been ritually chosen from within the tribe), but in Northern Ireland this is never the case. The Ulster victim—the Catholic slain by Protestants or the Protestant slain by Catholics—is a member of the alien, neighboring tribe, whose members are fated to choose yet another victim in their turn.

When liberals discuss illiberal violence, they customarily speak as though there were a qualitative chasm separating themselves and the people they know from the throwers of bombs—a custom reinforced for any traveler to Northern Ireland by the kindness and gentleness of all whom he meets. Who is violent? From this view the Northern Irish question centers around unseen members of the IRA and the loyalist paramilitary groups—the hidden stone at the bottom of the stream. What, though, if we were to think of violent acts as symptoms of a more widely shared animus, boils erupting on a skin tightly stretched over a whole community's fear and resentment? Paradoxically but logically, the sense of superiority of which Cairns speaks feeds off a sense of victimhood which is common in Northern Ireland. Of the ten words most frequently used by Catholics surveyed in 1977 to describe their group, reports Cairns, four were "long-suffering," "insecure," "deprived," and "unfortunate."[24] Looking as far back as 1847, Terry Eagleton finds a similar social ethos of angered grievance among the Irish, a phenomenon feared by the Anglo-Irish ruling class because it "might finally come to usurp the gentry themselves. This is what will happen in Ireland, a century on."[25] Yet whereas Eagleton tends to analyze the victims' hostility in terms of colonial oppression, others find it being produced domestically by practices of Catholic education such as those described recently by a middle-aged layperson: "It wasn't just physical—there was a ferocious humiliation and destruction of the personality. And because of the way in which young Catholics were treated, ritually and daily in those schools, I believe that the Catholic Church has some responsibility for the violence in Northern Ireland."[26] The question of what makes a few people actually bomb and shoot others, important as it is, finally matters less than the nature of the resentments, widely shared but repressed, which motivate those few.

In a work devoted to the literary theme of *ressentiment*—this latter term differs from "resentment" as signifying the vindictive response of an injured person, rather than the mere symptoms of injury—Michael André Bernstein espouses Girard's theory of violence in society, as opposed to Bakhtin's blither views of violence as carnivalesque disorder. Bernstein traces the tradition of the potentially violent, abject hero from Roman saturnalia, through Diderot *(Rameau's Nephew)*, Dostoievsky *(Notes from Underground)* and Céline, to the abject hero's emergence from fiction into such sordid realities as cult murder (Charles Manson). "Freudian neuroses," writes Bernstein, "may be specific and personal, but *ressentiment* is a herd phenomenon: the state of mind, temperament, and imagination of a being who suffers most from the realization that even his worst grievances lack any trace of particularity."[27]

Bernstein's abject hero, the loser, revels in his abjection, inventing it when necessary. His self-hate, as it becomes increasingly bitter over time, becomes a more and more dangerous tool of aggression against others, for the revel of self-abjection inevitably ends in the carnival of aggression. The abject hero begins as scapegoat, cultivating the scorn of others and introjecting it in a ritual of self-hate, but then turns it outward again, so that in a gruesome dialectic the victim-become-victimizer vents his introjected wrath outward on the victimizer-become-victim. Now imagine *two* such abject heroes, or two such herds, cultivating *ressentiment* simultaneously and mutually turning on each other as targets for the outward projection of their abasement. "Great hatred, little room." Heaney's holmgang.

Nationalism as *ressentiment* is a widespread phenomenon in today's world, especially since the collapse of the Berlin wall. Michael Ignatieff and Tony Judt reflect Bernstein's views when they find it to be a driving force in the separatist nationalisms of eastern Europe and Québec, as well as of Northern Ireland.[28] In his history of Irish nationalist conflicts, Robert Kee traces the theme of *ressentiment* back to the eighteenth century, when Protestant and Catholic secret societies in Ulster killed both each other's people (as ritual victims) and their own people (surrogate victims) as punishment for not measuring up to imposed standards.[29] By the late nineteenth century, when the early Sinn Fein had become "a rallying point for all radical, dissatisfied and potentially disappointed individual nationalists in Ireland," the nationalist myth provided a prism through which the heat of anger and resentment could appear as the light of sacred nationalism.[30] By a well-known process of political illusion, the nationalist myth came to be widely believed as true. In the spirit of such belief the Republic of Ireland was born, leaving behind it the partitioned residue of the six counties.

To analyze political attitudes in terms of inherited thought-forms is to move in the direction of politically responsible discourse, although not all would have it so. It is not unusual to hear that Irish problems have "a real basis in material circumstances and structural inequalities" (as of course they do), and are therefore not to be thought of as problems of "attitude and consciousness."[31] Why this opposition of materiality and mind? Eagleton is surely right when he claims that the oppressed are "ineluctably parasitic on their antagonists," in bondage to themselves. "The paradox or aporia of any transformative politics is that it demands, to be successful, a 'centred,' resolute, self-confident agent, which would not be necessary in the first place if such self-confidence were genuinely possible."[32] In order to wage a transformative politics, the oppressed person requires just that measure of personal independence that, because of oppression, he lacks. As the first step in such a transformative politics, Eagleton proposes the task of "going through" (*Durcharbeitung*, Freud's "working through") the particular identity which one experiences, bad as that may be, and ultimately arriving at a new self-definition on the hoped-for other side of the old identity. While Eagleton confines his discussion to the dialectical matrix of colonizer/colonized, I suggest that we may apply it just as well to that mutual oppression between "twins" which I believe to underlie the social malaise of Northern Ireland.

Looking to lyric poetry as a privileged terrain for such working through, however, we are normally not satisfied with labels such as "Irish/British," "Nationalist/Loyalist," or "Catholic/Protestant" as signifiers of identity; we seek fuller representations of a personal center or self, a working through which is appropriate to poetic art. Since the concept of the self is a disputed one, a further theoretical question must be posed. How is it that the self can provide a unified focus for both poetic technique and poetry's response to violence?

Postmodern theory largely rejects the concept of the self, presenting instead a fragmented view of personalities, as it does of texts and of cultures. The postmodern solution to the Northern Irish problem of embattled selves, on this account, would be to dissipate those selves into unconnected bits of cultural language and so to deny that there is anything to fight about. Postmodern doctrine requires that old identities be forgotten, not worked through.

In an interesting essay, Jim Smyth connects postmodernism with the political position that Northern Ireland can be saved by its future integration into European capitalism, a world that, in John Hume's words, "will elide all national and ethnic differences, eventually making conflict in Ireland irrelevant."[33] From this view, once again, the whole error lay in the positing of a unified consciousness; all liberal efforts to raise sectarian prejudices to a higher plane (viz. "Ireland's Fifth Province") were doomed from the start. Both international capitalism (by replacing outdated cultural centers with financial centers) and postmodern theory (by its ideological decentering) work to dissipate and fragment local and traditional *mentalités*. Smyth confronts Hume's "postmodern" optimism with skepticism, caustically foreseeing the transformation of Ireland into EEC-funded theme parks, with folk dancers at crossroads performing daily for groups of tourists, including one in Belfast which would feature daily simulated acts of terrorism. One doubts whether the move to disintegrate personal centers in art and thought and to "elide . . . all differences" in social politics can for long be taken seriously. Both an authentic working through of Northern Irish identity and a satisfactory approach to the poems which undertake this task require, therefore, an adequate theory of the self—a theory that does more than reiterate old romantic formulae about centers, roots, and the fixities of gendered and racial stereotypes.

While the post-Freudian Heinz Kohut, like the postmoderns, rejects any romantic notion of *the* self, posited as a metaphysical center of one's being, he nevertheless argues for an experienced "continuum in time, that cohesive configuration in depth, which we experience as the 'I' of our perceptions, thoughts and actions."[34] Allowing for the coexistence of several different selves in one person, Kohut posits the nuclear self as that state of integration which characterizes the healthy individual. Kohut develops his view of the nuclear self in the context of his work on narcissism (a term he uses for the basically healthy process of self-formation), and in so doing addresses the question of aggression. Kohut opposes Freud's belief that aggression springs from a basic drive which, if allowed to run unchecked, would make our lives brutish and short. Kohut describes the two selves that every infant begins to form after making the discovery that his selfobject (the mother) is not perfect (infinitely at his disposition): first the grandiose or assertive self which insists on having its way and, second, a self derived from the idealized parent imago, the self which desires above all to be loved and approved of by the selfobject. The developing person derives goals and ambitions from the grandiose self, and idealized values from the parent imago. Aggression or destructive rage comes not from a primal drive, but from the failure of one's earliest selfobjects—from the frustration one experiences in trying to form relationships. Healthy growth of the nuclear self requires that one learn to live with ambivalence, with the coexistence of "different and even contradictory selves in the same person."[35]

Kohut extends his idea of narcissistic rage to an understanding of social violence. The enraged person, offended by the failure of selfobjects, suffers from an internal defect whereby he experiences the offender "as a foreign body in an archaic world that must be populated only by obedient selfobjects." Such defects can cause both personal and, in a time of historical crisis, group regression. In the sector of the idealized parent imago the group regresses into vague mystical religiosity, and in the sector of the grandiose self it regresses into attitudes of intolerant certainty and arrogance toward other groups.[36] In the years following their defeat in the Great War, the German people experienced just this sort of crisis. Hitler's malevolent genius, in Kohut's view, lay "in his total resonance with the disease of the German self." Faced with failing selfobjects (parents, nation), he reinvested his whole personality in an archaic grandiose self, and it was precisely this aberration which qualified him as the charismatic leader of a people who were suffering from the same disease: "The core of the self, except for one nucleus of infantile grandiosity, is lost . . . . Such people . . . are no longer in need of selfobjects. They have acquired self-sufficiency. . . . [S]uch people become ideal targets for those who are in desperate need of selfobjects."[37] In other words, Hitler was able to reshape his *ressentiment* and that of a nation into its dialectical opposite by turning the abject self into a grandiose self, one which would treat any trace of otherness with the severest punishment. This grandiose self paradoxically became the idealized selfobject, the *Führer* with whom the Germans could identify, so that their ideals in turn would become those of an uncompromisingly grandiose self.

Interestingly Kohut also considers some of the few people who were willing to accept execution as the penalty for opposing the Nazi régime. Dietrich Bonhoeffer, the pastor-turned-plotter; Franz Jaegerstaetter, the conscientious objector; Hans and Sophie Scholl, the leaders of The White Rose in Munich, all managed to integrate their idealizing tendencies to an amazing degree, so that their ideals could inform their daily actions even under the greatest duress. All of them developed a profound sense of inner peace or, in Kohut's terms, narcissistic equilibrium.[38] At a time of national self-aggrandizement, only those few who dialectically opposed grandiosity with ideals, and thereby arrived at a state of personal balance, were able to oppose the prevailing trends.

Can one speak of a shared tendency to regression in Northern Ireland, similar to the one Kohut perceives to have existed in Nazi Germany? Segments of the Northern Irish population have, after all, suffered some of the same evils—loss of common dignity, unjust economic hardship—as did the Germans after 1918. Yet apart from Ian Paisley, whose following is mercifully small, no would-be demagogue has arisen in Ulster. Those who practice violence in Northern Ireland behave in ways completely opposed to the Nazis. Whereas the Germans, by sinking their desire for a parent imago into a representative of absolute grandiosity, lost their ability to integrate ideals into their national character, the people of Ulster, both Catholic and Protestant, may be seen to have sunk their tendencies to grandiosity—their ambition and personal goals—into idealizing tendencies, into their loyalties to religious traditions and inherited ways of thought. One finds little megalomania in the Northern Irish, whose *ressentiment* takes the form of submission to those very ideologies, green or orange, that maintain them in abjection. Cairns reports that, when polled anonymously, a majority of Northern Irish respondents declared themselves to be in favor of religiously integrated education, but that none of the same people ever questioned the segregated status quo. A veteran community worker tells Fionnuala O'Connor, "Locally people all understand there are no victories to be won: we're all net losers. Protestants don't really want to hold hands with Catholics and vice versa—on both sides they just want to be left alone. . . . I'm actually working towards benign apartheid."[39] A little more grandiosity, a little more youthful rebellion, might be just the thing, but as Cairns points out, the young are caught in "self-perpetuating feedback loops." Unable to wage the sort of transformative politics of which Eagleton speaks because they cannot think of any meaningful ways of changing their lives—lives predicated on the feeling of abjection and the necessity of self-defense against hostile outsiders—they do what they have always done, turning to violent action when threatened. Writing in the early seventies, Heaney got it right:

> Is there a life before death? That's chalked up
> on a wall downtown. Competence with pain,
> Coherent miseries, a bite and sup,
> We hug our little destiny again.[40]

To recapitulate: the Northern Irish Troubles furnish an example of how particular historical circumstances can aggravate a universal human tendency to mutual hostility. Are such tendencies best thought of as fatally rooted in the human psyche? We may agree with Girard that people are generally unable to live at peace with each other without the help of ritual or legal violence, but we may also agree that the work of finding peace instead of violence is a matter of strengthening, not weakening, human character. As Eagleton points out, it is one of the effects of oppression to erode people's ability to develop that centredness or confidence of thought which would enable them to overcome their subjection, anger, and proclivity to violence. The narcissistic project of self-definition, seen as the work of integrating opposite tendencies into a nuclear self, therefore presents itself as a theoretical avenue toward a more humane way of life in the *polis*.

In a time and place of severe oppression and violence, we turn to lyric poetry, which is the art-form of the self *par excellence,* and inquire whether this needed work of self-formation may not be going on within its lines. In order to make sense of such poetry, we must be willing to read it simultaneously in two ways: first as the work of an artist consciously making his or her stylistic choices; second as a partially unconscious strategy for the poet's personal survival in the dark times. It is not the critic's business to decide in what sense an utterance is crafted and in what sense unwitting, any more than it is to decide to what extent the "I" of a poem coincides with that of the "real" writer, but only to maintain a double sense of the writer as artist creating a beautiful object and the speaker as person getting on with the task of self-fashioning. Is it unreasonable to suppose that some of the most brilliant achievements of artistic form will incorporate some of the most revealing acts of self-formation?

Heaney ended his most recent pronouncement on poetry and violence, the Nobel lecture, with an image that seems to crystallize many of the themes touched on here. Saying that poetry "is both the ship and the anchor," Heaney uses the ship to symbolize the means of escape, of realizing the demands of the grandiose self, and the anchor to symbolize the means of holding on to the past and to the demands of the idealizing self. As such, poetry continues to be a stay against confusion, a means of countering violence. Heaney concludes that the work of poetry in dark times "is to touch the base of our sympathetic nature while taking in at the same time the unsympathetic reality of the world to which that nature is constantly exposed[,] . . . to persuade that vulnerable part of our consciousness of its rightness in spite of the evidence of wrongness all around it."[41]

Ironically, these words in praise of conscious artistry reveal their own unconscious strategy, whereby the poet asserts his claim to ethical innocence in an otherwise tarnished world. Of all the problems faced by the poetic self-fashioner, the would-be survivor of violence, perhaps the most troublesome is his realization that unsympathetic reality and evidence of wrongness are always to be found within the self as well as without. Aground in the marshes of complicity with violence and implicit guilt, the liberal poet's ship of self would, no doubt, prefer to weigh anchor and depart, but another force, the anchor-line of the traditional self, restrains it. My mortal enemy is my twin, presenting to me the reflection of myself, *mon semblable, mon frère.* By constructing the ship as an image of poetry (not the self), and by locating the evidence of wrongness in what surrounds consciousness (not in consciousness), Heaney tacitly is finding imaginative ways of absolving himself from a universal *malaise.* It must have been just as comforting for the audience at the Nobel lecture to hear that we are fundamentally all right as it is disturbing for the readers of Freud's *Civilization and its Discontents* to hear that we are fundamentally all wrong—*homo homini lupus.* The truth is even harder to face than either of these beliefs, and it is a truth which Heaney and the other poets discussed in this study confront courageously and in many different ways. The self, like the poem, is a place of ambivalence where meanings are not given but must be made; the self, like the poem, reflects what is around it and yet must always be fashioned. The poet's primary evidence of violence is the self in trouble; the poet's primary work of peace is the fashioning of that troubled self in poetry.

2

Seamus Heaney

"exhaustions nominated peace"

—"North"

It is generally acknowledged that Seamus Heaney is a great political poet and that he has written about the long Northern Irish struggle in such a way as to promote peace and understanding—an achievement which must have constituted no small claim to the Nobel prize for literature which he received in 1995. In his Stockholm lecture, he presents himself as one who long and slavishly pursued goals of political correctness and responsibility, "bowed to the desk like some monk bowed over his prie-dieu . . . Blowing up sparks for a meagre heat. Forgetting faith, straining towards good works. Attending insufficiently to the diamond absolutes," until the day when he began to credit poetry, "to make space . . . for the marvellous as well as the murderous."[1] We expect Heaney to transform this move away from politics into politics of the best kind, and he does: in the words cited at the end of the previous chapter, he affirms the power of poetry to counter the social evils surrounding us by its celebration of the human goodness within us.

Heaney's monk-like poet is the persona of "Exposure," the last poem of *North* (1975)—a turning-point in his development. In what follows I will look back on the way Heaney came to this point of political seriousness and on what he has done with it since then. His mental itinerary has been more complex and more interesting than he would lead us to believe. While developing a dialectic between the faint sparks of politics and the diamond absolutes of art in what he says about his poetry, Heaney has developed a very different tension in the poetry itself. There a sense of solidarity, even identification, with violent tribal culture undermines his wish for humanistic emancipation from social violence. Confident, then, as are Heaney's pronouncements about poetry's humanizing force in the Nobel and slightly earlier Oxford lectures, one detects beneath them old murmurs of self-doubt and a sense of guilt, a realm of unconscious personal need underlying the province of conscious artistic choice. Heaney's poetry of violence, at its best, exceeds the limits he sets for it in his criticism.

In a revealing text from "The Government of the Tongue," the first of the Eliot lectures delivered in 1986, Heaney borrows the image of Jesus writing in the sand from the story of the woman taken in adultery, a story which he had used over ten years before in his controversial poem "Punishment." In the lecture Heaney is discussing the seeming futility of poetry in a time of war, admitting that "no lyric has ever stopped a tank." Invoking the picture of Eliot composing "Little Gidding" during the second world war, Heaney asserts on poetry's behalf that "[i]t is like the writing in the sand in the face of which accusers and accused are left speechless and renewed."[2] The poet here is clearly cast in the role of savior, neither accusing nor accused. In the poem of 1975, however, Heaney plays the role, not of the savior writing in the sand, but of the "artful voyeur" who "would have cast . . . the stones of silence" when faced with the spectacle of contemporary women taken in adultery—Catholics caught consorting with British soldiers.[3] It is as though the redeeming poet of 1986, writing messages of grace in the sandy terrain of violence, has all but replaced the guilty poet of 1975 who watched violence and did nothing (except write poetry).

Heaney's next lecture, on Auden, reveals the continuing presence in Heaney's thought of the guilty bystander. Auden's career, as Heaney sees it, began as an attempt to rebel against his milieu, but ended with a return to it. Like Wilfred Owen, Auden connived in what he deplored (and here Heaney paraphrases the last stanza of "Punishment"); "he sensed the crisis in a public world . . . as analogous to an impending private crisis of action and choice in his own life."[4] In the private crisis, that is, the liberal bystander is compelled to confront his implicit involvement with society's collapse. It might have been possible for Jesus to be neither accuser nor accused, but how could anyone else manage the feat? What Auden discovers, and what Heaney so keenly feels, is that the poet himself requires absolution from the very sins that his poetry purports to heal. In 1974 Heaney wrote of his desire to be faithful in poetry both to historical reality and to "the perspectives of a humane reason."[5] For Heaney this is a personal dilemma before it is a poetic challenge. To speak from within the historical reality of Northern Ireland is to lose the perspectives of humane reason. To regain these perspectives, as Heaney does in Dublin and Oxford, is to write from outside one's sphere of authenticity, as remote from Northern Irish violence as Archimedes' hypothetical platform would have been from the world he longed to lift.

From *Death of a Naturalist* (1969) until *North* (1975), Heaney's poetry masterfully represents the dilemmas and travails of a person striving both to understand tribal revenge and to liberate himself from it—even to liberate himself by understanding it. In early poems about shovels as guns and frogs as predators, Heaney confronts the task of self-definition within the framework of a rural and Catholic tribal identity. He then goes on to search for poetic rituals of self-liberation, rituals which he typically hopes will free him from atavistic compulsions and be a healing balm for the troubled people about whom he writes. Ultimately these poetic rituals, invocations of corpses and of death itself, being a set of romantic devices, fail to make anything happen, leaving the poet of *North* in a deeply ironic stance at the end of his book.

Representing as it does his disdain for the dying fires of politics and his longing for the diamond absolutes of art, "Exposure" implicitly sets a goal which Heaney will pursue over a period of twenty years, as he distances himself more and more from political involvement, even while writing political poems. Yet in *The Spirit Level,* written after the cease-fire of 1994, Heaney revisits the mental terrains of violence that he had mapped out in *North,* reawakening many of the old tensions and trying to resolve them at a deeper level than before. There is in Heaney an acute sense of conscience that, however widely he gazes out at expanses of political space and historical time, unfailingly returns him to human facts, to a sense of reality which springs from within. Heaney's ability to include unconscious human need within his conscious artistic choices accounts for much of his genius as a poet of social violence.

I

In Heaney's early poem "Digging," a young poet attempts to fashion a self which is both consistent with his inherited identity (son of a farmer) and yet radically different from it (poet) by symbolically replacing the shovel with the pen ("I'll dig with it"). Running through the whole poem, as it might run through any poem of adolescent rebellion, is a discourse about the violence implicit in such rebellion. Descriptions of old men digging are but mechanisms to advance the young speaker's task of self-definition, a narcissistic task in Kohut's sense that he is torn between his grandiose impulse to rebel against, and his conformist impulse to submit to their tribal customs. Although the poet attempts to disguise rebellion as celebration, his professions of admiration for his forbears do little to hide his supercilious attitude toward the father who digs ("his straining rump").

Given this reading of "Digging," one which the poem relentlessly imposes on the reader, there is an uneasy oddness to the poem's first and last lines.

> Between my finger and my thumb
> The squat pen rests; snug as a gun.
> . . . .
> Between my finger and my thumb
> The squat pen rests.
> I'll dig with it.
> (*Death of a Naturalist*, 1–2; *SP*, 5)

Whereas the body of the poem advances the claim that the young man will write, not dig, the frames of the poem advance the disturbingly different claim that the young man in his writing will dig, not shoot. Implicit in both claims is the assumption that the young man, looking down on his father's earth-hugging labor from the elevated position of a window, will replace inherited tribal activity with deeds that are individually chosen. Explicitly he distances himself from tribal work; implicitly, in an artistically represented act of the unconscious, he distances himself from tribal violence, from shooting. Heaney alludes to this sort of psychological legacy in *The Listener* (1971): "I am fatigued by a continuous adjudication between agony and injustice, *swung at one moment by the long tail of race and resentment,* at another by the more acceptable feelings of pity and terror" (italics mine).[6] Heaney's itinerary, which was soon to lead him from Belfast to Dublin, may well be thought of more generally as a project of freeing himself from the long tail of race and resentment.

Seen from the familiar perspective of Marxist theory, the young man is changing social classes, replacing a form of physical work (digging) with one of mechanical reproduction (writing). A further aspect of oddness, though, resides in Heaney's analogy of pen to gun. Allen Feldman, also using Marxist theory, draws attention to a shift toward mechanization in modes of Northern Irish violence, as the traditional hard men who fought with their fists were replaced by gunmen. "In the ethic of the hardman," he writes, "the practice of violence is centered in the self. Hardness is an interiorized quality extracted from risking the body in performance. For the gunman, violence is an eccentric relation, an instrumentality that is detachable from the self, that transcends personal limits and attains magnitude."[7] It is precisely the physical performance of his ancestors which the young man of "Digging" forswears, for the implied reason that he lacks the older men's toughness ("By God, the old man could handle a spade . . . I've no spade to follow men like them"); his points of physical contact with the instruments of labor have been reduced to finger and thumb.[8] The young man's shift from farming to writing, a shift made possible only by the post-war modernization of society, ironically runs parallel to modernizing shifts in violence as chronicled by Feldman (56), who points out that "fair dig" is a synonym for "clean fight"—tropes of "pure" violence transgressed by automation. Although he omits his original comparison of pen to gun at the end of his poem, the young man's choice of the pen over the shovel, placed within the context of tribal violence, bears an uneasy resemblance to a choice of being a gunman rather than a hard man.

We have gone far from any idea of intentionality in this reading, but we have come closer to representations of unconscious process. On the one hand the poet perceives that the tribal, farming culture which nurtured him is "hard"—based on hard labor and illiberal in its attitudes. This hardness appears elsewhere in Heaney's earliest poems as a kind of violence which can burst out as quickly as Hopkins's "shining from shook foil"—the frogs in "Death of a Naturalist" seen as "great slime kings" gathered for vengeance, or the rat in the well in "Personal Helicon."[9] On the other hand the scribal digger reveals that his choice of a pen to replace the shovel, reverential as he tries to make it sound, represents a choice for a kind of hardness undreamed of by his spade-wielding ancestors. Such hardness comes not just from the new universe of mechanical reproduction, but also from a new depth in the experience of violence itself. Gunmen profess violence, whereas the liberal writer abjures it, but in Northern Ireland the writer, like the gunman, explores new depths of the violent experience. Each has his blind spot. The gunman knows what he is doing but does not appear to reckon with the enormity of the violence. The writer reckons with the enormity of social violence, but often does not appear to know what he is doing, to know that he is representing social violence within the theater of the self.

In his essay, "Feeling into Words," Heaney graphically charts the ways in which he rewrote the Wordsworthian project in his early poetry, discovering in his young soul the traces, not of immortality, but of an all too mortal connection to the sordid facts of contemporary politics.[10] While *North* (1975) continues to be the text most studied for an understanding of this drama, the short collection of prose poems, *Stations,* which appeared in the same year, usually escapes notice. Although a few poems from *Stations* appear in the *Selected Poems,* the complete volume, short as it is, was never widely published.[11] Heaney began the poems during his year in California (1970–71) as an exercise in retrieving spots of childhood time, but was unable to finish them upon his return to Belfast in September, 1972, where the recent beginning of internment had been followed by a sharp escalation of violence. Confronted with these profound civic disturbances, he discovered that "[his] introspection was not confident enough" to continue its work. Later, having moved to the seclusion of Glanmore, Heaney completed the poems, not returning to the original focus of boyhood innocence, but rather re-examining his youthful psyche within the perspectives of recent violence, because "then the sectarian dimension of that pre-reflective experience presented itself as something asking to be uttered also."

What exactly is this sectarian dimension? Shades of the prison house, the influence of a harsh outside world already imposing itself on an innocent consciousness? That would be the reader's Wordsworthian assumption, but imposed shadows can hardly be called "dimensions" of what they are imposed upon. While *Stations* does indeed chronicle, with uncharacteristic bluntness, the author's early confrontations with a hostile northern Irish Protestantism, the collection more profoundly locates the sectarian dimension of pre-reflective experience within the experiencing self. We are not to think of the boy's loss of Catholic innocence in a world of hostile Protestants; we are to think of the Catholic boy as always hostile to Protestants, as never any more innocent than they.

Why else would the first two poems, about the process of birth and an early accident, be entitled "Cauled" and "Branded" (4–5)? The child is already marked as a victim of social violence (if not also as one of its perpetrators) from the moment of birth. "Cauled" (that is, "called") confronts and revises the romantic doctrine of the pre-existing, unspotted human soul. The process stretching from pre-conception ("They thought he was lost") to birth ("They had found him at the first onset of sobbing") is one from which innocence is excluded:

> They thought he was lost. For years they talked about it until he found himself at the root of their kindly tongues, sitting like a big fieldmouse in the middle of the rig. Their voices were far-off now, searching something.
>
> Green air trawled over his arms and legs, the pods and stalks wore a fuzz of light. He caught a rod in each hand and jerked the whole tangle into life. Little tendrils unsprung, new veins lit in the shifting leaves, a caul of shadows stretched and netted round his head again. He sat listening, grateful as the calls encroached.
>
> They had found him at the first onset of sobbing.
> (*Stations*, 4)

Because calling or speech, rather than sexual activity, is imagined as the process of generation, the unborn infant's existence is compromised from the moment of conception by the social forms implicit in speech. Hence the call is also a caul, ". . . a caul of shadows stretched and netted round his head again." Unlike David Copperfield, whose caul at birth was seen as a sign of good luck, this Irish child's caul suggests ill fortune—the horrible hat of pitch poured over the heads of captives in earlier wars of rebellion and set aflame, or just the covering of those currently marked out for political humiliation, like Heaney's Belfast prostitutes "cauled in tar."[12] This child's caul, a membrane covering his head, is never quite shed. The last poem of the collection, about the young poet's pen-name "Incertus," ends, "Oh yes, I crept before I walked. The old pseudonym lies there like a mouldering tegument" (24). He both calls and cauls himself "uncertain," a figure not self-determining, something of a victim, as in the collection's second poem, "Branded," where Heaney remembers an early mishap of being kicked by a horse as a ritual of being branded with the crescent mark of the horseshoe.

This is not to say that Heaney is presenting a deterministic account of young people, always under the influence of social forces. In "Patrick and Oisin," Seamus is an elementary school student, studying his catechism in the family kitchen while the adults sit and gossip. The polysyllabic, latinate language of Christian doctrine is imagined as cut stone, the grownups' talk as "a back-biting undergrowth mantling the hard stones"—an echo of the "behind-backs" in the concurrent poems "North" and "Exposure." Patrick's theological terms, hard as the tablets of Moses, are opposed to the creeping softness of Oisin's everyday speech: "incised tablets mossed and camouflaged by parasites and creeping greenery." Patrick's hard surfaces, that is, confront human realities in ecclesiastically scientific terms that, barbarous as they may be ("morose delectation and concupiscence," "calumny and detraction"), do not disguise or hide such realities in the lush growth of inherited speech.

We are very far, here, from Celtically correct views of an "authentic" Irish culture occluded by a superimposed Roman (read English) set of conventions. It is, if anything, the opposite: the speech of Patrick reveals, while that of Oisin hides, the contours of normal behavior. In this short poem, Heaney raises an issue central to his poetry of the mid-seventies: are we to think of socially violent tendencies as imposed on people by unfortunate historical circumstances, as endemic to certain peoples but not others, or as basic human traits? Avoiding both the first of these views (that of post-colonial theory) and the second (ethnic essentialism), Heaney here proposes the traditional Christian view that underneath the camouflage of cultural discourse we must look within universal human experience for the realities of moral behavior. The reason why spots of spotless time cannot be found is that we are always spotted. Buried beneath the greenery of custom lie tablets of law, law which is always broken. Here and in *North,* by coming to terms with a violent society, Heaney's protagonist must come to terms with himself.

In *Stations,* this drama of self-knowledge plays itself out chiefly in poems about Protestants. Heaney's choices from *Stations* for the *Selected Poems* give the impression that the prose poems chronicle the writer's evolution up and away from the anti-Protestant and anti-British provincial mentality which nurtured him. We read of the tribally ignorant family in wartime gathered around the wireless to hear and applaud Lord Haw Haw's broadcasts, and of the father's awkward attempts to make friends with a demobbed Protestant soldier. Missing are poems about the sharper impressions which Protestant culture makes on the young man: the seductiveness he finds in unionist culture, his fear of fighting with Protestant boys, and his fear, as a young adult, of being surrounded by Protestants in the men's room of a pub.

Taken together the omitted poems provide an intriguing and complex representation of a culturally determined, but nevertheless individual, state of mind, one which combines attraction and repulsion, pride and humiliation, a need to belong and a need to flee. The first of these, "Sweet William," is in some ways the most important:

> In the gloomy damp of an old garden with its gooseberry bushes, strawberry plants and shot leeks, their blooms infused themselves into the eye like blood in snow, as if the clumped growth had been spattered with grapeshot and bled from underneath.
>
> Sweet William: the words had the silky lift of a banner on the wind, where that king with crinkling feminine black curls reached after the unsheathed flare of his

sword—and that was heraldry I could not assent to. And
the many men so beautiful called after him, and the very
flowers, their aura could be and would be resisted.
(*Stations,* 11)

To a young child, the flowers (known otherwise as pinks), which
symbolize King Billy, exercise an almost seductive attraction, one
both aesthetic and violent, "like blood in snow." The words "sweet
William" suggest a banner on which the child sees "that king with
crinkling feminine black curls" who "reached after the unsheathed
flare of his sword." He resists, of course, mentally gritting his teeth
and spoiling a line of pentameter (perfect through the first four
feet) with a verb ("assent") learned from catechism: "and thát was
héraldrý I cóuld *not assent to.*" Another mellifluous line comes
back to entice him, but this last is cut short by another violent act
of will, expressed this time in political ("resist") rather than reli-
gious language, as a "spoiled" poem of hexameters: "And the mány
mén so beáutifúl called áfter hím, / and the véry flówers, their áura
/ could be and would be re-sis-ted."
     The fluttering banner might as well be bearing the image of
sweet William Shakespeare or sweet Edmund Spenser as that of
King Billy. Since the banner is an emblem of war, the infusion of
red into the eye must be compared to blood in snow, produced by
spattered grapeshot. Yet even the grapes seem Keatsian, the flow-
ers and banners always strangely beautiful. Underneath the con-
ventional polarities (of which Heaney the critic is fond) between
vowel and consonant, female and male, Irish and English, peasant
and master, lies this bleeding infusion of red, this feminine reaching
for the unsheathed sword, these beautiful men and their flowers. In
a world where religious rivalries conspire to forge divisions of lan-
guage in the mind, the sensitive young man imagines the forbidden
pleasures of English (as opposed to its mere use) as he might imag-
ine the forbidden pleasures of sex (as opposed to its mere procre-
ative use). Violence lies less now in the spattered grapeshot than in
the force with which the young man averts his gaze from the flow-
ering red.
     Danny, a Catholic survivor of the Great War, crippled and
drunk, getting no sympathy from his tribesmen, presents the young
man with a caricature of forbidden Englishness in "The Discharged

Soldier." By rejecting him, Danny's fellow Catholics find another way to cover sweet William's heraldry, with its Keatsian gules, under the mouldy tegument or caul of sectarian hostility.

> Flanders. It sounded heavy as an old tarpaulin being dragged off a wet load. Their big voices that conceded nothing to pity or wonder moulded it over so that it was years before I could stare long and sadly into its gules. Flanders.
>
> . . . .
>
> My shell-shocked Pew, stamping the parish with his built-up hoof, proffering the black spot of his mouth.
> (*Stations,* 12)

Danny, then, is rejected as an English peon. When he is drunk, he is "full as the Boyne, . . . a bad-tongued godless old bastard." The boy, seeing him limp drunkenly home at night, like blind Pew, "proffering the black spot of his mouth," must in his turn play the role of Jim Hawkins, deciding what to do about "Flanders," the imagined far-away place of heroic treasures. Should he keep the secret to himself, or confide in some academic, patriarchal Squire Trelawney, residing perhaps at Queen's University? If the mouldering tegument is already here, so is the uncertainty of "Incertus."

The boy, of course, has his own inherited allegiances and sources of self-definition. When his people set up the pavilion for an annual Sunday football tournament, when the Protestant neighbors tear it down (because the Sabbath is being broken), and when his people play nevertheless, a chivalric ritual is being established ("The Sabbath-breakers" [13]). "Call it a pattern. We called it a tournament . . . Call it a pattern. We can hardly call it a pogrom." The headiness of pennanted branches and the "anthem" ("Faith of our Fathers," written by that most English of converts to Catholicism, Frederick Faber) at the Sunday festival do not give the Catholic boys enough courage to withstand their persecutors in the schoolyard, the beaters of drums in July, the bullets of the constabulary riddling the screaming boy in the IRA truck, or the two toughs tormenting the young man in the loo ("I thought he was going to ask me to curse the pope . . . The door was unexpectedly open and I showed them the face in the back of my head"—"Inquisition" [23]). Tournament or pogrom? Implacable or intimidated? The very concept of "enemy" is uncertain. During the war, the Ulster Catholics, thinking that England's enemy might be their friend, reassure each other that German bombs over Belfast are raining mainly on the Protestants and listen surreptitiously to pro-Nazi broadcasts; yet they are conscious of being styled "enemies of Ulster" by their pro-British countrymen. Placed in this milieu, where one always plays a betrayer's role, Heaney imagines himself as "a double agent among the big concepts." As he turns this metaphor into a conceit ("an adept at banter, I crossed the lines with carefully enunciated passwords, manned every speech with checkpoints and reported back to nobody"—"England's Difficulty" [16]), Heaney marks out the ground on which he will develop his political poetry a decade later in *The Haw Lantern*. There he will use allegory itself as a technique of crossing lines without harm, a technique, that is, of connecting pageant and pogrom, honor and humiliation, without being "caught" in the meshes of personal confusion. If England's difficulty is Ireland's opportunity, that opportunity is the sensitive Irish person's difficulty as he wonders which act of betrayal will be the least painful, or which avoidance of conflict will be the least shameful.

"Oh yes. I crept before I walked." The twenty-one prose poems of *Stations* present no running strides; not one of them develops the Wordsworthian trope of the unfettered boy running, skating, or rowing in solitary freedom. We never see this Derry child other than hemmed in, constrained. How else should we see him? Not everyone shares Wordsworth's romantic assumptions about what is natural and right; unfettered Wordsworthian freedom is a privilege reserved for boys who, unlike the boys of Derry, have much land and time and few obligations.

Yet young Seamus differs from Wordsworth's boy not only because he was born on the wrong side of the channel, hedge, or wall. The primary issues of *Stations,* those between which "Incertus" vacillates, are not the familiar English-Irish binarisms. Violence itself, and not the violence of any particular faction, inhibits the growing mind in these poems. The uncertainty of "Incertus" lies not between green and orange, or even between the Tricolor and the Union Jack; not between Catholicism and Protestantism; not between Ireland and England; certainly not between mother and father. The boy is torn rather between two ideals of self-definition. On the one hand he would like to glorify himself, indulge himself, enjoying unlimited power and pleasure. On the other hand he idealizes his surroundings, longing for approval and practicing "expert obeisance" (24). This young man's tribe, with its elaborate and strict rules of conformity, offers him constant reminders of duty and few occasions for self-indulgence. In a world where all children, Protestant and Catholic, learn to obey and to imbibe the values of a violently recriminatory culture, the scales are heavily tipped toward idealization, expert obeisance. The violence with which the child is cauled and branded is neither Protestant nor Catholic violence; it is a violence of mutually hostile attitudes. To be "good" is to learn hostility and mistrust, to repress as illicit pleasure the notions of intimacy and trust, and to live always as a victim of someone else.

Even the boy's one ticket out of this world, his schooling, is stamped with the spirit of tribal violence. Leaving primary school with a scholarship for further education, the boy is given reluctant congratulations by his teachers but already thought of as an outsider. In secondary school, although he imagines himself as a perfect knight, he can be so only as "champion of the examination halls," secluded from any real risk or adventure. "Scalding with lust inside [his] daunting visor," the boy knows that even to think of risk and adventure would constitute a betrayal of the Catholic code of chivalric conduct (20). His only experience of risk occurs in the gents, where he makes a cowardly escape from the verbal and physical threats of Protestant intimidators gathered around the sinks, in a poem ironically titled "Inquisition" (23).

One might think here of Stephen Dedalus's "silence, exile, and cunning," but Heaney's young man rather resembles Bloom, the Bloom humiliated by the Citizen. The milieu in which Stephen grows up, confining as it is, lacks that element of social persecution of one class by another to which Bloom is subject and which the young man of *Stations* experiences too, although in a different way. Neither the English hegemony of Stephen's Jesuit masters nor the petit bourgeois Catholicism of his friends constitutes the real challenge to the anti-Wordsworthian boy of *Stations*. To understand the latter's inherited cage of hostility, one would have to leave Dublin and come to the six counties.

The only way that Heaney's boy can overcome tribal violence is to overcome it in himself. He must find a way to negotiate between his grandiose and idealizing tendencies in a new way, rebelling against tribal tradition by preferring the former to the latter, choosing pleasure over duty and the inwardly imagined self over the socially required self. To a post-romantic, bourgeois reader, nothing seems easier. Prosperous, secularized, liberal milieux almost expect their children to indulge themselves, to be "creative," and even, within limits, to rebel. As studies of Northern Irish culture show, however, the children of Ulster are expected only to absorb and replicate their parents' attitudes. The best thing that could happen to allay the strife of Northern Ireland, says Cairns, would be wholesale rebellion of children from parents.[13] In a world divided between one's friends and one's enemies, a world to which one yet feels loyalties, it is hardly easy or even desirable to deny complicity with one's tribe and still retain one's loyalty, one's "roots"—yet that is precisely what the poet of *Stations* and, as we shall see, of *North,* wishes to do. Torn between loyalty with violence and peace with betrayal, "Incertus" must learn an exile and a cunning possibly more complex than anything Stephen had in mind. "The old pseudonym lies there like a mouldering tegument." How difficult to remove a covering, a caul, when its shadows are "stretched and netted round his head" (4, 22).

It is against this background of personal uncertainty that *North,* also published in 1975, may best be read. Ever since the collection's appearance, the critical tendency has been to inquire what these poems—poems which Heaney himself regards as his primary effort to deal with political problems in verse[14]—have to say, even if, to follow Heaney's own joke, they say nothing. The artistic achievement of *North,* whether the *North* of bogs and memory in Part 1 or the *North* of current affairs and caustic commentary in Part 2, lies not in what the poems "say," but in the troubled persona they represent.

As I have elsewhere argued in detail, the bog poems (beginning with "The Tollund Man" in *Wintering Out* [1972]) constitute a sequence of ritual poetically enacted so that the speaker may attain to consciousness, that is, to freedom from unconscious tribal violence.[15] Taken by themselves the bog poems offer a convincing psychodrama of mental liberation. Set within the context of *North*, however, Heaney's romantic trope of the descent into the under- world in Part 1 (following Orpheus, Virgil, Dante) jarringly en- counters his cynicisms of Part 2, where he implicitly insists on the failure of his romantic ritual without, however, completely negating his trust in such rituals. Whatever he says—from his opening uncer- tainties ("Brueghel, / You'll know them if I can get them true" [xi]) to those at the very end ("How did I end up like this?" [66])—Heaney offers his saying of nothing, his representations of confusion and anguish, as his most significant form of political statement.

As he puts it in a famous formulation, Heaney wished in the poems of this period to give an authentic artistic rendition of vio- lence without forsaking the requirements of humane reason.[16] In *Stations*, he attempts to maintain his loyalty to his tribal roots but at the same time to withdraw from such loyalty and to affirm his liberal enlightenment. In *North*, he would be both Antaeus and Hercules, a denizen of the earth and a champion of the sky. The ongoing uncertainty of *North* arises from the artistic dilemma that this project creates for the poet. By desiring to be both Antaeus and Hercules, earth-bound and sky-born, the poet requires of himself that he be both object and subject, participant and observer, native and anthropologist, at the same time.

In the dedicatory poems, this paradox appears as a specifi- cally technical problem (one which will reappear in Mahon's po- ems on paintings). When he poetically "paints" a tribal scene, Heaney first wishes to maintain the objectivity of a removed gaze, but then he also wishes to put himself in the picture. If he does this, however, he will also lose his objectivity. Thus he first imagines a treasured scene of his childhood, inhabited by a much-loved ances- tor, as a "sunlit absence," a space inhabited by the ticking of clocks. Such a personal interior is not enough, though. In "The Seed Cut- ters" he must expand his gaze outward in space and backward in time ("[t]hey seem hundreds of years away") to a whole commu- nity of laborers, searching for their political ("[t]hey kneel under the hedge") and sociological significance ("O calendar customs!"). Most importantly, the poet feels the need to invoke a fellow artist: "Brueghel, / You'll know them if I can get them true." There is more to this than asking Brueghel to vouch for the laborers' his- toricity, as though he were merely asking the old painter if he recognized the laborers. By the poem's end, the poet will require Brueghel's help because he, the poet, also wishes to take his place in the picture—and if he does, who will arrange the picture? In the sonnet's last sentence, the main verb is the imperative "compose," addressed to Brueghel: "Under the broom / Yellowing over them, compose the frieze / With all of us there, our anonymities" (*North,* xi; *SP,* 94). At two other crucial moments in *North,* when the poet will summon long-dead fellow artists for assistance (Tacitus in "Kinship" and Goya in "Summer, 1969"), the reason will be roughly the same: the poet cannot see and be seen, be subject and object, confessor and penitent, at the same artistic moment. In the terms of the bog poems, how can one represent oneself in a state of tribal unconsciousness? One cannot; another observer would be needed.

As every student of Heaney's poetry knows, P.V. Glob's accounts and photographs of corpses preserved in the peat of Northern Denmark for two thousand years provided the poet with "emblems of adversity" sufficient to make of the bog a powerful field of force.[17] Most striking of these images is the Tollund man, whose almost perfectly preserved head provides a shock to anyone who sees even its picture for the first time. To Heaney the face seemed like that of one of his father's uncles, a man he had revered in childhood. As I have argued elsewhere, "The Tollund Man" first represents the poet unconsciously identifying himself with the ancient victim of ritual violence, so that the man who stands naked awaiting burial in the fen as bridegroom to the goddess *seems* to be the poet himself.[18] The pilgrim recognizes the pull of this primitive religion as being strong enough to replace Christianity, to make him risk blasphemy in offering prayers to the saint and thus to the goddess of violence who requires human sacrifice. The seductive pull of this goddess, her fen, and the ideology of sacrificial death work strongly enough to lull the poet into a deadly fascination with the ritual.

But so much depends on a tumbril, one in which the poet, imagining his drive in a car through Jutland, also imagines himself riding to his death.

> Something of his sad freedom
> As he rode the tumbril

Should come to me, driving,
Saying the names

Tollund, Grauballe, Nebelgard,
Watching the pointing hands
Of country people,
Not knowing their tongue.

Out there in Jutland
In the old man-killing parishes
I will feel lost,
Unhappy and at home.
(*Wintering Out*, 48; *SP*, 63)

What exactly is the "sad freedom" which the victim enjoys? The freedom of realizing, sadly because too late, that the earth-mother's ritual of continuing life is a bankrupt mythology, a ritual that only kills. By becoming a victim, the socially unconscious person acquires consciousness, perhaps for the first time. Such, too, is the experience of the poet on his pilgrimage. At first he is devoutly fascinated by the goddess, but as he sees the people's pointing hands and hears but does not understand their speech in the "man-killing parishes," he becomes conscious of what is really happening. "Lost, unhappy" stands in balance as a mirror image of "sad freedom" ("lost" with "freedom," "unhappy" with "sad"). The pilgrim announces himself both as a bewildered tourist and as the inner emigré he will again become at the end of North. In either case he is a descendant of the Tollund man, free and even holy— not by succumbing to the goddess, but by realizing that the goddess will bring only death, not life.

"The Tollund Man" enacts a process of acquiring awareness. Enlisting our fascination with what fascinates him, Heaney coopts our sense of reverence before the numinous (we mentally tiptoe around the body and the bog). At the end, most powerfully, he asks us to feel what it is like to ride a tumbril, to know that the sacred grove is a fearful place simply because people get killed there.

"Blood sacrifice," a term with connections, however indistinct, to pagan ritual, Christian theology, Padraic Pearse, the IRA, and contemporary political violence in Ireland, occupies space in most discussions of Heaney's bog poems. For Edna Longley "the prototype developed by 'The Tollund Man' is a scapegoat, privileged victim and ultimately Christ-surrogate"—a prototype of Bobby Sands, as it were. She wonders rhetorically whether Heaney does not "in fact sacrifice some imaginative liberty to that 'dark-bowered queen,' Cathleen ní Houlihan."[19] The first of these two questions calls for a distinction. "Scapegoat" and "Christ-surrogate" refer, of course, to the idea of one atoning or dying for the sins of many. One gathers from Glob's account that the Tollund man was one of those given to the goddess of the fen as her yearly, springtime lover in a fertility rite, life given so that life may be received. Neither in Glob nor in Heaney's poem does this sacrificial act carry any clear connection to the notion of atoning for the sins of others. It can be argued, as Frazer, Weston, and Eliade do, that Christian ritual has its origins in vegetative ritual or, as Girard maintains, that all human sacrifice, including that of fertility cults, is meant to remove violence from within the community.

Primitive human sacrifice took different forms in different cultures.[20] Some tribes killed their man-god when his strength began to fail, transferring his soul to a more vigorous successor (the subject of Derek Mahon's "The Last of the Fire Kings"). Some dismembered a human body and buried the scattered pieces as seeds to ensure fertility ("That corpse you planted last year in your garden, / Has it begun to sprout?"). Others offered an individual to avenging demons to die as a ransom for the people. This last, oddly enough, is widely thought to be the Christian view of the matter, provided that God is substituted for the demons. For Freud, in *Totem and Taboo,* human sacrifice represents the triumph of patriarchalism: the sons, having longed to commit incest and parricide, must atone for their rebellion in fratricidal acts.[21]

For René Girard as well, violence is the original impulse that all communities must somehow contain. Breaking out, it perpetuates itself in a chain of vengeful acts. Violence itself cannot effectively stop violence; it only perpetuates it. Sacrificial rites therefore "serve to polarize the community's aggressive impulses and redirect them toward victims that may be actual or figurative, animate or inanimate, but that are always incapable of propagating further vengeance."[22] As a form of "good" violence, ritual finds a way of canalizing all the violent impulses of the community and redirecting them toward a surrogate victim whose expulsion or death allows the community to live in relative concord, free from mutual violence—until the next reenactment of the needed rite.

Girard's analysis would explain the phenomenon of the bog corpses, whose death promised that the participants in the rite, like the good folk in Shirley Jackson's gruesome story, "The Lottery," would be free from compulsions to internecine slaughter for another year. The Girardian model should not, however, be confused with Padraic Pearse's bogus theology of sacrifice, according to which the slain gunman reenacts the death of Jesus. The pagan rites, as analyzed by Girard, abate otherwise inevitable violence, whereas Pearsian sacrifice foments otherwise avoidable violence. The bloodless Christian sacrifice of the Mass has nothing to do with violence, neither propagating it nor showing the specific property of violence-healing that Girard discovers in pagan sacrifice. If one were to analyze the bog poems from a strictly Girardian perspective, one might conclude that the speaking persona is forsaking Christian ritual, ineffectual as it has been over thirty years in stemming the tide of violence. Rather he seeks out an older ritual that, by choosing a surrogate victim for the community's violence, did allay the community's propensity to destroy itself. While I do not think that Heaney is pursuing this exact line, his intentions will be better understood if these differences between pagan and Christian sacrifice are explored.

Further insight into Heaney's procedures in *North* comes from Jung who, in a departure from Freud's Oedipal theory, sees the dynamic of sacrifice as going on between the hero and the mother, the cruel mother of desires who represents *prima materia,* the wet, bottomless center of the unconscious. The mythic hero must travel into the place of danger (the minotaur's labyrinth, the cave of the mothers) to encounter the unconscious, but then must die so that the participant's libido may be freed from its regressive, infantile compulsions.[23] Seen as the actor in a psychodrama rather than as a mythic hero, the victim saves no one but himself by symbolically dying. By risking descent into this pagan bog and submitting to a primitive process that is both sacred and violent, the poet does not seek any kind of redemption, in either a pagan sense (free from compulsion) or a Christian one (free from guilt). Instead he attempts to see for himself, to encounter the original ritual of violence, to experience it without succumbing to it, and thus to emerge with a new understanding of himself both as a part and as no longer a part of that process.

Three poems in *North*—"The Grauballe Man," "Punishment," and "Strange Fruit"—continue the confrontation with primitive violence that began with "The Tollund Man." The Grauballe man's throat was cut; his face, unlike that of the placid Tollund man, shows signs of weeping and suffering. Having been absorbed into the first corpse's aura, achieving only the consciousness he imagined the original victim to have had, the poet now maintains a scrupulous psychic distance from the Grauballe man, allowing himself only one first-person statement, and that a careful narrative fact ("I first saw his twisted face / in a photograph"). Description by metaphor begins in a sympathetic vein (the tar-like quality of the body and his evident weeping) but quickly the metaphors become more far-fetched (instep like a wet swamp root, spine like an eel), until a clinically distant third person ("The head lifts, / the chin is a visor / raised above the vent / of his slashed throat") begins to intrude. Even when the slashed throat appears as a "door into the dark" (and here one imagines the poet again risking blasphemy or venturing into some inner place), still the poet keeps his distance, confining himself to rhetorical questions:

> Who will say 'corpse'
> to his vivid cast?
> Who will say 'body'
> to his opaque repose?
> (*North*, 29; *SP*, 110)

The two questions represent contradictory options, as does much else in these stanzas. The Grauballe man is too lifelike to be called "corpse," but too sepulchral to be called "body." He is, the poem continues, "hung in the scales / with beauty and atrocity." Does he embody beauty, like the statue of the Dying Gaul, or atrocity (from *ater*, meaning "black," this man's color), like the hooded victims of violence in Northern Ireland (where victims of the Protestant UDA are found hooded, slashed and dumped)? Is this a corpse or a foetus? The corpse-body is weighed in a scrupulous balance ("hung in the scales"): if the Grauballe man is a thing of beauty, he cannot be a political symbol, but if he is a political symbol, he cannot be a thing of beauty. First the poet, confronting his quasi-religious fascination with the goddess in "The Tollund Man," rejected that fascination; now he confronts his tendency to aestheticize the ugly and rejects that as well. Having created a beautiful Grauballe man, he erases that beauty and leaves only a corpse slashed and dumped. Having rejecting the violent rite as sacred in "The Tollund Man," he now rejects it as beautiful.

That is not enough. Now he must come to consciousness for a third time, confronting female victims of violence. The so-called "Windeby girl," the subject of "Punishment," was found with her head half-shaved, a blindfold around her eyes, and no signs of inflicted injury. She was about fourteen at death; Glob supposes her crime to have been adultery, her punishment drowning. The poet's objective distance, won with such apparent effort in "The Grauballe Man," again disappears in his relationship to this woman. Like the previous poem, "Punishment" (*North*, 30–31; *SP*, 112 f.) divides naturally into two halves—the first descriptive and the second (addressed to the girl) confessional. The poet begins by being connected to the woman, as though by a rope of prepositions ("I can feel the tug / of the halter, at the nape / of her neck . . . / on her naked front), but draws increasingly away to the distant kinds of metaphor employed in "The Grauballe Man" ("shaved head / like a stubble of black corn"). The noose (a torc or collar, not a means of strangulation), which closes the first half of the poem, winds the poet back into connection with the woman, enclosing "memories of love" within a symbol of ritual violence. By vacillating between the language of sympathy and that of artful voyeurism (he imagines her nipples and peers at her body, but masks his predatory gaze with the language of sympathy), the poet sets himself up as one of the woman's tormentors.

Those who find fault with Heaney's attitudes in this poem suppose that the speaker believes both the Windeby girl and the Belfast women to have been guilty of the offenses for which they are being punished. They also find that, by making the historical analogy in the first place, and by "understanding" the Catholic tribe's "intimate revenge," Heaney is at least accepting and at worst condoning this form of sectarian violence.[24] Such readings miss the point that the poet is identifying his position in the midst of sectarian violence—liberal *vir bonus,* shocked but inactive—as untenable.

A proper estimate of the poem's ethical stance can be reached by understanding its sensory components: elements of sight (the voyeur connives, or "winks at") and sound, or the lack of sound (the voyeur casts stones of silence and stands dumbly before the women's *numb*ered bones). The allusion to the woman taken in adultery ("Let him who is without sin among you cast the first stone") provides a key to Heaney's own artfulness. Silence in the gospel story implied that the observers were guilty, and therefore that the woman was not condemned. Heaney's artful voyeur, although he connives with politically correct liberals who are outraged by the way the women are treated, yet implicitly joins his tribesmen in exacting revenge by doing nothing to stop them. Adapting Hannah Arendt's phrase, "the banality of evil," used in her ethical analysis of the Holocaust, Padraig O'Malley ends his own analysis of Irish attitudes to the IRA with this observation: "The banality of evil has its counterpart in the 'banality of the good.' When the 'good' condemn the IRA as men of violence but are unwilling to confront the moral and political ramifications of their own passive and often self-serving actions, they are denying their own silent complicity in what they so earnestly protest."[25]

The poet of "Punishment" implicitly accuses himself of this banality of the good, first by limiting himself to distant and suspect statements about the appearance of the girl's corpse, and then with biblical references (the gospel story and the "numbered bones" of the psalm), by turning description into parable. When it comes to punishment, those who "understand the exact / and tribal, intimate revenge" but do nothing about it (including the poet himself) emerge as the most guilty of all. Having cleansed himself of unconscious fascination with the ritual as sacred and as violent, the liberal observer now encounters seven devils worse than the first; they paralyze him in the face of the evil he has just condemned.

"Strange Fruit," the last of the bog poems, should be read as a sequel to "Punishment"—the woman's answer to the artful voyeur (even though the second poem is about a different corpse). She cannot speak; she looks. This woman's severed head, a sacrificial offering, still shows a delicately formed, oval face with well-preserved teeth and wide-open, staring eye sockets. The symbol of the severed head, Heaney discovered just after his first reading of *The Bog People*, is an icon as fundamental to Celtic paganism as the cross to Christianity. From a Jungian perspective, it can function as a castration symbol, by means of which regressive impulses are allowed to die, cut off from the rest of the psyche, thereby freeing the psyche from the ritual.[26] There is a severing in this sonnet, figured in the abrupt change of voice between the octave and sestet, a manifest feeling of breaking finally from the old ritual "tug of the halter." The poet at first is merely describing an aesthetic ensemble, as he did with the Windeby corpse: here is the head, here are the teeth. But for the head being compared to a gourd, one wouldn't know that it had been cut off. Just at the octave's end, however, the broken nose and blank eyeholes appear in a more focused way, as a face staring back at the observer, challenging his objectivity. Then, in the sestet, the poet's erudite and cosmopolitan voice, quoting ancient history, comes as prelude to naming, not what the woman's corpse looks like, but what she is. She is murdered, she is forgotten, she is nameless (this too is named), she is terrible (that is, she terrifies), she is beheaded. These are all empirical statements, but they carry moral force, implicitly condemning the colonialist acceptance of atrocity in the name of civilization on the march.

> Diodorus Siculus confessed
> His gradual ease among the likes of this:
> Murdered, forgotten, nameless, terrible
> Beheaded girl, outstaring axe
> And beatification, outstaring
> What had begun to feel like reverence.
> (*North*, 32; *SP*, 114)

The woman's stare was meant for the axe, but now disturbs the beholder, forcing us to conclude that the artful voyeur, the executioner, and the pious observer all bear the same guilt ("axe and beatification"). Like the mythical Gunnar in "Funeral Rites," the actual woman of the Roum fen has open eyes, a symbolic embodiment of consciousness. In an interview Heaney has commented on the last two lines: "I discovered a manuscript of ["Strange Fruit"] a while back, and it had ended up with a kind of reverence, and the voice that came in was a rebuke to the literary quality of the emotion, if you like."[27] "What had begun to feel like reverence" began in "The Tollund Man" as the observer's posture of innocence. By now the observer has attempted a wide range of attitudes—avid scavenging, clinical distance, rhetorical questioning, self-scrutiny—and has found that none of them will do, that each one leaves the observer suspended between distance from the ritual and participation in cruelty, between identification with the victim and solidarity with the victim's oppressors. The end of "Strange Fruit," Longley rightly observes, capsizes the poem "and a good deal else in *North*."[28] She might have added that it is meant to do so.[29]

The bog poems undertook to overcome the atavistic savagery of ritual sacrifice by reenacting it in a conscious mode. The poet seemed to think that aesthetic configurations of the ritual would make him, the beholder, aware of the real savagery within those forms, as well as of his own part in contemporary, unconscious, political celebrations of the old sacrifices. With each poem, though, and with each fresh corpse, the expected enlightenment continued to elude the observer; every attained position disclosed fresh uncertainties and new ways of lapsing into old rituals. Most dramatically, in the concluding sestet of "Strange Fruit," as the observer retreats to his weakest line of defense (the cynicism of Diodorus), the brute facts of the woman's suffering speak for themselves. Here, fatally, the observer seems about to fall back once more from cynicism to his original awed reverence of "The Tollund Man," and so start the whole violent cycle again. But here he is outstared. Fact outstares ritual; the victim's consciousness outstares the observer's failed attempts to be appropriately conscious of the victim. The silence of those two eyes—a surd, a nonverbal event—renders full awareness of a horror that cannot be rationalized, and abruptly ends the experiment of the bog poems.

For all its pathos and risk-taking, the poet's experiment fails. At the outset of the sequence, he wanted to enter into his primitive picture, but needed another artist's eyes to see him there. Now, although his elaborate procedure of ritual has succeeded in drawing him into primitive space, and although he has successfully granted "the religious intensity of the violence its deplorable authenticity and complexity" from within that space, he is left confronting the inescapable need to have this violence and this version of himself seen by a humane observer.[30] What good is it to have survived the ritual of violence if one cannot then enter into the ritual of civility? And to do this, one must be accepted by the civil. Having endured the ritual of unconsciousness, the poet is afflicted by the ordeal of consciousness, of needing to be observed and approved of by one's "betters."

If Heaney were dealing only with tribal violence, his ritual might enjoy the dramatic success, the salving of the consciousness, to which it aspires. In fact, though, he is also dealing with his status as a colonized native, never free to work out the problem of his roots on his own terms. "As political radicals," writes Terry Eagleton in his Field Day pamphlet on Irish Nationalism, "our identity stands and falls with those we oppose. It is in this sense, above all, that they have the upper hand."[31] "Kinship," which immediately follows the bog poems in *North*, returns the "skull-handler, parablist" from the grave to upper earth, from subjective gazing to objective and painful awareness of those who observe him and his tribe with the lofty gaze of a colonizing mind. It is here that Heaney makes his final appeal to another artist:

> And you, Tacitus,
> observe how I make my grove
> on an old crannog
> piled by the fearful dead:
>
> a desolate peace.
> Our mother ground
> is sour with the blood
> of her faithful,
>
> they lie gargling
> in her sacred heart
> as the legions stare
> from the ramparts.
> (*North*, 38; *SP*, 119)

Tacitus, who "wrote up" the Celtic and Germanic peoples in 98 A.D., described ritual sacrifices to the goddess Nerthus as taking place on an "island of the ocean." Using the Celtic word for an ancient lake-dwelling, *crannog*, Heaney figures himself as a primitive Celt, submitting himself and his culture, a spectacle of primitivism gone wrong, to the scrutiny of a cosmopolitan visitor: mother ground grows sour with Irish blood ("sacred heart") as the Roman (British) legions stare down on them from the ramparts. Far from being the poet's teacher in sympathetic renderings of peasant life, as was Brueghel, Tacitus stares down on the poet from above, a judge rather than a helper. Heaney hopes for fair treatment. After all, Tacitus reported on the original devotees of the goddess dispassionately and without prejudice or rhetoric. Throughout *North* Heaney has been reading the photographs of bog victims and the hieroglyphs in the peat, reporting on them and on himself. Now he must accept solidarity with his tribe, become part of the picture, and ask someone else to describe it. "The goddess swallows / our love and terror," the poet-as-primitive concludes, implying the whole range of fear from primitive terror in the sacred grove to its historical sequel, the terrorism of the IRA. And love? That is swallowed too. Even the swallowing itself, the natural suctions of the bog and death, are terrible to speak of: the goddess has become most vengeful of late. Thinking with dread of Tacitus, the Irish poet can only hope that the Roman historian will treat him and his people more sympathetically than he now can treat them or even himself.

Part 1 of *North* ends with Heaney's well-known poetic parable of Hercules and Antaeus, in which the man of the sky, Hercules, represents the British colonizer, while mould-hugging Antaeus represents his indigenous Irish victim. The equally well-known cultural implications of the poem—that the chthonic culture of Antaeus, once Hercules removes him from his earth, turns into dreams, nostalgia, pap—are not more significant than the manner in which the poet imagines Hercules and Antaeus as opposed aspects of his own self. Brueghel was to have been the poet's master in realizing himself as Antaeus, and throughout the bog poems the poet manages to effect this realization in the hoped-for manner, one which would hallow the spirits of the tribe while freeing the subject from their compulsions. Such pieties, alas, are not to be tolerated by the poet realizing himself as Hercules, the grandiose and ambitious self which will have nothing to do with huggers of ancestral ground, whose only wish is to transcend tradition and aim higher. The cultural conflict between Hercules and Antaeus resolves itself back into an original narcissistic conflict, that of the child trying to be both the creative rebel and the faithful son. Now, however, the overlay of psychological, cultural and political contexts places the poet in a position of some discomfort. First playing the rebel who practiced violence against his violent tribe, turning the gun of his pen against his spade-wielding forbears, the poet now plays the role of the master, Hercules, violently turning his rational powers against Antaeus the Gael. In *North,* however, Heaney cannot identify himself both with Antaeus, carrying out blood-sacrifices on his island of the ocean and calling out to Tacitus for a fair treatment, and with Hercules-Tacitus, looking down on Antaeus (or from the upstairs window on his digging father) with the distance of rationality and, finally, of contempt.

As a commentary on the personal project of *North,* Part 1, "Hercules and Antaeus" does much to invalidate the seemingly powerful metaphors of the bog, metaphors by which the poet had hoped to remove himself from his culture's blood sacrifices. Following the desperate appeal to Tacitus, Heaney as Antaeus must allow himself to be extricated from his soil by Heaney as Hercules; his cosmopolitan persona rescuing but humiliating his indigenous, rooted self.

Part 2 of *North,* often described as a relieved return from digging into bogs to the more metallic surfaces of contemporary commentary, may better be read as another kind of digging. Abandoning the mythic conceits of Part 1, Heaney uses allusion and autobiography to engage in a literarily ironic and psychologically unsparing investigation into his actual self—not the symbolically imagined self of Part 1, but the self who lived and lives in specific places at specific moments. Significantly, at the end of "Whatever You Say Say Nothing," Heaney reprints the twelve-line poem which first appeared three years before as the dedication to David Hammond and Michael Longley of *Wintering Out* (1972). Beginning with a view of Long Kesh, "This morning from a dewy motorway / I saw the new camp for the internees," the poem concludes with a frank statement of anguish, the particular anguish felt by citizens who have learned to live with the horrors and wounds of a violent culture, but not to find remedies.

Is there a life before death? That's chalked up
on a wall downtown. Competence with pain,

coherent miseries, a bite and sup,
we hug our little destiny again.
(*North*, 54; cf. *SP*, 125)

There is little to distinguish between that hug and the mould-hug-
ging of Antaeus, the embrace from which he is weaned only by the
violent lifting of Hercules. Heaney could, in fact, only wean him-
self from an Antaean hugging of destiny by a Herculaean transfer
to the Republic. The reproduction of this poem in *North* serves, as
does "Hercules and Antaeus," to represent the poet's new dilemma:
either he rejects violence and his Antaean, Ulster identity by adopt-
ing a cosmopolitan, Herculean stance, or he rejects that alien posi-
tion and chooses to retain his violent identity. Having tried and
failed to emancipate himself from tribal violence, the poet now
must dig through the psyche he is left with, that of the repatriated
peasant-turned-poet, whose "hobnailed boots from beyond the
mountain / Were walking, by God, all over the fine / Lawns of
elocution" (*North*, 57–58; *SP*, 127).

Most of *North* 2, then, consists of autobiographical introspec-
tion, set out primarily in the complex poem "Singing School," whose
title is taken from Yeats's "Sailing to Byzantium." Crudely para-
phrased, Yeats's line says that the soul can only learn to sing if it
studies its own beauty. Imagining Derry, not Byzantium, as the place
where the soul must learn to sing, Heaney sets his title above two
citations: the first from Wordsworth's *Prelude* 1.301–5, where the
soul is "fostered alike by beauty and by fear," and the second from
Yeats's *Autobiographies*, where the poet's earliest memories include
the excitement of rifles being handed out so that Orangemen could
defend themselves against Fenians.[32]

Heaney, then, places himself as heir both to the first and last
romantic, a post-romantic who in 1975 is learning to sing by study-
ing his soul. Whereas Wordsworth's "fear" is that inspired by the
Sublime (the boy's discovery of fear when, by an "act of stealth" he
steals a rowboat and is frightened by a frowning black mountain),
Heaney is schooled rather by the "Ministry of Fear" (the title of
Graham Greene's tale of political intrigue). *His* act of stealth con-
sists of throwing biscuits, sent from home to him at school, into
Derry's Lecky Road in 1951. Like Wordsworth, Heaney is project-
ing himself into an unknown nocturnal world, but Heaney's ver-

sion of that world is an urban site of social repression. Yeats's singing school, Byzantium, is only for older souls who, since they can no longer create sexually, retire into aesthetic self-contemplation. But what about Yeats's Wordsworthian juvenile soul in its "fair seedtime"? By citing Yeats's passage about the Fenians, Heaney cunningly shows that Yeats too was fostered by fear as well as beauty, *political* fear of violence. As sons of Wordsworth (the boy in Grasmere), both Yeats (the boy in Sligo) and Heaney (the boy in Derry) turn for their sources of fear from Burke's (and Wordsworth's) Sublime to Burke's Ireland—except that, in Heaney's post-1922 childhood, the Irish place of political conflict has been reduced to the six counties. As romantics, Wordsworth, Yeats, and Heaney all believe that the primary job of the poet is to sing by studying the soul, but Yeats is made to correct Wordsworth by situating fear in society rather than in nature. For his part, Heaney holds Yeats to the implications of saying that soul should sing "[f]or every tatter of its mortal dress." These tatters, says Heaney, are the results of social violence, of the *ministry* of fear, of the Bogside and the Falls Road—and it is precisely *those* tatters which constitute monuments of the soul's magnificence.

Lucy McDiarmid, examining "The Ministry of Fear" as a narrative of education, shows how the classroom is a site of ideological conflict. Who owns culture? Who is to decide about language and style? Heaney here follows Joyce, Flann O'Brien and Kinsella in showing the classroom as a microcosm of a state which tyrannizes over culture.[33] I would add that this tyranny does not stop with culture, nor is it simply the prerogative of the state. The teacher initially instills inferiority in his Catholic students by telling them that they speak less well than Protestants. Then the strap comes out (for no known reason—it just "went epileptic"). Finally we see the young man coming home from a date in the family car, challenged at a checkpoint by police who hold a gun at his head, search the car, and read his love letters. "Ulster was British, but with no rights on / The English lyric: all around us, though / We hadn't named it, the ministry of fear" (*North*, 59; *SP*, 128).

So the poem ends—with a statement of cultural tyranny, but one couched in an unusually threatening way. This fear extends even deeper into the psyche than nervousness about one's accent. Authorities invade one's body, one's sexuality, and one's home (in

"A Constable Calls"). The language of lyric is the language of speech, and speech in Ulster partakes of the climate of fear, where accents, like first names and addresses, are subtle indicators of allegiance in a "land of password, handgrip, wink and nod, . . . Where tongues lie coiled" (*SP*, 124). And the state? The police are its representatives, but so are its schoolteachers: Catholics instilling repression into other Catholics, and Protestants doing the same for Protestants—all acquiring coiled tongues. Heaney's singing school, where he teaches himself elocution and the lyric, provides him with a way of emancipating himself from fear, of redefining himself. It is, however, a way fraught with paradox.

In summer, 1969, when rioting broke out in the Falls Road, Heaney was in Madrid. "Summer, 1969" takes three images by Goya from the Prado and sets them as icons of the conflict that the poet cannot see. This therefore is not poetry of witness, in which the observer testifies to what happened, and does so to bring a case against some guilty perpetrator. Because he is not at the scene of action, because he is neither guilty nor innocent of any specific deeds, Heaney uses Goya's drawings to advance from violence on the streets to violence in the psyche. After looking at "Shootings of the Third of May" and thinking of the shootings in Belfast, he passes on to the nightmare drawings, substitutes for those concealed horrors of which social violence is only a surface manifestation: "Saturn / Jewelled in the blood of his own children." Having passed from violence as historical incident to violence as disease, Heaney finally proceeds to an amalgam of the first two stages, violence as an ever-repeated ritual of mutual destruction: "that holmgang / Where two berserks club each other to death / For honour's sake, greaved in a bog, and sinking" (*North*, 64; *SP*, 132).

Heaney's conclusion to *North*, in "Exposure," unites the opposed themes of the book in counterpoint: the romantic theme of self-discovery and the ironic theme of political failure.[34] Having moved from Belfast to the south of Ireland in 1973, Heaney writes from his retreat at Glanmore. Walking in the evening rain, he cannot decide whether to think of the raindrops as the diamond absolutes of perfected art or as the societal mutter of "let-downs and erosions," that endlessly destructive process which has been his burden from the start. Throughout the poem, one voice struggles with the other. Lost comets and falling stars, alders dripping and damp leaves, all provide a romantic setting for the ironic and even desperate "How did I end up like this?" The poet tries first one model for alienation—Ovid in exile ("weighing / My responsible *tristia*")—which allows him to laugh at himself but also to glamorize his position as aggrieved artist. He passes from that to a second model, that of the wood-kerne—one of the peasant soldiers of a long-passed rebellion, taking refuge in the woods from the latest massacre. An archaic exemplar of the Eastern European inner emigré (Heaney's hero, Mandelstam), the kerne blends into the natural and romantic landscape, his long hair or glib matching that of the comet (a word derived from the Greek word for hair). For this poet, the "once-in-a-lifetime portent" of the comet symbolizes a dreamed-of chance to make the perfect statement, do the perfect thing—as though right action and right speech, the good and the beautiful, had at last come together in one expression. Ironic to the last, he also says that he has missed the sign.

The completed irony of the escaped wood-kerne only becomes manifest when one reads "Kernes," one of the prose poems from *Stations*. Heaney writes of a boyhood Protestant schoolmate, mounted on his bicycle as on a horse and defying the weaker Catholic boys ("I could beat every fucking papish in the school!") who, being poorer, must walk. With ritual cries of "Up King Billy" and "God Save the King," the young knight-at-arms rides defiantly through the knot of Catholic adversaries, who tacitly admit defeat: "One by one we melted down lanes and over pads, behind a glib he hadn't even ruffled."[35] Kernes are losers; they don't have the right stuff; they are cowed. But what if one were to fight? In "Exposure" the choices are clear: one either fights for the side (becoming an internee) or against it (becoming an informer). If one declares a plague on both violent houses, the only course left open is flight into the archaic forest, a stance that Heaney ironizes both in "Kernes" and "Exposure" in the would-be romantic but nonetheless self-mocking figure of the poet as fugitive.

My reading of *North* has tried to explain the sources and the various vectors of these poetic constrictions and tensions. From a Girardian perspective, Heaney writes of his Northern Irish "soil" as of a place always infected by ancestral spilling of blood. He widens his geographical perspective from Northern Ireland to the fuller area comprising Northern Europe and Scandinavia, and from the early modern history of troubled Anglo-Irish relations to the more extended history of Irish supplantings. Heaney sweeps out perspectival arcs and circles at the center of which his short lines, like drills, go in and down, down and in.

Heaney's mythical symbols for contemporary conflicts compel reflection. Was there ever a moment in Irish literary consciousness when someone was not supplanting someone else? "Balor will die," writes Heaney in "Hercules and Antaeus," implicitly reminding us with a heavy-lidded wink that Balor was an indigenous Irishman, supplanted by the Herculean Tuatha De Danaan, who in their turn were supplanted by the Milesians—the "original" Celts. Will the original Antaeus please stand up? Or will he have to be lifted up? Heaney's project of digging turns up layer after layer of violent replacements, so that one must give some credence to Girard's model of violence as always present in society. The dispossessed and their pap you have always with you.

To have demonstrated all this poetically, to have used myth and symbol to write a poetry of trenchant political commentary, would surely have been enough for one poet of genius. I think Heaney would agree; I think that is all he wanted to do. As his Oxford and Nobel lectures suggest, he would still like us to think of him as the poet who can first penetrate to a historical core of truth and then cleanse history by crediting the imaginative beauty of the ways in which such truth may be imagined. Heaney rescues the mind's ship, which had caught its anchor on a corner of terrestrial reality, releasing it again to the upper levels from which it came.[36]

Yet to have said all this is not yet to have said all that Heaney is doing in *North,* not even the most important thing. What preys on Heaney, what he keeps trying to "get right," is his own place in this picture, his sense of self; and it is precisely this anxiety, this unease, that communicates itself in his constricted lines, giving this poetry its true greatness. Heaney's narcissistic project, as I have called it after Kohut, emerges as a corollary of his poetic assumptions. As a new poet, he successfully wore Kavanagh's hobnailed boots as he walked (note—he did not stamp or tramp) on the British lawns of elocution. Those lawns were in Belfast, though, at Queen's University. Back home in Derry, the young man might seem to be walking on muddy fields in his new oxfords. The question, then, is one of self-imagining. How to remain faithful to the original project of authenticity—to be of one's own soil and a faithful son to one's own parents, while at the same time abandoning that soil for a different mental universe? How to adjust one's contradictory impulses to conformity and rebellion, to idealized and self-aggrandizing behavior?

Heaney admits that these dilemmas are not his alone: "I suppose I'm typical of the Catholics of my generation and experience, a marginalized, subcultural Catholic within an Anglophone culture." What is unique about Heaney is his ability to retain both elements of this conflict within his artistic psyche: that of Hercules ("The first thing a Catholic does in the outside world is to secularize his religion") and that of Antaeus ("but it remains inside you like a subterranean command").[37] Both sides are violent, endlessly engaged in combat within the self. To put the struggle in theoretical terms, the artist as a young man embarks on both his narcissistic project (conformity versus rebellion) and his poetic project (authenticity versus sophistication). He then discovers that he has really embarked on a moral project: how to avoid the guilt into which these projects plunge the one who embarks on them? Tribal identity is never innocent; it always entails participation in violent sacrifice. Liberal identity is never innocent; it requires the repression of the tribe. The barbarians in the mud look up to the soldiers on the rampart—will the troops come down or will the barbarians destroy themselves?

North is surely one of the great poetic works of this century. Had it only found a myth for social violence, or had it only made a political statement, no such claim could be made. Having opened the confines of the Northern Irish troubles, stretching his vision out in space and back in time, Heaney has also opened up the mind of one imprisoned in that social space, pushing against its confines, bringing to light its unique pain. To have artistically rendered a social impasse as a psychological impasse—to have represented anguish at the core of one's myth—is to have realized some of lyric's greatest possibilities.

2

Since *North* Heaney has continued to write political poems and, in his prose works, to vindicate for himself the neutral stance which these poems embody. Not until *The Spirit Level* does he undergo a confrontation with violence whose intensity matches that of *North*. By Heaney's own account, the writing of *North* was followed by a sense of relief and recovery:

> The line and the life are intimately related, and that narrow line, that tight line, came out of a time when I was very tight myself. Especially the poems in *North*. I remember looking at them when I was just going to send them out and saying: This is a very habit-formed book—these little narrow lines. Can I open this? And I wrote out a couple of poems in long line, and the sense of constriction went; and when the constriction went the tension went. I felt that I'd come through something at the end of *North;* there was some kind of appeasement in me.[38]

In the many political poems Heaney wrote over the next twenty years, this sense of appeasement did not abandon him.

Not that he stopped writing about violence. *Field Work* (1979), which followed four years after *North,* contains a wealth of poems about killings. *North,* with its archetypes, has no such gruesome, contemporary detail. Yet Anne Stevenson, shrewdly noticing that myths can be grimmer than news, says of *Field Work,* "I could wish, almost, that there was more 'pap for the dispossessed' in this beautiful, even-toned book, which continues Heaney's delicate exploration of language without touching the deeper chords of poems like 'Strange Fruit.'"[39] Hearing the same change in voice through different ears, Seamus Deane claims that, in *Field Work,* Heaney's "contemplative distance has vanished," that "the violence itself is pervasive, a disease spread," and that "[a]trocity is closer to him now as an experience."[40] Writing from his nationalist position, Deane sees Heaney as gradually acquiring the courage to ally himself with the victims of violence without being overwhelmed by that violence. Whereas he could only write about mythical victims of violence in *North*, argues Deane, he can now write about relatives and friends who have died.

Here Deane attends primarily to subject matter and not, as Stevenson does, to style. Heaney can now take dead acquaintances

as his subject matter, not so much because of his courage as be-
cause he has the stylistic means of distancing himself from their
sufferings. Other poems from *Field Work* engage the poet more
closely, such as "Oysters," in which he ruminates on the relation-
ship between art and economics. Distressed that his pleasure in
"toasting perfect friendship" at a seaside restaurant should be
spoiled by reflections on man's violation of ecosystems and the "glut
of privilege," he expresses anger at himself for spoiling a perfect
moment, but then concludes with a defiant *carpe diem*: "I ate the
day / Deliberately." The loud colors of the poet's pleasure, anxiety,
and anger are muted in his poems about sectarian violence, such as
"Triptych," which asks "Who's sorry for our troubles?" as a rhe-
torical device for expressing the political fact of Ulster's isolation
and imagines pastoral scenes (a girl bringing in fresh produce) in
contrast to violence. Soon the poet's voice fades entirely, to be re-
placed by a woman "prophesying" in abstract, moral terms about
northern mores ("My people think money / And talk weather").
Then when the speaker appears to feel an impulse ("everything in
me / Wanted to bow down, to offer up"), he is only finding an
ironic means of contrasting two gods—the old creator worshipped
by ancient Irish monks and the new army helicopter which hovers
over the land and demands the abasement of those underneath it.
The binarisms of "The Toome Road" (armored cars and quiet farms)
continue to leave the speaking self untouched. These are political
poems whose tropes—sentimental contrast of pastoral and belli-
cose themes, abstract prophecy, the ironic metaphor of helicopter
as mythical god—are used to make statements but not to reveal a
self.[41]

Such criticisms of *Field Work* should not be news to readers
of *Station Island* in which Heaney's murdered cousin, the subject
of an elegy in *Field Work* ("The Strand at Lough Beg"), inveighs
against that poem. He accuses the poet, first, of having removed
himself personally from a family tragedy (he did not come home
for the wake), and second, of having "confused evasion with artis-
tic tact"—of having used Dantesque imagery to invest a gruesome
event with elegiac sweetness.[42] The poet's *personal* evasion, then,
matches his *artistic* evasion, his distant stances in "Triptych" and
"The Toome Road." Does the cousin's critique (Heaney's self-cri-
tique, that is) imply that Heaney now rejects the earlier poem? Evi-

dently not: "The Strand at Lough Beg" is included in the 1990 *Selected Poems*. Elsewhere in *Field Work* ("Casualty"), Heaney candidly admits to having missed the funeral of another, much-loved victim. In his Oxford lectures of 1995, Heaney reveals that his non-attendance at funerals, at least those with a strong presence of the IRA, was a matter of personal policy.[43] Could it be that the dead cousin's critique tells us more about what Heaney thinks of nationalist views than about what he thinks of "The Strand at Lough Beg"? Heaney gives the last word of "Station Island" to Joyce, whose advice to the poet to abandon "the old whinges" and to "swim out on your own" forms the core of Heaney's own repeated claims for poetry's freedom from partisan politics. We must conclude then that Heaney himself does not believe that he confused evasion and artistic tact, or rather that artistic evasion is precisely what he was engaged in when he wrote *Field Work*.

Louis O'Neill, an obscure fisherman and the pub-crawling hero of "Casualty," is the first to represent Heaney's new (since *North*) ideal of the disengaged poet. In the aftermath of Bloody Sunday, the IRA had declared a curfew in the Bogside. O'Neill, valuing his night habits too much to be cowed by the strictures of the tribe, went out after dark and was blown up by a booby trap left for English soldiers and the RUC. "How culpable was he / That last night when he broke / Our tribe's complicity?" the poet asks, and relishes the joke of hearing O'Neill himself pose the question: "Puzzle me / The right answer to that one." That can be no puzzle for Heaney, who devotes his poem to opposing the tribe's complicity just as O'Neill did in his last moments of life.

O'Neill's art was fishing, just as Heaney's is poetry; when Heaney went out one morning in his friend's boat, he "tasted freedom with him" (including freedom from the violent tribe) because the two men could enter the realm of art

> and smile
> As you find a rhythm
> Working you, slow mile by mile,
> Into your proper haunt
> Somewhere, well out, beyond . . .
> (*Field Work*, 24; *SP*, 149)

Although the short lines here hark back to *North,* they show no trace of the previous book's anxieties. "Casualty," in fact, responds antiphonally to "Funeral Rites," where "each neighbourly murder" provokes in the poet a longing for "ceremony, customary rhythms," something to allay the pain. Now in part 2 of "Casualty," as he describes the funeral of Bloody Sunday's victims, Heaney writes of the ceremony's "swaddling band" tightening around the participants, "till we were braced and bound / Like brothers in a ring." What to make of such bonding? O'Neill and Heaney want no part of it. Like Joyce's Stephen and Heaney himself, O'Neill swam out past the nets; unlike them, he was destroyed as he swam. Whereas the legendary Gunnar, the hero of "Funeral Rites," embodies the tribe's best aspirations, O'Neill, the "dawn-sniffing revenant" of the latter poem, embodies the poet's rejection of any complicity in the tribe or even in the tribe's feelings.

The political poems of *Field Work,* like the book's nonpolitical centerpiece, "The Glanmore Sonnets," testify to the inner emancipation from violence which the poet has won for himself in *North.* The book's single attempt at a psychological encounter with violence occurs in "Badgers," whose symbolism and uncertain style (it includes an allusion to Eliot's "Gerontion") suggest that Heaney's acute preoccupation with violence is indeed on the wane. Of this poem, in which badgers stand for IRA members who pillage and are destroyed, Heaney says, "It's really about the relationship between yourself and the shadow self; the question of political solidarity with a movement becomes an extension of that."[44] The badger lying dead on the highway, and the "violent shattered boy" whose participation in violence brings him to a violent end, awaken in the poet a confused double reaction. Whereas he can rationally reflect that the badger, and hence the IRA man, is just "pig family / and not at all what he's painted," he can also feel that the dead houseboy's shoulders "could have been my own." Yet the poet drives past the animal, one suspects, with little more than the thought that there but for the grace of God goes he. A shadow is only a shadow, in the psychological sense that Heaney intends here, when it cannot be seen by its possessor. The very fact that the poet can see his violent shadow, allegorize it, and then explain the allegory, suggests that this shadow no longer goes in and out with him in the way that it once did.

Heaney achieves yet further distance from violence in "In Memoriam Francis Ledwidge," his elegy for an Irish Catholic poet who volunteered for the British army in the First War and was killed in France. The poem is written under the spell of Lowell, whose own elegy appears in the same collection. The bronze soldier who appears in the first line, the use of personal reminiscence, some of the diction ("dolorous and lovely"), and the use of quotations from the hero's letters all help to make of Ledwidge an avatar of Colonel Shaw in Lowell's "For the Union Dead." Heaney uses the serene nobility of Ledwidge as Lowell uses that of Shaw, to render judgment on the lesser men of his own day, although Heaney's poem lacks the self-condemnation which occurs when Lowell's persona, in the late 1950s, crouches to his television set and sees the faces of beaten black children rising like balloons. In "For the Union Dead," as Vendler says, Lowell "cannot remain immune from the corruption he describes. . . . The prophet has vanished; it is a sinner that speaks."[45] It is enough for Heaney that Ledwidge, because he was an artist, could fly by the nets of nationality and religion. Dying as a hero of such independence, he becomes "our dead enigma." The parallel, however, does not stand up: Lowell's Shaw represents a community (the Bostonians of old) whereas Heaney's Ledwidge does not (the Catholics of Ledwidge's day were no nobler than those of Heaney's day). Heaney only desires to replicate Lowell's tones of distance from, but not his guilty sense of solidarity with, contemporary degradation. Of Lowell, Heaney says, "The way we are living, / timorous or bold, / will have been our life" (31). Writing on Heaney from a nationalist perspective, Deane believes that both O'Neill, the victim of "Casualty," and Ledwidge are to be listed among the timorous, evidently because they reject solidarity with the tribe.[46] Not so—these two heroes embody Heaney's sense of the bold, those who overcome timorous conformity to tribal codes of violence. If the political poems of Field Work lack the complexity and depth of North, it is because Heaney must now vindicate for himself the psychological distance from tribal violence that he has already won.

Field Work concludes with a fearsome version of the "Ugolino" section from Dante's Inferno (Cantos 32 and 33). Earlier in the book, Heaney had already alluded to Ugolino's gnawing of Archbishop Roger's brain as a paradigm for the back-biting, head-devouring circle of poets into which he imaginatively casts himself in

"An Afterwards." In this funny but not-funny poem, the poet's wife, guided by Mrs. Virgil, visits him in hell and accuses him of caring more about his career than his wife and family. She does make allowances, though: "You weren't the worst. You aspired to a kind, / Indifferent, faults-on-both-sides tact." Heaney can laugh at his political tact, but will not abandon it; his sense of freedom from the tribe and its violence is complete. The real issues of "An Afterwards," career and marriage, point to areas where the poet's deeper interests and anxieties now lie.

In "Station Island," the long poem published in his book of the same name in 1985, Heaney again raises the issues of *North,* as if to live through them once more. As in the previous decade, he prescribes for himself a set of rituals which he will undertake to perform as a means of understanding his own consciousness. What Heaney now imagines, though, is no pre-Christian blood-sacrifice, but rather the well-known Catholic pilgrimage to Station Island in Lough Derg (Co. Donegal), where the faithful perform arduous spiritual exercises, depriving themselves of food and sleep and spending long hours in prayer (they walk the stations barefoot on the island's stony ground) in order to reach a state of spiritual cleansing and conversion. In each of the sequence's twelve poems, Heaney encounters a ghost from his past or remembers some moment from childhood. The voyage through personal memory is interrupted three times by visitations from literary ghosts—William Carleton, Patrick Kavanagh, and James Joyce—who take the poet to task for his enslavement to the ritual itself. Making frequent use of *terza rima* and occasionally alluding to *The Divine Comedy,* Heaney consciously walks in Dante's company. The island, indeed, is popularly known as Saint Patrick's Purgatory. It is evidently with the aim of purgation, not so much from his own sins as from his allegiance to the purgatory itself, that Heaney undertakes the penitential rite, emerging at the end into a paradise or free space of art. In his final, famous encounter with Joyce, Heaney receives absolution from the sins of religion and is baptized into art. "And don't be so earnest," barks Joyce, "so ready for sackcloth and ashes. / Let go, let fly, forget." Forget what? (Joyce himself never forgot anything.) If indeed Heaney has here written out some turning point in his poetic consciousness, then from what and towards what does he turn?

"Station Island" deals extensively, although not exclusively, with social violence. Early in the sequence, Heaney listens to the ghost of William Carleton (1794–1869), who wrote his own critical account of the Lough Derg pilgrimage and who converted from the Catholic to the Established church in an attempt to escape from both "hard-mouthed Ribbonmen and Orange bigots," as he characterizes the two houses in Heaney's poem. "Station Island," then, restates the premise of *North*—the folk rituals of Ireland, at least of Northern Ireland, are rituals of tribal violence—and adds another: the most violent of these are Catholic rituals. To complete his emancipation from violence, he must now write out his emancipation from religion. He considers the early death of a pious relative and finds a nothingness devoid of meaning which lurks within the rituals of death. He talks to the ghost of a young priest he had known who went on the mission, lost his vocation, and died of malaria. The priest wants to know why the poet is now visiting a place from which "the god has, as they say, withdrawn . . . Unless you are here taking the last look." The poet recalls his sexual initiation and allows Dante's Beatrice to be his patron saint. She guides him out of Saint Patrick's Purgatory into a Horatian, this-worldly spirituality of art and love, "the land of kindness" whose gentle paganism contrasts so markedly with the purgatorial and even infernal characteristics of modern Irish Christianity. He writes of his awakening to sexuality as a part of this emancipation, and listens to Kavanagh, who wrote his own critique of the pilgrimage ("Lough Derg," 1942) and who now tells Heaney that, in his day, men occasionally came here in search of women. (Heaney conveniently does not meet the ghost of Sean O'Faolain, in whose story, "Lovers of the Lake," a Catholic woman comes to the island in an effort to end her adulterous liaison and is pursued there by her lover, who comes to scoff but is won over and agrees to end the affair.)

Why is all this necessary? Wasn't *North* enough? Does Heaney feel compelled to renew his disavowals every ten years, or does the renunciation of "Station Island" represent something new in the development of his poetic consciousness? Heaney's escape from religion is a relatively easy matter: spritual scruples and a misplaced sense of duty are the young priest's problems, not the poet's. Religion serves only as prelude to violence, as we learn when we reach the poem's center. There the poet meets three recent victims of the

Troubles: William Strathearn, an old friend from football-playing days who was murdered in his shop; Colum McCartney, the cousin commemorated in "The Strand at Lough Beg" who here deconstructs his own elegy; and Francis Hughes, a neighbor who starved himself to death in the Maze Prison in 1981. Followed as they are by the poet's *aveu*, his cry of repentance—which in turn is followed by poems of tranquil release—these encounters comprise the sequence's dramatic crux.

Poem 7, the dramatic monologue of Strathearn, constitutes Heaney's most straightforward depiction of violent murder, seen from the eyes of a victim summoned to open a door late at night and half-knowing, as he goes down the stairs, that he is about to die. This moving recital, twenty-five stanzas of *terza rima,* brings us to the real business of the poem, accomplished in two stanzas. Remembering that Strathearn was "the one stylist on the team, / the perfect, clean, unthinkable victim" (that is, either he was clean and therefore, religiously, the perfect victim, or he was perfect and clean and therefore, morally, the unthinkable victim), the poet blurts out his feelings of unaccountable guilt:

> 'Forgive the way I have lived indifferent—
> forgive my timid circumspect involvement,'
>
> I surprised myself by saying. 'Forgive
> my eye,' he said, 'all that's above my head.'
> (*Station Island,* 80; *SP,* 237)

Heaney asks for and receives forgiveness for the position toward violence he has taken since *North.* Yet it is Strathearn who is saying Heaney's lines: "Forgive my eye." There is nothing to forgive. Strathearn was not, in the poem's context, any more involved in politics than Heaney; like the poet he specialized in perfect style. The false voice, the non-self, is that of the monk bowed over his prie-dieu, begging to be forgiven for sins he never committed.

As for Colum McCartney, the assassinated cousin who accuses the poet of literary evasion, Heaney deftly parries his thrust. In the first part of Poem 8, before meeting McCartney, he talks with the ghost of Tom Delaney, an archaeologist and friend who died at thirty-two of cancer. Heaney had visited his friend in the hospital, but failed to get any further in conversation than the normal banter of denial. Both Delaney and McCartney let the poet know—one gently and the other not—that he has been unsuccessful in meeting his human obligations to victims of tragedy. Heaney, that most Catholic of writers in his attention to conscience, is more than willing to admit his moral guilt as an imperfect human being, yet unwilling to compromise his vocation as an artist. Even if he has failed these men as a friend or relative, he has not done so as an artist. He is not, therefore, writing a "recantation of beauty," but rather a vindication of poetic art.[47] He has implicitly answered the words he causes his cousin to speak by writing, in the previous poem about Strathearn, the factual verses his cousin wanted for himself, but there too has arranged to remain circumspect and uninvolved. If he is timorous as a human being, as Deane puts it, he is bold as an artist.

In his third confrontation with violence, Poem 9, Heaney hears the words of the dead hunger-striker, the cause of whose death (when one starves, the digestive tract consumes its own organs) he imagines as symbolic of violence itself: "Often I was dogs on my own track / Of blood on wet grass that I could have licked." Here, for one important moment, Heaney's style drifts back ("I dreamt and drifted") to that of *North*, as he apostrophizes the dead young man in terms reminiscent of "Punishment" ("Little adulteress . . . My poor scapegoat") and of the bog poems in general: "Unquiet soul, they should have buried you / In the bog where you threw your first grenade" (*Station Island*, 84; *SP*, 240).

The scene that follows, that of the poet's repentance, presents a visual symbol in the form of a floating polyp, or an inverted flower, or a single breast, "My softly awash and blanching self-disgust." When the poet confesses and repents, the symbol is transformed into something bright, like a candle, and clear, like an old brass trumpet. These surreal images and their evident connection with pre-verbal feelings make it all the more imperative to understand what sins provoke this contrition.

> 'I repent
> My unweaned life that kept me competent
> To sleepwalk with connivance and mistrust.'

'I hate how quick I was to know my place.
I hate where I was born, hate everything
That made me biddable and unforthcoming.'
(*Station Island,* 85; *SP,* 240-41)

"Connivance" and "biddable" refer to an Ulster Catholic's attitudes toward members of his tribe; "mistrust" and "unforthcoming" refer to his attitudes toward those of the other side. Heaney confesses and repents, simply, of being an Ulster Catholic, and thus concludes Poem 9, "Then I thought of the tribe whose dances never fail / For they keep dancing till they sight the deer." Freeing himself from the evil breast of tribal dependence ("Long sucking the hind tit /Cold as a witch's and as hard to swallow / Still leaves us fork-tongued on the border bit," he had said in *North*),[48] he can now turn in tranquillity to "crediting miracles" (to use a later phrase): untrammeled recollections of childhood in Poem 10 and even, in Poem 11, the translation of mystical verses from St. John of the Cross as a penance once set for him by an enlightened confessor. This priest must, however, give way to Heaney's real spiritual father, Joyce, who appears in the final poem to dispense him from any further allegiance to nationalist politics ("That subject people stuff is a cod's game") and to enjoin on him the necessity of artistic work.

"Station Island," written so explicitly as a homage to Dante and resounding with so many echoes of *North,* never quite achieves the psychological drama of the earlier poems. In an article on Dante written at the time "Station Island" appeared, Heaney summarized his project in terms reminiscent of his programmatic statement eleven years earlier in "Feeling into Words." In "Station Island," says Heaney, "the main tension is between two often contradictory commands: to be faithful to the collective historical experience and to be true to the recognitions of the emerging self."[49] But what exactly does it mean to be faithful to a collective historical experience? To stay in Ulster? To engage in nationalist rhetoric? To attend IRA funerals? It is hard to imagine anyone less faithful to a collective historical experience than the protagonist of "Station Island," making his rounds in the company of Carleton, Kavanagh, and Joyce.

In his famous formula of 1974, written at the time of the bog poems, Heaney set himself this goal: "to encompass the perspectives of a humane reason and at the same time to grant the religious intensity of the violence its deplorable authenticity and complexity."[50] Here the conflicting claims of reason and the unconscious, *logos* and *mythos,* the individual and the tribe, idealism and fact, resonate strongly with the artistic data of *North.* When he writes "Station Island," Heaney is less concerned with the conflict between strong forces within himself and more concerned with his relation to a world around him, a world which knows him well. That concern had already begun in *North 2,* especially in its last poem, "Exposure," where the rueful wood-kerne weighs his responsible *tristia,* trying to say and do the right thing, and wonders if he has missed his magic moment of poetic greatness. Ten years later, Heaney is still publicly defining his role as a poet, but now has exchanged his earlier anxieties for a more relaxed self-assurance. There is something almost too self-conscious in the imperious way that Joyce recognizes Heaney as a latter-day Stephen Dedalus, as a chosen one. Anxious to avoid making this impression, Heaney argues that the Dante of "Station Island" is Mandelstam's innovative and rebellious Dante, not Eliot's patriarchal Dante, the icon of cultural orthodoxy. Heaney nevertheless has difficulty making us believe in the authenticity, in the immediacy of his crisis in "Station Island" or of its resolution. Rather Heaney is elaborately explaining, dramatizing, and contextualizing the crisis of a decade before. When the poet has Joyce advise him to "Let go, let fly, forget," we feel a certain nostalgia for the insouciance of private speech in *North,* where the poet did indeed let fly with a voice less concerned than now about the opinions of others. "And don't be so earnest," says Joyce, "so ready for the sackcloth and the ashes." "Earnest" here does not mean, one senses, "attentive to conscience," but rather "attentive to interviews and public statements." Preoccupied as it is with social violence, "Station Island" takes its place after the poems of *Field Work* in a long, but now hastening withdrawal from violence as a concern of the self.

Heaney's "widened gaze," of which Vendler speaks in discussing *The Haw Lantern* (1987), gives further evidence of the poet's increasing distance from violence as a personal problem; he has now reached, says Vendler, that moment "when the gaze of the artist widens beyond the private concerns of the self."[51] Allegory, Heaney's new-found technique for writing political poetry, permits him to write of tribal hostilities in a manner as remarkable for its serenity as was that of *North* for its anguish. The collection's opening poem, "Alphabets," explicitly discusses the poet's intellectual evolution from his "wide pre-reflective stare" ("wide" here in the sense of wide eyes, not Vendler's widened gaze) to the kind of mature, universal perspective symbolized by the "O" of the globe hanging from the alchemist's ceiling, with its allusions to Shakespeare's Globe Theater and to the globe seen by an astronaut in space. The child, once subjugated to the elements of first letters and to the attitudes of those who taught him, has now expanded his perspective, so that "the figure of the universe / And 'not just single things' would meet his sight."[52]

Not that Heaney could ever write a book of poetry without some soldiers in it, or some other threat to life and consciousness. His brilliant "From the Frontier of Writing" uses the menace of a border checkpoint as a symbol of the experience of writing. To drive a car across the border between the two Irelands was, until recently, to know the "tightness and the nilness" of seeing a gun pointed at one's head while one answered a soldier's questions and then advanced the car "with guarded unconcerned acceleration."[53] Amazingly, though, this array of inhibitory forces, these symbolic barriers to free expression, themselves become the means of entering into such expressive freedom. Heaney's alchemy transforms the border into a *mental* mechanism of inhibition, the *personal* barrier between everyday speech and writing. Thus when the guns are pointed at the driver, "everything is pure interrogation" (meaning self-interrogation), and when he passes the second checkpoint (at a border, one must always endure two of these), he emerges into a space whose images recall the conclusion of "Station Island": "And suddenly you're through, arraigned yet freed, / as if you'd passed from behind a waterfall / on the black current of a tarmac road."[54] This is deft indeed: Heaney dispels soldiers by allegorizing them. Real soldiers inhibit citizens, but allegorical soldiers symbolize the inhibitions writers experience when they begin to write. Having once responded to social violence personally by writing poetry, by unearthing his unconscious, the poet has now achieved such a conscious distance from that violence that he can imagine soldiers as an allegory of the very unconscious processes one undergoes in the act of writing.

The word "clearance," here meaning "permission to pass" (the on/off mike gives the "squawk of clearance"), becomes a touchstone for Heaney, most notably in the sequence of poems after the death of his mother, also published in *The Haw Lantern* and entitled "Clearances." In his elegy he imagines the moment of a person's death by comparing it to the felling of a tree, so that "the space we stood around had been emptied," "clearances . . . suddenly stood open." The mourner's empty soul becomes the newly barren plot of ground: "I thought of walking round and round a space / Utterly empty, utterly a source / Where the decked chestnut tree had lost its place." [55] This clearance in turn reminds us of an earlier moment in "Station Island," where the pious faithful endlessly do their rounds, rounds with which the poet cannot sympathize, aware as he is of a death whose meaninglessness obstructs faith:

> I thought of walking round
> and round a space utterly empty,
> utterly a source, like the idea of sound
>
> or like the absence sensed in swamp-fed air
> above a ring of walked-down grass and rushes
> where we once found the bad carcass and scrags of hair
> our dog that had disappeared weeks before.
> (*Station Island*, 68; *SP*, 290)

One wonders if the word "clearance" did not occur to Heaney, as it occurs in *The Haw Lantern*, first as a debased term for military control but then, as the poet's gaze widened and deepened, as a word for the emptiness of bereavement, an emptiness which can only be filled from within, from silence ("A soul ramifying and forever / Silent, beyond silence listened for"). Issues of love and loss, of death and belief, have clearly replaced those of political repression and personal freedom, so that military clearance to cross a border gives way to the clearance of space in the soul after loss. Ultimately the two uses of "clearance" converge upon the same point of consciousness, where the first (permission to cross a frontier) and the second (abandonment and silence) coalesce into the moment of poetic inspiration, the moment when some hitherto unsayable thing can be said.

If Heaney's allegorical distancing from violence gives him "clearance" to move away from the political and into the personal, it also provides him with that long-sought platform from which, with his Archimedes' lever, he can lift the earth of Ulster into the sky of humanistic art—a neater, gentler operation than Hercules' hefting of Antaeus. "From the Canton of Expectation" contrasts the ineffectual optatives of an older generation in its pre-Troubles speeches and prayers (the language of "would that we might") with the barbarous imperatives of a new, stone-throwing generation (the language of "give it to me now"). The poet condemns both groups for their fundamental disregard for "right action" (although he does not say what right action is) and takes as his hero Noah, "who stood his ground in the indicative, / whose boat will lift when the cloudburst happens."[56] Heaney here is looking to the group of Russian poets he admires so much—Tsvetaeva, Akhmatova, the Mandelstams, Pasternak—as models of writers for whom the writing of poetry *was* right action: right because they spoke the truth in a world where everyone else spoke lies.[57] Since Heaney deeply admires these heroes—Mandelstam writing "The Stalin Epigram" and waiting to be arrested—one wonders why he chooses Noah as his named patriarch. True, Noah was the one just man, but how did *he* "stand his ground in the indicative?" Heaney's answer is, by building the ark, a project which still echoes in the poet's ears with "hammerblows on clinkered planks, / the uncompromised report of driven thole-pins." Noah's carpentry stands for the honest art of "is," while the result of his work, the boat which "will lift when the cloudburst happens," stands for what the poet here hopes for as his own destiny, survival and personal peace.

Noah survived God's cloudburst, but Mandelstam did not survive Stalin's. The conflated persona of Noah-Mandelstam-Heaney raises a thorny question of motive. Does Noah-Heaney intend to save just himself or the world as well? What faithful remnant will the latter-day maker include on his boat when the rain starts to fall? Unlike Mandelstam, Heaney has no fear of being arrested for his honesty, although one cannot imagine any publicly articulate Irish person being quite at ease in a land of unpredictable and unreasonable reprisals. Like Mandelstam, Heaney wishes to stand his ground in the indicative. Like Noah, he wishes his work to be a refuge for others. Like Noah, finally, and unlike Mandelstam, he intends to survive the deluge. Although the precise tenancy of Heaney's ark is unclear at the poem's end, the likelihood of the lift-off is assured. Noah, Mandelstam, and Heaney speak, or act, on behalf of a remnant, a faithful few in a time of social catastrophe. Read in terms of its most basic motives, "From the Canton of Expectation" contains Heaney's condemnation of a whole culture and his desire to sail free from it, like the men in the boat stuck on the altar of Clonmacnoise: "The freed ship sailed, and the man climbed back."[58]

Heaney's widened gaze, or rather his more elevated vantage point, permits him greater freedom in the writing of political commentary then he ever enjoyed in the seventies. One remembers the almost infuriated sense of strictures which so effectively restrained the verses of *North* 2 ("where tongues lie coiled, as under flames lie wicks"). Now, instead of recounting the personal shocks he suffers from tribal ideologies, Heaney is able to examine those ideologies by means of allegory and, in "The Mud Vision," satire.[59] In *North* 2 Heaney sometimes speaks in the first person plural as if within a social cage from which the "I" cannot escape ("smoke-signals are loud-mouthed compared with us"). Now he ironically uses "we" (much in the style of Edwin Arlington Robinson's "so on we worked, and waited for the light") to speak, as a journalist might, in tones of casual objectivity about people whom he knows intimately ("we sleepwalked / The line between panic and formulae"). The vision— a great "rose window of mud" spinning in the air—means different things to different spectators. To the faithful it is a miracle, rousing them to a new sense of hope in divine intervention, a sense that providence has not abandoned the province. For the poet who made himself famous by writing about frogspawn and bog corpses, the "sullied yet lucent . . . original clay, transfigured and spinning," symbolizes his whole poetic *oeuvre*, his long-standing project of remaining faithful to fact and transcending fact. The mud is still there, sullied, but now spinning and lucent.

By saying "we," Heaney also allies himself in some sense with the Irish citizenry; although, as in the case of Noah, it is unclear just how far this alliance goes. In the poem's dramatic conclusion, people and poet share each other's fate. The vision ceases; the hope that it presaged a new age dies:

Just like that, we forgot that the vision was ours,

Our one chance to know the incomparable
And dive to a future. What might have been origin
We dissipated in news.
(*The Haw Lantern*, 48–49; *SP*, 298)

Is the poet-as-prophet here commenting, in his ironic mode, on the failure of a civilization to awaken to a sign, one which the poet understood but the people did not? In that case the sign might well be the poet's own work. To extend this possibility a step further, one recalls that right action in "The Canton of Expectation" was seen as standing in the indicative, being faithful to empirical reality—a faithfulness that brought salvation. The mud of things as they are lifts off (like the boat in the cloudburst lifting off from the mud) to become a vision of things as they might be but (because people are obtuse) will not be. Or is the poet truly rejoining the people and, as journalist, chronicling an event of collective loss? Perhaps both. Heaney, who was to turn fifty two years after *The Haw Lantern* was published, would soon write of "me waiting until I was nearly fifty / To credit marvels."[60] In context, those lines sound purely personal echoes, almost as though the only marvels one can credit at fifty are those relating to one's own feelings and attitudes. In "The Mud Vision," though, as in "Exposure," Heaney gives us the fleeting sense of a missed opportunity, as though he *might have* credited marvels which would have saved a populus—that would have been truly marvelous. Either, then, the boat did not lift off when the cloudburst happened (perhaps, like the mud vision, it disappeared), or it did lift off, but then it was only a coracle built for one, not an ark.

As their titles suggest, Heaney's most recent collections of poetry have tended to further his progress up and away from earthbound anxieties about social violence. *Seeing Things* and *The Spirit Level* gather within them poems of lightness and transcendence, of "walking on air."[61] Both in his Oxford and his Nobel Lectures, Heaney has justified the political value of his anti-political trajectory since *North*, successfully claiming for poetry, and for himself as poet, the charism of salving history's wounds. Now, when the Heaney of the nineties does return to themes of social violence, we expect him to speak from a stylistic eminence. The title of his most recent book, although it refers to an old childhood game ("Find me a bubble for the spirit level"), evokes levels of the spirit, implicitly promising elevations from the mundane to the lofty. And the promise is kept as Heaney chronicles his emancipation from a self which was once trapped in history. In "The Flight Path," however, and more fully in "Mycenae Lookout," Heaney re-enters the emotional underground of *North*, fully recovering his troubled self. This discordant note among the harmonies of Heaney's recent poetry—its almost heretical strain, given the assured syntheses of Heaney's lectures—opens up new depths in his poetry of social violence.

Much of Heaney's recent poetry about history, then, is spoken by one who has fully awakened from history's nightmare. In "A Sofa in the Forties" Heaney writes of the image with which he begins and ends his Nobel lecture: the sofa in his childhood home on which he and his siblings would pretend they were riding a train. "Ghost-train? Death-gondola?" asks the poet, imagining the sofa as the vehicle on which, without choosing to, "we entered history and ignorance": "Our only job to sit, eyes straight ahead, / And be transported and make engine noise" (*The Spirit Level*, 12; *SP*, 373-74). It was on this sofa that Heaney as a child also heard the wartime broadcasts of the BBC, transmitted in accents foreign to children living on a Derry farm. Although the poem leaves the child still traveling into history and ignorance, the Nobel lecture fastens on the radio broadcast as the child's introduction to a wider world, his first emergence from a pre-reflective self, his departure on a journey very different from that on which the sofa-train was careering as it headed into a dark tunnel. Now, in the Nobel lecture, he says,

> . . . it is that journey which has brought me now to this
> honoured spot. And yet the platform here feels more like
> a space station than a stepping-stone, so that is why, for
> once in my life, I am permitting myself the luxury of
> walking on air.
> I credit poetry for making this space walk possible.[62]

Both the poet and the lecturer equate, as it is customary to do, the cosmopolitan with the enlightened. One awakens from history's nightmare by advancing one's education, learning languages, visiting other cultures, and so on. No doubt. On the other hand, contemporary history is full of horrors perpetrated by highly educated ideologues and technicians. Even today many fine sofas bear their cargo of the supposed best and brightest into history and ignorance at no slower a rate than the long-ago sofa in Derry bore its uncouth children. There is something vaguely unsettling in this poet's stance, looking back from such a distance at a scene which, for all its childishness, could well symbolize one's own adult sense of being swept along by forces out of one's control, even while one is listening to the BBC news or NPR's "All Things Considered." Heaney's confident reading of the poem shows no trace of the unease which might arise for the reader who chances to see Heaney's sofa as a mirror rather than a photograph album. When I heard the poem's title, "A Sofa in the Forties," for the first time, I had the fleeting, unpleasant thought that "the Forties" referred not to a decade of this century, but to someone's age.

The poet maintains his far-away gaze when he sees his brother Hugh, the subject of "Keeping Going": "The piper coming from far away is you."[63] Here, Hugh is impersonating a player of bagpipes, using "a whitewash brush for a sporran." Little is said, though, to locate this scene in a specific time: participles are piled up ("coming," "wobbling," "pretending," "nearly bursting," "keeping," "biding") until some imperfects tentatively locate the action in a remembered past ("spring airs spelled lime," "smells brought tears"). Not only is the piper emerging from a distant time and visual space, as his unfamiliar form becomes more and more distinct (what we thought was a sporran turns out to be a whitewash brush), but also from a social distance. Hugh, that is, has "kept on" doing what they all did as children: he continues to tend a farm in Derry, keeping cattle and whitewashing walls.

One day a man was murdered against a whitewashed wall in the town, shot at point blank by an assassination squad (Heaney devotes sixteen slow-motion lines to the gory event). The whitewash brush, having become a sporran, must again become a whitewash brush; the wall must be repainted. The poet imagines his brother coming close to despair ("wondering, is this all? As it was / In the beginning, is now and shall be?"), but then reviving, "rubbing [his] eyes and seeing our old brush / Up on the byre door, and keeping going." This brush, a sentimental symbol, now functions ironically by dividing the different ways in which the two men cope with a sectarian killing. The brother, or whoever owns that particular wall, must remove the splattered gore. The poet, living far away, finds consolation by imagining the brush as a sporran—a poetic act of redeeming the mundane—and gratuitously supposes his brother to be deriving the same consolation when he sees that humble object hanging on its nail in the barn. "Which is he?" the poet asks in a poem about Saint Kevin, whom legend supposes to have kept his arms extended for the length of time it took a blackbird to nest and hatch her eggs in his hands, "self-forgetful or in agony all the time?" If a saint, then self-forgetful (the brush is a sporran); if a mere man, in agony (this brush is a brush). To credit poetry, for Heaney, is to credit miracles. In writing a poem for his brother Hugh, he expresses a wish to extend that credit to others, but tacitly acknowledges the difficulty of doing so. Hugh, like Saint Kevin, has kept going, but without benefit of miracles; they are the province of the poet, who has also kept going, but not as his brother has, not in Derry.

Poems about violence in *The Spirit Level* align themselves along two complementary axes. Some, like "A Sofa" and "Keeping Going," deal with the poet's itinerary through time, contrasting idyllic pasts with sordid presents, or pre-reflective pasts with reflective presents; others represent the poet's preoccupation with his present status in a politically sensitive Ireland. "Weighing In," although it begins with the remembered image of a 56–pound weight used on the scale in his family farm, turns this image to work as a symbol for the balancing act required of the contemporary poet, whose endless task is to weigh responsibility to others against responsibility to self. He imagines the job as no less onerous than that of Saint Kevin or brother Hugh:

> This principle of bearing, bearing up
> And bearing out, just having to
>
> Balance the intolerable in others
> Against our own.
> ("Weighing In," *The Spirit Level*, 21–23; *SP*, 382)

This a poem about tact, in which the poet expresses his longing "to refuse the other cheek," just once, and hit back—so that "weighing in" acquires its sense of what happens at the start of a fight. The "quick hit" and "drawn blood," of course, refer exclusively to words exchanged in a conversation between people well-known to each other, whose friendship causes the protagonist to pull his punches. The poet regrets this sense of civility: "A deep mistaken chivalry, old friend. / At this stage only foul play cleans the slate." At such a late stage in Heaney's development, does this poem herald a return of the repressed, the poet's nationalist "Papish burn?" The absence of specific detail about the conversation in question is itself a tactful omission, forcing us to believe in the emotion without knowing the emotion's cause. Whatever the slate may be which the foul play of a rude remark might clean, its dirt could never compare to the brains smearing the white wall in that Derry town.

Heaney's sense of distance from violence continues to expand in "The Flight Path," a poem about air travel. In it the poet, raised up from the world, contrasts the largeness of a house where goodbye kisses were being exchanged an hour before (thus a house of the past in air-time) with its present size, a speck on the landscape. As in "Weighing In," the axis of time gives way to the axis of space, as an image from childhood (a paper glider) prompts a brief exercise in autobiography, which then yields to current dilemmas, the balancing of forces within the poet's self. Will I be a localized Dubliner (even a cottage dweller at Glanmore) or an international traveler, commuting every year to Harvard? The seemingly world-weary poet quotes Horace's *caelum non animum mutare*: "Skies change, not cares, for those who cross the seas." Why then, in a poem about distances, the surprising section 4? Written "for the record, in the light / Of everything before and since," zooming back in time to a May morning in 1979 and down in space to a train on the way to Belfast, it presents to us the poet just off the red-eye from New York, being accosted by a stranger who enters his compartment, sits down, and (recognizing the poet—a detail modestly left for us to infer)

> goes for me head on.
> 'When, for fuck's sake, are you going to write
> Something for us?' 'If I do write something,
> Whatever it is, I'll be writing for myself.'
> And that was that. Or words to that effect.
> ("The Flight Path," *The Spirit Level*, 29; *SP*, 385)

What place on the highly sophisticated record of an international artist's flight path (Manhattan, California, Harvard Yard, Glanmore) does this incident have? When the man enters the compartment, he first reminds the poet of a "*film noir* border guard." This phrase condenses an anecdote included in the poem's original version, in which a British border guard detains a poet-friend in an English airport for having written, as a joke, an anti-British sentence on the entry-card next to "purpose of visit."[64] More importantly he reminds the poet of a recent dream in which a grim-faced individual, this man's prototype, importunes him to drive the van in a terrorist attack on a customs post. Following the recorded interchange, the poet reminds us that "the gaol walls all those months were smeared with shite." Thus the red eyes (including the poet's, presumably, after his flight) become the eyes of Ciaran Nugent, one of the hunger strikers in Long Kesh, who in his turn becomes the saddeningly familiar figure of Ugolino in "Dante's scurfy hell," endlessly gnawing the skull of his mortal enemy (an image last seen when Heaney applied it, in "An Afterwards," to the poets in their skull-biting circle of hell).

Most obviously this section of "The Flight Path" constitutes a reply to those, like Desmond Fennell, who have pilloried Heaney for not writing partisan poetry on behalf of the nationalist cause.[65] But why "for the record," when Heaney has expressed his political aesthetic so often and with such skill? His reply to the stranger does not come as news. We must suppose that Heaney is speaking about a private, not a public record of a self which dreams and imagines shifting identities and alternating roles. In this private record, the stranger functions antithetically as both a border guard and a terrorist attacking a border. Which border? Not only that between North and South, but also between conscious and unconscious. Here Heaney returns unexpectedly to the preoccupations of *North,* to that old, inner debate between conformity and power, between the obedient and the grandiose self. Now, however, the roles have reversed themselves. Twenty years before, the enactors of tribal violence ("each neighbourly murder") were those who conformed to their ancestors' codes—mould-hugging Antaeus—whereas the truly grandiose representative of power was Hercules. For the poet, longing to liberate himself from internees and informers and to pursue the diamond absolutes of canonical poetry, the border guard's name was Antaeus and the border's attacker, Hercules. Now, however, having ascended with Hercules on his flight path, the poet is assaulted by violent images of border guards who confine him to his liberal, international allegiance, and of terrorists who urge him to weigh in against such mistaken chivalry with a quick hit or even foul play. On the record's tape (if the plane goes down, there is always the black box), Heaney admits the voice of the terrorist, then puts the man in his place. No hijacking, please.

Having rebuked the stranger's partisan mentality, the poet might have returned to his cultural flight path, taking off from Belfast and heading east, south, or west. Instead of that, he considers the hunger strike, imaginatively entering the Maze prison (which that train to Belfast passes on its way north) and confronting the ravening violence of its inmates. It is still 1979, and while he is safely translating Dante (in his dream, the IRA man tells him that, after he's done his job, he'll be home "as safe as houses"), he sees the red eyes of the hunger-striker: "Drilling their way through the rhymes and images / Where I too walked behind the righteous Virgil, / As safe as houses and translating freely" (*The Spirit Level*, 30; *SP*, 386). Even as he rebukes the hostile stranger, then, the poet must again suffer from his sense of abandoning his people. More profoundly he must reflect that as a poet, he, too, exercises a disguised kind of violence. Heaney writes little about the hunger strike of the late seventies and early eighties, but when he does, he finds something that touches a nerve. In "Station Island 9," his moment of anguished repentance is preceded and therefore produced by the ghost of a hunger-striker who tells how he died, literally, by eating himself up from within. However high-minded and bold they may be meant to sound, the words "I'll be writing for myself" echo falsely in the poet's consciousness, sending back reverberations of blown-up borders and shit-covered walls, vibrations of hate and envy. Yeats, while praying for his daughter, declared that hate and envy were sold only in thoroughfares, but never in the minds of noble artists. Here Heaney, even as he vindicates his artistic nobility by silencing the terrorist, finds hate and envy awaiting him, ready for ambush on the thoroughfares of the mind.

Concluding the poem, Heaney returns us to a real roadblock so that he can tell a real policeman that he comes from "far away." And that is the end of the matter, as we leave the poetic pilgrim

climbing up to the "hermit's eyrie above Rocamadour," a moun-
tainous sanctuary in France, and seeing a dove which, like Yeats's
curlew, "kept on rising." Such is Heaney's way of "keeping go-
ing"—a perseverance in art for which the world gives thanks. What
makes "The Flight Path" a remarkable poem, though—a worthy
successor to the poems of *North*—is the baggage the poet takes
along on his flight, even opening it for inspection: that residual,
earth-bound hostility which one carries on every flight, no matter
how high. So Horace's *caelum non animum* turns back to the poet-
traveler's self. Even when one sky is changed for another, the bur-
den of violence in the self remains.

Since the cease-fire declared by the IRA in the late summer of
1994, a new sub-genre of "cease-fire poems" has begun to make its
appearance in Ireland, although the uncertain nature of that new
state of affairs in Ulster, subsequent relapses into hostility, and the
new cease-fire in 1997 have made poets and public alike increas-
ingly wary of "exhaustions nominated peace" (a phrase from 1975).
In "Mycenae Lookout" and "Tollund," his cease-fire poems pub-
lished in *The Spirit Level*, Heaney does not so much look forward
to social change as back at his own career, his "keeping going"
over that span of thirty years which has coincided with the
Troubles.

In both poems the poet represents himself as spectator of a
violent world: first he is a sentinel, then a tourist. "Mycenae Look-
out" consists of five dramatic monologues, all spoken by the watch-
man whose speech opens Aeschylus' *Agamemnon,* one of whose
lines provides Heaney with the poem's opening epigraph:

> May my king come home, and I
> take up within this hand the hand I love. The rest
> I leave to silence; for an ox stands huge upon
> my tongue.[66]

Like Aeschylus' watchman, the Irish poet sees but cannot speak;
his tongue is trampled on by cattle. Whereas he can see and imag-
ine violence "inside me like struck sound in a gong," he cannot
make that gong sound in the ears of others. Following all of Heaney's
claims to freedom of thought and voice, what are we to make of
this new version of the tongue's government?

And then the ox would lurch against the gong
And deaden it and I would feel my tongue
Like the dropped gangplank of a cattle truck,
Trampled and rattled, running piss and muck,
All swimmy-trembly as the lick of fire,
A victory beacon in an abattoir . . .
("Mycenae Lookout," *The Spirit Level* 34; *SP*, 387)

The poem can best be read as an echo or reprise of *North*. Whereas in "Kinship" Heaney the ancient Celt looked up to Tacitus and his legions on the Roman wall, asking for a fair report (later in the book he was the escaped wood-kerne), it is Heaney the watchman who now stands on the wall, looking down on history's participants. His heroic couplets in poem 1, a strangely formal choice of verse for a speaker with an ox on his tongue, recall the witty formal arrangements (*abab*) of "Whatever You Say, Say Nothing." The watchman leads a poet's inner life, imagining with his mind (he dreams of slaughters he cannot see), staring at the unseen (he looks "beyond the city and the border"), and weighing the ethical elements of what he considers ("I balanced between destiny and dread"). Heaney's poet-sentry admits that the war has altered his consciousness; although he took no part in it, it has "flawed the black mirror of my frozen stare." The watchman could tell the king that his adulterous wife is planning to kill him, but he does not; his only job is to look outwards. Having repeatedly argued on behalf of Joycean poetic independence ("I'll be writing for myself"), the poet here resumes the sackcloth and ashes which Joyce once told him to throw away.

In poem 2 Heaney returns us to "Punishment," with its slender lines and emaciated protagonist—and here Cassandra replaces the Windeby girl:

> Her soiled vest,
> her little breasts,
> her clipped, devast-
>
> ated, scabbed
> punk head,
> the char-eyed

famine gawk—
she looked
camp fucked

and simple.
(*The Spirit Level*, 36; *SP*, 388)

Because Cassandra is a spoil of war, a Trojan handed over as booty to Agamemnon, her debased aspect constitutes an implicit condemnation of the Greeks ("little rent / cunt of their guilt") and therefore a reason to do her in even before she starts speaking of Clytemnestra's wrongdoing. Witnesses who name the guilty are considered guilty of a yet greater crime by the guilty whom they name. By imaging Cassandra as witness and therefore guilty, Heaney recreates the position he himself had to occupy in "Punishment" while witnessing crimes against women. He is able to begin poem 2 with an implicit conclusion to the earlier poem: "No such thing / as innocent / bystanding." There is a further sense in which the Windeby girl, Cassandra, and the Belfast women witness violence: they are its passive victims, having first been violated and then punished for having been violated. The punished adulteresses and the guilty bystander finally coalesce in one person. Cassandra becomes the watchman, because to be abused by violence is to witness it. The watchman-poet becomes Cassandra, because to witness violence is to be guilty of imposing guilt on the violent. Witnesses are punished by those whom they observe, as whores are punished by those whom they service.

When, in poem 3, the watchman becomes the Grauballe man ("My soul wept in my hand . . . , my whole being rained / Down on myself"), he considers the mystery presented in that earlier poem, the relation between violence and beauty. Both *eros* and *thanatos* spring from human sources too deep for speech ("Our war stalled in the pre-articulate"). Dismissing the "claques" who need to be heard and seen on the center stage of politics, as Heaney does in *North* 2, the watchman prefers to gaze at those who are passionate in their violence; so he stands "watching as a man / Jumped a fresh earth-wall and another ran / Amorously, it seemed, to strike him down." This pair of deadly lovers corresponds symmetrically to "that holmgang" of *North* 2 "where two berserks club each other to death / For honour's sake, greaved in a bog, and sinking."

The watchman must therefore, in poem 4, raise the question of sex and violence in relation to the house of Atreus and its fall. Here Heaney recalls "North," where sex and violence, Viking-style, had a lumpish, persistent quality: "thick-witted couplings and revenges, / the hatreds and behindbacks / of the althing, lies and women, / exhaustions nominated peace." Now Heaney brings his allusion to that poem into sharper, more dramatic relief as the watchman speaks of Clytemnestra and Aegisthus: "Behind backs / each one of them confided / it was sexual overload / every time they did it." Now everybody's doing it—gods and goddesses thundering and thudding up in the clouds, or the men in the Trojan horse who almost mounted each other when Helen caressed the horse's side— everybody but the watchman, whose silence guarantees his favor with Aegisthus and his loathing of himself. What is the difference between sex and violence? If you thought *eros* was a life-principle and *thanatos* a death-principle, the watchman will tell you you're wrong. Lust ends in exhaustion; violence ends in death; yet exhaustion and death are nominated peace. So the watchman's familiar pun on "come": "the queen wailed on and came . . . , and the peace had come upon us." In between the first and second comings there is the betrayal and murder of Agamemnon.

In his final reprise of *North*, Heaney in poem 5 takes up the elements of his earlier metaphor and myth, the bog and even the bog's antecedents, the well, the omphalos of the family pump. Having just recalled the bath where Agamemnon was murdered (his "blood-bath"), the watchman now dreams of bathing in clean water, where the hero, "stripped to the skin, blood-plastered, moaning," can be cleansed and renewed. He envisages the well under the Acropolis as the truly sacred center of Athens, its "old lifeline," but also as its fatal weak spot when found by invaders, so that the downward and upward motions of "besieger and besieged, / the treadmill of assault / turned waterwheel" are co-opted into the fatal cycle of violence. Finally there is the well at Mycenae—the local well—into which both watchman and poet look and, in looking, find hope:

And then this ladder of our own that ran
deep into a well-shaft being sunk
in broad daylight, men puddling at the source

through tawny mud, then coming back up
deeper in themselves for having been there
like discharged soldiers testing the safe ground,

finders, keepers, seers of fresh water
in the bountiful round mouths of iron pumps
and gushing taps.
(*The Spirit Level,* 46; *SP,* 394)

Heaney has taken us to the bog—that watery center where the ritu-
als of violence were enacted year by year—and imaginatively trans-
formed it into the well, so that, instead of succumbing there to the
goddess of violence, the heroic survivor of violence is freed from
blood, made clean. Beyond that, he takes us back to the well of
"Personal Helicon" and to the source of his spiritual life, the water
pump in his family's courtyard.[67]

Is Heaney's cease-fire a peace or just another round of cou-
plings and exhaustions? Must the poet, for all his carefully chosen
positions and words, still assume guilt for the social sins which his
words have never changed, just as the watchman professed self-
loathing for his inability to deter Clytemnestra or save Agamemnon?
Like a subterranean fault line, "Mycenae Lookout" undermines
the structure of Heaney's aesthetic and political doctrines by throw-
ing into relief the troubled conscience of their author. Moving his
gaze even further outward (to Greece) and backward (to the
Mycenean age) than *North,* Heaney seems to be looking away from
the Irish conflict, but in reality is looking more deeply into both it
and himself. "Mycenae Lookout" is not a poem for "us," as the
grim-faced nationalist (one of the "berserks") demanded in the train;
it says nothing about one side or the other. Having extricated him-
self from tribal rituals of violence in *North,* Heaney here examines
the connections between art and violence within the artist's self;
when he tells the nationalist that he writes for himself, he states a
deeply ironic truth. In "Mycenae Lookout," he writes for himself a
kind of violence from which any real escape is impossible. Because
he is required to gaze far away from the immediate scene (poem 1),
he cannot speak to the moment; if he tries, his tongue turns from a
gong to a gangplank for cattle. Because he writes of violence imagi-
natively, as from the consciousness of one suffering violence (poem

2), he becomes guilty of leading others into guilt, a whore of violence. Because he loves beauty (poem 3), he must understand that the desire for beauty and the lust for blood are somehow joined in the deep, pre-articulate places from which our being flows. And because he understands desire (poem 4), he must understand how both sexual and violent impulses flow, in their turn, back to the wordless place called death. Poems 3 and 4, "His Dawn Vision" and "The Nights," thus provide a short view of the life span seen as a brief period of lucidity between one darkness and another, a short respite from that state in which our most longed-for desires and our most dreaded fears cannot be told apart. Relinquishing his post-*North* preoccupation with political and literary contexts, he again descends single-mindedly into the place of myth, and again emerges with a vision of violence as endemic to the human condition. Not since *North* has Heaney let himself down that far. If, in *North,* violence seemed to be an aspect of tribal culture, a mind-set which could be changed by anyone desirous of coming to consciousness, in "Mycenae Lookout" the outlook is far less optimistic. One may change skies and trains, but not one's violent animus.

What then is offered by poem 5, "His Reverie of Water," which represents nothing but Heaney's stock-in-trade, his images of water—and they mostly polluted by the blood of violence? Returning to the bath, the well, and the fountain—to the purest sources of life—Heaney recites his *credo quia absurdum,* his act of faith that, in spite of (or because of) what he, the watchman has seen, a source of humane life exists, a source of which he will write in verse. The poem's long last sentence begins by plunging a ladder deep into the well-shaft, so that seekers of water are "men puddling at the source / through tawny mud, then coming back up / deeper in themselves for having been there . . . , finders, keepers, seers of fresh water / in the bountiful round mouths of iron pumps / and gushing taps" (*The Spirit Level,* 46; *SP,* 394). In this aqueous act of faith, Heaney courageously follows Joyce's advice to stay away from political messages; he has nothing conceptual to offer, only an image, a *style.* The "bountiful, round mouths of iron pumps" speak of nothing but themselves, embodying no theory and prescribing no cure. Writing a poetry of guilt and contamination, he bravely offers no answer, but only brings water. While the phenomena of violence can be paraphrased in speaking of the poem, the healing images of water cannot. Heaney wages his whole poetic career, his "keeping going," on the salvific nature of poetry as an affirmation of death overcome by life, of the understandable overcome by the visible.

When the priest's ghost asks the unbelieving Heaney why he is going through the motions at Station Island, he suggests his own answer to the poet: "[Y]ou are here taking the last look." In "Tollund," at the conclusion of *The Spirit Level,* Heaney takes a last look at the bog poems. Dated September, 1994, the very moment of the first cease-fire, the poem fulfills a poetic promise made twenty-two years earlier ("Some day I will go to Aarhus"). It tells of a pilgrimage to Jutland, where "they dug him out," that first corpse whose spell launched Heaney on his imaginative descent into tribal violence.

Although written in six traditional stanzas of rhymed *abba* pentameter, "Tollund" is a postmodern poem, blithely demolishing a single myth into showers of commercial fragments, an older poet's benevolent joke about his youthful seriousness. It is Sunday morning (as in "A Kite for Michael and Christopher," Heaney waits until others are in church for his most important personal rituals), the poet is with friends or family, and now an unspecified but amicable "we" replaces the anguished "I" of the earlier poem. "I will stand a long time," promised the pilgrim-to-be, and so it is:

> That Sunday morning we had travelled far.
> We stood a long time out in Tollund Moss:
> The low ground, the swart water, the thick grass
> Hallucinatory and familiar.
> ("Tollund," *The Spirit Level* 80; *SP*, 410)

Familiar because hallucinatory: this is the place where all those atavistic dreams began. Now, though, "The scarecrow's arms / Stood open opposite the satellite / Dish in the paddock . . . Things had moved on." A sunny prosperity has put all the ghosts of the bog to sleep ("dormant quags"), relegating them to the status of artifacts by means of tourist signs and street signs. "Out there in Jutland," the young poet had predicted, "In the old man-killing parishes / I will feel lost, / Unhappy and at home." He was mostly wrong, partly right: he feels neither lost nor unhappy, but he does feel at home: " . . . it was user-friendly outback / Where we stood footloose, at home beyond the tribe." "Friendly" cancels "unhappy"; "footloose" (and the roadsigns) cancel "lost." And then "beyond the tribe." The postmodernist solution to tribal violence lies in capitalism: put everyone in a shopping mall or a theme park, and there will be no more ideological reasons for violence. Other kinds of warfare—poor against rich, gang against gang, corporation against community—will replace the old, but that is of no concern to the poet on this sunny September Sunday. For him to be "at home beyond the tribe" in Jutland does not mean that he has escaped his own tribe, but that, having at last followed that tribe back to its Nordic birthplace, he has found satellite dishes and a comfortable cottage industry of tourism. There is no tribe left. Things have moved on.

Like the bemused tourist telling of a visit to some island lost in the Pacific ("it could have been Fort Lauderdale"), Heaney keeps imagining Tollund as some other, more familiar place: first the idealized "Townland of Peace," the Irish community which might be but is not, and then, as he orients himself to the place's modernity, he realizes that "it could have been Mulhollandstown or Scribe," just another imagined, prosperously developing town. To find oneself "footloose, at home beyond the tribe," then, is to find oneself absolved by commerce, granted a reprieve from anxiety by the contentments of money. As the poem ends, this sense of well-being reaches inward to the soul:

> The byroads had their names on them in black
> And white; it was user-friendly outback
> Where we stood footloose, at home beyond the tribe,
>
> More scouts than strangers, ghosts who'd walked abroad
> Unfazed by light, to make a new beginning
> And make a go of it, alive and sinning,
> Ourselves again, free-willed again, not bad.
> (*The Spirit Level,* 80–81; *SP,* 410)

We remember that the force of "The Tollund Man" derived from the poet's fascination with the bog corpse, his identification with his subject. Here, then, the poet momentarily resumes that persona, not now as an interred corpse but as a ghost set free to walk in the light of day. It is difficult to identify the voice that speaks these lines. When I first read the words "Ourselves again, free-willed again," I recalled the gentle fox-trot of a forgotten song ("I'm wild again, beguiled again"). The abrupt, ambiguous sense of closure given by "not bad" (like *pas mal,* the phrase can mean just about anything you want) contributes to the sense of humorous dismissal of a subject, as though the speaker were light-heartedly withdrawing from a once-serious setting, changing the mood with a good line before he slips away. He has answered his own question. "Yes, we have lost track of the light," says Clamence at the end of Camus' *The Fall,* "the mornings, the holy innocence of those who forgive themselves."[68] It is just that light which Heaney strives to recover at the end of "Tollund" by forgiving himself.

In this last poem of *The Spirit Level,* Heaney makes a jest of precisely those concerns and poems which he so gravely reconsidered in "Mycenae Lookout." Both poems give readings of myths; and although the Greek myth is taken seriously by the watchman while the tourist makes light of the Nordic myth, the speaker of both poems is an imaginative traveler in an elsewhere which he implicitly compares to the unmentioned "here" of Northern Ireland, the land of fire and cease-fire. As *social* commentary, the two poems taken together represent the uncertainties which any sensitive observer might feel in this new state of affairs. Will the cease-fire merely herald a new chapter in the long tale of tribal hostility—that is the watchman's version—or will it instead, as the tourist suggests, bring in the end of tribalism, its Americanization, its exchange of tribal violence for urban, racial and economic violence? Or will Ulster become, as the tourist imagines that Jutland has become, a little place that time and the developers forgot, a "townland of peace" where there is just enough modernity but not too much ("light traffic sound"), where the scarecrow and the satellite dish face each other in gentle harmony?

As moral commentary "Tollund" strikes a sinister note in its protestations that "I'm okay and you're okay." Travels into myth should bring the traveler to silent amazement as he beholds what is noble with Keats's Cortez or what is despicable with Heaney's watchman. For tourists, though, it is quite the other way. As they travel they subsume the strange into the familiar ("It could have been Mulhollandstown"), so that each new experience, if the trip goes according to plan, reinforces a sense of personal well-being in the traveler. This well-being is guaranteed by his control over where he goes and even, as he sets forth armed with camera, what he will see. Whereas the voyager to Mycenae can only speak of the deep, muddy wells and the fresh water coming out of the pumps, neither of which he can explain, the traveler to Tollund explains every-thing, obscuring detail by explaining detail. Things have been resituated; things have moved on; things are user-friendly. We are starting again; we celebrate our imperfections; we claim our free will as ours. We're okay. The tone of "Tollund" is unquestionably one of laughing relief, as if to say "Thank God, that's over," but the laughter does not fully communicate itself. Rather it proves disqui-eting and isolates the speaker as an object of curiosity. It under-mines itself—but isn't postmodern writing meant to do that?

The antithesis between the personal and the political, as between the romantic and the modern, enjoys a hallowed status in today's criticism. When Bernard-Donals speaks of "the tension in [Heaney's] work between the impulse toward a highly personal poetry, and . . . the impulse toward poetry that could be called political," he is re-porting on the view of a very large majority, a majority which may even include Heaney the critic.[69] Throughout this chapter, I have implicitly argued that such a dichotomy tends to distort our under-standing of Heaney's best political poetry. Lyric poetry, whether romantic or modern, is the poetry of the self, and it is within the self that the conflicts of public life recapitulate themselves, often in an obdurate way which defies analysis or solution. It is part of Heaney's genius as a public poet that he has so extensively explored the self as the site of such conflicts and anxieties.

Heaney has undergone two long-term bouts of wrestling with violence in the self, the first of which concluded with *North*, while the second appears to have reached a moment of conclusion in just a few poems of *The Spirit Level*. In each case, Heaney has cavilled at his serious tone with a voice of irony, so that "Tollund" talks back to "Mycenae Lookout" much as *North* 2 does to *North* 1. The self-criticism contained in such responses contributes to the overall anxiety which Heaney represents in his poems of violence.

It is not unusual for critics to be impatient, as David Lloyd is, of any lyric poetry which gives the impression of "eliding" political realities by speaking of the self. In the world of Heaney's poetry, however, the self is the central political reality, the original building block of any *polis* or gathering of selves. Heaney's poetic selves are those places where dichotomies fail, where assailants and lovers, peace and death, loyalty and treachery, enlightenment and ignorance, embrace but are not reconciled. If politics is the realm where something can always be said and therefore done, the self is the nonpolitical place where there is nothing to say, but everything to be seen. Poetry, which makes nothing happen, is precisely the art form which makes us see this nothing, which makes this nothing happen. "Whatever you say, say nothing," said Heaney's mother to her son, and that is exactly what he has done, saying the nothing, the empty space of the self, where all rational formulations and actions finally end in a self-cancelling round. Who would want to say this nothing? It is a hard calling, one that Heaney the speaker of prose has often tried to conceal. Nevertheless it is in his brilliant faithfulness to that calling that his artistic greatness lies, and also his greatest contribution to politics.

3

MICHAEL LONGLEY

It took me a lifetime to explore
The dusty warren beneath the stage
With its trapdoor opening on to
All that had happened above my head
Like noises-off or distant weather.

—"Fleance"

So writes Michael Longley in the early seventies, assuming the role of Fleance, the son of Banquo who escapes his father's fate by hiding under the stage where *Macbeth* (here taken as a symbol for the whole Northern Irish political carnage) is being played out. Thus imagining himself as an innocent victim of other people's vile behavior, Longley the poet distinguishes himself from all the other poets in this study, even Medbh McGuckian, by his apparent refusal—one which finally proves deceptive—to admit or accept any personal involvement in the Troubles.

I say Longley the poet, because Michael Longley has in fact done more than any of these poets, except perhaps Ciarán Carson, to promote peace and civility in Northern Ireland during the conflicts of the past thirty years. As an influential officer of the Arts Council of Northern Ireland from 1970 to 1991 and as a founding member of the Cultural Traditions Group, Longley has worked tirelessly in the interests of promoting cultural diversity. In his autobiographical piece, "Blackthorn and Bonsai," Longley relates how he has struggled not only with plebeian prejudice but also with bureaucratic obtuseness in his efforts to bring performances of indigenous art to the people of Ulster, "to lift the community into consciousness and self-consciousness."[1] It may indeed be his very sense of nonparticipation in Ulster's ethnic hostility that has made Longley such an effective worker in the cause of promoting cultural understanding. For Longley the poet, though, this rigorous absence of personal involvement in any pattern of violence separates him from his colleagues. He shows no interest either in Heaney's pursuit of understanding such involvement or Mahon's flight from its consequences.

An exception must be made, however, for some of Longley's most recent work, written after a long period during which he published no books of poetry. Now, having relinquished his public work, he has produced two books of poetry which use the perspectives of Greek mythology (as Heaney has done) to develop new ideas and feelings about social violence. These latest works implicitly call into question the authorial attitudes of Longley's best-known poems.

The reasons for Longley's sense of separation from social violence are not obscure. Most obviously Longley was the son of British parents, born in Belfast. (Paulin, although he was born in England of a Scottish father and has lived in England for years, enjoyed the associations of his mother's large Irish family and has written from a far more indigenous Irish perspective than Longley, who had no Irish family.) "For reasons which I don't understand," Longley declared in a recent interview, "I find it difficult to get Belfast into my own poetry—unlike Ciarán Carson or, to a lesser extent, Derek Mahon."[2] Whereas both of these poets, one Catholic and one Protestant, have written of their rootedness in sectarian neighborhoods (the Falls, Glengormley), Longley's Protestant upbringing took place in the more mixed, cosmopolitan South Belfast, where religion and class divided social groups with lines less forbidding, though no less precise, than those to the northwest and northeast:

> I made friends with other pupils and started to explore
> the Lisburn Road. Belfast's more prosperous citizens have
> usually been careful to separate themselves safely from
> the ghettoes of the bellicose working classes. An odd ex-

ception is the Lisburn Road which runs south from the
city centre. Intermittently for about three miles workers'
tiny two-up-and-two-down houses squint across the road
at the drawing-rooms of dentists, doctors, solicitors: on
the right, as you drive towards Lisburn gardenless shad-
owy streets; on the left rhododendrons and rose bushes.
Belfast laid bare, an exposed artery.[3]

As Longley speaks of his upbringing, it becomes clear that the real
divisions were those of class, not religion. Michael and his twin
brother would come back from their all-Protestant school, and have
to change their speech from the Ulster diphthongs "cey-ek" and
"floo-er" to the purer British sounds of "cake" and "floor." "By
the age of six or seven," says Longley, "I was beginning to lead a
double life, learning how to recreate myself twice daily."[4]
      Longley and Mahon attended the same school and university
(though Longley is two years older): the Royal Belfast Academical
Institution and Trinity College, Dublin. Longley's reminiscences
about their friendship and student days serve to make the point
that he is his own man, and that neither he nor Mahon can fairly be
considered a product of Philip Hobsbaum's "Group," meetings of
which both attended in Belfast after leaving Trinity. Less concerned
to create a bohemian self than Mahon, and more interested in tra-
ditional poetic forms than Heaney and the other poets around
Hobsbaum, Longley avoided political means of self-definition from
the outset, preferring in his poetry the mythological, the natural,
and the personal, all for their own sake. In his "Alibis" (the word is
Latin for "elsewheres"), a parallel poem to Mahon's "Lives,"
Longley declares that "My one remaining ambition is to be / The
last poet in Europe to find a rhyme" (*Poems*, 104). Ironically, of
course, he does not here find one.
      Longley has often confessed himself incapable of writing about
the Troubles, a set of events too terrible to imagine poetically. "I
continue to be dumbfounded by the awfulness of our situation," he
said in the early nineties, adding that "all my political prognostica-
tions have been wrong."[5] Like Fleance fleeing from the senseless
carnage which is soon to include him, Longley accepts a position of
irrelevance, hiding under the stage and coming out again only when
the crowd has gone home:

In the empty auditorium I bowed
To one preoccupied caretaker
And, without removing my make-up,
Hurried back to the digs where Banquo
Sat up late with a hole in his head.
(*Poems*, 136)

Such ironies, like that of the unrhyming poet searching for a rhyme, preserve Longley from involvement in anything other than artistic sensitivity and a sense of victimhood. Both stances permit those who assume them to maintain a sense of purity.

"When the Troubles enter Longley's poetry," writes Peter McDonald, "the dominant perspectives are domestic ones."[6] Mahon, by contrast, uses the word "home" in a civic sense:

Perhaps if I'd stayed behind
And lived it bomb by bomb
I might have grown up at last
And learnt what is meant by home.[7]

Mahon, already living abroad in 1975, looks back at "home" as a world he left behind, including no doubt his immediate family but also the entire milieu from which he came. He considers home as an option for self-definition ("I might have grown up"), an option he consciously rejects. For Longley, on the other hand, there is no alternative to the milieu in which he lives. "Home is Belfast. Belfast is home. I love the place."[8] Even when speaking (in a letter to world-traveling Seamus Heaney) of "the sick counties we call home," Longley never imagines that there is any other place he might be living.[9] Whereas Mahon and Heaney, beginning with the home truths of personal experience, widen their gaze outwards to social concerns, Longley, when writing of the Troubles, proceeds in the other direction, collapsing public historical events into the immediate concerns of his personal life.

As a poet for whom the political becomes the personal, Longley's model is MacNeice, of whom he has written, "Fantasies, games of make-believe and above all a sensuous relishing of the external world were the antidotes he evolved to vanquish religion, darkness, loneliness and fears of death. These childhood antidotes anticipated in miniature the strategies of the adult poet. MacNeice's poetry began and continued as a reaction against darkness and a search for light."[10]

Here Longley is writing about himself as much as about MacNeice, for whom the voices that said "Come back early or never come" continued to echo in his mature poetry, at least in what he wrote about Ireland. Longley has represented his early childhood with care and detail, as did MacNeice, including the all-important nanny. Whereas MacNeice's nurse threatened him nightly with eternal damnation should he die in his sleep, though, Michael Longley's Lena was the great love of his life. "I began," he writes in his autobiographical essay, "by loving the wrong woman."[11] Lena, at twenty, proved indispensable when Michael and his twin brother were born. Since Peter, the twin, proved the more demanding infant, Michael fell more and more to Lena's care. The poet's mother herself had had a difficult childhood: her own mother had died in her infancy and was replaced by a shrewish stepmother; her retarded brother had abused her; she was partially lame and subject to periods of depression and irritability. "As my love for Lena deepened, my relationship with my mother grew more tense and complicated." Although Lena eventually moved to New York and although her former charge lost track of her, she remains the central figure of the poet's short autobiography. Going to New York with Paul Muldoon to do a reading, he wants to contact Lena and invite her but, afraid that the attendance will be poor and that she will be embarrassed, he does not. "The evening turned out to be a considerable success," he ruefully admits. "Lena could have been sitting in the middle of the front row." And Longley concludes the essay: "Since April 1979 I have been promising myself that some day I shall phone New York and talk across the Atlantic with Lena." One wonders why he does not, suspecting that he wishes his revery of childhood love to be left untarnished by the realities of old age, sickness, or possibly death.

As it turns to the bigotry and cruelty of sectarian life to which he was daily exposed as a boy, Longley's essay makes clear just how important Lena was and is to him. Offering Michael a welcome escape from competition with his twin brother for parental attention, Lena's unconditional love also solved the Kohutian dilemma of grandiose versus servile behavior. Gone were the opposing needs of imperious self-inflation (always in competition with a brother-enemy) and fawning idealization of parents. For whatever reasons—this or some other—Longley's poetry does not exhibit a self attempting to exorcise either its grandiose, violent tendencies or its unconscious allegiance to the standards of a degraded culture. As a boy he experienced his strongest temptation to loyalist bigotry in the form of salacious hate literature (accounts of Catholics mutilating their victims) which he read with the attention he would later devote to pornography. "I craved," he admits, "the bond of shared fears and superstitions." Yet here, as later in his adult writing, Longley is only an observer, an outsider looking in on a milieu in which he has no part.

The poet's father has long been known to readers of Longley's work. Major Longley fought in the First World War, survived the Somme, emigrated to Ireland as a commercial traveler, and died in 1959 from the lingering effects of wounds he had received in the war. Major Longley dominates his son's handful of well-known, elegiac poems about the Troubles. Longley's domestic style (to use McDonald's term) is nowhere more evident than here. Elegy can, of course, work well as political commentary; so Milton in "Lycidas" turns his lament for a drowned friend into a jeremiad against the established church. Longley, however, works his elegy in the reverse direction, by subsuming the public into the personal. When confessing himself incapable of writing poetry about the Troubles, Longley says to Dermot Healy, "I have written a few inadequate elegies out of my bewilderment and despair. I offer them as wreaths. That is all." As counterpoint to this statement comes Longley's belief in personal integrity: "You have got to bring your personal sorrow to the public utterance. Otherwise you are in deadly danger of regarding the agony of others as raw material for your art, or your art as a solace for them in their suffering. Atrocities of the mind."[12] On this account, "Lycidas" would fail Longley's test of appropriateness; Milton, he might say, rhetorically employs the death of a man he barely knew as an occasion for venting his wrath on the clergy. On the other hand one might also ask whether the poet who follows Longley's advice to be true to his own feelings might not run the risk of distorting the public dimensions of his poetry in order to satisfy personal requirements. In his well-known "Wounds," the poet recalls moments which his father revealed to him only in his last hours, juxtaposing scenes from the Somme with scenes from contemporary Ulster:[13]

> Here are two pictures from my father's head—
> I have kept them like secrets until now:
> First, the Ulster Division at the Somme
> Going over the top with 'Fuck the Pope!'
> 'No Surrender!': a boy about to die,
> Screaming 'Give 'em one for the Shankill!'
> 'Wilder than Ghurkas' were my father's words
> Of admiration and bewilderment.
> Next comes the London-Scottish padre
> Resettling kilts with his swagger-stick,
> With a stylish backhand and a prayer.
> Over a landscape of dead buttocks
> My father followed him for fifty years.
> At last, a belated casualty,
> He said—lead traces flaring till they hurt—
> 'I am dying for King and Country, slowly.'
> I touched his hand, his thin head I touched.
>
> Now, with military honours of a kind,
> With his badges, his medals like rainbows,
> His spinning compass, I bury beside him
> Three teenage soldiers, bellies full of
> Bullets and Irish beer, their flies undone.
> A packet of Woodbines I throw in,
> A lucifer, the Sacred Heart of Jesus
> Paralysed as heavy guns put out
> The night-light in a nursery forever;
> Also a bus-conductor's uniform—
> He collapsed beside his carpet-slippers
> Without a murmur, shot through the head
> By a shivering boy who wandered in
> Before they could turn the television down
> Or tidy away the supper dishes.
> To the children, to a bewildered wife,
> I think 'Sorry Missus' was what he said.
> (*Poems,* 86)

The construction of this poem as a double elegy, with parallel seventeen-line stanzas, includes several levels, all of them "wounds." The Battle of the Somme, in the summer of 1916, remains as a symbol of bellicose Ulster second only to the Boyne. The poet's British father was not a member of the Ulster Division (had he been, he might well not have survived, since virtually all of the Ulstermen died in that carnage); enlisting in England in 1914 at the age of seventeen, he mistakenly joined the London-Scottish "and went into battle wearing an unwarranted kilt. A Lady from Hell."[14] For all his bravery in battle, Major Longley, like his son, is only an observer of Ulster violence (he calls them wilder than Ghurkas). The "landscape of dead buttocks" represents the father's own regiment of dead Scots, grotesquely uncovered as they fell forward, while the chaplain, acting not unlike the poet himself, artfully restores decorum to the messy battlefield. Since the poet's father had part of his testicles sliced off by a piece of shrapnel (and since the poet owes his own existence to "skilled medical orderlies"), both the dead buttocks and the lingering wounds in the father's body, of which he finally dies, heighten the power of the poem as a double elegy. Wounds occur at two times in the father's life, and each occurrence is of importance to the son. Although the father's own view of the Somme is sardonic, contrasting the soldiers' rabid religious hate with the ineffective, decorous actions of the religious soldier (an implicit commentary on the contemporary scene), the final line of the first stanza, with its tender chiasmus (touch . . . hand / head . . . touch), changes the poem's tone into an elegiac tenderness. The vignettes from the Somme can only be known because the father tells them, and the father can only be remembered with delicacy.

Elsewhere Longley commemorates another relative who participated in the Great War: his mother's retarded brother, the one who had abused her and who was sent to the trenches but not given a gun. He was last seen after a raid walking around and filling a sack with the "littered limbs" of the dead. Although he disappeared and was never spoken of by the family, Longley chooses to retain him, too, as a symbol of violence, a memory residing in the wounded psyche of his mother and in his grandfather's occasional slips of the tongue when he "would call me Lionel. 'Sorry. My mistake. / That was my nephew. His head got blown off in No Man's Land.'"[15]

The father's role as observer is matched by the role of the elegist himself, whose actions—confined in the first stanza to the privacies of "I have kept" and "I touched"—now perpetuate those of the padre: "I bury" and "I throw in [objects to the grave]." Longley officiates at other funerals as well, notably that of his mother (who was a widow for nearly twenty years), where "The sexton is opening up the grave" in which the father lies and into which the poet places the difficult mother he has been caring for, saying good-bye with "I have handed over to him your pain."[16]

The bodies and regalia which the poet now symbolically buries in the family grave (with another sentimental inversion of syntax: "a packet . . . I throw in") serve to represent further ironies about Northern Irish violence. These dead soldiers, murdered by Irish Catholics, are themselves Irish Catholics by descent, born in England and ordered to police the war zones of Ulster. Their flies are undone (they were shot while in the gents), a reminder of the paternity they will never exercise; the point is repeated when the night-lights go out in the nursery forever. This robbing of paternity, in fact, emerges as the central motif of the stanza, just as the paradoxical preservation of paternity was the dominant idea of the first. The carpet slippers, the TV, and the supper dishes all provide the needed domestic setting for the absurd action of the shivering boy. The wife, to whom the boy apologizes, is "bewildered"; so is the poet's father as he admiringly but uncomprehendingly looks at the men of Ulster going over the top. Yeats, writing of the events of Easter, 1916, used this same word in a famous verse—"And what if excess of love / Bewildered them till they died?"—to offer a sympathetic explanation for "limbs that had run *wild*." To be bewildered in Yeats's poem is to be lured by an excess of love into an excess of action. To be bewildered in Longley's poem is simply to look without understanding. The father did not understand the screaming Ulstermen (but he admired them); the wife does not understand the shivering boy any more than we or the poet.

If we may call McDonald's domestic perspectives sentimental perspectives, as surely they become in the concluding lines of both stanzas of "Wounds," we may conclude that Longley's way of looking at and expressing social violence distorts both its topic and its poetic style in an excess of obvious emotion. The quaint tones which accompany the father's death and the tabloid "snaps" of the bus-conductor's home end by compromising the poem's attempt to find a serious political voice. Here Longley's own beliefs about public poetry come back to haunt him, or us: "you have got to bring your personal sorrow to the public utterance." The alternative to that, Longley believes, is rhetoric (Yeats's quarrel with others), the appropriation of other people's suffering for your own discourse, "atrocities of the mind." Longley's own option, however—what he believes to be the poetic quarrel with himself—runs the constant risk of capsizing into sentimentality: the dear old man, the wife and children. Ultimately Longley's problem is not sentimentality itself (as though every legitimate human sentiment were suspect in a work of art), but the fact that his "domestic perspectives" so thoroughly assume the nonparticipation of the speaking subject in the evils which he describes. Both those who curse the pope and those who defend the pope (by shooting Catholic soldiers who wear medals of the Sacred Heart) appear equally alien to this poet, sedulously maintaining his own bewilderment in the ordered cadences of blank verse.

In another dual elegy, "The Linen Workers" (one of a set of three entitled "Wreaths"), Longley considers the sets of dentures left lying in the road after ten men were massacred by Catholic operatives, comparing them to his "father's false teeth / Brimming in their tumbler." He saves the poem from sentiment by introducing a third set of teeth:

> Christ's teeth ascended with him into heaven:
> Through a cavity in one of his molars
> The wind whistles: he is fastened for ever
> By his exposed canines to a wintry sky.
> (*Poems,* 149)

Longley here is grotesquely reflecting on orthodox Christian belief—the ascension of Christ's whole body into heaven—in such a way as to satirize those beliefs and their power to wreak violence. If teeth go with Christ into heaven, then Christ goes with the teeth of the slaughtered into the dust: beside the dead workers are found "Wallets, small change, and a set of dentures: / Blood, food particles, the bread, the wine." Before the poem is over, though, the poet must *again* bury his father, giving him (back) his spectacles, small change and dentures. Longley's chance, it seems to me, for a fresh perspective is partially lost in his return to the domestic, to the sentimental.

All of these elegiac treatments of the Troubles focus (as, no doubt, elegy must) on specific tragedies, the daily tale of horror brought by the morning paper. The speaker is therefore guaranteed immunity from involvement in events so obviously foreign to him; it is not for him to consider the milieu out of which the day's crime arose, or of his own status within that milieu.

Another in this set of three short elegies, "The Greengrocer," praises the victim, who died putting holly wreaths and firs for Christmas on the pavement outside his shop, and requests that any of the Christmas characters ("Astrologers or three wise men") who might pass by "should pause on their way / To buy gifts at Jim Gibson's shop, / Dates and chestnuts and tangerines."[17] Longley's technique of listing small, everyday items as a way of emphasizing the brutality of murder reappears in a recent and much praised poem, "The Ice-cream Man," in which Longley tells off the vendor's flavors ("Rum and raisin, vanilla, butter-scotch, walnut, peach") and, over five equally long lines, enumerates the twenty-one varieties of wild flowers which he imaginatively sets on the man's grave.[18] What is it to surround the portrait of a crime with a frame of wildflowers and ice cream flavors? As John Bayley reads "The Ice-cream Man," it is to introduce crime into the place of flowers, the iron fist into the velvet glove, to realize the horror which stalks the beautiful.[19] Bayley senses in Longley's aesthetic a tacit response to the art-after-Auschwitz debate, to the notion that the beautiful never can or should represent the horror of genocide. Poetry never claimed to represent horrors, states Bayley, but only to transform them, echoing Longley's own idea that "[T]he artist needs time in which to allow the raw material of experience to settle to an imaginative depth where he can transform it."[20] By paying tribute to the dead ice cream man with his luxuriant recital of floral names ("thyme, valerian, loosestrife"), says Bayley, Longley follows in the steps of Paul Celan and even of the Irish bards and harpists, "[who] honored language at the same time that [they] honored the dead." Bayley claims, then, that Longley is politicizing the aesthetic, not aestheticizing the political.

I am not convinced. Longley's difficulty here lies in locating the lyric voice, the speaking self. He first addresses himself and refers to the ice cream man in the third person ("you bought carnations to lay outside his shop"), but then in the next line assumes the first person and addresses the dead man ("I named for you all the wild flowers of the Burren"). Longley here confronts Heaney's difficulty in *North*: how to be both part of the picture and the picture's maker? Longley's solution—to have both himself and the victim of violence be creators of beauty—runs the risk of trivializing his theme instead of burying it in loveliness. His poignant "tway blade, crowfoot, ling, angelica," reminiscent of Ophelia's musings but lacking the complications of character which give body to her song, again threaten to distort the sordid facts which the poem memorializes, not so much transforming violent life as merely sweetening it.

Longley's sense of himself as Fleance, as a voice separated from action and therefore as an almost victimized observer, appears subtly in other, earlier poetry. In a series of poems about war-poets (Edward Thomas and Isaac Rosenberg from the First World War, Keith Douglas from the Second), Longley characterizes them as bemused observers of details, admirable in their inability to comprehend the larger, awful picture:

> Wondering why there sang
> No thrushes in all that
> Hazel, ash and dogwood,
>
> Your eye on what remained—
> Light spangling through a hole
> In the cathedral wall
> And the little conical
> Summer house among the trees.
> ("Edward Thomas's War Diary," *Poems,* 134.)

Writing during the early seventies, when the Troubles were at their height, Longley composed epistolary poems to his fellow poets James Simmons, Derek Mahon, and Seamus Heaney, similar in style to Mahon's "Beyond Howth Head." There again he repeatedly imagines himself and his contemporaries as strangers, lost souls, "Sisyphuses come to budge / The sticks and stones of an old grudge."[21] Combining the letter-poem with the prayer-for-my-child poem, Longley interestingly imagines the war-poet as cast in the image of his new-born son, another potential, innocent victim of the surrounding violence. Of the baby son Longley writes, "About his ears our province reels / Pulsing like his fontanel," and goes on to say how, when it comes time to baptize the lad, he and the other poets, as priests of the muses, must "improvise" the holy water and font and so mock the "malevolent *deus loci*."[22] In this gesture of defiance, Longley manages to affirm poetic innocence in three ways—as free from sin, as free from the evil of the region, and as free from the evil of the region's religion. Longley's pun on "font" as meaning both large well and the small well of the infant's head reappears in a poem of the late seventies on "The War Poets":

> Unmarked were the bodies of the soldier-poets
> For shrapnel opened up again the fontanel
> Like a hailstone melting towards deep water
> At the bottom of the well, or a mosquito
> Balancing its tiny shadow above the lip.[23]

The sense of poet as child and as victim could not go much farther. "I am the solitary spectator," Longley again writes in the seventies: "A drenched fairground, the company advancing / And it is my head they hold in their hands. / The eyes open and close like a doll's eyes" ("The Fairground," *Poems,* 88).

In all his ways of writing about the Troubles—elegies, war poems, letter poems, poems about child-victims—Michael Longley has tacitly upheld his view of himself as a stranger to it all, a bewildered spectator of a violence which he does not understand and with whose proponents he has no sympathy. As a poet of nature (especially the landscapes and seascapes of his beloved Mayo) and of private, even erotic experience, Longley can boast of poetic accomplishments which lie outside the scope of these pages. He has avoided Heaney's soul-searching, Mahon's attempts at self-definition, Muldoon's self-ironies, Carson's urban wanderings, and Paulin's struggles to find a plausible Irish voice. Believing as he does in an unsullied private center of his experience, and insisting as he has on personal honesty in political poetry, Longley has established a speaking persona in his political poems which cleanses all traces of dirt as the objective is made to enter into the subjective. If he writes elegies to victims of the Troubles, he sees them as he sees his own dying father. If he thinks of himself as a war poet, he identifies himself with his innocent son. If he looks for a moment at an ice cream man lying dead on the sidewalk outside his shop, he must cover him with the flowers of his own idyllic sense of childhood and its ice cream flavors. In perhaps one of his strongest political lyrics, an epigraph to Simmons, Mahon, and Heaney, Longley characterizes the Ulster poet of the early seventies as lover, criminal, and child: a lover whose own words he cannot control, a criminal whose narrative comes forth under too much pressure and too late for it to matter, and a child whom no one can hear and who knows nothing but his own distress:

> for Derek, Seamus & Jimmy
>
> We are trying to make ourselves heard
> Like the lover who mouths obscenities
> In his passion, like the condemned man
> Who makes a last-minute confession,
> Like the child who cries out in the dark.[24]

Heaney, writing his own epigraph to *Wintering Out* in the same years, said:

> Is there a life before death? That's chalked up
> On a wall downtown. Competence with pain,
> Coherent miseries, a bite and sup,
> We hug our little destiny again.[25]

Heaney's "we hug our little destiny," his avowal of participation in Ulster's misery, is an act Longley could never perform in his poetry of the seventies. At this stage of his career, Longley's domestic perspectives, his maintenance of personal innocence and his transmission of that innocence to his sense of himself as a poet, qualify his poetry of social violence, preventing him from engaging with some of the deeper issues which appear in poems of his colleagues.

Having resigned from the Arts Council of Northern Ireland, Longley has entered a new, vigorous period of artistic creation.[26] He published *Gorse Fires* in 1991, which won him the Whitbread Prize, followed by *The Ghost Orchid* in 1996. Each of these two volumes includes seven adaptations from Homer, poems both dramatic and reflective, which constitute a new contribution from Longley to the poetry of the Troubles. Having lived through the Troubles during his mature years (they started as he and Heaney were approaching the age of thirty), and sensing that peace of a kind may be in sight now that he is approaching sixty, Longley casts a retrospective glance both on the recent history of Ireland and himself. The strategy of taking vignettes from Homer suits him perfectly, providing him with lyric moments of reflection or sensitivity within the epic frame-work of momentous events. By letting Homer's voice replace his own, Longley frees himself from the necessity of constructing an innocent or uninvolved self, and can therefore confront social violence with a new sense of immediacy. Although Longley's perspectives remain fundamentally unchanged, he now finds a better means of expressing those perspectives, of contributing significantly to the Northern Irish poetry of social violence.

Longley is not alone in seeking a sense of quietus as he writes of the Troubles at the century's end. Heaney's "Tollund," written in 1994, responds to "The Tollund Man," written twenty-two years earlier, replacing the famous qualifiers "lost, / unhappy and at home" with "Ourselves again, free-willed again, not bad."[27] Longley's first poem from Homer, in *Gorse Fires*, represents the homecoming of Odysseus, a topic he had already dealt with in a much earlier poem, "Odyssey,"[28] where the randy protagonist, making frequent stops for dalliance before coming home, represents his own father, then dying, who enjoyed a roving, amorous, post-war life before marrying and settling down. Whereas the earlier poem uses the myth for purely personal lyric purposes, with no tinge of politics, "Homecoming" emphasizes only Odysseus's exhaustion ("and put him to bed on the sand, still lost in sleep"), the result of long travail. Longley's possible intent appears in his brilliant adaptation of a line (as turned by Fitzgerald: "at mooring range, good ships can lie unmoored") depicting the harbor in Ithaca where the sailors land.[29] Longley turns this line to speak of the "Haven where complicated vessels float free of moorings / In their actual mooring-places." Here, then, the poet discovers a home where the self comes to rest without the entanglements (com-plicate: fold-together) of self-definition. Paradoxically Longley's greatest "complication" has always been his refusal to be defined by a mooring-line, an attachment to some partisan base; it was this reluctance which impeded his efforts to establish a self. Now, in his "Homecoming," the poet's self, like Odysseus's boat, can float free and be itself.

In much of what happens in these seven adaptations, all from the homecoming scenes in *The Odyssey*, Longley continues his work of personal revision, most notably in "Eurycleia," where Odysseus meets and is recognized by his old nurse. Here, ruminates Longley in an echo of his autobiography, Odysseus is more fortunate than he, still seeking Lena: "I began like Odysseus by loving the wrong woman / Who has disappeared among the skyscrapers of New York."[30] Whereas Homer's Eurycleia "touched the very flesh of [her] dear Lord," Longley's nurse "fondled [her] master's body all over."[31] Laertes, the hero's father, is brought back and loved again, while his mother, Anticleia, is appropriately nothing but a shade whom Longley renders even more ghostly by making his hero's encounter with her be merely hypothetical (summarized in the form: if you should meet your mother among the dead, and if you should talk with her, will she tell you "that this is what happens to human beings when they die?").[32]

This work of personal memory and revision, though, only serves as prelude to the last two adaptations of the series (which are interspersed in the collection, not grouped together). First Argos, the dog who remembered his master and died while welcoming him, stands as a symbol for all displaced persons, all victims of mass violence. Then Longley retells Odysseus's revenge on the suitors and the maids as an act which purges Ireland from the baneful deeds of the "Butchers" (an allusion to the Shankill Butchers, the perpetrators of a particularly bestial set of murders in Northern Ireland). Moving counter to his previous tendency to reduce public events to private concerns, in "Argos" Longley deftly succeeds in going from the particular to the universal, from the suffering animal to the suffering masses. This is a moment when he can convincingly say "we":

> like Odysseus
> We weep for Argos the dog, and for all those other dogs,
> For the rounding-up of hamsters, the panic of white mice
> And the deportation of one canary called Pepicek.[33]

Instead of asking, as before, that we collapse our concerns about public tragedy into concerns for a private life (of which we can know very little, given the short space of a lyric), Longley employs the well-known pathos of Homer's faithful dog to enlist our sympathy with a well-known and shared experience, and then transposes it to just that area of experience in which readers from bourgeois democracies have little or no share: the pogroms, the executions, the deportations. It is a small move, perhaps, but a significant one.

"The Butchers," with its harsh notes of violence, observes Lucy McDiarmid, is printed in *Gorse Fires* only a page after "The Ice-cream Man" with its lush tenderness. Remembering Longley's distaste for the "voyeurism" of those who write directly about the Troubles, McDiarmid suggests that, "coming after these occasional poems, 'The Butchers' expresses the outrage avoided by the poems with modern political subjects. Odysseus' 'whitewash and disinfectant' offer a drastic cleansing of all violated houses."[34] Odysseus applies these cleansers after ordering his men to drag out Melanthios' corpse "and cut off his nose and ears and cock and balls, a dog's dinner," the final act of revenge after dispensing with the suitors and the maids. The outcome of this purification (as Longley jumps from Book 12 to Book 24 of *The Odyssey*), is that Hermes can lead the gibbering, bat-squeaking souls of these slain off to the land of the dead. If McDiarmid is right about Longley's reticence when writing about the contemporary scene, it is worth asking further why he exchanges such discretion in discussing actual horror for such plain speech in describing, with Homer, mythological bloodshed (in comparison with which even Ulster's violence pales). I sense that Homer here gives Longley certain permissions not elsewhere available. While the news and television allow the poet only to consider the victims of the violent, it is in Homer that he can get at the butchers themselves, the perpetrators of violence. Here, for once, Longley himself turns violent by assuming the persona of Odysseus and by slaying the slayers. The house and outhouses which Longley must clean, at this point, are those of his own mind, since the only purgation of violence he can imagine (and here we remember Girard) inevitably perpetuates violence, serving up another dog's dinner.

Washed down and disinfected, the poet's mind can then imagine the ghost-life of the perished butchers. But why? What does the "dreamy region" of the dead contribute to his own lyric treatment of violence? Again Longley's version of Homer gives pause for thought. Where Fitzgerald (457) has Hermes go "to where the Dead inhabit / wastes of asphodel at the world's end," Longley writes of the place "where the residents are ghosts or images of the dead." The dead, in other words, are images of themselves. Writing in 1984 of Andrew Marvell, Christopher Ricks identifies what he calls "reflexive imagery" as a characteristic not only of Marvell but of contemporary Northern Irish poetry, the technique of presenting a thing as its own resemblance (he quotes liberally from Longley, as in "a knife-thrower / hurling himself"). Ricks suggests that, given the background of civil war shared by both Marvell and the Ulster poets, the reflexive image which "simultaneously acknowledges the opposing forces and yearns to reconcile them" may say the same thing about a poetic style of self-division in both the seventeenth and twentieth centuries.[35] In "The Butchers" Longley does indeed seek both to wreak revenge and then to reconcile the hard men of Ulster in their new state as harmless ghosts, so that Hermes plays the role of clergyman with his supernatural baton. I find it interesting that this reflexive image, if indeed it be a sign of self-division, appears at just the moment when Longley permits a fracture to appear on his hitherto impermeable surface, his appearance as a peaceful, bewildered poet. After revisiting his father, mother, and nurse, it is as though Longley himself arrives at a "home," a self which can at last admit its own small share in violence and mutilate a few villains; it is the moment when Longley can let his own complicated vessel float free of moorings in its actual mooring-place. Then, when the vessel ceases to be complicated, it starts to self-divide, to be an image of itself. That very self-definition implies mounting rage felt against the perpetrators of violence; it is only now that Longley can release even a small amount of such rage—rage that required five lines of flower names (recited through clenched teeth) to be repressed in "The Ice-cream Man." At just the moment of expressing such rage, however, the poet's lyric persona begins to divide, setting the enraged self over against the self which can will only humanistic sweetness and light. Longley's Odysseus, returning to Ithaca after years of wandering, finally discovers a home that is not merely domestic, a home named Ulster.

Longley's share in Odysseus's bloody behavior lasts only a

moment, though; he will not further investigate his political self. He has nevertheless won for himself a new ease of expression in writing of the Troubles, an ability to see and to say what he sees without needing any longer to sanitize such ugliness with lotions of domesticity. In *The Ghost Orchid* (1996), Longley presents another set of seven poems after Homer, this time taken both from *The Odyssey* and *The Iliad* (eight, in fact: the section on Hector comprises two very short lyrics). In a style absent from *Gorse Fires*, Longley embarks on a lofty mode of satire, juxtaposing the mores of Homer's heroes and those of Ulster's villains, a reductionist tactic which ultimately puts us all on the same moral scales which will weigh the violent and the nonviolent alike.

The satire works remarkably well, better than any of Longley's more anthologized political poems. Leaving *The Odyssey*, where the hero strives with himself, for *The Iliad*, where heroes strive with others, Longley deconstructs this strife by bringing it home to Northern Ireland. In "The Camp-Fires" (after *Iliad* 8), the ground outside the Trojan walls is debased by today's clichés ("no man's land," "killing fields"), while the iconic place-name of Ilium is qualified by its relation to Irish co-ordinates Tonakeera, Allaran, and Killary.[36] In "The Helmet" and "The Parting" (after *Iliad* 6), he reimagines Hector's farewells to his frightened baby and adoring wife as scenes from the home life of an Ulster hard man who prays "that his son might grow up bloodier than him" and who thus takes leave of his woman (Fitzgerald's Hector says, "As for war, that is for men"): "He: 'Leave it to the big boys, Andromache.' / 'Hector, my darling husband, och, och,' she."[37]

In the third of these scenes from *The Iliad*, that in which the defeated Priam comes to beg the body of his slain son Hector from Achilles, Longley's "Ceasefire" achieves an unparalleled greatness which may finally, if both the aftermath to Good Friday, 1998, and literary history prove kind, serve to nominate its author as the poet laureate of this possibly late moment of the Troubles. In June, 1995, in the era of John Major and the first ceasefire, it was my privilege, while attending a meeting of the American and Canadian Conferences of Irish Studies at Queen's University, Belfast, to attend a memorable evening in Whitla Hall, where the stage was shared by David Hammond, Seamus Heaney, and Michael Longley—a trio performing music and verse, just as it did in the sixties, when the

Troubles were beginning and the three men were starting their artistic careers. That evening Longley read this as yet unpublished poem:

I

Put in mind of his own father and moved to tears
Achilles took him by the hand and pushed the old king
Gently away, but Priam curled up at his feet and
Wept with him until their sadness filled the building.

II

Taking Hector's corpse into his own hands Achilles
Made sure it was washed and, for the old king's sake,
Laid out in uniform, ready for Priam to carry
Wrapped like a present home to Troy at daybreak.

III

When they had eaten together, it pleased them both
To stare at each other's beauty as lovers might,
Achilles built like a god, Priam good-looking still
And full of conversation, who earlier had sighed:

IV

'I get down on my knees and do what must be done
And kiss Achilles' hand, the killer of my son.'[38]

In two bold structural moves, Longley constructs a sonnet, and then divides each part from the other by an imposing numeral. Following the Shakespearean model, he posits each of the three quatrains as a separate moment in a problem, one to which the couplet will bring a conclusion. Dividing small lyric sections from each other by using roman numerals, barriers more suited to Homer's epic books, Longley insists on some kind of separation between each piece of the problem. The sonnet deals with the unthinkable: not just the reconciliation of mortal enemies, but their reconciliation after one of the sides has been defeated. It is unthinkable (quatrain 1) that the result of such a defeat—the shameful act of having to beg for a corpse—should turn into a gesture of sentiment (so, whereas Fitzgerald has Priam "huddle" at Achilles' feet, Longley has him "curled up"—the difference between abject shame and shared tenderness). It is unthinkable (quatrain 2) that the man who dragged Hector's body through the dirt, around the walls of Troy, should now have it washed and wrapped as a present. It is unthinkable (quatrain 3) that the two enemies should then dine together and gaze at each other's beauty "as lovers might." Each of these inconceivable actions must be considered separately; when we have finished pondering one, we must start afresh on the next.

How then can the couplet solve the problem, making it possible to think of the unthinkable? Having followed Homer through the three quatrains, Longley goes back for his couplet to the words Priam speaks to Achilles just before the actions described in the first quatrain. Whereas Homer represents Priam's visit to the Greeks as thinkable and doable only because Hermes has ordered him to do it, Longley squarely places the initiative with Priam, so altering Homer's sense. Fitzgerald's Priam declares "I / have brought myself to do what no man else / has done before—to lift to my lips the hand / of one who killed my son" (584). For Longley, Priam is only doing "what must be done." Why must it? For two reasons: as a moral person, Priam must do what is necessary to revere human life in death (and here he joins Antigone); as a defeated person, Priam has no other choice than to abase himself as he does. Longley thus fuses the ideal of moral obligation with the actuality of political circumstance and makes of this fusion the basis for unimaginable good. He secularizes the sense of moral obligation, removing it from divine command and placing it in the realm of human choice. Longley thus transforms mythological prelude, with its fundamental doubt about human agency (the god commands the unthinkable, and then the miracle occurs), into lyric conclusion, with its insistence on human agency (the hopelessness of suffering can be alleviated even under the worst circumstances by the performance of moral duty). Here, in a majestic stroke, Longley plays his favorite cards—domestic sentiment, reverence for natural life, erotic pleasure—in a new way. Rather than reduce public tragedy to a private domestic setting, he now offers the moral basis of the domestic—the sense of human obligation—as the force which achieves a solution to public tragedy. By refashioning epic, with its tale of human events shaped by blind fate or the gods, into lyric, with its turning of events into the form of considered human thoughts and feelings, Longley does indeed write poetry that makes things happen. What things? Not the things that historically happen, for they are the province of narrative, the tale of what "comes to be." In Longley's poem, what *might* happen *does* happen only when it happens as an act of the mind, as the voice which says, "I do what must be done." Constructed as it is in lyric, this action can *only* be an action of the spirit. As a poet of the late Troubles, then, Longley posits acts of the mind, of the ethical consciousness, as the only acts which can ever bring the Troubles to an end.

Before finishing, Longley proposes two further subjects of satire, God and himself. God, as the holder of the scales, represents the concept of fate, the basis for the gambler's question, "Who will win today?" So the transcendent, godlike symbol of snow falling turns into "a snowstorm of stones," as Trojans and Greeks go at it once again, and when God holds up the scales at noon to see whose pan will rise and whose will fall, the losers' faces, "when God thundered, would go white as snow."[39] This poem, too, presents itself in sonnet form—an antithetical sonnet, as it were, to "The Ceasefire." The fourteen unrhymed lines of "The Scales" present themselves in one stanzaic block, since there is no cognitive disjunction whatever between the three thoughts of divine power, random events, and violent action; it is all one, an all-too-familiar notion of fate.

And the poet himself? Returning now to *The Odyssey* and to the grisly tale of Odysseus' revenge on the suitors, Longley considers Phemios the poet, guilty of entertaining the suitors but trying to plead innocence because of his unimportance.[40] While the fawning Phemios speaks elegant English ("I beg you / Not to be precipitate and cut off my head"), generous Telemachus and his father speak a Scots-Irish dialect ("Dinnae gut him wi yer gully"). While Phemios pleads his inability to maintain any artistic integrity ("Overwhelmed and out- / Numbered, I gave poetry readings against my will"), Odysseus concedes to the poet a measure of "oul dacency," letting Phemios "hunker fornenst the altar of Zeus" while he slaughters the suitors and maids. Unlike the violently gruesome "och och" of Hector and Andromache, Odysseus' oul dacency, maintained over against spineless poets, matches the ethical nobility of Priam. We may well ask of whom the poet speaks, himself or some other man, but the answer must be left to Longley himself.

I have not yet mentioned the first and last of the Homer po-
ems in *The Ghost Orchid* because they act as a frame to the other
five, as well as to this entire latest moment in Longley's poetic con-
sideration of the Troubles. Like the first sequence of Homer po-
ems, the second begins by speaking of Odysseus lying down, not at
home but still in the midst of his voyages, as sleep "settled on him
like ashes and closed his eyelids."[41] The ashes are added by Longley,
reinforcing the sense of finality which informs all these poems about
journey's end. The final poem concerns Tiresias's prophecy that
Odysseus would die when, carrying his oar into a country where
men know nothing of the sea, someone would mistake it for a win-
nowing fan. There, said Tiresias, he must plant his oar in the ground
and begin to say his prayers to Poseidon in preparation for death.
"And death will come to me, a gentle sea-breeze, no more than /
An exhalation, the waft from a winnowing fan or oar."[42]

Here, as elsewhere in his most recent work, Longley speaks of
death as an imminent event. He imagines his own funeral and, in
"Ghetto," the deaths awaiting those deported to the camps in Po-
land.[43] In "The Oar" it is his own death, the death of the inner
Odysseus, which rises before him. The strange sounds that death's
winds make—the gentle ones of "waft . . . winnowing," and the
somewhat more ominous "or oar"—are meant to enchant and
soothe epic violence, in the way of Yeats's incantations in "Easter,
1916." The elegiac note, so often used by Longley in the past, here
sounds at its truest, as an elegy for the striving self. To change the
ocean's gale into a soft breeze and to lay the warrior to rest, is the
work of these last poems, which lay epic to rest within lyric. The
poet who once refused to engage with social violence now enables
his poetic self to overcome history, no longer finding poetic power
in domestic narratives but rather in lyric alternatives to all narra-
tive.

4

DEREK MAHON

The ancient fears mutated
To play, horses to rocking-horses . . .
                              —"The Hunt by Night"

"Once upon a time it was let me out and let me go," Derek Mahon
wrote in 1995, implicitly referring to his Fire King's utterance in
1975, "I am through with history."[1] The only way one can really
be through with history is by suicide, which is what the Fire King
intends, having no choice other than to die by his own hand or as
the victim of violence in a Northern Irish world of "sirens, bin-lids
and bricked-up windows." Born in 1941 and raised in a Protestant
suburb of Belfast, Mahon has often written of sectarian conflict
from the perspective of one who wishes to flee but is constrained
by a contradictory impulse to remain and be who he is.[2]

Heaney has called Mahon the Stephen Dedalus of Belfast,
and the comparison offers a useful starting point.[3] Joyce's sensitive
child, the young man as an artist, perceives the strictly conservative
milieu which has fostered him as violent—the Dedalus's Christmas
dinner is a scene of rage, Catholic school a scene of punishment,
and the afterlife a scene of torture. The Joycean solution is to flee
from the sow who eats her farrow, but then to write endlessly of
the escaped-from place. Mahon left Belfast early enough—he at-
tended Trinity College, Dublin, and after a brief stint of teaching in
Northern Ireland, moved to Dublin at age twenty-seven, then to
England at age thirty. In his poetry, however, he has repeatedly

wrestled with the angel of Northern Irish violence. While it is true to say that "the problem of belonging or not belonging to a people is one of the main sources of [Mahon's] metaphysical unease,"[4] what more pointedly disturbs the poet is his inherited share in that people's culture and behavior. Mahon's best poems engage him in the daunting task of self-construction: making a good self in a bad place and finding poetic strategies for dealing not just with a violent environment, but more importantly with the residue of social violence, the antagonisms and resentments that the poet finds within himself.

Even before the outbreak of the Troubles, Mahon's earliest characterizations of his Belfast milieu, like Heaney's portraits of Derry, contained strong elements of potential aggression. In a poem of the sixties, "Glengormley" (the name of the suburb in which Mahon was raised), he imitates the breezy but bitter tones of MacNeice's "Sunday Morning" and adds his own sinister evocations of bloodshed in ancient Ulster, a mythic world of monsters and giants "who tore up sods twelve miles by six / And hurled them out to sea to become islands."[5] The MacNeician element lies in the poem's ironic casting-out of the mythical: in today's suburban havens, with their hedges and watering cans, we are safe from monsters and giants. "The sticks / And stones that once broke bones will not now harm. . . . Only words hurt us now." While the poem's irony works historically—appearing as it did in the late sixties, it foretells the transformation of sectarian conflict from words into sticks, stones, and bombs—there is more to it than that. Expressing his longing for release and self-fulfillment, the poet invokes the age of giants because that was also the age of saints and heroes, "landing at night from the conspiring seas, / Bring[ing] dangerous tokens to the new era." The parental world of the present, however, replacing mythic adventure with the enforced conformities of hedges and watering cans, has ordained a new kind of symbolic oppression, a tyranny of the established order in which "the unreconciled, in their metaphysical pain, / Dangle from lamp-posts in the dawn rain." Ironically professing allegiance to the present, "a worldly time under this worldly sky," the poet concludes that there are no selfobjects to idealize, only sanctions to fear: "By / Necessity, if not choice, I live here too."

While he does not say by what necessity he continues to live in this damaged world (in fact he had already said good-bye to Northern Ireland by the time the poem appeared in a book), Mahon hints at an inner compulsion to self-denial. Because saints and heroes—those who could provide their own standards of self-worth—have disappeared along with monsters and giants, the would-be hero must search within his social environment for a means of self-definition. Mahon thus bears witness to a split, in Kohut's terms, between the grandiose escapist self and the idealizing conformist self, such that the former can only conceive of itself in archaic terms, the world of the present having been fully occupied by a repressive culture of parental standards. Had Mahon lived in a Yeatsian world of romanticism and revival, he might more easily have chosen the option of saint and hero, reviling the quotidian world of Paudeen. In the intervening years, however, such romantic impulses had been coopted by the patriarchal ideologies of extreme sectarianism; saintliness and heroism had been bought up and placed, along with hate and envy, among the wares peddled in the thoroughfares. It is the particular curse of politico-religious violence that it turns narcissistic self-magnification into a code of obedience to an ideology of coercion. That is why the speaker, as he manifests anxiety about being a mythic hero in Glengormley, confesses to an even deeper fear of societal rejection. The poet cannot risk dangling from the lampposts of the unreconciled. As the Stephen Dedalus of Belfast, Mahon presents a paradoxical inner conflict. Will I indulge my mythic, grandiose self, or will I choose conformity to an inherited, idealized order? Each choice commits him to a world of violence—the sticks and stones of mythic self-inflation or the lampposts of a repressive bourgeois milieu. Mahon will play Stephen's card, attempting to transcend Ulster paradoxes by flight into a more liberal environment, but will discover that he cannot so easily escape the fundamental problems of social hostility.

Many of Mahon's best poems may be read as artistic strategies for resolving this problem of identity. Not that self-fashioning and poem-fashioning are the same. Whereas the person to be self-fashioned is always there, hedged around with countless givens, the lyric poem to be written is pure possibility. As an unborn entity, it makes strong prior demands, insisting that it not be versified prose, that it not be agitprop, that it not be the unmediated whining of a suffering self. In Mahon's early dramatic monologue, "An

Unborn Child," the as yet unencumbered consciousness, declaring both its egocentricity and its innocence, represents the poem to be written as much as the infant to be born.[6] It is as though poems had their own nuclear selves. Whereas the individual's social context acts as a corrective to personal ambitions, poetic ambitions correct the poet's social self. The poet's compulsion to say something to his community, to be relevant, must be corrected by the poem's own demands, its grandiose ambitions, to be its own lyric self.

Mahon has responded to these dilemmas by imagining his lyric self in three distinct phases. First (*Night Crossing, Lives*) he uses dramatic monologue, allegory, and conceit as ironic modes of imagining the immediate in terms of the far-off, invoking exotic elsewheres and aliases without ever forsaking the actual. Secondly (*The Snow Party*) he uses these polarities (London/Belfast, here/ elsewhere, present/past) as another ironic mode of imagining the self in a double manner. Constantly setting himself over against the violence from which he is trying to escape, the poet dialectically encounters that very violence within himself. Thirdly (*The Hunt by Night*) he uses objective meditation, most notably in poems about paintings, to submerge the self into a consciously crafted environment (the painting) which is yet also a scene of social chaos, so that the authenticity of being rooted and the integrity of being free may finally be achieved in the same movement.

Mahon's first step in social self-definition is to imagine himself as other than what is immediate, the given, in spite of the fact that the given thoroughly conditions his imaginings. Dramatic monologues (the voice of Van Gogh speaking of sunflowers) or the more allegorical voice of the unborn child provide the poet with ironic modes of yoking an elsewhere with a here and now, just as "Glengormley" first imagines Northern Ireland to be a site of monsters and giants, but then denies it that privilege by returning it to "a worldly time." Such a poem as "Homecoming," written in the voice of a jet-lagged diarist returning from the United States to an Ireland where nothing has changed because the speaker (in spite of his voyage) has not changed, manifests in a different style the same search for extreme ways to express one's identity.[7]

Lives (1972), the collection in which "Homecoming" first appeared, marks a turning point in Mahon's early development of

strategies for escape. The book's title poem, another dramatic mono-
logue, spoken by an entity which has endured multiple incarna-
tions over the centuries, reads at first like a satire on Heaney's
exercises in poetic archaeology ("I was a torc of gold"). Perhaps
Mahon makes fun of his fellow poet, to whom he dedicates the
poem, because he experiences the need to imagine other forms of
being even more obsessively than Heaney. Mahon soon abandons
his satirically exotic representations of the actual and begins a free
play of fantasy, imagining all sorts of possible incarnations—as an
oar, as a bump of clay in a Navaho rug, as a tongue of bark at the
heart of Africa.[8] These objects cannot be representations of any-
thing. The point of the exercise is to become something else, any-
thing, as long as it is not here or now.

Unfortunately for the poet, the brilliance of the exercise ne-
cessitates its failure. The act of imagining without at the same time
signifying—gratuitously to become a random object, say, "a tongue
of bark"—implies that the imaginer has achieved the sophistica-
tion necessary no longer to need grounding in a here and now. Like
Proteus, though, he must pay for the power of becoming anything
by giving up the power to be anything. "It all seems," he confesses
in his most recent incarnation, "a little unreal now," now that he is
an anthropologist with a credit card and the latest technology: "I
know too much / To be anything any more." Having imagined
himself as living all those lives, Mahon implicitly admits himself
guilty of the "insolent ontology" of ever imagining that one could
both be what one is and have been what one was—or both be
what one is and expect to be what one wishes to become. Whereas
the ontology of *Night Crossing* required that what is not ironi-
cally represent what is, the insolent ontology of *Lives* capriciously
seeks to transform what is into what is not. In either case, the
poet has yet to find any strategy to solve Parmenides' paradox—
that if being is and not-being is not, one can never be what one is
not. The higher the flight of fantasy, the harder the subsequent
fall into Belfast.

Nowhere does this poetry of imaginatively ironic leaps speak
more poignantly than in another short lyric from *Lives*,
"Ecclesiastes." Written in the same prosodic arrangement as
MacNeice's "Autumn Journal"—a longer line followed by an in-
dented shorter line, in syllabic dactyls—Ecclesiastes accomplishes

the tour de force of consciously imagining himself to be what he already is, unconsciously and unwillingly: a member of Belfast's Protestant community. "You could grow to love it here," we may paraphrase the poet as telling himself, "purist little puritan that you are, and shelter your cold heart from the heat of the world: from women and children." As a lyric poet, to be sure, the speaker is already both purist in his dedication to form and puritan in his examinations of conscience. As Ecclesiastes, though, Mahon characterizes himself as a puritan John the Baptist who does "not / feel called upon to understand and forgive / but only to speak with a bleak / afflatus" (and here one thinks of MacNeice's self-inculpating diatribe against Ireland in "Autumn Journal 16"[9]). Inveighing against his people, Ecclesiastes finally inveighs against himself. By giving up the vocation of itinerant preacher or wandering minstrel, the speaker accepts his people's call to be king—that is, to be responsible for, to embody their sectarian despair.

> Bury that red
> bandana, stick and guitar; this is your
>   country, close one eye and be king.
> Your people await you, their heavy washing
>   flaps for you in the housing estates—
> a credulous people. God, you could do it, God
>   help you, stand on a corner stiff
> with rhetoric, promising nothing under the sun.
> (*Lives,* 3; *SP,* 28)

Ecclesiastes was a sophisticated anthropologist who knew too much to imagine any kind of change that could be desirable ("there is nothing new under the sun"). The poet is already "stiff with rhetoric" in this highly rhetorical poem. The extreme of escape, evoked in "Lives," comes around to meet the extreme of entrapment in "Ecclesiastes" and, at that meeting point, suggests a disturbing idea about lyric poetry and social violence. Here, as in MacNeice's "Autumn Journal 16," the language of lyric draws close to the idiom of violence. Note the conjunction in this poem between cleverness of speech and coldness of heart, where bleak afflatus replaces the plainer language of understanding and forgiveness. Preferring wit to sentiment, the hard to the soft, Mahon's poem promises nothing, makes nothing happen. The irony which dominates Mahon's earlier poems of escape now turns into self-irony; we start to hear the language of social violence as terms of self-hate mutate into terms of hate for others: "a bleak afflatus . . . God help you."

The primary tropes of *Lives*—imaginative reincarnation and multiple identities—although they serve to liberate consciousness from its initial bondage to the here and now, prevent their protean subject from establishing any identity and therefore from finding any ground to take up, any position to establish. The grandiose self repeatedly attempts to deny its actual surroundings and just as repeatedly falls back to the point from which it started. Like the anchor on Heaney's legendary ship, it is the conforming self, intact and unchanged in the speaker's mind, which prevents the grandiose self from enacting its dreams of escape and change.

Mahon's poems about reincarnations and suburbs, or the voices of unborn children and preachers, offer little specific comment on civic disturbances. It is not that Mahon has nothing to say about the early Troubles, but that his attempts at poetic political commentary, notably in the Audenesque verse epistle, "Beyond Howth Head," lack any strong poetic or moral bite, that conscious center of speech which poems like "Lives" so earnestly seek.[10] It is not until his next volume, *The Snow Party* (1975), that Mahon, having already sought escape from the actual by imagining multiple selves, now begins to construct polarities—double geography (here and there), double time (now and then), double cultures (Japan and Europe)—which permit him to gain distance from, and therefore to comment on, the Troubles.

This change of perspective from *Lives* is heightened by the appearance of the first poem in the collection, "Afterlives." In parallel sets of stanzas, "Afterlives" presents two places at dawn: London, where the poet is waking up, and Belfast, to which he is returning on the night ferry "for the first time in years." London is the place of civility, of the rational faith that the power of good, love, and poetry will always prevail over dark, irrational places such as Belfast, where light is reduced to a naked bulb burning at the ferry dock. Nevertheless the poet concludes by rejecting his London frame of mind,

What middle-class cunts we are
To imagine for one second
That our privileged ideals
Are divine wisdom

and accepting what he has left behind in Belfast and missed ever
since:

Perhaps if I'd stayed behind
And lived it bomb by bomb
I might have grown up at last
And learnt what is meant by home.[11]

Previously the urbane anthropologist compulsively reverted
to the voice of his twin, the rabid Ulster preacher (since both spoke
from a position of assumed superiority and a corresponding lack of
self-awareness). Now a single consciousness, speaking in a consis-
tent voice, successfully distinguishes between two places and two
modes of being. From a Belfast perspective, the speaker can see
that his London liberal stance of rational *vir bonus* is a childish
posture, a vague kind of well-wishing. From a London perspective,
he can take the full measure of "home," when home is a place of
sectarian violence. Like the balanced lyrics in which they are set
forth, these insights resolve into a paradox: either the self seeks
emancipation for its grandiose impulses by flight from home, at the
price of abandoning rootedness in ideals and a corresponding sense
of growth, or the self returns home at the price of clipping its wings.
The impulses to fly away and to come back are equally strong,
equally distorting to the nuclear self and equally resistant to inte-
gration with each other. The best thing about this poem is that it
makes no attempt to resolve its own paradoxes. The worst thing is
that its dialectical ironies are too simplistic in their identification of
places with lives—as though London were an Athens of rational
thought or Belfast a den of tribal darkness. At least, though, the
poet is successfully sorting out the two contradictory aspects of his
persona.

In "The Snow Party" Mahon finds a more successful else-
where. The seventeenth-century Japanese poet Basho and his friends
gather in MacNeician fashion to watch the beauties of falling snow.

From the poem's perspective, the ancient Japanese city is here , and its elsewhere is an occidental there, the western reader's world of sectarian violence:

> Elsewhere they are burning
> Witches and heretics
> In the boiling squares,
>
> Thousands have died since dawn
> In the service
> Of barbarous kings.
> (*The Snow Party*, 8; *SP*, 57)

Basho is so far removed from "elsewhere" that he is oblivious to its ways (the poet must remind us of them). Mahon's insoluble problem, though, lies in appropriating Basho's pacific aesthetics—in becoming Basho—without succumbing to the feeling of unreality which such an insolent ontology breeds and therefore relapsing into the circular self-accusations of "Afterlives." It is, after all, history which provides Mahon with his escape to Basho's Nagoya—the same worldly time in which barbarous kings burn witches and heretics. In the sequel to "The Snow Party," Mahon's Fire King declares, "I am through with history." Elsewhere is here again.

The Fire King rules over a people (their bin-lids lend them a decidedly Northern Irish character) who see fit that each king shall die at the hands of his usurper and that the murderer-become-king will die in his turn at the hands of the next usurper. Determined to break "the barbarous cycle"—he dreams of Nagoyan silence, cold and timelessness, but is surrounded by European noise, fire and history—the Fire King plans to die by his own hand. In his analysis of sacred violence, René Girard speaks of such "temporary sovereigns, both comic and tragic, who are ceremonially sacrificed at the end of their brief reign. . . . The surrogate victim dies so that the entire community, threatened by the same fate, can be reborn in a new or renewed cultural order."[12] The Fire King, as his people's designated victim, becomes the scapegoat upon whom the community projects its violence, lest that violence turn inward and destroy the community.

The Fire King imagines that his society might be otherwise—

frugivorous, peaceable—but knows that his people insist on violence,

> Demanding that I inhabit,
> Like them, a world of
> Sirens, bin-lids
> And bricked-up windows—
>
> Not to release them
> From the ancient curse
> But to die their creature and be thankful.
> (*The Snow Party*, 9–10; *SP*, 59)

In the Fire King's view, the ancient curse pertains only to this doomed, carnivorous society; in Girard's view, the curse is a universal one, as much on the fruit eaters of Basho's Nagoya as on the meat eaters of Mahon's Belfast.

A more recent poem, "Rathlin," provides a third exploration into the cycle of violence. The sparsely populated island of Rathlin lies off the extreme northeast coast of Ulster. Mahon imagines it as having been well populated in an ancient age (its name figures in Irish mythology), but deserted ever since the "unspeakable violence" which killed the island's last inhabitants: "A long time since the last scream cut short— / Then an unnatural silence; and then / A natural silence." Here, as in "The Last of the Fire Kings," history comprises the unspeakable and the unnatural: "Bombs doze in the housing estates / But here they are through with history."[13] At the poem's end, we rejoin Girard and his theory of violence as an original and therefore inescapable feature of society: leaving the island and "the infancy of the race," one is unsure "whether the future lies before us or behind." The era of giants and monsters may be over, but the era of inhuman violence is not.

These three poems express what I have called Mahon's second stage of self-definition, his second attempt to solve the problem of the dissatisfied self in a violent society. After ironically characterizing here in terms of elsewhere ("Glengormley"), and after tentative moves toward escape from here by means of such tropes as reincarnation and multiple selves ("Lives"), Mahon confronts violence and the self through a poetry of polarity. No less than the first attempt, this one is also rendered in an ironic mode. Desiring to be "through with history," Mahon takes refuge in Basho's Nagoya, an elsewhere so ethereal as to be nothing more than a fairyland. Nagoya can only be offered to consciousness through history, and it is from the nightmare of history that Mahon's Fire King, like Stephen Dedalus, is trying to awaken. Beginning with London and Belfast, Mahon stretches his polarities further and further apart, and in so doing uncovers the sameness which underlies difference. Thus, by thinking of ancient Japan instead of modern Britain, he universalizes the terms of history and thereby translates them into terms of the human condition. The cultural differences between London and Belfast are in a sense greater than those between Nagoya and its European elsewheres, and these are in turn greater than the differences between the Fire King and his people. The further we go from the here and now, the more clearly we realize that history is a form of violence mandated by human circumstance. The Fire King's wish to resemble Basho can only lead him to self-destruction, since the traditions of the Fire King's culture will not tolerate his dream. The elsewhere of Rathlin Island, now a bird sanctuary, turns out to have been the "here" of primal Irish violence. To be in any here and now is to be immured in violence; to think that it could be otherwise is to be a "middle-class cunt."

That insulting and now expunged epithet[14] provokes one further reflection about this stage of self-definition, a reflection inspired by Girard's claim that the murdered king can be a comic figure as well as a tragic one—a royal fool, a companion to sacred clowns, North American tricksters, and a host of other hallowed buffoons. The Fire King is a royal successor to middle-class buffoons, as he admits. One need think only of the treatment of public leaders by the media to realize that abasement continues to function as an instrument of social violence, a form of aggression carried out to satisfy a public filled with resentment against "the system." Public leaders, in this view, serve society as scapegoats, absorbing violence by subjecting themselves to exposure and ridicule. In Girard's structuralist analysis, one begins with violence and humiliation as givens, that which people are always inflicting on each other. For Bernstein, however, humiliation is something the abject hero is always inflicting on himself.[15] Might not abject heroes make good scapegoats? Since self-ridicule and self-abasement constitute a potent germ of hostility against a world perceived as alien, growing from simple resentment into such social violence as that in Northern Ireland, it would seem to be an elegant move to appoint abject heroes as scapegoats in order to free the populus from its own abjection-resentment. Uriah Heep (that symbol of villainous self-abasement—the character you love to loathe) may be seen as an icon of scapegoating or ritual sacrifice. We free ourselves from *ressentiment*, with its compulsions to violent retaliation, by driving Heep, the unabomber, or whoever the current pariah may be, into our psychic wilderness.

Mahon's self-criticisms, at this stage of self-definition, establish a tonality of abject *ressentiment*. Representing his consciousness as desiring to escape from its embeddedness in violence while still preserving its cultural identity, Mahon ironizes that consciousness, portraying himself as a comic, not a tragic, persona: the middle-class liberal fool who thought he could rise above his roots and now must learn what is meant by home. It is precisely by that term of contempt that Mahon conceives of himself as the last of the Fire Kings, longing wistfully to be a creation of Flann O'Brien, an imagined Irishman "who descends / At two milk churns . . . and vanishes / Where the lane turns," but who is condemned by the bin-lid-banging people "to die their creature and be thankful." The only solution to this entrapment in violence is self-inflicted violence, the Fire King thinks. But this is surely a gruesome paradox, since the king's function as scapegoat is to save the people by absorbing into himself the accumulated violence which they inflict on him, lest they inflict it on each other. The Fire King thinks he will cure the disease by killing himself; instead, not knowing that what he thought was a symptom of disease—his ritual murder at his people's hands—was really a sacrificial cure, he has reverted to the original disease, self-inflicted violence. Just as Mahon's lyric comment on violence presented itself in a violent idiom in "Ecclesiastes," the middle-class liberal's tones of self-contempt and the Fire King's tones of abjection speak for a consciousness which constantly returns to the personal source of the violence from which it is trying to escape. The preacher, instead of changing the people, colludes with them in potentially violent self-abasement. The would-be liberal is really middle-class; the king is really a fool; we cannot even look at Basho looking at snow without also looking at heretics burning in the squares of Europe. Every step forward is a step back. Well may the visitor to Rathlin wonder "whether the future lies before us or behind." As he flees from history, Mahon's persona constantly meets itself and wants again to flee.[16]

At this point Mahon's poetic self-development will have reached an impasse, one beyond which only a masterful imagination could go. In "A Disused Shed in Co. Wexford," Mahon finds a new set of imaginative techniques for repositioning himself in relation to social violence and so passes to a third stage of self-definition. Having exhausted the thought of a peaceful, different place, he now accepts the violent "here" and looks within it for hidden places of peace: "Even now there are places where a thought might grow." Thoughts, we learn, grow in abandoned mine shafts, empty houses on Indian compounds, and (in this poem) in a shed, locked up on the property of a resort hotel which was abandoned during the Black and Tan War. In the shed an allegorical host of mushrooms— one at first takes them to represent Irish Protestants—await the liberation which comes to them when a journalist opens the door for the first time in fifty years and takes their picture with a flash bulb. (The hotel may reproduce that ghastly pile, The Majestic, in *Troubles*, a novel by J.G. Farrell, to whom the poem is dedicated.) Such an exotic inventory of forgotten objects reminds us of "Lives," but here, as in Heaney's digging projects, the objects are imagined as found, not imagined as imagined. Like Heaney, Mahon now seeks the elsewhere hidden in the here, the other time hidden in the present.

   This uncharacteristically solemn poem (six ten-line stanzas of blank verse) strives for and often attains a Yeatsian language of pathos: "This is the one star in their firmament / Or frames a star within a star" (*SP*, 62–63). (That describes the keyhole of a dark shed, seen from within.) It is unclear just whose thoughts might grow in such a place: those of the mushroom-inhabitants, or those of the visiting journalist who enters the shed and considers the sorry scene? It must be the mushrooms' thought, even though, being allegorically condemned to remain in their shed, they have no voice to express what they think. Hence the poet's requirement of a double stance, whereby he first impersonates the mushrooms, but then interprets them from a distance. In the first stance, the mushrooms "have been waiting for us in a foetor / Of vegetable sweat since civil war days," listening for a sound, but only hearing the occasional truck changing gears at the end of the lane. Let us call this part of the poem (stanzas 2–4) the organic allegory—the use of mushrooms to depict an abandoned people. Farrell's Majestic having been an Anglo-Irish refuge until the superannuated guests were forced to flee by the fighting of 1919, one can take the denizens of the shed to signify today's superannuated unionists who hang on in constant expectation of something better and in constant experience of something worse. But what thought of theirs has really grown? The mushrooms strain toward the door and groan for deliverance. Working by personification (mushrooms listening, hoping, groaning), the organic allegory limits itself to a static representation of social suffering.

In the second part of the allegory, however, the poet intervenes. First within the narrative: the lock of the shed is cracked, the hinges creak, and the team of journalists, "the flash-bulb firing-squad," walks in. Confronted by this assault of modernity, the "powdery prisoners of the old regime . . . lift frail heads in gravity and good faith." The poet-journalist then intervenes in a second way, by *interpreting* the mushrooms:

> They are begging us, you see, in their wordless way,
> To do something, to speak on their behalf
> Or at least not to close the door again.
> Lost people of Treblinka and Pompeii!
> 'Save us, save us,' they seem to say,
> 'Let the god not abandon us
> Who have come so far in darkness and in pain.
> We too had our lives to live.
> You with your light meter and relaxed itinerary,
> Let not our naive labours have been in vain!'
> (*The Snow Party,* 36–37; *SP,* 62–63)

This is no longer the voice of a ventriloquist, speaking for the mushrooms, but that of an all too visible, all-knowing visitor who says, "You see," and "They seem to say," who imposes on his allegorical mushrooms the full burden of representing both social disaster (Treblinka) and natural disaster (Pompeii).

These wider references, however, introduce a false note into the poem. Although they seem to elevate the status of the mushrooms, their real purpose is to elevate the tone of the poet's voice from the abasement required of it by the terms of the organic allegory ("vegetable foetor," "a trickle of masonry") to the high tones of a trans-historic interpreter. The poet is in the shed but not of it, entirely comprehending the mushrooms' plight but unwilling to be counted as one of them. Writing about this poem in 1985, the period of his own allegorical poems of distance in *The Haw Lantern*, Heaney speaks of Mahon's "long perspective . . . of detached compassion."[17] Yes, but the detachment finally works against the compassion. Let us call this second stance the interpretive allegory, following on the organic allegory; a move of dissociation following a move of association. The place where a thought might grow turns out to have been one where an *observer's* thought might grow. The mushrooms' thought, truly hidden and silent, would have been like the unheard tree in the forest. The poet's need at the end for noise and light—the popping flashbulb and the resonating flourish—reveals a residual discomfort with his assumed identity.

Mahon has said that he rarely reads this poem in public, preferring to do "A Garage in Co. Cork," a more comic and perhaps more convincing poem about abandonment—here the family abandoned its own pathetic gas station and left for the States or the mainland, never to return to such pathos.[18] If we agree that the latter poem's dingy specificity and its witty bit of mythology make for a more satisfying piece than the possibly cloying sentimentalities of "A Disused Shed," we do so in collusion with Mahon himself, sharing his unease in having to decide between mushroom-being and journalist-being (like Belfast-being and London-being). It is precisely this discomfort, though, which constitutes the greatness of "A Disused Shed," giving witness that the poet is still trying to decide how to escape from being personally implicated in a violent society while yet remaining faithful to the realities of his being. Mahon attempts to cut this Gordian knot in "A Disused Shed" by poetically identifying himself with some of the victims of cultural violence, those victims who comprise his own milieu. Although the poet's failure to imagine how he can simultaneously personify his allegorical victims and explain them—how he can write simultaneously in the first and third persons—finally weakens the poem, his willingness to enter into social suffering rather than escape from it points the way to new possibilities of self-imagining.

A poem from the late seventies, "Autobiographies," provides further evidence that "A Disused Shed" speaks not only for a forgotten people, but that it also tries (unsuccessfully) to identify the speaker with that people. Recalling his early childhood during the Second World War, the poet remembers himself looking at a newspaper. As he does, he pictures the inmates of a concentration camp in much the same way that he pictures the mushrooms in their shed.

> Gracie Fields on the radio!
> Americans in the art-deco
> Milk bars! The released Jews
> Blinking in the shocked sunlight . . .
> A male child in a garden
> Clutching the *Empire News*.
> (*Courtyards in Delft*; SP, 85)

Appearing in a poem of autobiographical self-searching (the plural title implies a plurality of selves), the hidden people emerging out of prison and into memory partially symbolize the remembered child. Later the poem recalls an old summer hotel, like Farrell's Majestic, as the site of sexual awakening. The spin of the hotel away from conscious memory matches the spin of people away from the hotel, as they buy discount travel packages and go on holidays to North Africa, "Far from the unrelaxing / Scenes of sectarian strife."

Taken together, "A Disused Shed" and "Autobiographies" exhibit parallel tracks of historical and psychological symbolic narratives, parallel *recherches du temps perdu*. Hidden objects, peoples and selves—mushrooms, Protestants, and the speaker—converge as they symbolize each other. One can attempt to retrieve "lost time" as a forgotten residue of one's life or as a wasted segment of history. In the disused shed, one hears no echo of the Fire King's "I am through with history;" now it might be "History is through with me." As people forsake the unrelaxing scenes of sectarian strife, the poet's expatriate psyche, in spite of its exodus, experiences itself as such an unrelaxing place, and therefore finds itself reckoning with social violence not as an aspect of "home," but as a personal attribute, whether inherited or acquired.

In this third stage of self-definition, Mahon has abandoned the polarities and ironies of the previous stages, no longer styling himself in terms of contempt as a middle-class liberal who might have done better to stay home. Instead of oscillating between extreme options of grandiosity and conformity, the poetic persona strives for an integrated self by reaching out to disparate places and times, bringing them together and overlaying them on a fictive center, so that past and present, here and elsewhere now constitute concentric circles, the framework of a nuclear self. No longer imagining historical choices, all of them flawed, Mahon now imagines and begins to accept a self which is inescapably part of some large historical process—a self, therefore, which shows ravages similar to those of a war zone or to the collective psyche of a beleaguered people.

Such a mental procedure, in which one considers a fixed object instead of alternating between opposites, calls to mind the technique of the emblem, the visual figure which calls forth thought and words. Mahon's final move in this third stage of self-definition, undertaken in poems of the late seventies and early eighties, occurs in poems about two paintings. Both works have painted over a residue of violence which the poet as observer will rediscover and which the poet as composer will reintegrate into his own poetic canvas. Retrieving his journalist's voice from "A Disused Shed," Mahon now speaks partially as a docent, explaining private images from the museum of his own mind, and partially as a psychologist, explaining shared images of our common consciousness.

"Courtyards in Delft" characterizes a Dutch painting of 1659. The visual resemblances between the Dutch courtyard and those of Protestant Ulster are not lost on us; neither is the final alexandrine flourish (a seventeenth-century convention in English verse), invoking "sword upon parched veldt and fields of rain-swept gorse," a reference to those paragons of Dutch heroism, the Afrikaaners (the veldt), and King Billy (the gorse). Mahon's politically realist aesthetic resembles that of the domestic realist de Hooch, announced in the opening line: to shed "oblique light on the trite." By painting the mundane, the artist paints it in, renders it inescapable because aesthetically tolerable. The docent is less concerned to explain the peaceful scene that de Hooch has shown (the young woman waiting for the man to come home) than the lewd and violent bits he has left out: "We miss the dirty dog, the fiery gin." By referring to other genre paintings of this period and pointing out what de Hooch has eschewed in this particular one, Mahon sheds an oblique light on the painting as a kind of dike, keeping out "the esurient sea" of moral and social chaos. Yet when the paint disintegrates, he muses, the dikes will burst and the dirty dogs will return, esurient, to their sea of gin.

Once again—by now it seems inevitable—the docent concludes with a word of personal explanation:

> I lived there as a boy and know the coal
> Glittering in its shed, late-afternoon
> Lambency informing the deal table,
> The ceiling cradled in a radiant spoon.
> I must be lying low in a room there,
> A strange child with a taste for verse,
> While my hard-nosed companions dream of fire
> And sword upon parched veldt and fields of rain-swept gorse.
> (*The Hunt by Night*, 9–10; *SP*, 120–121)

This could be the child from "Autobiographies," concealed under the stairs, only now concealed because he is different: he has a taste for verse rather than for fire and the sword. Both Belfast's Stephen Dedalus and his unsympathetic contemporaries, the young artist and the violent young loyalists, have been painted over, like the lewd drinkers and the dirty dogs. Both poet and warriors belong equally to the subtext, or subcanvas, of this picture-poem.

The poem as painting, or the poem which explains the painting, is a poem which reflects upon itself. Every representation of a social reality, even such a highly realistic one as that of de Hooch, rearranges, adds and omits details for its own purpose. One can only surmise on the purpose of the painter in 1659; we infer that the poet's purpose in 1983 is to arrange his consciousness within a social setting. Re-inserting the child with a taste for verse, together with his companions with a taste for violence, into the painting,

Mahon concisely centers both his own consciousness and his environment in one ensemble—a far different thing from saying "I am through with history." Mahon brilliantly uncovers this ensemble in a domestic city-scape of 1659, thus locating his historic consciousness "lying low" at the origins of planter history. The original datum of that history, revealed as having been painted over or painted out, is one of passionate urging to some form of violence. To have a taste for verse is neither to be innocent of violence nor to be unscathed by it but only, as when a small boy is afraid of bullies, to find violence extremely troublesome.

In "The Hunt by Night" Mahon has found his most succinct and convincing solution thus far to the problem of the civilized consciousness adrift in a world of social violence.[19] Here, in contrast to "Courtyards in Delft," the docent omits autobiography from his explanation of Uccello's canvas (of 1465). This painting too is a palimpsest but, as the opening lines of the poem make clear, what the docent finds lying under the renaissance canvas is not a self-portrait but a cave painting: "Swift flights of bison in a cave / Where man the maker killed to live." The poem's narrative idea is a simple one: as time passed, ancient images of fear and death changed to more civilized images of fear and death; hunters and animals mutated to the pageantry and ceremony of courtly art, as in Uccello's canvas, and later to the decorations and toys of the nursery. The high style, though, provides but a thin veneer over the old images, which evoked the smells and cries of ravening beasts; our high-mannered hunt by night can do little to mask the terrible night hunt it has never ceased to be.

Mahon uses every strategy he can find to emblematize historical development in reverse. The six-line stanzas follow an abccba rhyme scheme and a 2–3–4–4–3–2 scansion. The poem even ends with a palindrome: Spectacle pu*t on* for fun / And *not* for food." The poem's discourse follows the same regressive pattern, starting from the neolithic cave and proceeding to the renaissance display, but then characterizing the latter as poised over vanishing points into which the dogs' cries recede, as do all our civilizing manners, back to their predatory beginnings.

Mahon has, however, achieved his vision at a price. The idea of violence as essentially bestial is neither new nor immensely helpful.[20] Some of the criticism directed (I think mistakenly) against

Heaney's *North* might be recalled here—that to resolve social violence into its universal origins is to trivialize it in any particular instance. Nevertheless the trope of caves and beasts works in Mahon's poem, not because it gives the final word about violence but because it gives the poet a means of moving to some non-autobiographical place. It may be asking too much of a metaphor that it simultaneously provide both subjective understanding of the self and objective understanding of violence; both poets use their metaphors for subjective understanding.

It is worth noting that Mahon and Heaney turn to archaic metaphors for self-understanding at different moments of the self's itinerary. Heaney, as we have seen, uses the bog poems as strategies for resisting seductive icons of social violence, contemplating the bodies and objects that are turned up only to wrench himself away from their fascination. The bog poems, coming at the mid-point of Heaney's struggle with the violent self, function in a way that resembles Mahon's dialectical poems, like "The Snow Party" and "The Last of the Fire Kings,"where Mahon is struggling between opposite poles of consciousness. "Courtyards in Delft" and "The Hunt by Night," coming at Mahon's last stage of self-definition (they are therefore parallel to Heaney's allegories), reveal how widely Mahon's resolution of the problem differs from Heaney's. Mahon elects to consider sophisticated works of art from the high Italian and Dutch periods, but systematically penetrates behind their surfaces to the images of violence which they hide. Nor is there any question of the poet's identifying with these images or resisting them, since he already sees himself in the picture, whether autobiographically, as in "Courtyards in Delft," or just because he sees images of human nature, as in "our hunt by night, / So very tense, / So long pursued, / In what dark cave begun / And not yet done." Whereas Heaney has chosen "the long perspective . . . of detached compassion," which he attributes to Mahon in "A Disused Shed," Mahon's own choice in "The Hunt by Night" is to abandon perspective entirely in favor of a primitive scene in which the independent observer no longer has a place and from which the writing self can no longer escape. In this sense "The Hunt by Night" works as the dialectical opposite of "A Disused Shed." Whereas the earlier poem indulged in the language of compassion ("What should they do there but desire?") while retaining an independent point of view (that of the journalist), "The Hunt by Night" adopts a distantly objective language ("the hunting horn / At once peremptory and forlorn") while abandoning an independent, observing consciousness: it is the final ironic function of the language to make this loss plain.

In one sense the itinerary which began with "Glengormley," a place where monsters and giants could no longer walk, has reached its furthest antithesis, a dark place of predatory adventures. In another sense the poet has only returned to his Northern Irish place of origin. "By necessity, if not choice, I live here too"—in this cave where the hunt by night dominates all other activities.

The violence with which Mahon contends in his poetry is no specific set of historical misdeeds. Historical narration and analysis can trace the Northern Irish we-they mentality to its political origins, but such narrative does not constitute explanation. Beginning with a structuralist description of tribal violence and of the rituals invented to appease it, one can better understand the Troubles as an aggravated kind of social malaise, one which could affect any group of people but which happens to have found in Ulster a particularly congenial set of circumstances for its tumescent growth. This malaise, when described in terms of narcissistic rage or *ressentiment*, can finally be seen as the self-destroying impulse of the disgruntled individual, turned outward on others.

If social chaos can indeed be discussed in a framework of narcissism, then poetry such as Mahon's can be read as a source of enlightenment. Lyric, after all, is the most inward of literary art forms, situating itself within a consciousness. By attending carefully to the modalities of Mahon's lyric voice, one can follow his imaginative work of constructing a self which will somehow be free from violence—free, that is, from the narcissistic rage of the stunted self. Since Mahon so consistently places this troubled self in a social context (and not in nature, as the romantics, or in the web of autobiography, as the confessionals), his artistic obedience to the command "Know thyself" commits him to an exploration of social violence.

Mahon starts at the point where Heaney arrives in the Sweeney poems, at the impulse to flight, to imagine himself as other and elsewhere. I have called this the poetry of fantasy, the narcissistic development of the grandiose, high-flying self. Mahon then copes with this "insolent ontology" by developing a poetry of dialectical opposites, polarities by which he attempts to yoke, however harshly, his desire for flight and self-aggrandizement to his desire for submission and inherited ideals, even if these latter are never allowed to emerge from the surrounding darkness. Mahon's inner debate can never advance beyond the paralysis of paradox, though, since grandiose flight into an elsewhere always returns to the demands of a here, a place in which one can never survive. Brilliantly, in "A Disused Shed" and "Autobiographies," Mahon hits on a new strategy. Instead of oscillating between two poles of consciousness or two selves, he starts to integrate them both into one conscious center or one integral self. By attempting to imagine himself as both prisoner and liberator, both mushroom and journalist, he assumes a voice together with the understanding of that voice. In his two poems on paintings, Mahon takes further steps toward integrating his self by replacing it consciously within its original milieu—first as the child hiding from violence in the painted courtyard, but finally as a mind (just a flickering light) participating in violence on the painted cave wall.

There are no answers to violence in Mahon's poetry. Its ironic complexities, begun in "Glengormley" and concluded here, are beautifully symbolized by the triple negative with which "The Hunt by Night" ends:

> As if our hunt by night,
>   So very tense,
>
>   So long pursued,
>   In what dark cave begun
> And **not** yet done, were **not** the great
> Adventure we suppose but some elaborate
>   Spectacle put on for fun
>   And **not** for food.
> (*The Hunt by Night*, 30–31; *SP*, 174–75)

(All this is to say that the hunt is just for food.) What makes us able to live with these ironies is the artistic dignity that Mahon brings to the depiction of human violence within the self, combining dark fatality with the pleasures of artistic wit. If "foetid bestial howls"

are what we primally utter, we do well to listen to ourselves utter-
ing them in the beautiful yet entirely appropriate harmonic settings
which Mahon has devised for their accompaniment.

In *The Hudson Letter* and *The Yellow Book*, Mahon's most recent
collections, we find the poet in a far different mental world from
that whose geography we have traced in earlier works. The self of
these poems—that of an aging, lonely man—has no further interest
in escaping from identification with a violent society. Writing *The
Hudson Letter*, he is a solitary in New York; writing *The Yellow
Book*, he is a solitary in Dublin. Ulster is a barely remembered
foreign country when he goes home for his mother's funeral. "Once
upon a time it was let me out and let me go, " he confesses, "and
now it's take me back and take me in."[21] He roams the streets of
New York, eyeing vagrants and bar-dwellers, a stranger to all. He
writes verse observations about life in the nineties, but always from
afar (with the birds, he gazes from on high on the "Mondrian mil-
lions lunching far below," the "alien corn of Radio City").[22] Sounds
are either intrusions on privacy or overheard. Bridget Moore, the
girl from Co. Cork writing home to her mother in 1895, does in-
deed connect vitally with the city ("it's all fire and sunlight here in
the New World"). She does so in striking contrast to the poet him-
self, however, whose more conventional moments of psychological
insight ("encoded mysteries of the human heart," "innermost si-
lence of the heart") occur in a vacuum, unrelated to any particular
human situation.[23] Mahon's random, gloomy attention to the sor-
did sights and sounds of the city around him expresses personal
loss rather than any further interaction between a self and a soci-
ety.
    As his title suggests, Mahon in *The Yellow Book* claims kin-
ship with Wilde and the aesthetes of the 1890s. By putting a cen-
tury between his imagined self and the current *fin-de-siècle*, he
perpetuates his stance of outsider (who in the 1890s would have
imagined himself a contemporary of Sheridan or Goldsmith?). And
yet, in spite of such distancing, Mahon does occasionally reveal
insights which continue his previous work as a poet of social vio-
lence. The poem "An Bonnán Buí" ("The Yellow Bittern") wryly
imagines a bird found dead in winter as an image or companion of
the poet, also figuratively dying of thirst. He thinks of enforced

sobriety as one instance of a more general victory of psychiatry over inspiration: drunk geniuses are disappearing in today's "world-clinic where the odd learn to renounce / their singularity for a more communal faith."[24] He goes on intriguingly to repeat a few strains of "Glengormley," written thirty years earlier, as he asks "And the lyrical madness? If no saint or hero, / no goddess 'all saints and sober men' revile . . . can we still expect / to know the Muses' wicked, intolerant smile?"[25] The saints and heroes of "Glengormley," it will be remembered, were those of ancient Ireland, whose values had been replaced by the Northern Irish bourgeois culture in which Mahon was raised. It was that bourgeois mentality, in turn, which perpetuated the narrow sectarian hostilities from within which the young poet called, "Let me out and let me go." Curiously, though, Mahon now appears to set Ulster sectarianism in league with all the other odd-but-real mentalities (like drunkenness and poetic inspiration, one supposes) which the new age of materialist "wellness" is stamping out:

> No dope, no 'Kubla Khan'; no schizophrenia, no *Chimères*,
> do we love one another and build the shining city
> renouncing the sublime for a quieter beauty
> or fight to the death about the nature of reality?
> Do we want the Renascence art-and-poison paradox
> or a thousand years of chocolate and cuckoo clocks?
> Do we choose peace to please some foreign power,
> war-like itself elsewhere, or do we prefer
> the intransigence, bittern, of our native Ulster,
> the bigots shrieking for their beleaguered 'culture'?
> Do we give up fighting so the tourists come
> or fight the harder so they stay at home?
> Waving and drowning, the restored spirit floats
> in blue water, the rising tide that lifts some boats.
> (*The Yellow Book*, 27)

This is decidedly odd. Why on earth should Mahon wish to lump Ulster bigotry with the sublime, with saints and heroes, with sacred rage? In order, no doubt, to ironize on alcoholism by twinning the specious identification of drunkenness and genius with the equally specious identification of fighting over philosophy and fighting over parade routes. In order also (and here the poet's direct address—"bittern"—to his avatar reveals his mind) to repeat his new cry, "We have been too long in the cold—Take us in; take us in!"[26] Observe in the lines quoted above the pronoun "we." "Do we want . . . ," "Do we choose . . .": that is the generalized, editorial "we," the French *est-ce qu'on veut* which is addressed to no one in particular. "Or do we prefer, *bittern*, . . .": that by contrast is a specific address to one other person (albeit a dead bird), an address which therefore establishes a community of sorts. Community, it seems, is what the poet most of all wants, even with a dead bird, yes, even (a final capitulation) with the other citizens of "*our* native Ulster" (these citizens are immediately characterized as shrieking bigots). In the final question, the poet bizarrely supposes that he still lives in Ulster, and that he faces a choice between fighting or not fighting the sectarian battles from which, in fact, he fled long ago.

Reading these and other scattered passages in his recent writing, one senses that Mahon is turning instinctively to Ulster as an emblem of his spiritual condition, although that condition has nothing whatever to do with Ulster. He is a lonely, alienated man looking bitterly at a postmodern world which is superficially united by material bonds but which appears to him as fracture, chaos ("I can see a united Ireland from the air, / its meteorological gaiety and despair"[27]). Writing of loss and consequent despair, he rejoins his fellow Ulstermen in his sense of being forgotten, lost. Mahon has not yet, however, touched on the more sensitive question of cause and effect: why and how did *his* despair happen? Because his rhetorically confessional postures in these recent poems ('in youth a frightful little shit," "I too have been homeless and in detox / with baaad niggas") never address the specifics of moral responsibility, Mahon is unable, now, to confront the links between violence and emotion which so powerfully inform his earlier poems. Whereas the speaker of "Courtyards in Delft" and "The Hunt by Night" felt perpetually threatened by his sense of involvement with unknown violence, the speaker of *The Hudson Letter* and *The Yellow Book* exhibits a sense of guilt for his own deeds of violence, or whatever he did to alienate others and leave himself in the plight he now laments. That, I think, is the profoundest effect of "An Bonnán Buí," in which the poet's ironic vindication of his guilty stance—disorder masquerading as inspiration—includes a shocking expression of solidarity with the violent culture against which he had once set the whole force of his thought and work. It is as though Mahon, in a sinister reprise of "The Hunt by Night," were admitting that his own work was not "the great / Adventure we suppose," but yet another version of the primal hunt, the violence.

Mahon achieves a gentler and certainly more objective perspective on Ulster in the elegy for his mother, "Death in Bangor." As he returns to Co. Down for her funeral, Mahon imagines himself as a Platonic protagonist striving to liberate himself from illusion: "The figure in the *Republic* returns to the cave, / a Dutch interior where cloud-shadows move, / to examine the intimate spaces."[28] Home, then, is identified both with the courtyard in Delft and with the primal scene of violence in "The Hunt by Night," and beyond that, with Plato's cave, where those who cannot see things as they are remain chained to each other in perpetual bondage. Like her son, the poet's mother had an "idea of the beautiful, not unrelated to Tolstoy / but formed in a tough city of ships and linen." Mahon's litany of Belfast remembrance, including such familiar items as revolvers and drums, Brookeborough and the B-Specials, is replaced by his mother's innocent humming of popular songs and her needlework. With death, the humming ends:

> All artifice stripped away, we give you back to nature
> but something of you, perhaps the incurable ache
> of art, goes with me as I travel south
> past misty drumlins, shining lanes to the shore,
> above the Mournes a final helicopter,
> sun-showers and rainbows all the way through Louth,
> cottages buried deep in ivy and rhododendron,
> ranch houses, dusty palms, blue skies of the republic . . .
> (*The Yellow Book*, 53)

It is this "incurable ache" which first makes the Platonic sufferer imagine that he can break his chains and turn from illusion to reality, but which then changes even that imagination into suffering when he realizes that his best efforts at transforming reality are mere artifice, like his mother's Dresden figurines. As the poet travels south to Dublin after the funeral, Plato's *Republic* becomes the Irish lowercase *r* republic (his mother "innocently hummed 'South of the Border'"), a materialist refuge imagined as the only alternative left to the old violent cave.

"An Bonnán Buí" and "Death in Bangor" give only brief glimpses into a terrifying but compelling world of thought, that cave which Mahon explored so well when writing his best work. Poetry, said Yeats, is the quarrel with oneself, rhetoric the quarrel with others. In his recent poetry, Mahon quarrels abundantly with himself; yet when he transforms that self-quarrel, however briefly, into his quarrel with Ulster, we feel his poetry broadening and deepening, more fully engaging us in the massive questions he once proposed and with which, in some obscure way, he is still engaged: what can the incurable ache of art do to overcome the insoluble effects of violence, whether in the self or others?

5

PAUL MULDOON

Once they collect his smithereens
     he doesn't quite add up.
         —"The More a Man Has the More a Man Wants"

Paul Muldoon's poetry abounds in scenes of sordid violence, made all the more perplexing by the joking style used to describe them. The visitor to Muldoon's Ireland regularly encounters explosions and murders, bodies raped or chained to fences—catastrophes unidentified by historical coordinates and unexplained by poetic reflection.

Although born in 1955 (he is six years younger than Paulin and seven years younger than Carson), Muldoon began to publish his major work in 1977, not long after Heaney's *North* and Mahon's *The Snow Party*. In this astonishing production between the ages of twenty-two and thirty-two—*Mules* (1977), *Why Brownlee Left* (1980), *Quoof* (1983), and *Meeting the British* (1987)—Muldoon represents a self that, more than that of any other Northern Irish poet, allows existing violence to invade and fracture it. Muldoon never asks, as Heaney does, how he can mediate between uncivil violence and the civilized self ("How with this rage shall beauty hold a plea?"); he always knows that beauty has no rights against rage. Instead Muldoon asks what remains, what can be salvaged, and whether the fragmented self can be restored. When a body is blown to smithereens, he observes, the pieces never quite add up. Representing those pieces in his fragmented style, Muldoon embodies a humpty-dumpty self which, in spite of the best efforts of horses and men, can never be put together again.

How then can one discuss a poetic self in Muldoon's poetry? "One cannot," has seemed to be the verdict of much critical writing on Muldoon, as it follows the poet's deceptive example in rejecting romantic assumptions about a unified consciousness. Such a rejection may, however, betoken the fullest activity of a self—a point fully taken by Stephen Burt when he writes that "Muldoon's compelling subject is the doubt and duality inherent in any personal identity, in our senses of who we are and how we know."[1] More generally critics have tended to explore the connections between Muldoon's formal innovations and his political positions. Edna Longley finds in his poetry what she calls "the politics of form," observing that "the politics of Irish poetry can be more revealing than the poetry of Irish politics."[2] Interested as she is in questions of classification (from what poets does a given poet descend? to what group, region, or school of thought does he belong?), Longley is chiefly preoccupied with Muldoon's projects of felling poetic family trees (the Yeats tree and the Heaney tree) and of garbling the familiar clichés of regional and nationalist discourses. When compelled to acknowledge the human source of these formal strategies, Longley limits herself to conjecture ("the core of ice in Muldoon's imagination, possibly where religion has frozen").[3] Clair Wills, although ideologically at odds with Longley, joins her in reading Muldoon's poetry as an artistic representation of certain abstract political ideas (thus Wills's "politics of poetic form"). For Wills, Muldoon's transgressions of artistic form (such as a sonnet of fourteen words, one word per line) constitute an implicit commentary on imperialist borders; his eclecticism a commentary on late capitalist ideas of ownership; his postmodernist techniques of fragmentation a particularly devastating commentary on romantic-imperialist ideas of origins and identity.[4] This way of reading Muldoon, a joining of the formalist and the thematic, has fostered debates about the political significance, or insignificance, of Muldoon's extravagant style. One chorus of commentators is aggravated by the political irresponsibility, as these critics see it, of Muldoon's notorious playfulness, his games with words and allusions.[5] These voices are met by those of others, such as Longley, who finds that Muldoon's postmodernism constitutes a trenchant form of social commentary, "grounded in Northern Irish culture," since "Catholic Ulster seems to have incubated its own de-construction."[6] Longley goes so far as to suggest that Muldoon's most fundamental deconstruction is aimed at Western epistemology.[7]

The best that can be said for these arguments, whatever their formal or political bias, is that they successfully depict Muldoon as a satirist. If send-ups of nationalist discourse constitute a form of political commentary, so be it, but there is relatively little one can say about such commentary. If repeated protestations of uncertainty by a poetic voice constitute an "epistemological scruple," so be it—but what is there to be inferred from that about epistemology itself? Arguments concerning either politics or knowledge must be rational in order to be arguments. Does Muldoon's formal arrangement of *Madoc*, a sequence of short poems whose titles present a list of philosophers from Thales to Hawking, constitute a statement about Western thought, or is that also a joke? When we find that the only relevance of the poems to their philosopher-titles is often concealed in one catchword (thus "hemlock" for Socrates, "geld" for Origen, "Carthage" for Augustine, and so on), we tend to take Muldoon's own advice not to take his philosophical references too seriously.[8] Arguments about Muldoon's poetic-political statements, whether couched in formal arrangements or not, are undermined by what they assume about poetry as statement. Peter McDonald has now brought to this discussion a much needed corrective, first setting forth some of Muldoon's most recent and most beautiful formal arrangements (in "Incantata" and "Yarrow"), and then observing that these arrangements constitute an implicit argument against all criticism which reads poetry primarily for its (political) content.[9]

One need not stop there. My own preference is to read Muldoon's poems as formal enactments of a lyric process, the play of some active mind in personal response to life's challenges. In the early Muldoon, as in Heaney and Mahon, I find borders and possessions, origins and identities, to be less compelling than some imagining sensibility's efforts to deal with issues of self-definition in the specifically bordered context of Northern Ireland. Seen from this perspective, Muldoon's poems paradoxically render inaccessible that sense of self which the poems' persona wishes to achieve, not only by representing the fragmenting effects of social violence, but by enacting such violence in their fragmented language and style. In his more recent work, Muldoon's vaulting structures as well as his short, quotidian lyrics, betoken a sense of personal resolution, a self's new-found ability to find repose within complexity.

Like Heaney and Mahon, Muldoon reveals the need to construct a nonviolent yet authentic self from within a violent society. Of the three, Muldoon sets about this process of self-construction with the highest degree of intellectual rigor, one which might have been impossible to attain had he been the first to attempt it. Using abstract concepts in *Mules* to represent a self discovering that it has been born into a state of violence, Muldoon then turns, in *Why Brownlee Left*, to a more narrative mode of self-definition, chronicling the development of the self in such a way as to show a socially produced yet fatal pattern of self-destruction. Having further explored the correspondences between social and mental chaos in *Quoof*, Muldoon then writes *Meeting the British*, a book about expatriation which implicitly asks whether flight from Ireland can liberate the consciousness from its destructive tendencies. His negative answer comes as less of a surprise than the ever-novel ways in which that answer is expressed. Muldoon's exuberant love of innovation, his stylistic optimism, serves to bandage his pessimism—if not to heal, at least to hide.

Muldoon uses tropes of similarity and non-distinction in *Mules* (1977) to characterize the legacy of violence inherited by everyone born into his society of Northern Ireland. René Girard, as we have seen, traces the genesis of violence to a pair of siblings who desire the same thing and fight—not because of the thing, but because the desire of one is imitated by the desire of the other. Mimetic desire, as Girard describes it, uses the object of desire only as an occasion for manifesting itself. One's enemy appears as one's double; brothers and twins classically symbolize the impulse to violent conflict as a unique, spontaneous event in human life and society.

"Lunch with Pancho Villa," a lyric satire on *poésie engagée*, characterizes "revolution" as being what the word means, an interchange of positions, so that front doors turn into back doors. The speaker's identity revolves between that of Pancho Villa and his double, the young interviewer. Addressing the young man, Villa speaks of a deadly circularity:

> 'Look, son. Just look around you,
> People are getting themselves killed
> Left, right, centre
> While you do what? Write rondeaux?'
> (*Mules,* 41–43; *SP,* 19–21)

The young man's circular poetry (rondeaux) cannot be distinguished from the circularity of the political world ("look around"), where the coordinates of political space ("left, right, centre") have become smudged in chaotic outbursts of violence.

"Armageddon, Armageddon" conjoins the cosmic and local ("Armageddon/Armagh"), so that Orion and Sagittarius become Hunter and Archer (Protestant Will Hunter appears in three other poems in the book), rival farmers of opposite religious loyalties: "Were Twin and Twin at each other's throats? . . . Had Hunter and Archer got it into their heads / That they would take the stars in their strides" (*SP,* 35–41)? The poem's local violence is described in terms of gruesome twinning: the poet's father is "torn between his own two ponies, / Their going their different ways" (an ironic result of his father's inability to decide which horse to bet on). Once this violent act has been committed, there are no more stars—such is Armageddon—and the poem ends in darkness. Muldoon's purpose is not to elevate local violence to a cosmic level, but to satirize the indignity of such violence by the absurdity of the comparison. At the poem's end the poet, under the stars, is picking up a beetle and setting it on its tiny feet "to have it walk in the paths of uprightness." Like Swift, Muldoon joins great and small as a satiric device for commentary on social violence, although in fact both writers employ the device to intensify the very social violence they depict.

Violent twinning reappears in "The Centaurs," where Protestant beast (King Billy) and Catholic beast (Cortes) are identically violent, as is the third beast, Saul of Tarsus, whose conversion to Christianity is depicted as the cause of his metamorphosis from human to violent animal.[10] The familiar trope of twin religions, though, provides less interest in this poem than a second and, for

Muldoon, more important dimension of twinning, the yoking of human and animal within each individual centaur. He employs this hybrid symbol again in "Vaquero" (where a horseman, lashed to his saddle, has been riding dead for a week) and in "Mules."[11] Because the mule, like the centaur, unites within itself two kinds of being, it typifies violence. Even its conception is violent; having loosed the male jackass and the female horse in one field, the two owners wait for the act of coupling, "tense for the punch below their belts, / For what was neither one thing or the other." Responding parodically to the Yeatsian shudder in the loins of the jackass, they "had shuddered / To think, of their gaunt, sexless foal." The mule might be thought to have sprung from the earth were it not for the equine afterbirth, which "trailed like some fine, silk parachute, / That we should know from what heights it fell." Metaphor transforms the gross afterbirth into evidence of the beast's angelic origins. Muldoon evokes the sense of mixed identity (angel or beast?—"neither one thing or the other") as both the source and product of conflict—the shudder, the punch below the belt.

If the first dimension of twinning, the indistinguishability of Hunter from Archer, of twin from twin, provides Muldoon with a social, horizontal coordinate, this second, vertical coordinate enables him to turn from social to personal perspectives, as in the ironies of "The Mixed Marriage." The marriage of Muldoon's parents was socially, not religiously, mixed: both were Catholic, but his mother was a schoolteacher and his father a farm laborer. Hence the twins Castor and Pollux, offspring of Leda and Zeus, embody two separate spheres of existence within the poet—not the social Catholic-Protestant polarity, but the vertical, inner split between civility and violence. As an aspirant to the world of culture, the poet's mother inhabits a world of twins ("The world of Castor and Pollux . . . She could never tell which was which"), a world in which genteel oblivion to difference and ferocious insistence on difference dwell side by side. His mother's attempts to ascend from crude faction-fights to airy non-difference produce only uncertainty, the inability to tell which is which.

> I flitted between a hole in the hedge
> And a room in the Latin Quarter.

When she had cleared the supper-table
She opened *The Acts of the Apostles,*
Aesop's Fables, Gulliver's Travels.
Then my mother went on upstairs

And my father further dimmed the light
To get back to hunting with ferrets
Or the factions of the faction-fights—
The Ribbon Boys, the Caravats.
(*Mules,* 72; *SP,* 32)

Girard's model of twinning as the pattern of social violence
here gives way to Kohut's model of identity-formation, the task of
mediating inwardly between two rival identities, represented by
the "mixed" marriage of the mother who ascends to the liberal
plane of enlightened, humane letters and the father who descends
to the dim light of ferrets and faction-fights. The child can only
vacillate: "I flitted between a hole in the hedge / And a room in the
Latin Quarter." The paternal, earthbound hedge school symbol-
izes, as it does in Heaney's "Ministry of Fear" and Friel's *Transla-*
tions, the conformist option of adhering to traditional violence.
Although the imagined bohemian world of a Paris university
(which Muldoon never attended—like Heaney and Friel, he stud-
ied in Belfast) offers him the grandiose alternative of intellectual
self-inflation, the mixed marriage leaves the child experiencing
the division between paternal fascination with violence and ma-
ternal efforts to transcend violence as being itself an irreducible
inner conflict.

Pervading *Mules* is the question "Who am I?"—not an unex-
pected one for a poet in his twenties. There are two sets of ques-
tions here. The first, set out on a horizontal axis, concerns similarities
and differences, my status among others: am I Catholic Archer or
Protestant Hunter? Archer confronts Hunter, twin and twin at each
other's throats. The second, set out on the vertical axis (angelic
parachute or earthy afterbirth?), asks about the elements of which
I am composed: am I Paris bohemian or Armagh Taig, upscale horse
or downscale jackass—or just mule, neither one thing or another?
Trying to answer these questions, the self encounters ironic polari-
ties. One remains downstairs to confront violence, but then is fi-

nally coopted into it. The other tries to escape violence by going upstairs, but in so doing implicitly promotes that violence by denying it. If it is true, as Girard claims, that one's brother is one's enemy, then the romantic project of uniting things in the imagination appears to be a project for violence. "How with this rage shall beauty hold a plea, / Whose action is no stronger than a flower?" So Heaney questions, in his search for the civilizing power of art.[12] Muldoon's implied answer to this question is a disturbing one: rage infests the root from which the flower blossoms.

In *Why Brownlee Left*, Muldoon's search for identity turns from the abstractions of *Mules* to more concrete elements of personal narration, as in "October, 1950," a sonnet about his birth:

> Whatever it is, it all comes down to this;
> My father's cock
> Between my mother's thighs.
> Might he have forgotten to wind the clock?
> (*Why Brownlee Left*, 9)

As imagined, this act of conception is crude and ill-timed (cock and clock), random ("anything wild or wonderful") and meaningless ("whatever it is, it leaves me in the dark"). Thinking of himself as the product of a chance sexual encounter or whim (a favorite word of Muldoon's), the poet locates the sources of his being in the random flow of history. But history is violent; therefore the sexual sources of his being are violent. Elsewhere Muldoon compares the soldiers cautiously emerging from opposing trenches to greet each other on Armistice Day to "Friday-night lovers, when it's over" who "congratulate each other / And exchange names and addresses."[13]

Sex and violence appear in "Cuba" as two emergencies which occur simultaneously during the poet's childhood—the Cuban missile crisis and the first time that the poet's adolescent sister stays out all night. The girl's father sends her off to confession when he hears of the American ultimatum, since "this Kennedy's nearly an Irishman / So he's not much better than ourselves. / And with him only to say the word." If he were in Kennedy's position, the father reasons, he would no doubt have already pushed the fatal button.

Irish patriarchy, then, embodies a double violence, the first of which threatens the world with destruction (Kennedy's nuclear threat and "my father . . . pounding the breakfast-table"), and the second of which threatens a young woman with eternity in hell ("Maybe you should make your peace with God").

It serves Muldoon's purpose to portray his sister's sexual experience as romantically innocent.

> I could hear May from beyond the curtain.
> 'Bless me, Father, for I have sinned.
> I told a lie once, I was disobedient once.
> And, Father, a boy touched me once.'
> 'Tell me, child. Was this touch immodest?
> Did he touch your breast, for example?'
> 'He brushed against me, Father, Very gently.'
> (*Why Brownlee Left*, 13; *SP*, 47)

If we can imagine May in her white muslin evening dress as pure and innocent throughout her night-long sexual adventure (not because her breasts were untouched but because they were touched gently), then, the poem suggests, we can suppose the existence of some self whose sexuality is the badge of its innocence and integrity, hemmed in by a patriarchy which contaminates that self in the name of both war and religion. This romantic idea of sexuality (make love not war) reappears in a five-line poem entitled "Ireland," where the poet looks at an empty car whose engine is running as either a refuge for lovers or, more probably, the means of escape for terrorists who are "hurrying back / Across two fields and a river" (*NSP*, 47).

The very ambiguity of the parked car, though, like the comparison of enemy soldiers to partners in casual sex, pairs sex with violence at the same time that it dialectically opposes them. Although love is opposed to war, it can never be separated from war, and therefore the patriarch's own use of sexuality ("my father's cock between my mother's thighs") can never be innocent. But if so, if "it all comes back to this," one wonders how the children can ever be innocent, even if they are girls in white named May.

Muldoon invokes the romantic, sexual self only to ironize on the thought of the impossibility of such a self existing in a violently patriarchal world. Saying a last good-bye to his lover in "Something of a Departure" (this last word signifying both leave-taking and perversion or departure from the norm), the poet first ironically characterizes her as an angel:

> Would you be an angel
> And let me rest,
> This one last time,
> Near that plum-coloured beauty spot
> Just below your right buttock?

But then, having inventoried her thigh, breast, wrist, and ankle, as body parts which "might yet sprout a wing," he concludes by altering her persona:

> So put your best foot forward
> And steady, steady on.
> Show me the plum-cloured beauty spot
> Just below your right buttock,
> And take it like a man.[14]

Muldoon's ironic transformation of the adorable female angel to a male object of sexual cruelty, after his ironic reduction of personal identity to gross copulation (cock between thighs) and his ironic conjunction of adolescent sexuality and nuclear holocaust, expresses the logical collapse of his represented quest for an innocent identity. Having suggested in "Cuba" that innocent female sexuality is corrupted by a violent male patriarchy, he also suggests in "October, 1950" that, since the original sexual act originates with the patriarch, there can be no such thing as innocent sexuality. When transformed from female angel into male prostitute, the innocent sexual self can never emerge from its mythic status (the angel in the white dress) because it is always compromised by the violent male.

Turning from sexuality to the politics of the classroom, Muldoon transposes these reflections to the context of Northern Irish violence in "Anseo," a poem in three sonnets which anatomizes the male-to-male propagation of violence by Ulster Catholics:

When the Master was calling the roll
At the primary school in Collegelands,
You were meant to call back *Anseo*
And raise your hand
As your name occurred.
Anseo, meaning here, here and now,
All present and correct,
Was the first word of Irish I spoke.
The last name on the ledger
Belonged to Joseph Mary Plunkett Ward
And was followed, as often as not,
By silence, knowing looks,
A nod and a wink, the Master's droll
'And where's our little Ward-of-court?'

I remember the first time he came back
The Master had sent him out
Along the hedges
To weigh up for himself and cut
A stick with which he would be beaten.
After a while, nothing was spoken;
He would arrive as a matter of course
With an ash-plant, a salley-rod.
Or, finally, the hazel-wand
He had whittled down to a whip-lash,
Its twist of red and yellow lacquers
Sanded and polished,
And altogether so delicately wrought
That he had engraved his initials on it.

I last met Joseph Mary Plunkett Ward
In a pub just over the Irish border.
He was living in the open,
In a secret camp
On the other side of the mountain.
He was fighting for Ireland,
Making things happen.
And he told me, Joe Ward,
Of how he had risen through the ranks

To Quartermaster, Commandant:
How every morning at parade
His volunteers would call back *Anseo*
And raise their hands
As their names occurred.
(*Why Brownlee Left*, 20–21; *SP*, 49–50)

In his interview with Muldoon, John Haffenden misleadingly
refers to "Anseo" as dealing with "the possibilities of behaviouristic
conditioning" (a comment to which Muldoon replied in terms
equally misleading: "If [the poem] works, it works because every-
thing in it is absolutely dead-on, the details are really accurate. It's
fiction, of course").[15] It is not helpful to speak of Joe as
behavioristically conditioned; he does not whip anyone. The one
action he causes to be reproduced, the saying of *Anseo* at roll call,
is the very thing he did not do as a truant boy, which is why he was
whipped.

Exactly how then does violence reproduce itself in this poem
of social mimesis? There is nothing here about Protestants or the
British (although Joseph Mary Plunkett was one of the leaders of
the Easter Rising); the master and his students are all Irish Catho-
lics. The Catholic master teaches Joe not how to deal violently with
the world, but how to be a victim of violence. Joe learns to submit
to whipping and even to fashion beautiful whips. As a non-event,
Joe's silence stigmatizes him as both guilty and as victim. When it
was called, the name Joseph Mary Plunkett Ward "was followed,
as often as not, / By silence, knowing looks." The missing sound,
Anseo, is a word in Irish, "the first word of Irish I spoke," adds the
poet. Joe's silence at roll call is matched by his silence in punish-
ment: "After a while, nothing was spoken." In symbolic silence,
Joe identifies himself by carving his initials on the whip.

Now Joe has replaced the master who whipped him—not as a
torturer of his "pupils" but only as one who hears them reply *Anseo*.
What is being transmitted from master to Joe and from Joe to his
men is the persona of victim. The process requires three steps. First,
when the name occurs, it can be cancelled by the appropriate Irish
word *Anseo*, "meaning here, here and now, / All present and cor-
rect." Second, when this order of subservience is broken, it is bro-
ken by silence, and then replaced by a ritual of violence. In Girardian

terms, Joe now becomes a scapegoat. In the third stage, Joe has restored order and is enforcing it on others, but now that order itself is a violent one: the men who respond are "making things happen," wreaking violence either upon enemies or (what is just as likely) upon fellow Catholics who displease the IRA—who are not, symbolically, saying *Anseo* when their names occur. The ritual of violence has been elevated to a higher, more violent level: Joe does not inflict violence on his men, but he and his men inflict violence on their fellow men and women. What has caused this elevation? The question sends us back to the second stage, the scapegoating ritual, when the victim makes his own whip . The silence whereby Joe becomes a victim (not answering to his name) develops into the silence whereby Joe *is* present and bearing the whip he has beautifully fashioned (bearing his silent initials) for his silent torture. By means of this progression, the silent victim in the first sonnet becomes the silent means of his own victimization in the second, and hence the origin of an entire army's violent deeds in the third.

Violence in this poem originates in the moment of silence and non-presence when one becomes a victim; as such, one becomes a scapegoat for the community's shared violence and, no less, one learns to become the means of inflicting that violence upon oneself. Having learned to become an object of violence, therefore, one learns to become its source. In the last sonnet, Joe has assembled an army of fellow victims who all answer to their names in a new order of violence, and who make things happen: they seek new objects, silent partners who must learn in silence first to become objects, then sources, of violence.

The underlying theme of "Anseo," self-inflicted violence, reappears in "Immram," the long poem with which *Why Brownlee Left* concludes. The first of Muldoon's picaresque long poems, to be followed by "The More a Man Has the More a Man Wants" and "Madoc: A Mystery," "Immram" is based on an Irish travel-text, *Immram Mael Duin*, which dates at least to the eighth century. Mael Duin (aka Muldoon) sets out on a voyage to find the murderer of his father and seek revenge. After visiting all his islands and having all his adventures, the original protagonist learns from a hermit that it is better to forgive than to avenge, and so turns to a life of piety. In the nineteeth-century translation upon which

Muldoon's poem is based, the ancient hermit says, "Slay . . . not [your father's murderer], but forgive him, because God hath saved *you* from manifold great perils, and ye, also, are men deserving of death."[16] Tennyson's version (Muldoon calls it "dreadful") turns this same passage from a religious to a political statement about cessation from violence: "Thy father had slain his father, how long shall the murder last? / Go back to the isle of Finn and suffer the Past to be Past."[17]

Muldoon finds Tennyson's poem so dreadful that he rewrites it in the picaresque style of a Raymond Chandler thriller, set in Los Angeles, whose protagonist must find the persecutor of his father. The first stanza will suffice to indicate the style, as well as to point out some of the poem's central problems:

> I was fairly and squarely behind the eight
> That morning in Foster's pool-hall
> When it came to me out of the blue
> In the shape of a sixteen-ounce billiard cue
> That lent what he said some little weight.
> 'Your old man was an ass-hole.
> That makes an ass-hole out of you.'
> My grand-father hailed from New York State.
> My grand-mother was part Cree.
> This must be some new strain in my pedigree.
> (*Why Brownlee Left,* 38; *SP,* 58)

The term "ass-hole" (freshly immigrated to its American spelling) is defined first as the condition of being a victim—subject to the intimidation of men like the wielder of the ass-hole-appropriate pool-cue—and secondly as an inherited characteristic of inferiority. The problem about being an ass-hole, then, is identical to the problem about being violent: is it a question of what one becomes, or of the way one was born? Muldoon's implicit answer to this question is that the two possibilities amount to the same thing. To learn violence as May and Joe learn it—at home, in church, at school—is tantamount to being born violent. Small wonder then that Irish Muldoon should call British Tennyson's advice to "suffer the Past to be Past" dreadful, since the past always reproduces itself in the Northern Irish experience, as if by a genetic code: one is born a victim ("that makes an ass-hole out of you"), destined to make victims of others. Because he wants to know more about his father, though (*why* was he an ass-hole?), the protagonist sets out in search for his father's persecutor.

Muldoon's itinerary, following the trail of a Raymond Chandler sleuth—his encounters with a stripper and his near misses with death, his cocaine sniffing and his getting knocked out by thugs—provides the stuff of carnival, a ludic succession of mishaps which construct the speaker-sleuth as an abject hero. In tales such as *The Big Sleep*, Chandler's hero must simultaneously allow himself to be taken ever further out of the bounds of rational experience (assuming the classic picaresque posture of a Candide or a Tom Jones, whose flight from one sort of abjection always leads to another), and at the same time come ever closer to the object of his quest, as though derangement and reason were convergent tendencies. To this classic paradox Muldoon adds another: he ventures further and further into rootlessness (lotus-eating Los Angeles) in search of his paternal roots. Muldoon's logical premise ("Your old man was an ass-hole. / That makes an ass-hole out of you") can thus be rephrased as follows: if one's origins lie in abjection, then in order to find those origins one must venture further and further into the ritual of abjection; hence the need for the abject carnival.

In search of the true story of his father, the protagonist learns that he was a small-time drug runner for a millionaire with the British name of Redpath who now occupies the top two floors of the Park Hotel. The ludic impulse which leads the picaresque hero on to self-destroying abjection (strippers, cocaine, murder) has already led the father into abject enslavement to a crook. The father had to flee "from alias to alias," while Redpath enjoys respectability. At the end our hero is taken up in the elevator to see Redpath and discovers that his father's persecutor (he against whom the original protagonist sought vengeance) is also the hermit of the original tale (he who advised the protagonist to abandon revenge). Redpath lives on the top two floors of a hotel and eats only Baskin-Robbins ice cream, an eccentricity which serves to identify him as Howard Hughes:

He was huddled on an old orthopaedic mattress,
The makings of a skeleton,

Naked but for a pair of drawstring shorts.
His hair was waistlength, as was his beard.
He was covered in bedsores.
He raised one talon.
'I forgive you,' he croaked. 'And I forget.
On your way out, tell that bastard
To bring me a dish of ice-cream.
I want Baskin-Robbins banana-nut ice-cream.'
(*Why Brownlee Left*, 47; *SP*, 67)

Muldoon's brilliant stroke—having the father's persecutor first re-place the hermit who advises forgiveness, and then having him for-give his victim—returns us to the dialectic of victimization. In "Anseo" the process whereby the victim of violence must in turn become its source is one which takes place within a community, on a horizontal plane. Now "Immram" transposes this process onto a vertical axis, so that the protagonist ascends in the elevator to be forgiven by his father's persecutor. In political terms, whereas "Anseo" addresses violence as a tribal phenomenon, "Immram" deals with it as a condition of hegemony, the domination of under-lings by overlords.

We normally suppose, Bernstein points out, that life's every-day order, its quotidian superstructure, is menaced from below by the powers of protest and unreason. In fact, he observes, the con-verse is true; our greater menace comes from what is above. "Rather than thinking of ordinary existence as a fragile superstructure ev-erywhere vulnerable to the upsurge of forces from its repressed underground base, it would be more accurate to see the under-ground as the secondary phenomenon, a tenuous and partial resis-tance to the pressures of the normative. It is the normal that structures the underground and not vice versa."[18] In Muldoon's version of this dialectic, the quotidian superstructures make for violence. First the IRA terrorists repeat what was said in the school-room. Then, by voyaging to the seat of hegemonic power and ex-periencing an ultimate form of abjection, Muldoon's itinerant sleuth is authorized to return to Foster's pool-room. "It all comes back to this": parents, from the moment they beget their children, create abject victims and (therefore) perpetrators of violence, handing them on to schoolmasters, employers, and the highest of the higher-ups, who all work together to maintain their charges in this double state of abjection and ferocity, resentment and *ressentiment*.

By yoking the concepts of history and sexuality—the original sexual act is always that of the patriarch—Muldoon takes apart the romantic myth of innocence and associates the erotic with the violent. Turning to rituals of socialization (the classroom), Muldoon locates a silent absence underlying vocal presences, and finds in this absence the space in which victims are created and endowed with the means of propagating their victimhood as sources of further violence. Muldoon finally expands the ritual to its broadest ludic scope, imagining an abject society in thrall to its own superstructures, presided over from his top floor by the richest man in the world, who forgives his abject victims for being abject, and forgets.

Muldoon considered social violence as an abstract question of identities in *Mules*, then transposed this dialectic to a more dynamic mode in *Why Brownlee Left,* conceiving of history and sexuality as ludic rituals of humiliation whereby victims are born and sent forth to create more victims. Then in *Quoof* he addresses the all-important question implied by the scenarios he has created: how can the individual consciousness survive in this carnival, where boys silently fashion the whips with which they will be beaten and where men accept forgiveness from their tormentors? Here Muldoon moves dramatically to the question of self by deconstructing—exploding would be a better word—the politically correct categories of colonialism and hegemony that haunted *Why Brownlee Left.* The symbolic father for whom the poet searches and from whom he escapes now takes flesh as his own father, and then mutates to another symbolic figure—his poetic father, Seamus Heaney. Sex and hallucinogens provide forms of dangerous play, as Muldoon's poetry moves away from cultural abstractions and towards the figure of a self struggling to maintain identity amid experiences of fracture and dissolution.

Quoof begins where *Why Brownlee Left* ended. The protagonist of "Immram" had returned to "Foster's Pool Room," his search for his father the ass-hole having led only to the finding of his foster-father, the man who had made his father an ass-hole. Muldoon starts his new collection with a citation concerning eskimo culture, where the "old foster-mother was a great shaman" who could change her sex by making a penis from a branch.[19] This kind of father can only be found through magic, or in altered states of mind. In *Quoof* the poet simultaneously seeks and flees his father, a mushroom farmer, by moving to Belfast and taking psilocybin. Still both farm and city are sites of violence: the father, "one of those ancient warriors," opens the barn door to let in the Trojan Horse with its shipment of horse manure; the young people tripping in Belfast are thinking of "the fire-bomb / that sent Malone House sky-high."

What is new here is Muldoon's degree of personal involvement. The poet, as Carol Tell writes, is trying to escape Northern Irish violence, yet "every evasion of reality is deeply tinged with guilt."[20] Like both Heaney and Mahon, Muldoon at first conceives of this escape as a flight from his tribal background, but finds that background inescapable. The last sonnet of "Gathering Mushrooms," printed in italics because its voice is that of "the ancestor," calls out, "*Come back to us . . . Your only hope is to come back . . . Lie down with us and wait.*"[21] These lines bear echoes both of the poet's poetic father Heaney, answering a call ("Lie down in the word-hoard") to write a poetry of digging and self-examination, and of his tribal parent, affirming that cement and dung constitute our true domain, "the soiled grey blanket of Irish rain" (an allusion to the dirty protest of the previous decade, when internees in Long Kesh refused to wear prison uniforms and had only their blankets to wear). By placing these lines at the beginning of *Quoof*, Muldoon makes it clear that he is continuing the poetic struggle with violence that began in *Mules* and *Why Brownlee Left*, the same struggle already waged by both Heaney and Mahon.

In the father poems which comprise the first half of *Quoof*, Muldoon struggles with the legacy of male sexuality, pondering the fact that he is fated to imitate his father, performing mutely an endless series of actions for which no proper words can be found. No matter how far the son may depart from the father's domestic sexual role, the resistance of sex to language will always remain, and therefore the implicitly violent aspects of the sexual act will realize themselves in a widening variety of ways. In Muldoon's well-known sonnet, "Quoof," the first and last lines (ending with "word" and "language") symbolize the poem's concern for imagining sexual performance as a speech act:

How often have I carried our family word
for the hot water bottle
to a strange bed,
as my father would juggle a red-hot half-brick
in an old sock
to his childhood settle.
I have taken it into so many lovely heads
or laid it between us like a sword.

An hotel room in New York City
with a girl who spoke hardly any English,
my hand on her breast
like the smouldering one-off spoor of the yeti
or some other shy beast
that has yet to enter the language.
(*Quoof,* 17; *SP,* 77)

Language and sexuality play against each other, not just in a
simple contrast, but also as a means of contrasting father and son.
Thus, in the octave, two of the rhyming pairs deal with the father's
sexuality (brick/sock, bottle/settle), while the other two (word/
sword, bed/heads) deal with the son's. The father's sexuality, either
trivialized ("red-hot") or diminished ("half-brick . . . old sock") by
its qualifiers, remains confined to a scene of childhood. The son
carries to bed the word for the hot object instead of the object
itself—carries it indeed into many beds and many heads. The son,
when he transforms his father's inarticulate sexual brick-in-a-sock
into a word (the poet calls it a family word, although the poet's
father claimed he first heard the word from his children[22]), gains a
mercurial kind of mobility (strange beds, many heads), but loses
the power of connecting with his partner. Language, the sword-
word (a biblical image), lies between lovers as between Tristan and
Iseult, signifying their separation from each other.

The sestet offers two pictures of non-speech: an English-speak-
ing man with a non-English-speaking prostitute, and the abomi-
nable snowman (two pictures which match in their rhyming of "city"
with "yeti" and "breast" with "beast"). This tableau of non-speech
(the sestet has no main verb) is also a tableau of sexual non-perfor-
mance and personal absence. The man's hand on the woman's breast

functions as the yeti's spoor, signifying what is absent (the missing beast, the missing action of sexual fulfillment). The shy beast, like the word "quoof," has yet to enter the language of normal human communication. Sexuality, inherited from the father, remains an incomprehensible word, an act outside of the sphere of communication, and hence something bestial—something shy, that is, something that can only be guessed at by its traces.

The purpose of these wry exercises in nostalgia only begins to emerge when the focus of *Quoof* shifts from Muldoon's biological father to his poetic father, Seamus Heaney—from Freudian to Bloomian anxiety. It would be tedious to note all the allusions to Heaney in poems entitled "Yggdrasill," "Mink," and "The Frog."[23] Muldoon's focus here is not on Heaney himself, but rather on Heaney's early attitude to the Irish troubles, when he sought emblems of historical conflict in crude natural objects—the frog and the shovel. "The Frog," a satire on Heaney's political poetry, concludes:

> There is, surely, in this story
> a moral. A moral for our times.
> What if I put him to my head
> and squeezed it out of him,
> like the juice of freshly squeezed limes,
> or a lemon sorbet?
> (*Quoof*, 29; *SP*, 83)

Muldoon's burlesque of Heaney's attempts to squeeze morals out of natural phenomena, to find "images and symbols adequate to our predicament," speaks for itself. In "Aisling," which contains allusions to Heaney's "Sloe-Gin" and "The Haw-Lantern," secretions again are used as satire: the unspecified woman of the aisling leaves a venereal lemon stain on the poet's sheet, while a "saline drip into [a] bag of brine" supports the latest hunger-striker to have called off his fast (*SP*, 84).

Muldoon would not, of course, be writing back to Heaney so acerbically were he not so closely engaged with Heaney's own questions. Since Heaney believes that "it would be possible to encompass the perspectives of a humane reason" in considering Irish social turmoil, Muldoon must deny this by violently squeezing out all

Heaney's abstractions or essences, letting the juices run off and down. In doing so Muldoon can implicitly claim that he takes conflict *more* seriously than Heaney—so seriously that he refuses to concede that any "moral for our times" can be found. What is most fascinating here is that Muldoon expresses his refusal by casting Heaney as a companion to his own father and expressing nostalgia for Heaney's pieties in a way parallel to his nostalgia for his own father's care of family and farm. Yet such piety is no longer possible because it does not square with the facts and because the writer's consciousness cannot permit it. He has taken the family word into too many strange beds; he has escaped from parental mushroom farming by taking psilocybin. Muldoon's derangements are those of a person who will not allow himself the sort of unified consciousness Heaney evidently enjoys. Some of this difference might be accounted for if we could compare Muldoon's experiences of early adulthood, just as the Troubles were beginning, with those of Heaney in the late fifties and early sixties. It is precisely because he longs for certainties he can no longer find that the speaker of Muldoon's poems obsessively returns to the disappointment he experiences at not finding them.

In the long sonnet sequence with which *Quoof* ends, "The More a Man Has the More a Man Wants," Muldoon unites the abstract preoccupations of *Mules* (twinning, mutual hostility) with the developmental patterns of *Why Brownlee Left* (fathering, the carnival of abjection), transposing both themes into a new key, one in which he represents desire blocked by its opposite, violence. As the pub song from which the poem's title is taken would have it,

> *The more a man has the more a man wants,*
> *the same I don't think true.*
> *For I never met a man with one black eye*
> *who ever wanted two.*
> (*Quoof,* 61; *SP,* 106)

Does desire oppose destruction as a counter-force, or does desire itself dialectically generate chaos? Muldoon chooses the latter option: it is man's activity of desiring which gives him his black eye. As "The More a Man Wants" traces the parallel courses of eros (the derangements produced by dangerous sex and substance abuse) and politics (the explosions of terrorist warfare), it becomes clear for Muldoon that erotic violence is a metaphor and symptom of political violence and not the other way round.

The poem performs a carnivalesque exercise in twinning. The Irish protagonist Gallogly (or "gallowglass" or Ogalala Sioux) is matched by a Mescalero Apache, Mangas Jones; the latter specializes in mescalin, while Gallogly will and does ingest anything he can put his hands on. Jones and Gallogly, the noble and ignoble savages, finally coalesce into one person who is blown to bits by a terrorist bomb. They in turn are matched by a female pair: ignoble Alice on endless drug trips and noble Beatrice, Dante's ideal woman, who is found as a terrorist victim one Sunday morning, naked and chained to a church fence, but who then reappears as the spirit of 1798 and finally as an internee of the 1980s. Lewis Carroll's Alice A. easily becomes Gertrude Stein's Alice B., eating hash brownies at a tea party to which Beatrice is invited: "the three of them sat in the nude / round the petits fours / and repeated *Eros is a Eros is Eros*."

The figure of an Apache and the recurrence of native American words and themes all lend themselves to consideration of "The More a Man Wants" as a discourse about colonialist subjugation. Jacqueline McCurry argues that Muldoon condemns the Irish in America for doing unto the native Americans as they had been done to by the British.[24] Interestingly, though, it is American Mangas Jones who occupies the position of superiority in this poem, while Gallogly plays Caliban, running from the police, terrorizing innocent citizens, "fistfucking" his mind with drugs, lying down in frogspawn and lapping the yellow earth of a freshly dug grave. Read in the context of post-colonial discourse, Muldoon's doubling of Jones and Gallogly serves to demolish any idea of the "native" as a pure, original person corrupted by the colonizer. As I read the poem, Mangas Jones and Gallogly represent aspects of a single but fragmented consciousness, one which seeks to keep alive the myth of a "native soul" but which always debases that ideal in the violence it wreaks both upon itself (drugs) and upon others (terrorism). In his tenth sonnet, written in strict Shakespearian form, Muldoon uses the fifth line to cite line five of Shakespeare's tenth sonnet, where the young man is reproved for his refusal to love others, a refusal which Shakespeare traces to his friend's failure to love himself: "For thou art so possessed with murd'rous hate, / That 'gainst thyself thou stick'st not to conspire." Muldoon's tenth sonnet is the only one in which Mangas Jones and Gallogly appear side by side as two distinct people (they appear as one conflated and disintegrated person at the end); the line from Shakespeare interrupts the speech of an observer who is trying to identify the two men:

> 'I'll warrant them's the very pair
> o' boys I seen abroad
> in McParland's bottom, though where
> in under God—
> *for thou art so possessed with murd'rous hate* —
> where they come from only God knows.'
> (*Quoof*, 44; *SP*, 89)

On this account Mangas represents Gallogly's anti-self, but represents it to no useful end, since the two selves exercise murderous hate against each other. Arriving in Ireland on a charter flight from Florida as "excess baggage," the noble Apache can never be integrated into the consciousness of the Irish boor. Mangas is identified as the exploded corpse at the end because his hand (the red hand of Ulster) is clutching the same pebble of quartz he was carrying at customs upon arrival—not a magic symbol but just the little pebble from Frost's "For Once Then Something," a poem which derides the bogus wisdom of those who are thought to be versed in country things.[25] Muldoon deconstructs romantic nationalist pieties in the bathetic doubling of Jones and Gallogly, just as he does in the doubling of Beatrice and Alice, A. or B.

Throughout *Quoof* Muldoon satirizes the Irish sexist myth of the nationalist siren. In the thirty-sixth sonnet of "The More a Man Has," Muldoon takes up some lines of his "Aisling" as he questions the true identity of Alice A.: "Was she Aurora, or the goddess Flora, / Artemidora, or Venus bright?" Whereas Muldoon's aisling woman became a victim of her own terrorism in the person of a hunger-striker, Anorexia in the present poem is replaced by "Helen fair beyond compare / That Priam stole from the Grecian sight." But Helen is not the right answer either; for the real Alice/Beatrice, Muldoon returns us to the first poem of *Quoof*, "Gathering Mushrooms":

We were thinking only of psilocybin.
You sang of the maid you met on the dewy grass
And she stooped so low gave me to know
it was mushrooms she was gathering O.
(*Quoof*, 7; *SP*, 71)

The context of the earlier poem, it will be remembered, was escape
from the tribal father—the young people "tripping" through Belfast
where, however, their exploded consciousness was likened to a ter-
rorist bombing. The conjunction of drugs and terror now comes full
circle (the "O") in this thirty-sixth sonnet of "The More a Man Has":

Was she Aurora, or the goddess Flora,
Artemidora, or Venus bright,
or Helen fair beyond compare
That Priam stole from the Grecian sight?
Quite modestly she answered me
and she gave her head one fetch up
and she said I am gathering musheroons
to make my mammy ketchup.
The dunt and dunder
of a culvert-bomb
wakes him
as it might have woke Leander.
And she said I am gathering musheroons
to make my mammy ketchup O.
(*Quoof*, 57; *SP*, 102)

Muldoon's explosion of Ireland's erotic nationalist myth be-
gins with "Eros," desire for ecstasy—eros is eros is eros. Desire for
hallucination and desire for sexual gratification converge on the
deceptive figure of a woman. She who speaks the aisling is named
Anorexia and has a venereal disease. She who gathers mushrooms
is preparing the terrorist bomb inside the mind and finally the ter-
rorist bomb in the street. The round O, a symbol dear to Muldoon,
reappears in the poem as the peephole in the jail through which
Gallogly spies on Beatrice and as the pebble of quartz in the Apache's
hand; it has been seen already as the O marked on Uncle Pat's
forehead by the gun barrel pressed to it one night by the B-Spe-

cials.[26] The final word of *Quoof,* "Huh" (it replaces the missing one-hundred-fiftieth sonnet), vocalizes this empty icon. Spoken in the poem by the uncomprehending garage attendant, the sound is echoed at a deeper level by the poet staring into the chaos that always underlies consciousness.

Muldoon began, in *Mules,* by representing his violent society abstractly as a series of hostile twinnings. In *Why Brownlee Left* he followed with more dramatic representations of the ways in which violence is established by rituals which create victims and breed them to become victimizers in their turn. *Quoof* then turned to the question of how the individual consciousness is to save itself from the compulsions of abjection and *ressentiment.* Engaged in the Kohutian project of grandiose self-definition, the young man turns from paternal mushroom-growing on the farm to rebellious mushroom-tripping in the city, and from the politico-naturalist pieties of Heaney, his poetic father, to burlesques of Heaney's serious style. The long process begins with the search for the patriarchal father in "Immram" and ends with the squeezing of juice from the poetic father's frogs. It leaves Muldoon, in "The More a Man Has," seeking to use the emancipatory masks of his personae—masks of drug-taking and sexual activity—to construct a self which can look unflinchingly at the realities of violence while remaining free from its compulsions—an endeavor reminiscent of Heaney!

Ironically Muldoon depends for his self-definition on the very techniques he uses to define violence itself—twinning or doubling, and the abject carnival. Earth-hugging Gallogly is doubled by an import, the Mescalero Apache, and both are simultaneously exploded. Domestic Beatrice is doubled by Alice A. and Alice B. (sex and drugs) and ends up as an internee. "The More a Man Has the More a Man Wants" comprises a ritual of self-definition, an erotic attempt to construct a self through wanting and having. As its title implies, the poem immediately takes away from its personae all that they acquire, since having always leads to wanting—that is, to not having. If enactment of desire provides the self-aggrandizing means by which the persona hopes to escape both from tribal transmission of violence and liberal acquiescence in it, that enactment or carnival also turns the self back upon itself so that it meets its double, its violent sibling. The aesthetic pattern to which Muldoon therefore returns, at times obsessively, is the circle. If "Immram" is a voyage, it is only a circular one which lands the protagonist back where he started. In *Quoof* the O appears with increasing regularity to symbolize both the return of the self upon itself and the futility of the self's original enterprise in seeking liberation from accustomed patterns. Expressed dramatically or ironically, the explosion of the terrorist bomb responds to the search for freedom through self-aggrandizement or mind-expansion. Muldoon's attempt to escape from the ritual of servitude and abjection necessitates participation in the carnival of desire and fulfillment, but this latter ritual always leads its devotees back to the enslavement from which they started.

If *Quoof* represents a persona's futile attempt to achieve an emancipated self-definition from within a violent culture, *Meeting the British* represents the same persona's attempt—one no less futile—to find that freedom in a new culture. Muldoon the expatriate clearly thinks of the place he has left as a place of violence. Images of bloodied faces, a rabbit assailed by vicious dogs, and a body bag with its tagged toe appear in dreams and chance moments of association, violent images springing out sporadically from the unconscious of a person who has consciously said good-bye to all that.[27] As in *Quoof*, though, when Muldoon's speakers flee from one place to another, they usually return to the place where they started. Having sought freedom from old cultures by importing new ones (the Mescalero Apache), the self now exports itself to the Apache's land but finds, as the book's title suggests, that one but meets the same old people. This book on immigration, whose first poem begins in the new world ("Ontario": its title begins and ends with an "O") and whose last, a long poem structured as a corona, ends in the old (a Belfast shipyard), ceaselessly ponders its own circularity.

Implicit in the formal design of the circle is the question whether anything can really be changed—a question of high interest to the self which seeks redefinition or repositioning. Whereas Yeats's circle—the moon in its phases—provided its poet with a dynamic mechanism for self-alteration, Muldoon's circular mechanism for change is never more than ironic: one circles around to meet oneself. Nevertheless Muldoon's itinerary leads him through several interesting fields of thought, notably the economics of exportation and the metaphysics of identity and change.

What is the expatriate poet? An economic item, Muldoon suggests, a piece of goods for export. In a sonnet set in early adolescence ("Profumo," 16; *SP,* 118), the poet's mother, already characterized as a snob in "The Mixed Marriage," urges her thirteen-year-old son to give up his girlfriend on the grounds that she is an unworthy piece of goods, a cheap import next to a valuable export ("you and she are chalk / and cheese"). "Away and read Masefield's *Cargoes,*" is her final if improbable piece of advice to her son. Masefield's short lyric depicts three epochs of cargo, listed in order of descending value. First comes the classical quinquireme of Nineveh, with its exotic cargo of apes and peacocks; then, later in history, a Spanish galleon carrying mere currency ("gold moidores"), and finally the contemporary dirty British coaster loaded with junk ("cheap tin trays"). Masefield's "Quinquireme of Nineveh from distant Ophir" reappears in the first and last lines of "7, Middagh Street," the long, concluding poem of *Meeting the British*, as an emblem of poetic cargo. The valuable exports of expatriate poets (Auden, Muldoon), brought to foreign markets for barter, turn into cheap imports, tin trays from dirty British coasters.

The connection between questions of trade and questions of violence emerges in "Christo's," where Muldoon conceives of all Ireland as a kind of cargo ready for packaging. Sheets of black plastic appear first as garbage bags on which dogs are peeing, then as black protest flags at the time of the hunger strikes, then as the coverings farmers use for haystacks, and finally as a creation of Christo, a series of sheets stretching from Dingle to Belfast ("the whole of Ireland would be under wraps / like, as I said, 'one of your man's landscapes'"). The poem thus envisages the black wrapping of Ireland as subhuman (the dogs), quotidian (the farmers), political (the black flags), artistic (Christo) and, no less jokingly, religious ("Your man's? You don't mean Christo's?").[28] While jests about rural or even literary Ireland-as-commodity are not new,[29] Muldoon's inclusion of political hostility, "the wearing of the black,"[30] as an item of cultural export, is startling—as is his suggestion that packaging, the mechanism of export, is also a mechanism of repression. Weighted down as they are "by concrete blocks, old tyres; bags of sand / at a makeshift army post," the black sheets serve simultaneously to symbolize, to hide, and to package for foreign export the idea of Irish internecine violence. These three functions, predicated of "the island," match the consciousness of the poet who is also seeking for strategies of simultaneously hiding and manifesting political violence. By characterizing the poet's own literary career as a kind of packaging, "Christo's" represents the writer's introjected hostility as yet another scene of repressed, and then expressed, violence.

Muldoon's best-known poem about barter, "Meeting the British," is normally read as lyric, political satire, yet its voice—that of the native monologist—speaks also in the tones of an artist confronting a personal dilemma. Native Americans during the French-Indian War meet the British, brilliantly characterized in the Meissonier painting reproduced on the jacket of the Wake Forest edition of *Meeting the British* (although it depicts Napoleonic troops), as soldiers forcefully appropriating the virgin territory of the new world. The incident in which General Jeffrey Amherst gave blankets infested with smallpox to the natives as barter has become famous in the annals of colonialist atrocities:

We met the British in the dead of winter.
The sky was lavender

and the snow lavender-blue.
I could hear, far below,

the sound of two streams coming together
(both were frozen over)

and, no less strange,
myself calling out in French

across that forest-
clearing. Neither General Jeffrey Amherst

nor Colonel Henry Bouquet
could stomach our willow-tobacco.

As for the unusual
scent when the Colonel shook out his hand-

kerchief: *C'est la lavande,*
une fleur mauve comme le ciel.

They gave us six fishhooks
and two blankets embroidered with smallpox.
(*Meeting the British*, 24; *SP,* 121)

The poem arranges its elements in beautiful, almost ghostly
pairings, presenting resemblances (the lavender of the sky matches
that of the snow, but also the lavender scent of the colonel's hand-
kerchief) and convergences (the two streams coming together and
the two voices speaking French) before presenting smallpox as the
final aesthetic touch (the blankets are embroidered with it, to match
the Colonel's handkerchief). In stanzas 7 and 8, where an *abba*
rhyme interrupts the pattern of couplets, the handkerchief is pro-
duced to counter the foul smell and taste of the Indians' willow
tobacco. It is a deliberate interruption; the word "scent," had it
been placed at the end of the previous line, would have provided a
couplet well within the boundaries of Muldoon's conventions of
rhyme: "As for the unusual scent / when the Colonel took out his
hand-" The division of "handkerchief" over two lines further com-
plicates the matter, implying that what might have been the exten-
sion of a hand in a gesture of friendship turned into the fastidious
shaking-out of a handkerchief in a gesture of repugnance. The hand-
kerchief, then, interrupts pairings of resemblance and convergence
(sky with snow, stream with stream, language with language). When
such pairings become dramatized by gestures (the peace pipe), the
British can no longer stomach them and therefore replace given or
natural pairings with an artificial one (lavender sky with lavender
scent and embroidery), an artifice which leads directly to an arti-
fice of murder (embroidered smallpox).

As post-colonial discourse "Meeting the British" manipulates
images in ironic pairings. As personal discourse the poem manipu-
lates sounds in ironic pairings of voice. "No less strange," says the
native American speaker, than the sound of two streams coming
together was the sound of his voice calling out in French: even
stranger is the Britishness of the same speaker's voice, reciting its
poem in English and beginning with a very British line of iambic
pentameter. The word "lavender" belongs wholly to the speaker's

English vocabulary before he hears the French speaker use it, explaining in French what the speaker had already explained, with far greater felicity, in English (lines 2–3). Although the speaker of the dramatic monologue is native American, the voice is the voice of Muldoon—and for a reason. His book is a collection of poems largely about becoming an expatriate poet; "Meeting the British" thus paradoxically means "Coming to America." Having symbolically imported the Mescalero Apache into native Irish consciousness, Muldoon now exports that hybrid consciousness (Apache-Irish) to the land of the native American and . . . meets the British. Attempting to go west from Ireland, he finds himself going east; attempting to appropriate an American tribal voice, he meets a British voice, the voice of one listening to speakers of a foreign language. Exporting himself as Irish and playing with a politically correct analogy of native Irish to native American, "native" Muldoon finds himself in the paradoxical position of bartering with the British. "In the dead of winter," then, Muldoon depicts a consciousness replicating itself in completely new circumstances, but replicating that consciousness just as the old one was, frozen solid in its own identification with violence, whether tribal or colonial. His ironic depictions of colonialism and trade serve as a metaphor for a consciousness which seeks but does not find the means of changing one thing for another.

Muldoon's search continues, however, in the poems he devotes to metaphysical questions of identity and metamorphosis. As in the poems about exchange and barter, these poems about changes in essence play grimly with themes of violent destruction. "Sushi" takes place in a restaurant, where we enter into the middle of a discussion on art and reality. Although we never learn what the dinner companions are arguing about, the poem itself debates the ontological status of an artwork. At first the chefs in the sushi-bar are merely performing culinary operations—"fastidiously shav[ing] / salmon, tuna and yellowtail," but then become artists who "had scrimshandered a rose's / exquisite petals" on the sushi with a carrot. When an apprentice cook submits this work of art to the Master,

> it might have been alabaster
> or jade
> the Master so gravely weighed

from hand to hand
with the look of a man unlikely to confound
Duns Scotus, say, with Scotus Eriugena.
(*Meeting the British,* 41–42; *SP,* 129–30)

This sushi is not sushi. It is alabaster or jade, not because some-
one capriciously says it is, but because of the beautiful
scrimshandering the apprentice has wrought. Does the being of an
object depend only on its being named, or does its being as it were
predate naming? The Master knows the answer to this question,
since he knows the difference between Duns Scotus and Scotus
Eriugena. The latter, a ninth-century Platonist from Ireland with
pantheistic leanings, taught that essences emanate directly from the
being of God. On the other hand Duns Scotus, a fourteenth-cen-
tury nominalist from Scotland, taught an early version of the doc-
trine that the only difference between one thing and another is in
its verbal sign, which Scotus indecorously termed *flatus vocis.* One
of the dinner partners, like the chef weighing the sushi-art from
hand to hand, refuses to talk, to be vocally flatulent, whereas the
other can't stop talking. Three key words emerge from the unusual
rhyme scheme: the poem consists of rhyming couplets, except for
three lines, occurring at the beginning, at the exact center, and at
the end of the poem, whose rhymed end-words are "arguing," "erog-
enous," and "Eriugena." In the first line, then, "arguing" means
conversation. During the course of the poem, however, as mere
cooking becomes high art, "arguing" is identified as an erotic ac-
tivity ("erogenous") and is thus transformed to a higher philosophic
activity, the sort of *disputatio* which one would associate with the
name "Eriugena." We are left, nevertheless, with an unanswered
question about the status of this very poem: is it merely a *flatus
vocis,* a vocal fart, or is there something here which could be "gravely
weighed" (the very tautology suggests substance)?

The references in "Sushi" to metaphysics, both eastern and
western, find resonance in "The Soap-Pig," an elegy for Muldoon's
former colleague in the BBC, Michael Heffernan, whose "favourite
word was *quidditas.*" When the speaker throws up in a basin,
"Anne-Marie looked on, her unspoken, / 'That's to wash, not boke
in'" (*SP,* 124–28). Anne-Marie is affirming the basin's quiddity, so
grossly abused by the speaker. When dying, Heffernan deliberates

on whether two six-foot boards (intended for the coffin) on which tea is set is really a table, or "merely a token / of some ur-chair, / or—being broken— / a chair at all." In any case, as nominalist Ockham would say, "the mind's a razor / on the body's strop." Death answers all metaphysical questions. The soap-pig is a bar of soap, but then only a sliver in a dish as, each morning, the poet shaves, an action which reminds him both of his father (the shaving brush) and his mother (the wash-stand's marble top) and, therefore, to the final end of them both, of Heffernan, of us all, and of the soap: a "pool of glop."

Muldoon rings a further variation on this metaphysical theme, one which resonates with the *leitmotiv* of violence in *Meeting the British*. On several occasions body parts are taken as objects to be played with or on, so that they lose their connection with any known body. In "The Lass of Aughrim," the poet hears an Indian boy in the Amazon playing a haunting air "on what was the tibia / of a priest / from a long-abandoned Mission." The boy has presumably cannibalized the missionary for this high aesthetic purpose. In "The Wishbone," while spending Christmas alone with his aging father and after watching "the Queen's / message to the Commonwealth / with the sound turned off," he cooks a frozen chicken, "the wishbone like a rowelled spur / on the fibula of Sir ___ or Sir ___." In a poem which expresses such resentment to Britain, the wishbone may well, as Michael Hofmann feels, "suggest some Dantesque atrocity," some ultimate punishment of British nobility, as the "Lass of Aughrim" suggested a gruesome end for missionaries.[31]

It is enlightening to consider the poems of export and barter, such as "Christo's" and "Meeting the British," as engaged in precisely the same argument with themselves—an argument about change—as the poems of metaphysics, such as "Sushi" or "The Soap-Pig." Although at each stage of Muldoon's work the terms of the question become more cosmopolitan (so that the question of why Brownlee would leave has given way to new questions, as it were, of what Brownlee might do when he arrives elsewhere), the question itself, and the intense tones in which it is put, remain the same. How can one escape from the embarrassments and constraints of one's self-defining circumstances, and still remain oneself? Both the glop of dessert carried out of a building during a bomb alert and the glop of soap on the washbasin serve as images of mortality, of descent into non-language and, finally, non-being. First sinister barter of embroidered blankets between British and native Americans, then gruesome play with body parts and reflections on words and things, lead the mind to thoughts of violence and dissolution, thoughts which finally raise questions of political identity. The poet's liberal decision to pronounce a plague on both Irish houses and to go elsewhere does nothing to alter the structures and distresses of a consciousness always aware of what it means to be reduced to a glop of nameless matter.

The fascination of *Meeting the British* lies in Muldoon's explorations of this *hantise* at ever more advanced areas of artistic consciousness, culminating in "7, Middagh Street," his masterpiece on the plight of the expatriate poet. In 1939 W. H. Auden emigrated to the United States, where he met and fell in love with Chester Kallman; in the autumn of 1940 he moved in to 7 Middagh Street, a house in Brooklyn owned by George Davis, then the fiction editor of *Harper's Bazaar.* Davis gathered around him a community that included, at one time or another during those few months, Benjamin Britten, Peter Pears, Carson McCullers, Gypsy Rose Lee, Salvador Dali, Louis MacNeice, and a trained chimpanzee.[32] Superficially these names and Muldoon's treatment of them give the impression of a *vie de bohème* in which Auden and MacNeice, vainly trying to escape from the complexities of their political and artistic commitments in time of war, took refuge for a season. By thus characterizing Auden and MacNeice as embracing a form of high silliness, Muldoon is able to represent his own consciousness as trying, equally vainly, to escape from itself in time of another war.

Formally "7, Middagh Street" represents this circularity by imitating the device of "La Corona," a sequence in which Donne attaches poems to each other by repeating the last line of each preceding poem in the first line of the poem which follows it. Thus the line "it won't be over till the fat lady sings," which ends the poem on Britten, echoes itself in the ensuing line, "The fat lady sings to Der Rosenkavalier," which begins the poem on Kallman. The first line of the first poem is repeated in the last line of the last poem (hence Muldoon's "quinquireme of Niniveh" at the very beginning and very end).

Muldoon's closed circle, as the quinquireme travelling on it informs us, is also a trade route from Belfast to New York and back. Especially back: whereas at the poem's beginning the whole exotic line of Masefield is cited ("Quinquireme of Niniveh from distant Ophir"), in the last line the foreman of a Belfast shipyard is refusing hard-up MacNeice a job—he will not even let him "caulk a seam / on the quinquireme of Niniveh." The poem carries artists as supercargo, listed in the titles of its sections: Wystan, Gypsy, Ben, Chester, Salvador, Carson, Louis. By his insistent lampooning of these characters' erotic lives (he derides Auden's love for Kallman, Lee's profession as stripper, McCullers' infatuation with Auden's wife Erika Mann, and MacNeice's failed courtship of Eleanor Clark), Muldoon characterizes them as high-class whores, commodities in the art market. Here, too, the formal device of the corona serves Muldoon's purpose; one thinks of Arthur Schnitzler's camp comedy, *La Ronde*, in which A sleeps with B, B sleeps with C, and so on to X, who ends the play by sleeping with A. Such irony is given a further twist by the depiction of Auden seeking to escape from crass mercantilism through romantic love ("out of the realm of Brunel and Arkwright / with its mills, canals and railway-bridges / into this great void / where Chester and I exchanged love-pledges"), only to discover that his lover is nothing more than a cruiser, so that neither one can be more to the other than a commodity. The poem's formal circle draws itself tightly around the inner dynamic of expatriate escapism, characterizing the literary expatriate as a piece of cargo inescapably consigned to a trade route which will land it back, in slightly damaged condition, where it began.

This brilliant exercise succeeds only at the cost of being unfair to Auden, whose influence on Muldoon is evidently a complex one. On the one hand, he uses Auden as a stick to beat Yeats for the older poet's seriousness in wondering whether "that play of mine sen[t] out certain men" to be shot ("certainly not," replies Wystan). As in his burlesques of Heaney in *Quoof*, Muldoon here is at pains to deny the possibility of poetry ever having a constructive part to play in the conduct of life.[33] He therefore has Auden ruminate on the uselessnes of having participated in the Spanish Civil War and the Chinese revolution. In this ironic tone Muldoon relishes the opportunity to ventriloquize through Auden's mouth:

For history's a twisted root
with art its small, translucent fruit

and never the other way round.
The roots by which we were once bound

are severed here, in any case,
and we are all now dispossessed.
(*Meeting the British,* 46; *SP,* 134)

Muldoon thus knocks Auden off the pedestal where he had placed him, now condemning Auden for abandoning his ironic stance. Muldoon lampoons not only his sexuality, but also his conversion to Christianity and, most damningly, his high-minded politics. Auden matched his leap of faith in joining the Anglican church, Muldoon callously suggests, by his leap into Chester's bed. After Britten comments on Auden's legendary dirtiness and Kallman represents himself as a whore, MacNeice (who also laughs at Auden's confusion of religion and sex) makes light of the fact that Auden was re-converted to an artistic seriousness about politics after seeing a newsreel at a movie theater in New York's German quarter where the audience applauded Hitler—a seriousness which Louis compares to the attitude of a stylite, adopting ridiculous postures in the fond hope of some remote better state.

What seems to irritate Muldoon is Auden's conversion to Christianity and his penchant for a poetry of serious meaning. As a poetic father, Auden does much for Muldoon, teaching him to be witty to the point of acerbity, to be both allusive and elusive, and to express the irony inherent in every human effort at high seriousness—the horse scratching its rump on the tree at the moment the Savior is born. How maddening, then (we imagine Muldoon feeling as he follows Auden on the path of expatriation), to find his model becoming a Christian and writing such didactic drivel as the "New Year's Letter"! It is as if expatriate Auden were leading Muldoon through the closed circles of a political-artistic hell—good!—but then, intolerably, pointing the way out of the inferno to some imagined salvation and embarking on that way, leaving his charge behind—as though Virgil had gone on to the Paradiso, leaving behind him a disillusioned Dante.

Here one may label Muldoon as a postmodern, refusing meanings and indulging in the fragmentations of wit, but to do so is to miss his nostalgia for meaning. In the case of Muldoon, a poet equally adept at the poignant and the caustic, what begins as nostalgia ends as ridicule. If Muldoon lampoons Heaney as saying, "There is, surely, in this story / a moral . . . for our times," that is finally because Muldoon wishes that there were such a moral. After the capitulations to meaning of Yeats, of Auden, and of Heaney, it is as if Muldoon were still holding the line, still saying, "No surrender to meanings." Muldoon's world, like that of his predecessors, is meaningless to the extent that it is violent, but it is left to him, he believes, to insist on this fact without flinching. His caustic wit, however, is undermined by the distress he suffers from this new vocation to be a prophet who must resolutely deny that there is a moral for our times.

As the last speaker in "7, Middagh Street," "Louis" functions as an alternate voice for "Paul." Muldoon, that is, escapes from the embarrassment of his sonship to Auden by assuming the persona of his fellow Ulsterman. Louis MacNeice arrived at 7 Middagh Street as a guest of Auden in late October, 1940. Having come to America in pursuit of a lover who eluded him, MacNeice then decided to return home, sailing for England in late November. Wishing to be as clever and honest, as sardonic and sincere as MacNeice, Muldoon has MacNeice satirize both Auden and Yeats for their naive politico-artistic sensibilities, but then has him satirize his own, and therefore Muldoon's, efforts at dealing with the realities of a violent world.

Upon his return to England, MacNeice wrote that "The expatriates do not need anyone else to act as their *ersatz* conscience: they have consciences of their own and the last word must be said by their instinct as artists."[34] It is precisely this emphasis on conscience which dominates, even torments, "Louis" in Muldoon's poem, as he evokes twin images of Auden in New York and of his own father, the bishop, in Ulster—both men trying in vain to understand human nature bent on cataclysmic self-destruction. The poet's art and the bishop's religion provide only vague refuges for idealistic minds; the bishop's preaching "into the wind" is as ridiculous as Dali's political surrealism ("and the very painting of that oyster / is in itself a political gesture"). Yeats attempted, in his elegy for Eva Gore-Booth and Con Markievicz, to transform radical political action into radical artistic action, so that the poem would constitute a fire-bombing of time. Here, though, Muldoon's Louis inverts Yeats's attempt by reducing art's dreams to the rude awakenings of politics. Yeats's words, "Bid me strike a match and blow," no longer apply to the artist's destruction of time. They have been appropriated by Sir Edward Carson, whose voice Louis hears as he imagines himself being covered with kerosene prior to being blown up. If the expatriate lives by his conscience, that conscience is always being returned to its own primal scenes of violence.

Return is what this circular poem enacts, so that Louis returns to Europe and the poem returns to the violence from which it had tried to escape in the person of Auden. The bloody Northern Irish faces which appear in the book's first poem, "Ontario," now reappear in the guise of Lorca, a victim of the Spanish Civil War, who "lay mouth-down / in the fickle shadow of his own blood." Having opened with Masefield's quinquireme of Niniveh sailing to the new world, "7, Middagh Street" now returns to a Belfast shipyard where Louis, showing up for work after drinking all night in a pub ("Muldoon's"), is rejected as an outsider by one of his fellow Ulster Protestants:

> The one-eyed foreman had strayed out of Homer.
> 'MacNeice? That's a Fenian name.'
> As if to say, 'None of your sort, none of you
>
> will as much as go for a rubber hammer
> never mind chalk a rivet, never mind caulk a seam
> on the quinquireme of Niniveh.'
> (*Meeting the British*, 62; *SP*, 153)

I have read *Meeting the British* as a collection in three parts, all dealing with fathers: the poet's own father, then his immediate literary father, Heaney, and finally the collection of artistic ancestors gathered in New York in the autumn of 1940. Muldoon has consistently joined issues of violence and identity, expanding his consideration in each successive collection of poems, so that early themes of family identity and twinning led to strategies of separation from parental dominance and then strategies of separation from British dominance. Ironically, though, Muldoon's postmodernist style of fragmentation, ostensibly designed to dismantle unitary, hegemonic structures, emerges as a form of violence turned back upon itself. By characterizing itself in ever less coherent complexes of feeling and expression which can only be restrained, paradoxically, by ever more elaborate formal structures, his poetic persona increasingly imagines itself as a place where violence happens. As a site of twinning and mutual destruction, this consciousness exemplifies the kind of *ressentiment* which endlessly fuels sectarian strife. When Muldoon turns to expatriation, the twentieth-century's last strategy for dealing with such an impasse, he makes that yet another closed circle of self-destructive violence. It is in this context that his poems about his fathers become bitter burlesques, ironically ridiculing ancestors for the foibles from which the present descendant cannot escape. His experiments with mushrooms lead him back to his father's mushroom farm, and his poetic fragmentations of consciousness, requiring him to mock both Heaney's and Auden's quests for meanings, lead him to his own failures to find meanings.

At this stage of his artistic career, just before the extravaganza of *Madoc*, Muldoon's early poetic treatment of violence reaches its term. He has gone a step farther than either Heaney or Mahon, who attempt to escape from violence only to find it inhabiting their consciousness. Muldoon imagines violence as a primal chaos of the mind, representing his own attempts to escape violence as, finally, a kind of violence he inflicts upon himself. One may read Muldoon's postmodernist poetry as a set of mordant leftist attacks on traditional political or literary structures, but I suggest that the sharper bite of his wit will be felt by reading him as a disciple of the poets he is at pains to satirize—Auden, MacNeice, and Heaney. Muldoon, no less than they, is a poet in search of meanings, trying to resolve the personal dilemmas occasioned by his situation as a lyric poet in a culture of violence. Violence, he finds, is a primal condition; his only refuge lies in the wit of self-awareness. Gone are Heaney's appropriations of Stevens' violence from within redressing a violence from without. Muldoon's mind remains a place where twin turns against twin, and where the escapee hides in his prison. His quips and clever rhymes serve to keep consciousness in a state of constant questioning, perpetual awareness of itself. In that sense, his instruments of self-inflicted violence—his fragmentations—may also constitute his means of healing that violence. The best that can be said for Muldoon's self-destructive consciousness is that it knows what it is doing. As long as he can conceive of the quivering jelly of the violent mind as "a trifle," a blob of dessert in the middle of a bomb alert, then the damage can be contained. Muldoon's ultimate stay against chaos is to prevent sincerity.

Muldoon's most recent work, however, has begun to represent a self more at peace with itself, if not more removed from violence. His poems of the nineties are tantalizing indeed, since they so clearly represent themselves as lyrics with violent themes, but then hide the lyric persona in their length and obscurity. There is nothing surprising, to be sure, in Muldoon's double wish to be a self and to hide that self, or even to deny it. "Madoc: A Mystery" might best be read as a sequel to "7, Middagh Street," as the poem of a persona coming to terms with a new world. Like the poetry of Heaney after *North* (the period from *Field Work* to *The Haw Lantern* covers Heaney's late thirties and early forties; *Madoc* appeared in the year Muldoon turned forty), Muldoon now shows an increasing desire to distance himself from his old anxieties of self-definition and to worry instead about his standing in the turgid world of authors, both dead and living.

   "Madoc: A Mystery," an elaborately constructed fantasy of what would have happened if Southey and Coleridge had carried out their scheme to start a utopian community in America, must initially be read as an extended comment on colonialist violence, one in which Britain ravages the new world much as it had ravaged Ireland (a focal point of the story is Ulster, Pennsylvania). But what exactly is the comment? Neither Muldoon's levity about violence nor his explicit descriptions of its gruesome details, can be put into context without locating a speaker with some concern, some argument. For Edna Longley the real argument of the poem is an in-joke, having to do with the rivalry between Coleridge and Southey, that is, between Muldoon and Heaney.[35] Whether that's all there is to it, or whether Muldoon is indeed launching an attack on Western epistemology ("At any moment now, the retina / will be in smithereens"[36]), must await the light to be shed by further explications along the lines established by McDonald and Wills. It is in the works following *Madoc*, in any case, that Muldoon fully turns to issues of the poetic self.

In *The Annals of Chile* and its companion volume *The Prince of the Quotidian*, Muldoon's thematic concerns and his style take a new turn. Although much remains obscure, especially in the very long poem "Yarrow," a new kind of lyric self, with a new set of concerns, begins to emerge from the poetry. Three human events— the death of Muldoon's mother (in 1974), the death of his former lover, Mary Farl Powers (remembered in the elegy "Incantata"), and the recent birth of his daughter, Dorothy Aoife Korelitz Muldoon—now preside over the writer's consciousness, drawing forth unexpected strains of the tender and the serious. Readers who had grown accustomed to Muldoon's caustic send-ups were amazed by the cadences of "Incantata," both rapturous and plangent. In the longer and more complex elegy "Yarrow," written for his mother, Muldoon revisits the scenes of his childhood from his distance in time and space—he is now in his forties and lives in Princeton. Clair Wills has argued convincingly that the poem's intricately in-terlocked (and masked) rhyme schemes, and the insistent repeti-tions of words and phrases, enact the poem's central concern, its "search for 'relief' from the endless repetitive diet of violence, grief and loss in both state and family. . . . It is clear that what he is searching for is not a new focus or a new subject-matter, but a means to create something new out of the same materials—the memories of his childhood, Irish literature, and Irish history."[37] If this is true then Muldoon has indeed altered his perspective radi-cally from *Meeting the British*, where in brittle ironies he expati-ated on the impossibility of creating anything new out of the new materials sought for in the new world of America.

Since the issue of the poetic self predominates *The Prince of the Quotidian*, I will end this chapter by turning to this shorter and perhaps less well-known collection of poems. Generically the poem of daily life is short, confined to a here and now (although they may parody the Glanmore sonnets, Muldoon's quotidian poems also descend from them), whereas annals are lengthier, extending themselves far over history and geography. The words "Prince" and "Quotidian" (one thinks of Kavanagh's "I am king of . . . every blooming thing") suggest the lyric self's concern with its own being, in contrast with "annals," an unpoetic genre-word suggesting historical and impersonal perspectives in which the self may easily hide.

Muldoon rewrites his lyric self in this sequence of thirty-one poems, written one each day during a month of January, a time when his wife was pregnant and he was bringing forth *The Annals of Chile*. Muldoon reflects on three aspects of his being. As an Irishman living in the United States, he puts himself in touch with the now-distant land of his birth. As a writer, he puts himself in touch with the professional world of writers and critics. As an incipient father who is busy writing two lengthy elegies, he puts himself in touch with birth and death. Whereas both extension in space and the moral altitude of literary accomplishments (his "high ground") provide Muldoon with ways of distancing himself from violence, his meditations on death and, more especially, on birth require that he again confront violence as it appears within consciousness.

In a pair of poems from the first week of the month, Muldoon juxtaposes the two stylistic elements whose discord establishes the book's tension. The poem about a "Twelfth Night bash" establishes a literary atmosphere of carnival, with a guest list of authors living and dead (Elaine Showalter, Oscar Wilde), as well as the cross-gartered symbol of an ampersand. On the following day, "The Feast of the Epiphany," the poet meditates on a desolate back yard, hoping for his own epiphany: "I wait in vain for some small showing forth."[38]

In this latter poem, remarking dejectedly that few birds are using their feeding station (it is a mild month), Muldoon humorously longs for deer to come out of the forest "to prune the vines / from the picket fence / or vault the five-foot chicken-wire cordon / round our herb-garden." Having gone to the trouble to build such a fence to keep out marauders, why does he wish them to maraud? He also notes glumly that his "lemon-peel / and bacon-rind mobile / is losing something of its verve." What balancing act does this mobile represent? A later poem, again mentioning the mobile and the bacon-rind, makes it clear that Muldoon is alluding to, and largely dwelling in, Robert Lowell's "Home After Three Months Away."[39] Lowell, writing on his return from an institution where he had been recovering from mental illness and wondering whether his small daughter could still be his child and he her father, presents Muldoon, a father-to-be, with an anti-self. The image of bacon rind governs Lowell's poem. At first they are the literal gobbets of meat which a nurse hung on trees during the winter as homemade feeding stations for birds; at the end they symbolize the diminished condition of the sufferer returning home: "Cured, I am frizzled, stale and small." If Muldoon's bacon rind calls up all the horrors of Lowell's plight—the father unable, from personal decline, to exercise his fatherhood—the lemon-peel does the opposite. As yellow ("xanthous"), it represents a pervasive color in this volume, exemplified in this poem by the finch and elsewhere personified as one of Achilles' horses (named "Xanthus"); one thinks of upward flight, heroism, or the celestial path of art. Finding that his balancing act between the grandeurs of art ("the prince") and the fallenness of everyday being ("the quotidian") is losing its verve, the poet longs for an epiphany, even if it comes as an invasion against the small cordon of order that he has built around his life. The carnival of the "Princeton heavy hitters," in which Muldoon characterizes himself typographically ("&") as cross-gartered Malvolio, gives way to the Epiphany for which a single individual longs, an individual whose defenses against disorder make him fear disorder all the more, even to the point of hoping for some real disorder to overturn his feeble defenses.

Like the original epiphany, the "invasion" for which the poet hopes will be the birth of a child. While awaiting that event (still several months off), he reviews his familiar self-conceptions: expatriate, poet. For the book's epigram Muldoon has found a delightfully ironic passage from a letter written in 1795 by Wolfe Tone, describing his brief sojourn in the fledgling United States—specifically in Princeton, where "I . . . began to think my lot was cast to be an American farmer." Elsewhere Muldoon caustically contradicts a statement by Seamus Deane who "has me 'in exile' in Princeton." "I'm not 'in exile,'" he replies to Deane, "though I can't deny / that I've twice been in Fintona." Fintona, a town in County Tyrone not far from where Muldoon grew up, was once used as a case study for documenting discrimination against Catholics. Muldoon, who now enjoys the privileges of a good income and a good reputation, has escaped exile by leaving Ireland.[40] Such paradoxes constitute another balancing act, another mobile, swinging uneasily between

distance and nearness. One day's poem, a two-liner written men-
tally as the poet reads the newspaper on the commuter train be-
tween Princeton and New York, sets this mobile atilt: "Weehawken.
Kearny. The Oranges. I'm filled with dismay / by news of two mur-
ders in The Moy." (*Prince of the Quotidian*, 19). The first line
"takes place" on the New Jersey commuter line, the second in
Muldoon's home county of Armagh. Both lines are five-footed: the
first filled with syllables, with Oranges, with dismay, the second
stripped down to a bare fact, even missing a syllable in order to
emphasize the solitary "two." The poet's own consciousness dwells
in the place of fullness (if he is filled with dismay, he can also be
emptied of it, and presumably will be when he turns the page of his
newspaper), and yet is haunted by the emptiness which his abun-
dance can never quite replace.

Such hauntings can be beautiful as well as ugly. Only those
who have driven their cars through the maelstrom of a car wash
can appreciate how the poet, performing this humble task with a
copy of Nuala Ní Dhomhnaill's poems on the seat next to him, is
transposed to another place:

> a wave broke over a rock
> somewhere west of Dingle;
> my windshield was a tangle
> of eel-grass and bladderwrack.
> (*Prince of the Quotidian*, 38)

The alternation between ugliness and beauty (the car wash and
Dingle, bacon rind and lemon-yellow) somehow coincides with the
alternation in the poet's consciousness between nearness to vio-
lence and distance from it. On a weekend trip to New Orleans,
Muldoon is preoccupied with thoughts of another birth—that of
his newborn nephew—and prays that he may be another Prince of
the Quotidian, finding surprising beauty in every ordinary detail of
life. Yet he ends his "prayer for my nephew" with this Yeatsian
coda: "yet let him not, with Alejandro O'Reilly, / forget the cries of
the bittern and the curlew" (*Prince of the Quotidian*, 26). As Wills
has explained, Muldoon uses two expatriate Irishmen of colonial
history as opposing symbols: O'Reilly, a Royalist mercenary in the
pay of Spain, and Bernardo O'Higgins, the Chilean liberator.[41] The

man reading the newspaper in the commuter train must mediate between O'Reilly and O'Higgins, as between two antithetical versions of exile. By introducing these two political figures into the equation, Muldoon admits social violence into the fabric of the quotidian, the daily experience of consciousness. In one of his imitations of Heaney, Muldoon allows himself the same invasion of consciousness so familiar to readers of *Station Island*:

> I open the freezer. The blood-besmirched
> face of Kevin McKearney
> implores me from a hospital gurney;
> 'Won't you at least visit my grave in March?'
> (*The Prince of the Quotidian*, 23)

If social violence sporadically invades Muldoon's consciousness, the strain of violence peculiar to professional authors appears to inhabit his mind on a daily basis, occupying no small place in his recital of the quotidian. However he may feel about being far from Ireland, there is no question about his desire to be far from Irish literary politics. Scorning Field Day's "old whines in new bottles," he asks why the Irish "band of balladeers and bards" should "add up to so much less than the sum of its parts" (22). The violent aspect of literary in-fighting appears when the poet exposes his feelings of vulnerability to others' criticisms of his own work. In one day's sonnet, assembling a number of the barbs used against him in the octave, he reserves the sestet for the figure of Erasmus, first seen as his ideal reader, the only reader who might be willing to look for a pattern in the crazy quilt of his verse, but then imagined as the writer himself, tortured by readers as a heretic whose "viscera are cranked out by a windlass / yard upon 'xanthous' yard" (29). (Here the golden color of "xanthous" clashes with the degradation of "innards," as lemon peel with bacon rind.) In a hotel bar during a conference, he finds "a dozen off-duty windlass men," critics and cultural commentators, ready to crank out the innards of their literary victims (34). Paradoxically Erasmus's role is to "steel himself, then somehow to exhort / the windlass-men to even greater zeal." The real Erasmus, as Peter McDonald points out, is not the humanist but an early Christian saint Erasmus, one of whose legends is that of the cranked-out innards. For McDonald, then, the writer-as-martyr "steels" or strengthens himself in his dedication to poetic form, obdurately submitting himself to the misguided intrusions of politically correct criticism.[42] The verb also carries echoes of Shakespeare's sonnet 24, where the eye "steels," engraves, or inscribes images in the heart. As a martyr the writer steels himself against the torture of misinterpretation. As a poet the martyr writes himself, repeatedly providing innards and exhorting the windlass men to even geater zeal.

In another poem after Heaney ("Glanmore 9," "Station Island 12"), a caustic voice (no doubt the poet's own anima, although the parallels with Heaney make it sound like that of an irritated spouse) criticizes the poet for writing what it considers to be the inane stuff of this collection: "Who gives a shit about the dreck / of your life?" (40). The voice then turns to the figure of Erasmus: "you know that 'Erasmus' stuff is an inept / attempt to cover your arse." "Leave off laundry-lists and tax-returns / and go back to making metaphors" is the accuser's parting shot of advice.

Even though there are no laundry-lists or tax-returns in this book, and even though "Erasmus" *is* a metaphor, the writer cannot easily dismiss the accusing voice. What force does the ironic figure of Erasmus (and here we think of the writer) have for Muldoon—this icon of the humanist, the patient decoder of arcane texts, the honest cynic, and the dangerous heretic (Muldoon's version of Heaney's Noah, it seems)? Is he merely created, as the accuser says, to garner sympathy for his creator? Then why create and dismiss him almost in the same breath? When the accuser says, "Go back to making metaphors," s/he operates on the principle that "golden" (or "xanthous") poetry provides an alternative to the "dross" and "dreck" of quotidian life, including politics. But then the requirement that poetry do this becomes in its turn another kind of orthodoxy, so that formalist critics, too, would join the windlass-men as members of an inquisition, examining each line for political content and/or for its "golden numbers." As seen in these short poems, the act of critical reading exemplifies a kind of violence, the sort which examines statements and identities, and punishes as it does so. Following Heaney in his poems about civic and literary backbiting ("Whatever You Say," "An Afterward"), Muldoon transposes literary hostilities into the forum of his own consciousness, where violence is self-inflicted.

Elsewhere Muldoon imagines the mutual acts of writing and examination as natural and inevitable. As a coda to these few poems about literary-political torture, he writes in *The Annals of Chile* that "the windlass-women ply their shears." It is now July, not January, and the poet is in the operating room where his daughter is being delivered by Cesarean section. Doctors and nurses reach in to the mother's body and draw forth the child, an event which Muldoon ecstatically describes in a shower of verbal bubbles (arranged according to the letters of the alphabet). At the end of the poem, happy as it is, he looks again at the medical practitioners now ready to sew up his wife:

> Dorothy Aoife Korelitz Muldoon: I watch through floods of
>   tears
> as they give her a quick rub-a-dub
> and whisk
> her off to the nursery, then check their staple-guns for staples.
> ("The Birth," *Annals*, 31; *New Selected Poems*, 159)

The windlass-men, the professional readers and commentators on Muldoon's poetry, become the windlass-women, those who deliver his child. The violence which surrounds the business of bringing forth art is as necessary as that which surrounds the bringing forth of children. So too perhaps, in each case, is the violence of self-criticism and despair. If art provides a stay against confusion—so that Heaney's Noah stands fast and Muldoon's Erasmus steels himself—it is not because art transcends violence or provides some alternative vision to politics. Art itself is subject to violence. Muldoon's vision in *The Prince of the Quotidian* perceives miracles (Heaney's word) appearing from within the context of violence. If the deer crash the fence, that will be an epiphany. Erasmus lets the windlass-men wind out his intestines; a poem is born. The windlass-women do it for his wife; a child is born, an epiphany occurs, "some small showing forth."

Presided over by the awaited birth of a child, *The Prince of the Quotidian* looks for resolutions to its besetting dilemmas—political and professional violence—in the mysteries of birth and death. The book's opening scene shows a car with a bassinet (not a baby) approaching the darkness of the Holland Tunnel, when "a man with a belly like a poisoned / pup careened towards us, much the worse for drink" (11). In another poem this damned soul reappears as an avatar of the poet himself: "That man with the belly like a poisoned pup / was once a strange child with a taste for verse" (25). This foreshortening of life, in which innocence and decrepitude reflect each other, takes a political turn in the one poem from *The Prince of the Quotidian* that Muldoon reproduces in *The Annals of Chile*, where it is called "Sonogram":

> Only a few weeks ago, the sonogram of Jean's womb
> resembled nothing so much
> as a satellite map of Ireland:
>
> now the image
> is so well-defined we can make out not only a hand
> but a thumb;
>
> on the road to Spiddal, a woman hitching a ride;
> a gladiator in his net, passing judgement on the crowd.
> (*Prince*, 21; *Annals*, 29; *New Selected Poems*, 146)

Once again Heaney has provided the model for this poem; in his "Act of Union," the child *in utero* provides tropes for considering both political and psychological issues. Whereas Heaney's poem works by allegory (the father is Britain, the mother the colony, the baby-to-be the colonized citizen already angry at the fatherland), Muldoon's poem plays with the imaginative aspects of a visual symbol. In the earlier stages of pregnancy, images are still unresolved; the abstract image of the mother's uterus resembles a satellite map, an equally abstract image of Ireland. This map or image of a "body politic," as it becomes more sharply defined, reflects the parallel actions whereby the child grows and the beholder, in his satellite, zooms in on the object of his vision—as if the satellite had come so far down to earth that one could see, as from a hovering helicopter, the hand and thumb of an infinitesimal person. With this poetic sharpening of vision, abstract ideologies are exchanged for human close-ups; the outline of a physical person appears. The images of hand and thumb then pass the observer on to political events which are both factual and symbolic: a woman hitching a ride; a gladiator in his net. The three images provide a foreshortened view of life, from the womb to the road to the end of the road, when the trapped gladiator, not waiting for the crowd's verdict, passes his own judgment—presumably thumbs up, if the image is physically identical to that of the hitchhiker. One can only admire Muldoon's artistic courage throughout *The Prince of the Quotidian* in picturing these most intimate moments in the process of birth—sonogram, delivery, post-operative procedures—as various forms of political torture involving nets, windlasses, and guns. It would be wrong, though, to look for some one-to-one correspondence between the natal and the political, as one would do with Heaney's "Act of Union." The two terms of Muldoon's analogy are linked by a third: the feelings of being trapped, eviscerated, or categorized ("stapled") which he, as an Irish writer in the States, experiences on a day-to-day basis. Here as elsewhere in this book, the poetry of political statement and the poetry of sentimental declaration both collapse and are resolved into the symbolic language of an experiencing self—the self of the writer.

In the final day-poem of the collection, a six-liner whose *abccba* rhyme scheme symbolizes return, the poet (who two days earlier was whispering the name of his daughter-to-be to a friend on the telephone) finds himself required to return to his own parent. The voice of his conscience instructs him:

> 'Above all else, you must atone
> for everything you've said and done
>
> against your mother: meet excess of love
> with excess of love; begin on the Feast of Saint Brigid.'
> (*Prince*, 41; *New Selected Poems*, 150)

This command will of course be honored by the long elegy, "Yarrow," in a book which the poet dedicates to his mother, Brigid Regan, who died in 1974. It is by the birth of the poet's child, though, that the child's father will definitely meet excess of his mother's love with an excess of his own. "Atone" is not the sort of word one expects to find in Muldoon, and certainly not set in a sonorous end-rhyme which brooks any equivocation. If, as we said at the conclusion of *Meeting the British*, the poet's ultimate stay against chaos is to prevent sincerity, the conclusion of *The Prince of the Quotidian* presents a sincere self committed to a new kind of quotidian order. As commentators unwind for us the manifold contents of "Yarrow" and the rest of *The Annals of Chile*, let them keep this self in view. Muldoon's last day-poem, after all, is programmatic. Written on the last day of January, it concludes, "Begin on the Feast of Saint Brigid." The Feast of Saint Brigid falls on the first of February.

6

TOM PAULIN

Simplex plays the pipe indeed
But the soldiers pay no heed.
                    —"The Caravans on Lüneburg Heath"

Tom Paulin's poetic voice, as it champions enlightenment politics, cannot withstand its own anger. In his argumentative essays concerning literature and politics, including the polemical introduction to *The Faber Book of Political Verse* which he edited, Paulin has continually spoken in favor of poetry that argues passionately for a cause, following the example of his hero, Milton. Paradoxically, though, Paulin the artist has always found it difficult to achieve the univocal, outraged resonance of "Avenge, O Lord, thy slaughtered saints." Paulin's own outrage, a fire maintained by the friction between his democratic ideals and the base politics of the world in which he lives, often consumes itself in congested anger over past betrayals of Ireland by England and a hopelessness about the future of Ulster Protestantism—"a sense of inferiority and a gut aggression that flares when you're crossed."[1]

Like the Heaney of *North*, Paulin seeks full consciousness of political reality. Yet, whereas Heaney seeks rituals for rousing himself into consciousness, Paulin often attempts to put himself to sleep so that he may wake up again in a different place, some free and equal republic, although he finds himself again experiencing the horror of a gloomy city under a dictatorial régime (Northern Ireland) or a bourgeois "tennis-suburb" where money is the tyrant

(England, where he now lives). Paulin cannot decide which angers him most—the way Britain deals with Protestant Ulster or the way Ulster Protestants themselves behave.

Paulin cannot easily be classified along territorial or confessional lines. His father was Scottish, his mother Irish; he was born in Leeds. His family moved to Belfast, his mother's home, when his father took a teaching position there. Paulin himself has been much influenced by the nationalist ideals of the United Irishmen, an originally Protestant society which provided the impetus for the rebellion of 1798. He has written, notably in *The Field Day Anthology*, as a spokesman for the best traditions of Ulster Protestantism.[2] Almost two hundred years after the failure of Wolfe Tone's rebellion, Paulin still believes in what he considers Tone's ideals to have been— the radical political thought which inspired the revolutions in America and France. Paulin thinks the subsequent history of Irish agitation for independence, notably that of the IRA, to have constituted a sectarian and self-interested betrayal of Tone's original ideal. In his view De Valera's Catholic state of Ireland has more in common with its professed enemy, monarchic imperialism, than with the nonsectarian republicanism which might have been its original foundation: "Like the ideologues of the old provisional IRA, [British conservatives] have a cyclopean vision of an island inhabited entirely by people of the same religious creed and ethnic origins."[3]

Paulin's politics, then, are puritan—in the originally privileged sense of that now overused word: he passionately chooses "the free way, not the formal,"[4] rejecting hierarchies in religion and government, longing for a republic of free consciences. Because these ideals are so far from the realities of the world in which he writes, Paulin's poetry secretes much of its bile from his sense that both puritan religious culture and English literary culture are dying: Britain's political jettisoning of Ulster and its cultural jettisoning of the literary canon are two forms of Thatcherite contempt for the past.[5] Like Heaney Paulin envies Mandelstam and other Russian or Polish poets who, however much they suffered, knew the satisfactions of heroism, of resisting régimes known to be evil. Longing to gain his freedom by speaking in clear, unequivocal messages—the kind that Milton spoke—Paulin writes bitterly of ambivalence and frustration.

But this anticipates the Paulin of the eighties, the period of Ulster's "defenestration" by Britain in the Hillsborough accord of 1985. Before telling his wrath to England, he tells it to his own Protestant culture of Northern Ireland. In his first collection of poetry (1977), although recognizing the beauties of a church "as neat and tight as a boat" where the lessons are read "in an accent sharp as salt," he sees his home as a "town on the wrong side of the border" where the faithful intone the refrain, "My heart is stone. I will not budge."[6] Such poetry is pre-political, in the sense that it expresses feelings about a place, not a rationally drawn set of conclusions as to what is wrong with it and what ought to be done.

Paulin writes first of a violence which is neither that of terrorism nor that of the intractable hostility existing between Protestants and Catholics; it is the fanatically oppressive rigor of Ulster politics, of "Not an inch" and of "No surrender." "In the Lost Province," a Miltonic sonnet of stately exhortation, relies on classical structure for its satire:

> As it comes back, brick by smoky brick,
> I say to myself—strange I lived there
> And walked those streets. It is the Ormeau Road
> On a summer's evening, a haze of absence
> Over the caked city, that slumped smell
> From the blackened gasworks. Ah, those brick canyons
> Where Brookeborough unsheathes a sabre,
> Shouting 'No surrender' from the back of a lorry.
>
> And the sky is a dry purple, and men
> Are talking politics in a back room.
> Is it too early or too late for change?
> Certainly the province is most peaceful.
> Who would dream of necessity, the angers
> Of Leviathan, or the years of judgment?
> (*The Strange Museum,* 16; *SP,* 27)

Lord Brookeborough, the Northern Irish Prime Minister who boasted that he never employed Roman Catholics as servants, here joins Paulin's roster of "the daylight gods," the Creons of this world whose dedication to enforced order always defeats the Antigones, the defenders of principle.[7] The stylistic devices of the octave—reminiscence, description, evocation—serve not only to represent the sordidness of Northern Irish life, but also the speaker's original subjugation to it (that ironic "Ah"). In his transition to the sestet, Paulin exchanges this conformist voice for one that is more grandiose and rebellious. Whereas in the octave the city was slumping into dark canyons, now the perspective elevates itself to the dark sky, an eminence from which the speaker can view the men talking politics—the Brookeboroughs and their sabres—in perspective, reduce them to size. The concluding ironic statement ("Certainly") and the two rhetorical questions are spoken by some vocal power which prophesies and threatens to enact what it foresees—very like the "avenging Archangel" of Ciarán Carson in its promised revenge against enforced, inescapable order.[8] The poem implicitly makes its demand for a newly constructed self, since the violence implicit in these grandiose lines has nowhere to go in real time and space (unless one chooses to build barricades and throw stones at riot police), and therefore must turn inwards. But what new, violent man replaces the old conformist who once lived in the Ormeau Road? Surely not a disembodied voice in the dry, purple sky?

Although Paulin emigrated to England, he does not, as Mahon does, poetically imagine his escape from the "caked city" as a matter of physical flight. Whereas Mahon devotes considerable creative energy to his realization that London and Belfast, symbolizing the rebellious and conformist selves, occupy two parts of his mind, Paulin implicitly takes this realization as understood in some of his earlier poems, where he imagines the process of liberation as one of sleep and awakening. So, "Before History":

Mornings when I wake too early.
There is a dead light in the room.
Rain is falling through the darkness
And the yellow lamps of the city
Are flared smudges on the wet roads.
Everyone is sleeping. I envy them.
I lie in a curtained room.
The city is nowhere then.
Somewhere, in a dank *mitteleuropa*,
I have gone to ground in a hidden street.

This is the long lulled pause
Before history happens,
When the spirit hungers for form,
Knowing that love is as distant
As the guarded capital, knowing
That the tyranny of memories
And factual establishments
Has stretched to its breaking.
(*The Strange Museum,* 1; *SP,* 20)

Sleep, the poet imagines, provides him with an escape from history—not in the conventional sense of losing consciousness, but because, when he awakens, he enjoys a few moments of altered consciousness before the real-world engines of time and space start up again. The short sentences, with their unconnectedness and lack of specificity, permit Paulin the double move of recreating his mind while characterizing his city, Belfast or London, as just another dreary site of oppression, like a middle-European city under Stalinist régimes. What then of recreation? If this early-morning stupor can be called the pause before history happens, what would constitute both the rebuilding of history and the rebuilding of the self?

Beautifully, in an eight-line sentence whose syntax replaces the pointillist utterances of the first stanza, Paulin conceives of an exact parallel between the artistic achievement of form, the personal achievement of love, and the political overthrow of a dictatorship. Paradoxically he alludes both to the impossibility of such an overthrow (love as distant as the guarded capital) and its imminence (tyranny stretched to its breaking), an imminence guaranteed by his awareness that factual establishments are only as strong as the mental states of those who concede to their power. In the tradition of the aubade, however, his fantasies are undermined by a presiding irony, the call of day to the waking sleeper. Habitual memories and factual establishments cannot, after all, be allowed to break down, so we awaken and succumb once again to their tyranny. Imagining his self before history as that of a revolutionary in hiding ("gone to ground in a hidden street"), Paulin must abandon his dream of overthrow whenever he gets out of bed, resuming his disguise of respectability or abandoning his disguise of rebellion. The daylight gods win every time.

There is a more subtle way in which Paulin here refashions his poetic consciousness. The *mise en scène* in a tawdry locale, the combination of sensuous detail ("flared smudges," "lulled pause,"), philosophical abstraction ("history happens," "love is . . . distant"), and oracular pronouncement ("the tyranny . . . has stretched to its breaking") are all reminiscent of Auden writing, as in "September 1, 1939," his own sensuous detail ("[f]aces along the bar"), philosophical abstraction ("the international wrong" . . . "universal love"), and oracular pronouncement ("Those to whom evil is done / Do evil in return").[9] Having written that "the puritan-republican tradition ends in England with the early Auden," Paulin would like to think of himself as a perpetuator of that tradition, while distancing himself from Auden's preoccupations with the English upperclass.[10] By saying that he has gone to ground, Paulin casts himself as a subversive, not only in matters of love, memory, and politics, but also in matters of literature. Like Wilde, Auden, and Orwell, he wants to attack British repressions of love, memory and freedom from within the British literary tradition. Unlike those writers, he wants to do so from outside the British social establishment, writing like Jude the obscure on the outer walls of Britain's intellectual fortress.

Paulin more dramatically performs the ritual of sleep and awakening in "The Strange Museum," where he dreams of waking up:

> First I woke in an upstairs drawingroom.
> The curtains had been pulled back, but the house
> was empty. It was furnished and oddly
> quiet. A patriarch's monument.
> (*The Strange Museum*, 32–33)

The structure (four nine-line stanzas) and the Victorian gothic imagery ("a crazed / Scottish-baronial style, foolish with turrets") offer allusions to the conventions of such exotic romance-poetry as Keats's "The Eve of Saint Agnes." Like Porphyro, the dreamer is lost in a house and pursued by its master, "some dead, linen millionaire." Like Porphyro, too, the dreamer longs for his Madeline—but she is not in the dream ("Had you been there we would have made love / In that strange museum"). Far from being a castle of romance, though, this is a museum of fraudulent theology where servile spirits are "locked / in a fierce doctrine of justification." This cruel doctrine includes a "god of curses," an insane, malevolent presence loose on the house grounds, a "vindictive shadow" who wants both lovers dead. Recognizing the place as the house he once lived in, the speaker declares that he is "through / with the polite dust of bibles, the righteous pulpits," and wakes up later "in a tennis suburb," freed from the strange museum's cruel religion, looking forward to secular tranquillity and sexual love without fear of vengeance. To be freed from the god of curses, however, is to fall prey to the daylight gods, the pragmatic rulers of secular life.

In an essay on Joyce's *Ulysses*, Paulin characterizes Stephen's famous saying, "History is a nightmare from which I am trying to awake," as an effort of the imagination "to free itself from the past, to make the leap into imaginative freedom."[11] Whatever "awakening" means to Paulin, it is clear that one does it with open eyes; his efforts to free himself from the historical unconscious are highly literate and conscious. In a long poem at the end of *The Strange Museum*, "The Other Voice," he reviews the various places his mind has inhabited, recalling the voice he might have were he still in those places.[12] He thus passes through, and leaves behind, the established Church (childhood), flower-child communism (student days), the bourgeois civility of the tennis suburbs ("a glass of wine, . . . a volume of Horace"), doctrinaire Marxism ("identikit opinions"), and literature for its own sake ("What does a poem serve? / Only the pure circle of itself"). At the poem's conclusion, Paulin invokes the image of Osip Mandelstam, walking "through the terrible night" after he has spoken out against the régime. "In the great dome of art," he has Mandelstam say, ". . . I am free of history." And again, "Beyond dust and rhetoric, / In the meadows of the spirit, / I kiss the Word." Why cannot Paulin himself say these words? Paulin's nightmare, one feels, includes all of the bogus positions (liberalism, Marxism, aestheticism) which Paulin the critic rejects precisely because they, too, are products of a tyrannical history which keeps its subjects from attaining to consciousness.

Although no one would want to relive Mandelstam's sufferings, Paulin clearly reveres Mandelstam the martyr as much as he admires Mandelstam the artist, sensing that only by such suffering might one ultimately awaken from history. The Word, for Paulin, is the gospel proffer of the free and equal republic of consciences, but since no such republic exists or can exist in western society as we know it—since no such Word can be said or heard—one can only imagine how such awakening to truth might happen. Paulin finds himself caught between the extremes of an ultimate, lived idealism which he can only imagine and the bitterness of an actual world, the only one which he can experience.

The higher Paulin's idealistic leaps, the more jarring his falls. The highest leap of all occurs in "The Book of Juniper," the longest and most discussed of the poems in *Liberty Tree* (1983), which presents the ideals of Wolfe Tone (flanked in his saint's niche by Mandelstam on one side and Joyce on the other) in the form of a scripture or liturgy.[13] Paulin, who elsewhere derides romantic views of nature as the products of a consumerist culture, here appropriates the wild landscape of Inishkeel, a small island off Donegal, for his own humanist ideal.[14] The juniper tree—green, close to the rugged ground, a survivor of all harsh conditions—symbolizes an idea and a will which remain ever fresh for Paulin. The first voice we hear is Tone's, as he dreams of an original Edenic happiness but awakes to the severe tasks which lie before him. He is answered antiphonally by Mandelstam, who prays for sacramental nourishment from the Word. In a characteristically self-negating move, the poet answers both voices, reminding them that there is just history, no sacraments or, at the very most, some sacramentality in pure fact:

> "There is no word
> and no comfort.
>
> Only a lichened stone
> is given you,
>
> and juniper,
> green juniper."
> (*Liberty Tree*, 22; *SP*, 47)

At the poem's end, after a complex tour through juxtaposed scenes of idealism (a Zen garden) and sordid pragmatism (an Austro-

Hungarian casino where Europe is being gambled away before the Great War), the poem returns to Ireland, where the French forces of 1798 are landing on the coast of Mayo in their failed invasion of Ireland:

> On this coast
> it is the only
> tree of freedom
> to be found,
> and I imagine
> that a swelling army is marching
> from Memory Harbour and Killala
> carrying branches
> of green juniper.
>
> Consider
> the gothic zigzags
> and brisk formations
> that square to meet
> the green tide rising
> through Mayo and Antrim,
>
> now dream
> of that sweet
> equal republic
> where the juniper
> talks to the oak,
> the thistle,
> the bandaged elm,
> and the jolly jolly chestnut.
> (*Liberty Tree*, 27; *SP*, 51)

In a rare moment of self-confident idealism, Paulin follows his "I imagine" with two imperatives, bidding us "consider" the mitred helmets of the redcoats meeting the green tide of popular resistance and, no less urgently, "dream" of that republic where British and Irish trees can all talk to each other. Part of the poem's effectiveness comes from Paulin's yoking of allegory with a historical meditation on what might have been but was not. Trees, as Frost reminded his

neighbor, do not cross stone walls, and the green tide never rose—
yet a suitable lyricism can persuade us to consider that the trees
might cross walls, or dream that the green tide rose. Were the poem
only an exercise in allegory and historical musing, it would not
succeed. It does succeed because its voice is that of an experiencing
self who, revisiting the wild Donegal coast every summer ("The
tides parted and I crossed / barefoot to Inishkeel"), finds in the
taste and feel of a juniper branch the shadowy "sacrament" of an
ideal: "Spicy, glaucous, / its branches fan out / like the wind's
shadow." The very failure of the ideal—the fact that it has no in-
carnations in current political time and space—helps to render its
sacramental manifestation in berry and branch believable. "The
Book of Juniper" is a vacation poem, about the way one feels dur-
ing those precious two weeks in August when the idyllic experience
of one's Donegal heightens one's longing for a more perfect world.

There are two senses in which "The Book of Juniper" places
itself in the Wordsworthian tradition of envisioning better worlds
in nature—the implied contrast between the decadent and the pure,
and the fact that Paulin, like Wordsworth, longs for the unrealized
promise of the French Revolution. Wordworth, however, forgets
his political disappointment by internalizing his natural vision, ap-
propriating it for the construction of an inner world. Refusing
Wordsworth's solution, Paulin externalizes his vision through alle-
gory, transforming bushes and trees into the symbols of a visionary
politics and thereby condemning himself to even bitterer disappoint-
ment, since the self which crossed barefoot to Inishkeel must rue-
fully cross back at holiday's end.

The tart freshness of the juniper, then, soon turns sour. One of
Paulin's original "liberty trees," a patriarch of his political creed, is
the Presbyterian preacher William Drennan (1754–1820), with his
Calvinist doctrines of free conscience. Drennan is remembered to-
day for his role as a poetic champion of the United Irishmen. Paulin
identifies his own political ideals with the originally Protestant na-
tionalism of the United Irishmen, but sees the history of that move-
ment, both politically and religiously, as one of fatal compromises.
The Miltonic tradition of religious freedom as a basis for political
freedom sits better with Paulin than other aspects of Calvinism,
such as the doctrines of sin, predestination, and election. Two sets
of images are at war in Paulin's poetic representations of Northern

Irish Protestant culture. The first, or "polite," set appears at the beginning of "Presbyterian Study," with its display of a clean, spare, bright, quiet and—most importantly—empty space.

> A lantern-ceiling and quiet.
> I climb here often and stare
> At the scoured desk by the window,
> The journal open
> At a date and a conscience.
>
> It is a room without song
> That believes in flint, salt,
> And new bread rising
> Like a people who share
> A dream of grace and reason.
>
> A bit starchy perhaps.
> A shade chill, like a draper's shop.
> But choosing the free way,
> Not the formal,
> And warming the walls with its knowing.
>
> Memory is a moist seed
> And a praise here, for they live,
> Those linen saints, lithe radicals,
> In the bottled light
> Of this limewashed shrine.
> (*Liberty Tree*, 49; *SP*, 62)

In each of the first four stanzas, the first and last lines establish a parallelism between empty physical spaces (quiet lantern-ceiling, songless room, starchy and chill, limewashed shrine) and mental acts (conscience, reason, knowing, memory). This room is surely nothing now but another museum, only it is not strange: the writer is not trapped in it; he climbs up to it by choice. This shrine of long-dead patriarchs, the purity of whose beliefs ("the free way, not the formal") determines the writer's own convictions, may once have been a real space, but today it exists only in the writer's mind. In real spaces like schoolrooms, purity has been forgotten. Thus the last two stanzas, preoccupied with the present, fill up with a second set of images, those of dirt and violence: "dingy smiles . . . dungy pattern . . . a jacked corpse." In the dingy and dungy "lost provinces," the corpse of Irish Protestant culture has been jacked (folded up like a jack-knife) and pitched overboard.[15] Who murdered it? That is the mystery. Was it the bullies from the British mainland or was it the Irish themselves, abandoning the rugged beliefs of their Calvinist fathers in favor of an hysterical demagoguery? In "Desertmartin" Paulin makes it clear that the violence of British soldiers pales in comparison to that of the citizens they watch over, men whose self-righteousness is the original cause of violence in the province. (Desertmartin is the name of a predominantly Protestant town near the Derry-Antrim border and also near the place where, on the night of February 6, 1981, Ian Paisley gathered five hundred men brandishing their gun licences and vowing to oppose the growing *entente* between Great Britain and the Republic of Ireland.)

> At noon, in the dead centre of a faith,
> Between Draperstown and Magherafelt,
> This bitter village shows the flag
> In a baked absolute September light.
> Here the Word has withered to a few
> Parched certainties, and the charred stubble
> Tightens like a black belt, a crop of Bibles.
>
> Because this is the territory of the Law
> I drive across it with a powerless knowledge—
> The owl of Minerva in a hired car.
> A Jock squaddy glances down the street
> And grins, happy and expendable,
> Like a brass cartridge. He is a useful thing,
> Almost at home, and yet not quite, not quite.
>
> It's a limed nest, this place. I see a plain
> Presbyterian grace sour, then harden,
> As a free strenuous spirit changes
> To a servile defiance that whines and shrieks
> For the bondage of the letter: it shouts

For the Big Man to lead his wee people
To a clean white prison, their scorched tomorrow.

Masculine Islam, the rule of the Just,
Egyptian sand dunes and geometry,
A theology of rifle-butts and executions:
These are the places where the spirit dies.
And now, in Desertmartin's sandy light,
I see a culture of twigs and bird-shit
Waving a gaudy flag it loves and curses.
(*Liberty Tree*, 16; *SP*, 43)

The ironies of Protestant identity first appear on line one, a definition of "faith" by means of Desertmartin's location on the map, the facts of its political geography. Here at the dead center of a faith, the classic Protestant antinomies—word over law, grace and the spirit over the letter—are reversed, so that God's word withers and his law is enforced by a British soldier (who comes, more's the irony, from Scotland), while free conscience under grace calls out for a Paisleyite demagogue. The owl of Minerva, goddess of both war and wisdom, must stay in its car and accept protection. In Paulin's Desertmartin, baked light, charred stubble, scorched tomorrows, Moslem sand-dunes and rifle butts, twigs and bird-shit find their home. Everything is denatured: whereas the Presbyterian study was whitewashed with lime, Desertmartin's nest is smeared with birdlime and decorated with a flag (the Union Jack— see the muddy jacket and the jacked corpse of the previous poem) to which Protestant loyalists give their allegiance in spite of British distaste for Ulster. Finally, though, the owl-poet does get out of the car, and by the end of the poem its voice has risen in pitch to the level of an old Protestant preacher. "These are the places where the spirit dies," Paulin intones, railing at *his* wee people for deserting that spirit and following their Baal, Ian Paisley, the Big Man.

Paulin thus assumes in the same poem the postures both of an alienated, cynical observer of Protestant culture and of an impassioned Protestant prophet, although that double stance is an awkward one at best. Is this a flaw of the poetry itself? Paulin, one might argue, falls into his own trap, adopting the very tones he professes to loathe, railing at his people for following Paisley but using Paisley's own tone of voice (". . . where the spirit dies"), and so betraying a humorless lack of self-awareness which undermines the effectiveness of the poem as either witness or judgment. Looked at from another perspective, though, Paulin's self-contradictions skillfully reproduce the tonalities of the culture which they represent. At the dead center of a faith, Ulstermen cling to a dead faith; they cannot give it up and they cannot revive it. They are loyal to England but England is not loyal to them: they cannot give England up and they cannot rejoin it (so they love and curse their gaudy flag). The poet's inability in this poem to find an archimedean space, an emotional platform from which to view a fallen world in perspective, constitutes a poetic strategy for representing a dying culture. The poetic voice of "Desertmartin," whether it is unable to avoid or whether it chooses to adopt the very shrillness which it condemns, accurately transmits a sense of impasse, of unavoidable social evil hanging over Ulster.[16]

Paulin therefore blesses and curses the same faith in nearly the same breath. In "Father of History," he still venerates the symbolic representatives of Protestant culture whose accents ("a spiky burr / like a landrail crecking in the bracken") provide vestigial echoes of the Fathers of 1798, echoes now to be heard only in an historical library ("the Linen Hall stacks," "McCracken").[17] Ambiguously the poet digs the Fathers up—not as corpses but, following his hero Mandelstam's sacramental way of speaking about the Word, as food, an almost eucharistic memorial restoring to modern consciousness what was lost in antiquity.

Opposing the pieties of "Father of History," and printed on the opposite page from it in *The Liberty Tree*, stands "Off the Back of a Lorry," a lyric collection of vulgar vignettes gleaned from the popular culture of Ulster.

A zippo lighter
and a quilted jacket,
two rednecks troughing
in a gleamy diner,
the flinty chipmarks
on a white enamel pail,
Paisley putting pen to paper

in Crumlin jail,
a jumbo double
fried peanut butter
sandwich Elvis scoffed
during the last
diapered days—
they're more than tacky,
these pured fictions,
and like small ads
in a country paper
they build a gritty
sort of prod baroque
I must return to
like my own boke.
(*Liberty Tree*, 33; *SP*, 53)

The bark, cinnamon things, and Linen Hall of "Father of History" are now exchanged for zippo lighters, quilted jackets, and chipped white enamel. The conjunction of Northern Irish and American culture ("rednecks," "Elvis") brings back the figure of Ian Paisley, about whom Paulin has written a brilliant essay.[18] Paisley, who likes to point out that thirty-six immigrant Ulstermen signed the Declaration of Independence, claims a direct connection between yesterday's Protestant call for freedom in America and today's Protestant call for freedom in Ulster. Paulin acknowledges this connection, yet knows that all is changed utterly, and so chooses the dying Elvis (another American of Scottish-Irish descent and another demagogue of a sort—Presley/Paisley) to symbolize doubly the Northern Irish Protestant mind: first as a dead figure who is remembered and uselessly longed for ("Elvis lives!"), and second as one who stands for the decline of an authentic folk culture to the commercialized and cheapened idiom of "Grand Ol' Opry." Here then, opposing the Victorian elegance of Belfast's Linen Hall, is "prod baroque," an incoherent collection of tasteless items which constitute the Northern Irish Protestant *mentalité* and which are to true Protestantism what the small ads in a country newspaper are to the country itself—culturally inauthentic but factually true. Paulin has spoken elsewhere of "some sort of Scottish Calvinism beating at the back of my mind,"[19] a force which sends him (down) to the sweet yams of cultural memory but also (back) to grosser items, as the biblical dog to its vomit—another version of the impasse encountered in "Desertmartin."

In writing about one of Paulin's more difficult poems ("Politik"), Gerald Dawe offers an insight into this ambivalence. He is commenting on the following lines:

I'd be dead chuffed if I could catch
the dialects of those sea-loughs,
but I'm scared of all that's hard
and completely subjective.
(*Liberty Tree*, 30)

Dawe finds it inconsistent that Paulin should express the desire to catch a dialect at the same time that he is in fact catching it (by using the dialect expression "dead chuffed," meaning "pleased"). One cannot be scared of a thing and make use of it at the same moment. Dawe concludes that, since Paulin cannot decide whether or not to enter into the experience of the culture he is depicting, his poetry lacks an authenticating consciousness or believable voice.[20] Isn't the point rather that Paulin's ambivalence, his sense of exclusion from what is already his, constitutes precisely that mental experience or authenticating consciousness which the poem seeks to release? Unable in "Politik" to recapture the tonalities of speech heard in childhood, unable to equate today's Ian Paisley with yesterday's William Drennan or to find the sacramental Word in a fried peanut butter sandwich, and yet forced to keep trying, to keep returning, the poetic voice candidly and believably confesses, "I'm scared."

Paulin offers a key to this political and poetic ambivalence in his introduction to "Northern Protestant Oratory and Writing," the section he has edited for *The Field Day Anthology of Irish Writing*.[21] The piece vacillates between criticism and praise. "Protestantism," Paulin confesses, "can protest its integrity too much and mask an argument with a series of self-images and personal testimonies." Paulin then juxtaposes this admission to a series of statements about the Protestant mind which read as though they were his own attempts at self-definition: it is "a passionate seriousness about politics and a self-justifying energy and sense of personal integrity that seem strangely innocent;" it is "feisty, restless, argumentative, never quite at home in this world." Perhaps Paulin says most about himself when he writes, "There are moments in Protestant discourse when consciousness for its own sake, consciousness as subject, erupts and dominates. This sense of consciousness as process, as an end in itself, can be observed in much American writing, and it is rooted in puritan ideas of private judgment and personal testimony." Just a few lines later, however, he characterizes this mentality as "a solipsistic universe gnawed at its edges by anger and incoherence." I can think of no better phrase than that to describe the corpus of Tom Paulin's own poetry.

Much the same conjunction of opposites that we find in Paulin's style—idealism and vulgarity, innocence and degradation—may be discerned in traditionalist Ulster Protestantism, a culture whose members feel themselves increasingly betrayed, as the Britain to which they have been so doggedly loyal continues to make common cause, as they see it, with their mortal enemies in Catholic Ireland.[22] Increasingly isolated between two worlds, both of which it perceives as hostile and alien, conservative Ulster increasingly turns in upon itself.

In an important essay on the thirties in England, Paulin characterizes the British spies Burgess, Maclean, and Philby as the intellectual sons of Auden and Orwell, who in turn were descended from Oscar Wilde: all members of an upper class infected by self-disgust, turning their sharp wit against their own kind. A more general spread of this infection to the British ruling class as a whole, Paulin implies, is now being acted out in politics as modernized Thatcherites, driven by self-loathing, reject their less modernized cousins in Northern Ireland for having remained embarrassingly faithful to Britain's pristine, outmoded ideals. What Paulin does not fail to add is that the Northern Irish cousins themselves are consumed by self-hate, a hate hysterically projected outward by demagogues and terrorists. Paulin's own ambivalence—the prod baroque and the dog's boke—succeeds in representing precisely this self-hate. Paulin's impurities—his jarring diction, his inconsistencies—embody the dividedness of a Northern Irish Protestant consciousness, "gnawed at the edges by anger and incoherence." Paulin's own resentment of Ulster's Protestant, self-righteous violence is itself the key to his artistic representation of that violence: such resentment is a form of self-hate, and such self-hate is at the heart of social violence.

A certain weariness sets in as one reads poems—"images of our own disgust"—whose most enlightening aspect is their speaker's lack of enlightenment: he would be dead chuffed if he could catch accents, he "can't pray, / end, or send this letter," he must return to his own boke.[23] In at least one short poem, though, Paulin achieves enlightened self-understanding, and thereby reaches a new level of brilliance in writing the poetry of social violence. The poem, entitled "Of Difference Does it Make," carries its own bit of historical background: *"During the 51–year existence of the Northern Ireland Parliament only one Bill sponsored by a non-Unionist member was ever passed."*

> Among the plovers and the stonechats
> protected by the Wild Birds Act
> of nineteen-hundred-and-thirty-one,
> there is a rare stint called the notawhit
> that has a schisty flight-call, like the chough's.
> *Notawhit, notawhit, notawhit*
> —it raps out a sharp code-sign
> like a mild and patient prisoner
> pecking through granite with a teaspoon.
> (*Liberty Tree,* 51; *SP,* 64)

The poem, like the notawhit, is a rarity: the fact that Paulin is uncharacteristically writing about the other side gives his poem just the kind of "imaginative leap of freedom" which he elsewhere longs for but denies himself. Here is a history poem, a part of history not heard in canonical narration (at least not in Protestant Ulster history); its voice must therefore be listened to as carefully as one would listen for a rare bird-call. The sight and sound of the word "chough" answer both the sound of "chuffed" and the sight of "lough" from the already-discussed couplet in "Politik," a poem which develops a parallel trope of listening to history (by a kind of auditory carbon-dater which picks out Ulster gutturals from the soundwaves of the past). "Schisty" contains the term for splitting rock (the activity of the pecking prisoner) and suggests "schism," another word derived, as is "schizoid," from the Greek root meaning "to divide." By moving from sound to the felt resistance of stone walls, the poem invokes the whole complex of Ulster's modern history, in which Catholics and Protestants are divided from each other—literally, in Belfast, by stone partitions. More deeply than any topical reference, though, lies the general sense of isolation experienced by anyone whose efforts for change make no difference, not a whit. After the Anglo-Irish agreement of 1985, Paulin would soon testify to the same sense of political helplessness which he here attributes to the early Catholics of the republic. Paulin's almost inaudible tones render the isolation and helplessness, the sense of violent incarceration that each side inflicts on the other, as desire for freedom of conscience mutates into the self-loathing tyranny of conscience.

Now bitterness sets in, as the tone of *Fivemiletown*, Paulin's volume of 1987 (the late Thatcher period), turns stridently from the loftiness of "The Book of Juniper" to more caustic accents. Until its long concluding poem, "The Caravans on Lüneburg Heath," *Fivemiletown* constitutes a dead end, a place where both idealism and outrage have nowhere to go.

Paulin's ambivalence about his Protestant inheritance intensifies in "Why the Good Lord Must Persecute Me," a sequel to such poems from the previous volume as "Desertmartin."[24] Portraits of Calvin and Farel stare down at the poet from a bulletin board in his study ("fierce *féroce* feral stiff / a pair of stone pricks"). Nursing a hangover ("I've just had a liquid shite") under Calvin's eye, he ruminates on the clichéd word *tradition*, a word which will "squeak if you touch it / then break up like a baked turd / into tiny wee bits." Paulin curses his theological inheritance and yet holds it in honor, despises it as shit and yet experiences that same shit as physical discomfort, allows it to crumble into "tiny wee bits" yet admits that it can't be rubbed out.

The legacy of the enlightenment, no less than that of the reformation, leaves the poet at an impasse. The place called Fivemiletown, Paulin tells us, is five miles from its three nearest villages.[25] It may, therefore, be thought of as the center or eye of a Masonic triangle, a symbol which evokes some of Paulin's most somber thoughts. "We have the Orange Card, and we will play it," said Randolph Churchill and the followers of Edward Carson. "Now for the Orange Card" sees the exchange of letters between Tone and the French ("enlightened, protestant, and *juste*") transformed into a "french letter" or condom. It alters the Masonic rationalist symbol of the pyramid, first into a mark branded on cattle, then into the signet ring on the finger of a butcher who slaughters animals and rapes young women. The second stanza, beginning with political satire, ends with a confession:

> Now a daylight god
> has opened the sixth book
> and must go down into the ground
> like Achilles—
> Achilles strapped in leather,
> a pushy jerk
> on his night journey.
> I can smell his seed
> and know it's wasted;
> it can't belong.
> While up in the world there
> the roads are straight and secular,
> everyone says what they mean
> under the stamped sun
> and the earth is bent
> by blades and machines.
> All I want
> is to snatch a sleaked song
> till a wetness slicks and grows
> on your dagged black hairs
> —but what nature is
> and what's natural,
> I can never tell just now.
> (*Fivemiletown*, 10–11)

The daylight god (Creon, the bureaucrat, the Thatcherite traducer of ideals) is forced to open *The Aeneid* and follow Virgil into the underground night of the unconscious. Why? Because the coopting of rational ideals by pragmatist politics in this century has led to ceaseless outbreaks of unconscious violence, symbolized by the masonic pyramid on the butcher's signet ring. As for the daylight god's sexuality, he can only masturbate, a mechanical ex-

ercise in futility which Paulin compares to the rhythms of mecha-
nized society. In a later poem Paulin writes of the ticks of time
"falling like seed / onto barren ground," of "scouring the dust / for
Onan's cock / and that annoying little clock."[26] In the conclusion
the speaker admits that he, no less than the daylight gods, has dif-
ficulty "just now" in distinguishing between what is natural—sex
with love, productive sex—and what is not.

Clair Wills argues persuasively that Paulin, like Muldoon and
McGuckian, uses sexuality as a subversive political trope, writing
out narratives or symbols of sexual escapades as ways of overturn-
ing systems of imposed order. Much the same statement, though,
could be made about the traditional form of the aisling, in which a
sexual relationship is made to represent a form of civic life (so that
the maid longs for her lover as Catholic Ireland longs for the Stuart
monarchy). As I read Paulin's idiosyncratic poetry of sexuality, it is
the fictional self that holds my interest—the fiction that order and
disorder, repression and desire, are forces experienced by some imag-
ined person. One may, without losing the dimension of political
commentary, avoid reading the poem as mere code for such com-
mentary by keeping in mind this inferred person as the source of
lyric reflections.

Paulin's sexual script does not oppose revolutionary libido to
imperial repression; rather it evokes bad sex as symbolic of bad poli-
tics. The male daylight god, the "pushy jerk," is abusive, not repres-
sive; the poet dreams of escaping him and finding some other god,
some other sexuality, but what that preferred sexuality is, "I can
never tell just now." Paulin chooses a variety of sexual scenarios in
Fivemiletown for playing out his masterplot of sex without love: an
abusive male-female liaison in "Waftage: An Irregular Ode," a taste-
less episode of male-female casual sex in "Breez Marine," and an
equally tasteless episode of male-male casual sex in "Really Naff."[27]
All three of these poems—dramatic monologues spoken by a male
adventurer—make it clear that the sexual other is nothing but an
accessory to self-gratification. The political other, in the climate of
which Paulin writes, is nothing but an accessory to self-promotion.

There is a counterplot to be found in "Fivemiletown," osten-
sibly an account of the poet's courtship. In this dramatic mono-
logue the opening lines imagine an idealized sexual encounter—as
though this poem were to be an erotic "Book of Juniper":

The release of putting off
who and where we've come from,
then meeting in this room
with no clothes on—
to believe in nothing,
to be nothing.
(*Fivemiletown*, 15–17; *SP*, 80–82)

Remembering the often painful details of early courtship (the messages one left, the places where one waited), the poem develops the narrative of events leading up to this first sexual release—a release from history. The removal of clothes, creeds, and identities betokens a sexually "free and equal" condition, although this condition, like that of the poet's dreamed-of republic, can only be approached through the specifics of some history. In lines as rhapsodic as those in which he stands on the shores of Inishkeel and crushes berries in his hand, Paulin gives us an equation between "true" love and "true" civic polity, between abuses of sexuality and abuses of civic freedom. Such equations, trite as they may sound when reduced to prose, provide Paulin the poet with emotional energies for representing social violence as intimate experience. If Paulin refuses to render his landscape inwardly in "The Book of Juniper," but insists that it be a model for public life, so in "Fivemiletown" he implicitly proposes that mutual nakedness be thought of as a public condition, an alternative to life with the daylight gods of quotidian existence, those pushy abusive jerks. As an expression of this ideal, however, "Fivemiletown" leaves unanswered the question of how Paulin might extend his metaphor, of how one might spell out the correspondences of shared civic life to shared sexuality.

It is not until his most recent volume, *Walking a Line*, that Paulin has in fact begun to speak in this unusual language, comically advancing the notion of sex as a kind of free speech. "L," a poem in praise of the tongue, rehearses in graphic detail the tongue's ability to enter various human apertures: ears, armpits, "the bum" where "[it] searches the *mons pubis* / for a fleshy button / a tiny wee *cep*." Paulin enters a plea for recognition of the tongue as a noble instrument both of sexuality and speech:

with a fur of tannin on it like a mole
and hiding a soft saggy underbelly
this tongue thing's a supple instrument
kinda decent and hardworking
and often more welcome than the penis
—too many poems speak for that member
maybe it's time I unbuttoned my tongue?
(*Walking a Line,* 19–20)

Paulin's poem invites comparison with Robert Graves's more fa-
mous but inferior "Down, Wantons, Down," which gratuitously
concedes overarching powers to the penis, thus implying masculine
power over others. As opposed to Graves's tone of nod and wink,
implying that everyone has had an experience which could only be
had by men, Paulin leads his reader into areas which, although
they are socially marginal, are equally open for exploration to any-
one, male or female, who has a tongue. Waxing humorously lyrical
about the erotic tongue ("like a heifer drawn to the rocks / it loves
to lick salt / and dwell on the sea's minerals"), Paulin forces consid-
eration of oral sexuality as an experienced or an imagined activ-
ity—not political code, not yet allegory.

When he finally does present his allegory in the last line
("maybe it's time I unbuttoned my tongue?"), he does so in two
ways. First by substituting the tongue for the penis as a sexual mem-
ber, he establishes a form of bisexual or ungendered sex, a free and
equal erotic republic in which sensual exploration replaces the use
of one body by another for the release of a pent-up expression of
power. Secondly he vindicates this view of sexuality as a kind of
free speech, the language of decent and hardworking citizens who
deserve to be heard—as opposed to the silencing of the other by the
penis. By contrast Paulin continues to invoke abusive phallic activ-
ity in other recent poems such as "A Taste of Blood," in which the
woman's clamped oyster is invaded by the man's claspknife, an
activity which ends in "blood and fuckyous / between them," or
"A Hard Sell," in which "a ramstam fuck / the split bamboo / has
its own guilt / its own pleasure."[28]

"L," then, offers an answer to the concluding question of "Now
for the Orange Card," the question of what is natural. While sexual

desire in the earlier poem cannot be distinguished from the butcher's desire for slaughter and rape, in "L" it presents itself as the erotic longing of decent and hardworking citizens for a mutuality of both pleasurable sensations and expressed thoughts. In its detail, its humor, and its logical coherence, "L" provides a far more satisfying sexual analogy for modes of existence than the masculine language of total release and nothingness in "Fivemiletown." These are poems, of course, not essays in sexual politics; Paulin nowhere argues the respective merits of genital and oral sexuality. What he does do, by overturning the traditional distinction between "natural" and "perverted," is to replace a symbolic sexual order of domination with one of freedom and equality.

Like Heaney after *North* and like Muldoon after *Meeting the British*, Paulin after *Fivemiletown* has started to move away from outrage, shifting his attention to other concerns, to more abstract considerations of the artist and society (especially in the poems about Paul Klee), of nature and culture, and of Irish history. It remains to be asked how Paulin sought to write his way out of the particular impasse in which he found himself, the state of introjected rage in which selves construct themselves as victims and, hence, perpetuate violence. Paulin's own escape from the labyrinth opens up at the end of *Fivemiletown* in a long and challenging poem, "The Caravans on Lüneburg Heath."[29]

Paulin overcomes his obsession with violence, as Heaney had in *North*, Mahon in "The Hunt by Night," and Muldoon in "7, Middagh Street," both by widening his scope of reference in space and extending it back in time, as far back as the seventeenth century and as far afield as Germany, where he finds a friendly colleague in the person of Simon Dach (1605–59), a poet who flourished obscurely during the aftermath of the Thirty Years' War. Paulin bases much of his poem on Günter Grass's historical novella, *The Meeting at Telgte*, which describes a group of poets who came together after the carnage which had devastated Eastern Europe to revive their common commitment to learning and beauty. Following Grass in considering the Thirty Years' War as a prototype of the Second World War, Paulin advances the character of Martin Heidegger as the antitype of Dach the humanist—Heidegger the intellectual who remains at the center of power by conniving with an evil régime before the war and lying about his actions after it. By opposing Heidegger and Dach, Paulin confronts himself, another intellectual living at another time of hostility and betrayal, "a bust-up, dirty time to be alive."

Although Paulin begins his poem with sardonic, dead-end rhetoric ("we've had x years of blood and shit / and some of us have written poems / or issued too many credos through the press"), he manages to disengage from this familiar stance by two strategies. First he consciously negates his own voice by constructing himself as "Simplex," a name which can connote either idiocy or single-mindedness. By assuming both kinds of simplicity, Paulin is able to abandon his earlier self-importance and imagine himself as an artist in pure dialectical opposition to military force: "*Simplex plays the pipe indeed / But the soldiers pay no heed.*"

Second, Paulin has his twin, Dach, provide him with a place of refuge: the "Cucumber Lodge," a small bower in the backyard of the poet Heinrich Albert's garden by the river Pregel in Königsberg (more recently the Pregolya in Kaliningrad, Lithuania), where weekly meetings were held.[30] Mindful of Spenser's bowers and Keats's "wreathed trellis of a working brain," Paulin's lyric imagination hits on a complex of sensuous items which convincingly evoke artistic and civic ideals. With its allusion to Isaiah 1.8 ("the daughter of Zion is left like a booth in a vineyard, like a lodge in a cucumber field, like a besieged city"), Paulin-Dach's modest hut is just the place for representing idealists as refugees:

> we treated cucumbers like art objects
> and loved the slippy gunge that cauls the melon seeds
> every stranger was made welcome in our house
> you brought a bottle or a spondee and got tight
> you cast your bread upon the waters of the Pregel
> (*Fivemiletown*, 56; *SP*, 103)

Because Paulin can talk to Dach (he never talked to Tone in "The Book of Juniper"), he is able to find a new comic seriousness, a way of detaching himself from anger: "Simon, you're the It that isn't there / you're the reader and the writer / the crowd's buzz." Because Dach can talk to Paulin (Tone never did that), Paulin can find a more vibrant rhetorical *timbre* in dealing with political horrors, more telling because less personally aggrieved:

is there anything can shock us now?
the Virgin of Magdeburg charred in a ditch
the sleeping girl they shot because she married out
why give a shit if what you write doesn't last?
could you feel could you really feel any joy
watching the nation states rising up like maggots?
(*Fivemiletown*, 59; *SP*, 105-6)

Crimes of sacrilege (wrought by the faithful upon their own cult-objects) and of sexual violence (wrought by the tribe upon its own kin), brutalized bodies playing host to political infestation— these are all Paulinian motifs. Yet the question, "Is there anything can shock us now?" spoken by the jaunty Simon, who also confesses that "I dreamed and wanked in a cage of swelling vegetables," here serves to remove just that note of shock and outrage which compromises poems like "Desertmartin." Simon Dach's successor, *Simplex* (Simple Simon) can view social violence, for once, with a controlled, objective rage. "Brueghel, / You'll know them if I can get them true," promised the Heaney of *North*.[31] Dach helps Paulin, as Brueghel helps Heaney, to get true what had seemed most familiar but most resistant to language.

Enter Martin Heidegger, "the West's last thinker, part woodcutter / and part charlatan," who implicitly accuses the poet of complicity with corrupt governments. Like Heaney, Paulin requires a means of standing outside himself and examining his own failures—if failures they be—to protest against what he sees going on around him. By agreeing to dismiss Jewish faculty from the university of which he was the rector in the thirties and by publicly distancing himself from his Jewish mentor, Edmund Husserl, Heidegger managed to retain his respectability during the time of the Third Reich.

For Paulin, Heidegger's politics are no worse than his metaphysics, his post-romantic search for deep origins. There is an element of carping at Heaney's bog poems in the figure of Heidegger digging in the Black Forest; Paulin leaves it unclear whether Heidegger is digging trenches, digging graves, or digging for "ontic particles" as part of his program for delving to the roots of Western thought. Paulin thus aligns himself with Muldoon and Carson in finding "digging projects" inherently suspect because they assume unacceptable acts of the past to be phenomena of organic growth. Paulin's question about "what nature is / or what's natural" here returns as an objection to any project for going to the "roots" or origins of Western social developments. Such a critique (the aligning of Heidegger and Heaney) seems ironic, though, since Heidegger's digging was a bogus means of justifying the present, in Paulin's view; whereas Heaney in "Punishment" digs in order to sever the present from the past, and even to examine his possible culpability in contemporary violence.

Heaney serves as a model for implicit self-accusation when Paulin considers the guilty figure of Heidegger, "a survivor like you and me." In what, Paulin wonders, did "This old smooth fuck" differ from so many others who have to bend principles in order to survive the realities of unwelcome systems, and yet assure themselves that they are not, after all, the active perpetrators of evil? Such are university teachers, who live "on the quiet side of the stink." Paulin, whose salary is paid by a social system which he loathes, cannot but consider himself as Heidegger's *semblable, son frère.* "Guilt is not my subject," he has Heidegger say, turning his eyes away from Bonhoeffer being led to the gallows. Paulin will neither turn away nor reassure himself of his innocence. As Simplex he maintains his black insouciance, playing the cabaret master of ceremonies who is and is not a part of the show:

> *Simplex sees the final strike*
> *Devastate that evil Reich.*
> *Simplex says I'm going now*
> *You can read this anyhow.*
> (*Fivemiletown,* 63; *SP,* 110)

In one deft stroke Paulin now brings together the narrative elements of this poem at their center in the speaker's consciousness. Following the exit of Heidegger, the poem turns to a scene on the same blasted German heath of the Thirty Years' War, only now it is the place where the Germans are surrendering to the British in 1945. He imagines this act as a sexual one, as Muldoon does in "Truce"[32]: "they signed the instrument of surrender / then lit cigarettes the way young people used to / after sex in the daytime." Paulin, who was born in 1949, imagines this act as some part of his own birth:

"now I can get born again." The Field Marshal who received von Friedeburg's surrender was Montgomery, one of the four field marshals from Ulster whose names graced the four sections of the primary school which Paulin attended as a child. So it is that

> . . . one tight thread
> links Lüneburg *Heide*
> to the Clogher Valley
> —provincial world history
> or the seedbed of soldiers
>
> *Dill Alexander*
> *Montgomery Alanbrooke*
> they're crimped on my brain tissue
> like patents or postcodes
> their building's the hard rectangle
> that kitted me out first
> as a blue British citizen
>
> which signifies only
> that this flattened trashcan
> has more than enough room
> for Tommy's wee collection
> of aesthetic judgments
> decals
> further descriptions
> loony tunes
> or Free State referenda
> (*Fivemiletown*, 66; *SP*, 113)

Tom Paulin was born and grew up as a Tommy, a little British soldier, written upon as a piece of tracing paper by the lines of British imperialism. World history became provincial history; the seedbed of soldiers produced the attitudes of the lost province, the pushy jerks who waste their seed on the lost tribe. Paulin, the field marshals, and the hard men of Ulster are all stamped like postmarks from the same hard rectangle.

But here Paulin is flirting with danger. By feeling himself to have been traced on, stamped, kitted out, Paulin faces the same threat that confronts Heaney at the end of "Strange Fruit," the threat that, at the end of a long and difficult process of self-freeing, he will slip back to the point from which he began—the mistake of becoming a part of what he condemns. In "Desertmartin," inveighing against Ulster Calvinist rigidity, he ended by speaking in rigid Ulster Calvinist accents. At the end of "The Caravans," having inveighed against the imperialist warfare of nation states, is he to capitulate to his earliest identity, his "stamp" of British imperialism?

Heaney's final escape lay in aesthetic gazing, in confronting the victim's stare and recognizing her irresolvable otherness. As for Paulin, who also now requires a final means of stepping outside of himself, salvation lies in irony, a kind of self-mocking of which neither Heaney nor even Muldoon is capable. "Tommy's wee collection" includes his views on literature, his political maxims ("decals"), his journalism ("further descriptions"), his poems ("loony tunes") and even his paeans to the free and equal republic of conscience (ironically called "Free State referenda"). None of this is to be read as self-deprecation, whether sincere or otherwise. Paulin merely suggests that the writer can only succeed at characterizing and judging social violence by writing from that stance of objectivity which can be gained by "working through" his subjectivity, in Eagleton's sense. Having learned from Dach to refuse seriousness ("bring a bottle or a spondee"), Paulin can negate any claims his artistic talent might have lured him into making for his right to teach, preach, or prophesy. To have so thoroughly comprehended his artistic and political thought—comprehended the ways it was formed within social confines—is to have gained a new sense of self.

Paulin concludes,

so in all this melt
of incident and hot metal
there's still time to stop over
on the road to Damascus
—a light a voice patch of stamped earth
and if you ask my opinion now
I'll tell you about our musical *Kürbishütte*
then hand you a cucumber
and say it doesn't exist
(*Fivemiletown*, 66; *SP*, 113)

After such knowledge, what change of heart? Remembering that Paul was on his way to persecute others when converted, Paulin offers us, if not the possibility of conversion, at least that of stopping over for a night on the road to our evil encounter, stopping in the *Kürbishütte* or cucumber lodge, where the poet will descant to us on the unreality of all things, beginning with cucumbers and ending with Damascus. Paulin's irony finally succeeds in bringing forward the guilty observer, the compromised self. Dach-Paulin represents the noble resister—yet what does such resistance amount to, other than idle versifying? Heidegger represents the corrupt collaborator—yet which of us, dependent on a state-run and market-driven intellectual establishment for our livelihood, is not?

By placing the cucumber lodge on the road to Damascus, finally, Paulin affirms the ultimate requirement of conversion if real political change is ever to occur. "There is no 'Northern Ireland problem,'" writes Steve Bruce, "for which there is a solution. . . . The fundamental fact that even the most constitutional nationalists and even the most liberal unionists have incompatible desires combines with a lack of consensus within each camp to make substantial agreement seem an insubstantial hope."[33] How could one imagine such desires being reconciled, such inter-tribal communication being achieved; how could one hope for a million changes of heart? Political mythologies of conversion usually work the other way: first the wall comes crumbling down, as in Berlin, and then the people (so we like to believe) destroy their mental walls. Good poets, like Paulin at his best, implicitly contest such mythologies, insisting that the only walls which really matter are those built in the mind. Paulin can only say this, however, by representing the poetic self coming to political self-knowledge. It is in his progress from disembodied voice ("these are the places where the spirit dies") to ironic self-image ("Tommy's wee collection") that Paulin makes his most telling contribution to the Northern Irish poetry of violence.

7

CIARÁN CARSON

I loved its cold-jolt glug and fizz, tilted bottle upheld
    like a trumpet
To the sun; or so it might be, in the gargled doggerel of
    this dumb poet.
                                 —"Zulu"

Ciarán Carson likes to characterize his speech and even his thought as incoherent. "I was trying to complete a sentence in my head, but it kept stuttering," he says in 1987, telling how the experience of being in a Belfast riot, and more generally of being surrounded by social violence, impedes direct speech.[1] He repeats this claim to unintelligibility in 1996, writing of "the gargled doggerel of this dumb poet," but now does so in a triumphant manner, his bottle of orangeade held up to the sun like a trumpet.[2] It is in the implied battle between style and personality which these two lines enclose, the battle between verbal and personal versions of coherence, that Carson wages his own lyric war with social violence.

    Like Longley and McGuckian, Carson still lives and works in his native Belfast; of the three, he is the one truly urban poet. His well-known trope of the city map and his long lines, simulating rhythms of demotic speech, give his poems a tone of authority, the old-timer's voice. Carson's rambling narrative reproduces stylistically his thematic preoccupation with maps and with wandering around Belfast. His itineraries, like his stories, never go in a straight line, but lead up one street and down another. We fear getting lost; we rely on our guide.

These very techniques, however, initially serve to confuse our understanding of his poetry as it refers to violence, since they tend to hide the speaker behind such a mask as a local savant might wear when he speaks to ignorant strangers. Reading Carson (unless you are from Northern Ireland) is like walking into a Belfast pub—not a tourist's pub like The Crown, but one of those which Carson himself frequents: either you understand nothing of what is going on and quietly feel like the fool you are, or you pretend to understand, playing the fool.[3] Carson initially uses style to repress personality and therefore to confine his representations of violence to the evasions of mannered idioms. At length, however—almost, one senses, against his will—a persona does emerge and a position is taken. A bottle is raised to the sun.

After *The New Estate* appeared in 1976—a first collection which labored under the influence of Heaney—Carson felt the need to find a distinctive style. Taking a position as an expert in traditional music with the Arts Council of Northern Ireland, Carson did not return to poetry until 1983. He had by then read the American C.K. Williams's *Tar*, whose long, nine-beat lines, adapted from Whitman and Ginsberg, provided him with a means of adapting traditional, narrative speech forms to lyric. Shortly after reading *Tar*, Carson tells us, he finished *The Irish for No.*[4]

The differences between Carson and Williams, however, tell us more than their similarities. The long, sharply cadenced lines of *Tar* render their disclosures of the speaking persona with unambiguous force. Such parallels of rhythm and revelation may be found on any page; here is the beginning of "My Mother's Lips":

> Until I asked her to please stop doing it and was astonished to
>   find that she not only could
> but from the moment I asked her in fact would stop doing it,
>   my mother, all through my childhood,
> when I was saying something important to her, something
>   important, would move her lips as I was speaking
> so that she seemed to be saying under her breath the very
>   words I was saying as I was saying them.[5]

This insistent beat of forceful, personal speech is not at all what Carson says he heard when he read *Tar*—rather it was "the voice of someone thinking, working things out, trying to say it right; a voice which, for all its assurance, was strangely modest, puzzled, saying, well, I finally don't know any more about this than you; the voice of the storyteller who leaves the listener to draw his own conclusions."[6] There is only one conclusion to draw about Williams's overbearing mother, and he draws it for us; the modest, diffident voice Carson heard evidently came from somewhere else. Again (to compare poems about pub talk), in "The Regulars," Williams's expectoration—"the shits"—leaves no room for doubt about the do-nothing regulars: "In the Colonial Luncheonette on Sixth Street they know everything there is to know, the shits."

As Carson begins a long pub narrative in "Dresden," the rhythm is slacker, the discourse more oblique, and the point of view far less certain: "Horse Boyle was called Horse Boyle because of his brother Mule; / Though why Mule was called Mule is anybody's guess. I stayed there once, / Or rather, I nearly stayed there once. But that's another story."[7] Whereas Whitman and Ginsberg, and after them Williams, use the long line for self-exposure and self-criticism, Carson's early long line, like much rambling narrative, consists of stratagems for avoiding direct speech. The more we hear, the less we know. Carson's preoccupation with assembling large quantities of small objects—the shards of a crumbling city, the points on a map, the etymologies of a name, all that "confetti"—coheres with his love for the shaggy dog story: all seem calculated to hide the speaker's intention. Indeed, such hiding is itself one of Carson's professed intentions. Extolling narrative for its indirection and ironic distance, Carson offers his opinion that "overwhelming, deeply-felt emotion, doesn't necessarily make for good poetry," and adds, "I don't particularly want to write about how I feel."[8] Nor does he.

In its evasiveness and its conscious departure from Heaney's person-centered style, Carson's poetry constitutes an implicit challenge to the critical methods at work in these pages, an implicit rejection of the poetic self as a bogus, late-capitalist myth. The best studies of Carson have in fact avoided considering the self in his poems, preferring to focus on wordplay and post-colonial discourse (Batten) and the textual play of postmodernist aesthetics (Corcoran). It may also be, however, that Carson's loquacious evasions are themselves part of a personal agenda, a self's way of dealing with experience. There is a distinct self, hidden and shy, in Carson's poems, which is working things out, which is modest and puzzled (all the things that Carson says of Williams's poetic voice)—a lonely soul in a troubled city. Familiar neighborhoods are destroyed or altered, disorienting him; British troops survey and harass him at checkpoints, offending him. Unable to generate a strong personal center, he turns nostalgic, recalling how places used to look and how his parents and other figures of his youth used to look in them. The Joycean project of refashioning a strong, non-tribal self, so central to Heaney, Mahon, and even Muldoon, holds no interest for Carson, who remains in Belfast. Yet by his evasions—the long narratives, the play with maps, words, and things—Carson constructs a surviving self, one which perpetually negotiates with loss while seeking to understand the origins of violence. Precisely because he keeps his tribal identity, Carson can look upon that violence from a privileged vantage point. Even more than the *emigrés*, his colleagues, Carson performs a dialectical leap as he both suffers violence and imagines himself as its origin. Carson is indispensable to this study of poetic self-construction because he refuses to perform that construction in the ways that anyone else does.

Carson announces his programmatic avoidance of direct speech in the title of his first major collection, *The Irish for No*. Surrounded as he is by the omnipresent Protestant slogan, "Ulster says no," Carson reflects on the fact that the Irish language lacks the words "yes" and "no." He likes to tell it slant, imagining circumlocution as the language of wise, peaceful people, in contrast to the bluntness of the violent. In a recent collection of essays on traditional music, *Last Night's Fun*, Carson imagines the pub (of course, it has to be the right pub, where the crack is good and the music is inspired) as a model of civic concord, a euphoric *polis* where the barbarians (first tourists, but then readers, when the pub turns into a poem), understand neither the music nor the jokes and keep a respectful silence.

So the crack is good in Carson's narrative poems, although here, as when it is served in the pub with strong drink, such rambling talk primarily serves the needs of the speaking self—needs for dissipating guilt and acquiring innocence. The story of Horse Boyle, who once flew over Dresden in the gun-turret of a bomber and now lives in a junkyard, takes four pages—scenes from Horse's life, a tale of a young terrorist, and reminiscences about the old village schoolmaster—to bring us to the real story ("now I'm getting round to it") of that one terrible night. As the bombs fell, we learn, Horse imagined that "All across the map of Dresden, storerooms full of china shivered, teetered / And collapsed, an avalanche of porcelain, slushing and cascading: cherubs, / Shepherdesses, figurines of Hope and Peace and Victory, delicate bone fragments" (*The Irish for No*, 15). In one sense the poem works beautifully, because of its irony, as a reflection on brutal destruction and as a way of establishing Horse's rural junkyard as a little war zone. Like Dresden, or Belfast, or all of Ulster, it is littered with broken objects, people, dreams. In another sense, however, the poem works as an exercise in avoidance. By imagining all the smashed crockery and by remembering how he once accidentally broke a favorite childhood figurine, "a milkmaid standing on the mantelpeice," Horse adroitly sentimentalizes the carnage of the Dresden bombing. He thus transforms the crime of genocide in which he participated into the destruction of a Dresden porcelain figurine, an accident of which he paradoxically becomes a victim. Not that Horse, who joined the RAF for lack of other work, should need to beat his breast for having obeyed orders in the war. Yet clearly, throughout this long poem, both speaker and protagonist express their need to discuss violence graphically without looking at the shadows that violence casts in their minds. In Eagleton's terms, the man in the junkyard— be it Horse's backyard or the whole of Belfast—is experiencing his identity but not working through it. In the case of art after Dresden, like art after Auschwitz, prettiness, even the tinkling of pretty things being smashed, sounds a false note. "Dresden" is off-key; it betrays the hidden anxieties of its speakers as they try to preserve something within them from breaking.

The last and most important thing to shatter is consciousness. "Belfast Confetti," one of Carson's nine-line "sonnets" whose long lines and shortened strophes serve to expand the unit of speech but contract the formal structure of thought,[9] gives scope to the expression of this fracturing while limiting the thought process which would belie it:

Suddenly as the riot squad moved in, it was raining exclamation marks,

Nuts, bolts, nails, car-keys. A fount of broken type. And the
  explosion
Itself—an asterisk on the map. This hyphenated line, a burst
  of rapid fire . . .
I was trying to complete a sentence in my head, but it kept
  stuttering,
All the alleyways and side-streets blocked with stops and
  colons.

I know this labyrinth so well—Balaclava, Raglan, Inkerman,
  Odessa Street—
Why can't I escape? Every move is punctuated. Crimea
  Steet. Dead end again.
A Saracen, Kremlin-2 mesh. Makrolon face-shields. Walkie-
  talkies. What is
My name? Where am I coming from? Where am I going? A
  fusillade of question-marks.
(*The Irish for No*, 31)

The term "Belfast Confetti," as a reader might guess, means "shrap-
nel," or any of the stuff that gets thrown during a riot. Here, as
elsewhere in Carson's writing, the snowstorm also includes the sym-
bols of printed language, the symbols of a map, the sounds of gun-
fire, and the sounds of questions fired at citizens by soldiers in a
riot squad. The suddenness of the poem's beginning, with no con-
text of time, place, or causality, establishes the incoherence which
is the poem's theme. Every chaotic event finds its equivalent in an
expression of thought—thrown objects and type symbols, a burst
of rapid fire and hyphens or dots, dead ends and full stops, "a
fusillade of question marks." The poem belongs on the newspaper's
front page, not with the editorials; it reports without comment on
the chaos caused by the riot squad. Conforming to the convention
of the sonnet, though, as it moves from the longer to the shorter
strophe, the poem then ceases to narrate and starts to ask ironically
deep, personal questions ("Where am I coming from? Where am I
going?"), which are really nothing other than a security check at a
police line. Carson's questions of identity have been reduced, like
broken porcelain, to the panic-driven, stuttering dialogue of a citi-
zen under police interrogation during a riot in the Falls.

All this makes good reading (the book was an instant success, as poetry goes), but constitutes an interpreter's despair. Could such skillful poetry be doing nothing more than representing civic chaos as causing mental chaos? Successive sonnets, like pictures in a photographic essay, suggest just that, as they assume different clever perspectives to repeat the same idea. "Campaign" deals with dismemberment: a man is shot nine times by his questioners but reappears as a bartender, "his almost perfect fingers flecked with scum." Urban destruction is characterized as an unlovely sexual act in "Night Patrol" ("the whole Victorian creamy facade has been tossed off / To show the inner-city tubing") and, in "Smithfield Market," to a more general decomposition ("Maggots seethe between the ribs and corrugations").[10] One senses that the poet is leaving his most important questions unanswered, even unasked. Why is this happening to me/us? What is my own political, moral or emotional position on the matter? When the riot squad moved in, what was I doing, and why? What should I do now? The speaker implicitly represents himself as merely a victim of violence, wandering around with a victim's assumed innocence and confusion. But this posture, given the sophistication of the poems, can hardly be taken seriously. Like Horse Boyle the poet is designing and writing his own labyrinth—not a map of the city but rather an inner maze in which he can always go around a corner, eluding confrontation with himself.

At the end of the sequence, however, just as it seems that Carson has finished pulverizing consciousness together with the city, reducing both to a rubble of artifacts, landmarks, and words, the postponed confrontation occurs. An exercise in memory and nostalgia, "Slate Street School" arranges small items methodically under the gaze of an ordering mind. In the next-to-last sonnet, "The Exiles' Club," Carson portrays a group of men now living in Australia who gather each week to reconstruct every detail of the Falls Road as they remember it (and as it no longer is), including "the names and dates carved out / On the back bench of the Leavers' Class in Slate Street School." Even more methodical in his recollections than the Australians in theirs, Carson adopts the ordering principles of the school itself, its weights and measures, and even its religious doctrines, to categorize everything, including snowflakes. Then, in the unexpected finale of the last sonnet, the speaking persona suddenly rises from the page as the avenging Archangel and declares his purpose of burying Belfast forever:

> Back again, Day one. Fingers blue with cold. I joined the lengthening queue.
> Roll-call. Then inside: chalk-dust and iced milk, the smell of watered ink.
> Roods, perches, acres, ounces, pounds, tons weighed imponderably in the darkening
> Air. We had chanted the twelve-times table for the twelfth or thirteenth time
> When it began to snow. Chalky numerals shimmered down; we crowded to the window—
>
> *These are the countless souls of purgatory, whose numbers constantly diminish*
> *And increase; each flake as it brushes to the ground is yet another soul released.*
> And I am the avenging Archangel, stooping over mills and factories and barracks.
> I will bury the dark city of Belfast forever under snow: inches, feet, yards, chains, miles.
> (*The Irish for No,* 46)

Having revisited a site of his childhood, the poet now takes the child into himself, allowing its resentments and its grandiose, avenging voice to become his own. This outburst requires that the entire poem be reread as a catalogue of causes for neighborly hostility— a deadening quantification of all experience, including religious practices and the experience of nature—causes which make for a wish to destroy the whole system, the whole place.

Carson as avenging Archangel brings a dramatic contrast to Carson as "lost, unhappy and at home," bemused by surveillance, violence, and unwanted urban change. The latter persona, the one we encounter in most of these poems, implicitly plays the role of victim ("I know this place like the back of my hand, except / My hand is cut off at the wrist"[11]). By now we recognize this gambit of a self which is developing first personal, then tribal animosity toward others. As Corcoran points out in his discussion of this poem, revenge is the commonest and most dangerous tribal emotion in Belfast.[12] Does the victim, then, merely repeat a familiar cycle as he turns to revenge? Or, to argue a contrary possibility, might he be a herald Angel, singing of some counter-force to victimhood, some desire to build a strong new self whose vengeance consists not of reprisal, but of burial and new beginning? Does Carson's avenger take his place in an ironic cycle of violence, or does he express dialectical opposition between an old violence and a new?

The answer to this question, I think, lies in the title of Carson's book and the poem after which the book is named.[13] It is to break the cyclical repetition of "No" that Carson elevates the very opposition of "yes" and "no" to the status of a dialectical question. "The Irish for No" contains multiple allusions to "Ode to a Nightingale," in which Keats develops options (drink, suicide, and art) for dealing with life's horrors, options to which he must say yes or no. Although writing in a light, parodic style, Carson sets himself the same task as Keats in his ode: how will I deal with the horrors of a world where "youth grows pale, and spectre-thin, and dies?" It matters little whether the horror's cause is tuberculosis or the Troubles, whether death is a certainty or a risk; in either case the artist must face the issue and respond. Like Keats, Carson considers drink ("Bacchus and the pards and me" are drinking at the Eglantine Inn on the Malone Road) and suicide (the Belfast businessman "who drilled / Thirteen holes in his head with a Black & Decker"). Like Keats, he prefers the famous third option of flying from horror on the viewless wings of poesy. At the poem's beginning, seeing through a window (the Keatsian casement) "a yin-yang mobile," Carson makes this object symbolic of the Irish for no, or for yes. Because there are no such words in Irish, he implies, the graceful passage from one to the other, the dialectical yin and yang, symbolizes that artistic state of mind which transcends the rigid, violent cycle of "no."

Keats has helped the poet to do what Horse Boyle could not, has made him face the horror and choose the method of self-construction he will use to oppose it. Now, however, Carson encounters a problem of style. Although he cannot and will not write a Keatsian poem, he cannot just write simulated pub talk either, avoiding issues of violence and mortality by talking endlessly about them. Ulster's cycle of tribal opposition must be responsibly faced as a personal and as an artistic question. Carson's problem, then, lies not with Keats but with Heaney, who has already redefined Irish poetry by his exercise of such responsibility. Carson, like Muldoon, feels it necessary to satirize Heaney as a step toward poetic self-liberation: "Empty jam-jars. / Mish-mash. Hotch-potch." Having said "yes" (or its Irish equivalent) to the artistic choice of both Keats and Heaney, Carson struggles to oppose their styles in muted parodies.

In *The Irish for No*, even while using tropes which allowed him to side-step the inevitable tasks of his calling, Carson turns a sharp corner, calling forth a self and beginning to construct that self in the face of the violence which surrounds it. While "the unfed cat toys with the yin-yang of a tennis ball, debating whether *yes* is *no*," Carson begins to write seriously of tragedy in a lyric mode, to write from within the self.

Belfast Confetti (1989) is a darker book than *The Irish for No*, declares Carson. He does not say why, except to observe that there are many enclosed spaces in it.[14] Yes, the darkness inhabits inner spaces. Poems of nostalgia lose their innocence; poems of contemporary violence prohibit the poet from remaining innocently on the outside as a journalist. In *Belfast Confetti* Carson's lyric reflections, as well as his long narrative, "Queen's Gambit," allow the patterns and events of the war zone in which he lives to replicate themselves within his mind.

These replications extend even to such conditions of consciousness as time. "Ambition," which deals with personal growth through time ("one step forward, two steps back"), represents full human development as escape from some unspecified enemy. The escape, however, is as difficult as evasion from a soldier holding a gun to one's head ("if time is a road, then you're checked again and again / By a mobile checkpoint"). This central metaphor, not dissimilar to that used two years earlier in Heaney's "From the Frontier of Writing," internalizes surveillance as a condition of being in time. "Just then the border passes through him," writes Carson in another poem from this collection, "like a knife, invisibly, as the blip of the bus is captured on surveillance radar."[15] In characterizing time as a repressive soldiery, Carson is less concerned with tracing the effects of soldiers on citizens, as he did in "Belfast Confetti," than with making time itself the ultimate oppressor, as Yeats does "In Memory of Eva Gore-Booth and Con Markievicz." The soldiers in Carson's version of the parable are bored: "one of them is watching Wimbledon." Tennis, imagined as a yes/no game of either/or, not a yin-yang game of both/and, raises the subject of other, darker games of *sic et non*. What is the contrary of ordering death? *"Did you give the orders for this man's death? / On the contrary*, the accused replies, as if he'd ordered birth or resurrection." "The present is a tit-for-tat campaign," Carson writes in the same poem, "exchanging *now* for *then*." Given that Carson, as early as "The Irish for No," imagines cyclical or recurrent opposition ("Ulster says no") as violent, and the alternative state of mind (yin-yang, both yes and no) as nonviolent, it follows that time, being a then-or-now, yes-or-no game, is an inherently violent process.

If time is a condition of consciousness and if time is violent, then to be in time is to be in a condition of violence. The principal character of "Ambition" is the poet's father, a postman whose nationalist activities got him in enough trouble with the authorities to prevent his promotion—"so one story goes. . . . My mother's version is, he lacked ambition. He was too content to stay / In one place." Although nurtured on his father's clichés of yin and yang (*"one nail drives out another . . . one hand washes the other . . . God never shuts one door, but he opens up another"*), the poet must abandon those old saws as he tries to advance into the future—to play the tennis game of yes or no. The old clichés are useless: the door God shuts is a prison door on the father when he spends seven weeks in jail as an internee (an uncle spends seven years). At the poem's end, as at its beginning, father and son are climbing a mountain outside of Belfast, the father leading and the son catching up: "He stopped and turned, / Made two steps back towards me, and I took one step forward." It is not just that the son has more ambition than the father; it is that he has learned a new language, that of *sic et non*. Carson here destroys the framework he had built up in "The Irish for No," where he aestheticized the indirections of pub talk, its yin and yang, and opposed it to Ulster's yes and no. Here he consigns the old people and their yin-yang language to a *then* which must always be exchanged for a *now*. *Now* is one of Carson's darkest confining spaces.

The corollary of *now* is *here*. The aesthetic privilege of tran-

scendence, tentatively asserted in "The Irish for No" and negated
by time in "Ambition," is now negated by the here of Belfast in
"Queen's Gambit," another long narrative poem. We have come
a long way from the avoidances of "Dresden." No longer content
to maintain his distance from violence, merely describing or imag-
ining it, Carson here uses the tricks of narrative to enter con-
sciously into violence, assuming the role of an imagined
participant.

Not that the narrative is easy to follow: in this story of a double-
cross, told from the multiple perspectives of the various actors, it is
difficult to know what is going on, or who is who. By adopting this
strategy, Carson can amplify his idea of consciousness as condi-
tioned by surveillance:

> I'm constantly amazed at the amount of surveillance that
> goes on here. You're being watched all the time: spies in
> the sky, cameras, bugs in telephones. And yet, for all this
> massive input of information, they don't appear to know
> what is going on. . . . Maybe they've got too much infor-
> mation. . . . Information has to be directed by someone
> who stands outside the information. . . . [M]ost people
> don't know the totality of what's going on around them.
> I've lived in Belfast all my life and I still couldn't tell you
> a fraction of what's going on. All I can do is tell you
> stories.[16]

At the poem's beginning Carson adopts the voice of an in-
former ("Now they're seen together . . . they're now in the interior
. . . Much of this is unintelligible, blotted out by stars and aster-
isks"). The queen's gambit, a risky chess opener, renders one's back
pieces vulnerable by a seemingly foolhardy advance of pawns,
thereby (if the gambit works) inducing the opponent to attack pre-
maturely and so fall into a trap. In this narrative, the first pawn, a
female shop assistant, "informs" the British army that a small-time
crook, Mad-Dog Reilly, is planning a post-office robbery. She is
followed by a second set of pawns, a group of nationalist men in a
Ford Sierra, who then attack the post office, further drawing out
the opponents. Unbeknownst to the soldiers, a third set of pawns is
waiting in a mail truck, so that when the soldiers attack the Ford,

the mail truck ambushes the soldiers, firing on them with a gatling gun, scooping up the men in the Ford and driving off. The soldiers of England have been suckered by the other side's queen's gambit. The ever-changing narrative voice of "Queen's Gambit" now begins to ruminate on its own confusions as it compares information to lists of numbers and names, to pencil rubbings, bad photostats, and old films with missing reels. As Carson says, such playing with "information" cannot go on forever; someone has to tell a story. The question is, who? In mid-poem, when we are still in the dark as to who, what, and where, comes this:

But the Unknown Factor, somewhat like the Unknown Soldier, has yet to take
The witness box. As somone spills a cup of tea on a discarded *Irish News*

A minor item bleeds through from another page, blurring the main story.
It's difficult to pick up without the whole thing coming apart in your hands,

But basically it invokes this bunch of cowboys, who, unbeknownst to us all,
Have jumped on board a Ford Sierra, bound for You-Know-Where.
(*Belfast Confetti*, 37–38)

With the ironically self-contradictory "unbeknownst to us all" and "You-Know-Where," the bemused narrator becomes the omniscient narrator and the confused reader starts to be in the know: even the cowboys will be under surveillance "unbeknownst to themselves," but known to us. In the all-important last section, the full story is told to the narrator (whose voice in the first person is heard here for the first time) by his barber:

My newly-lowered ears in the barber's mirror were starting to take on a furtive look.
A prison cut—my face seemed Born Again—but then, I'd asked for *short*.

And I've this problem, talking to a man whose mouth is a
  reflection.
I tend to think the words will come out backwards, so I'm
  saying nothing.
(*Belfast Confetti,* 38–39)

Several things are happening here. The narrator, who is say-
ing "I" for the first time in six pages, now impersonates a criminal
on the run, obliquely suggesting that he is changing his appearance
to avoid detection. He is adopting the look of a convict in order
not to be caught. The barber, seen only in the mirror, is imagined as
a symbol of inversion, of words coming out backwards, and yet it
is he who finally tells the story straight. We are left to conclude that
the fictional narrator—the man in the barber's chair—knew the
story all the time, and that it is he who is telling it to us back-
wards—that is, through the mouth of the reflected barber who is
telling it straight, and who knows nothing of the double-crossing
female accomplice. Looking at the cuttings of his hair on the floor
"like commas on the chessboard tiles," the narrator leaves the bar-
ber "to a row of empty mirrors," and turning on to the street where
the post office is located, begins "to feel like a new man."
    Why new? Because of the haircut, but also because he has
finally taken control of his story. Having started the poem in a
familiar manner (the passive spectator, confused by a welter of un-
decipherable data), the speaker of "Queen's Gambit" finds a way
to "stand outside the information," as Carson puts it. By becoming
the omniscient narrator, Carson gains power over his story. The
poet can enjoy his own story because he takes responsibility for it.
Knowing the story before the barber tells it to him, he imagina-
tively becomes an accomplice to the plot, someone in the know,
someone who therefore must change his appearance, someone who
enjoys the bliss of having pulled a perfect move on the enemy. To
say all this is simply to say that Carson has brilliantly written out
the grandiose unconscious of his poetic persona, the violent, tribal
self which he could never express in "straight" language. "I've lived
in Belfast all my life and I still couldn't tell you a fraction of what's
going on. All I can do is tell you stories." That sense of helpless
victimization, providing the motivation for grandiose violence, in-
cludes a sense of helpless ignorance. What Carson does here is to

vent his grandiose self, not as the protagonist in a story of violence, but as the unseen master of that story. Responding to all those small deaths suffered at the hands of surveillance and subjection ("the border passes through him like a knife"), Carson here constructs a narrating consciousness which knows what it hears in advance.

Carson's narrative poems, like "last night's fun" at the pub, revel in fantasy, extending the imagination across boundaries of space, time, and convention. Like *The Irish for No, Belfast Confetti* is divided in the middle by a section of nine-line "sonnets." Using the short lyric, Carson turns to a new construction of the self amid violence, one which is truer to social fact. Having mentally participated in a bit of nationalist derring-do in "Queen's Gambit," Carson now abandons the fiction of soldiers-and-robbers for poems about a different kind of Belfast violence, that which the Irish wreak upon each other. In his citation of a Belfast ordinance of 1678 at the head of his sonnet section, Carson rudely changes Mad-Dog Reilly, the protagonist of "Queen's Gambit," from a folk-hero preying on the British to a cur who preys on poor citizens:

> that the Mastive dogs belonginge to . . . Inhabitants dwelling in this Corporation . . . have ffallen upon severall men and boyes upon the Streets and Lanes of this Towne . . . and have pult them to the Ground, Torne their cloathes and Torne some of their ffleshe and eaten the same Insoemuch that many Inhabitants ffeare their lives to walk the streets or laines either by night or day for the said dogs and Bitches. . ."
> (*Belfast Confetti*, 44)

No longer the bemused wanderer of *The Irish for No*, this speaking persona is a mordant commentator on the mutual destructiveness of his own people. "Last Orders" (the last drink of the evening or, if a bomb goes off, of one's life) is another poem about surveillance, but now the speaker is being watched by the proprietors and patrons of the pub he is entering:

> Squeeze the buzzer on the steel mesh like a trigger, but
> It's someone else who has you in their sights. Click. It opens.
> Like electronic

Russian roulette, since you never know for sure who's who,
   or what
You're walking into. I, for instance, could be anybody. Though
   I'm told
Taig's written on my face. See me, would *I* trust appearances?

Inside a sudden lull. The barman lolls his head at us. We order
   Harp —
Seems safe enough, everybody drinks it. As someone looks
   daggers at us
From the *Bushmills* mirror, a penny drops: how simple it would
   be for someone
Like ourselves to walk in and blow the whole place, and our-
   selves, to Kingdom Come.
(*Belfast Confetti*, 46)

This scene of Russian roulette causes more anxiety than the
fusillades of question marks to which we are accustomed in Carson's
poetry. Now one does not know who is watching or what will hap-
pen. No questions are asked; one's identity consists of superficial
appearances, interpreted randomly. "I could be anybody" is the
contrary of "Taig's written on my face." Who knows when Catho-
lic identity, or presumed Catholic identity, might be one's downfall
(as might be the case about Protestant identity, real or presumed, in
some other venue)? In the sonnet's sequel, where the barman is a
demon invented by Dante and Catholic Harp is opposed to Protes-
tant Bushmills, an enlightening thought occurs to the speaker: "how
simple it would be. . . ." It is not that he is still afraid of random
violence, as in the first strophe. It has suddenly occurred to him
that *he* could walk in and blow the whole place, himself included,
to Kingdom Come. In a sense Carson is hewing to the Keatsian
lines sketched out in "The Irish for No": he imagines escaping from
the inferno of a death-haunted life, first by inebriation (blushful
Hippocrene or Harp), and then by self-inflicted death ("now more
than ever" or "blow the whole place"). As in "Slate Street School,"
the speaker achieves enlightenment by imagining that he could be
the one to enact destruction; he could be the avenging Archangel.
Here, however, the speaker aims his concealed wrath neither at the
patriarchal school system of his memories nor at the monarchical

system of military surveillance, but at the Northern Irish fratricidal system of everyday hostility. Carson thus takes the notable step of invoking his grandiose self to overthrow, not the imagined oppression of an authoritarian force, but (if only in his imagination) the experienced oppression of social tensions, tensions which require him to submit to a rigid, self-imposed discipline.

Things get worse. "The Mouth," like its companion piece, "The Knee," concerns violence wrought by Catholics upon each other when the IRA punishes errant members of the tribe for loose speech. In the first poems about surveillance, humans were reduced to electronic signals in retrieval systems; now they are reduced to body parts while the poet's voice reduces itself to the ventriloquized voice of the victim's assailants ("There was this head had this mouth he kept shooting off . . . We thought it was time he bit off more than he could chew"). In this poem, the murder victim can only be identified from his toothmarks in the apple he was eating when he died, an image Carson uses again in "Jawbox." "He bites it," one says, meaning "bites the dust," but Carson means the apple, as though to have lived were the original sin. The bite into the apple also betokens memory's seizure of the past in the act of remembering:

> He bites into the core, imagining his mouth's interior.
> That twinge, an old occlusion. The tooth he broke on the rim
>   of the jawbox
> When he was eight.

> . . . One bite from the apple, as the victim's Ford Fiesta trickles
> Up the driveway. The car door opens. The apple's thrown away.
> (*Belfast Confetti*, 92–93)

Transforming the Proustian thought of a life recaptured by a single bite into the titillating idea that a forensic expert might identify a mutilated body only from its toothmarks in that same apple, Carson continues to move the zone of violence inward, replacing his yin-yang mobile of yes and no with this double image of the apple: the core of your life, the rind of your death.

It is in the short essays on Belfast, inserted into *Belfast Confetti*, that Carson brings his constructed self into sharpest confrontation with the violence surrounding him. These essays, he tells Rand Brandes, had originally been intended for a separate book on the city, but the project was unfinished; hence the inclusion of the existing work in this collection.[17] They are well-adapted to the poems, amplifying the poet's favorite tropes with a wealth of information—thus an excursus into the multiple etymologies of "Belfast" (each with its own connotative suggestions), another into the historical vagaries of Belfast maps (some showing what is no longer, others what was never to be), and another, after Foucault, into the connections between British military surveillance and Bentham's punitive Panopticon.

For the interpreter of Carson's poetry, though, the most interesting essay is "Question Time." It seems at first as though there is nothing new here, as the essay begins with the by-now familiar theme of the bemused city-dweller revisiting the sites of his youth and getting lost. "I know this place like the back of my hand," says the speaker, but finds the place strange, thus invoking again the image of the hand which, like the red hand of Ulster, has been cut off from the body. The piece gains in interest, however, as the poet recalls the time when, as a boy, he would disobey his father's admonitions and venture onto Cupar Street, a boundary between the Falls and the Shankill. Inevitably, one day, he and his friends are accosted by a group of tough Protestant boys who challenge them to declare which of the two they prefer—the Union Jack or the Tricolor. The boy escapes his tormentors only to get a thrashing at home for having run this risk.

The essayist recalls this initiation into internecine terror by narrating its sequel, an event from the recent past. One Sunday afternoon he is riding his bicycle along the so-called Peace Line, a thirty-foot wall which runs through the territory of his memories. At last discovering how one might voyage into the Shankill, he does so and eventually rides back into the Falls. There he is ambushed by a group of men who haul him off his bike, drag him into a deserted lane, pin him to the wall with his legs spread apart, and barrage him with questions:

> *You were seen coming from the Shankill.*
> *Why did you make a U-turn?*
> *Who are you?*

Where are you coming from?
Why did you stop when you seen the car?
You know the car.
The car. Outside Sinn Féin headquarters.
(Belfast Confetti, 61)

The questions go on for another forty-one lines. The "speaker,"
whose answers to the questions are not recorded, can only save
himself from torture and death by answering trivia questions about
the houses in the Falls, thus proving that he really is a local, an old-
timer like the men in Australia who can reconstruct the names carved
in the desks at the Slate Street School:

Where are you from?
Where is he from?
The Falls? When? What street?
What was the number of the house?
How far down the street was that?
When was that?
What streets could you see from the house?
Cape Street? Yeah.
Frere Street? Yeah. Where was Cape Street?
Again. Who lived next door?
Next door again.
(Belfast Confetti 62)

"The questions are snapped at me like photographs," says Carson,
meaning photographs of places and people no longer there. He can
only save himself by arranging the pictures into an obsolete map.
"I am this map," Carson concludes, ". . . a map which no longer
refers to the present world, but to a history, these vanished streets;
[nevertheless] a map which is this moment, this interrogation, my
replies." To become the map of the past is to experience obsoles-
cence, death—the same kind of death, one infers, which the speaker's
assailants inhabit by custom: " . . . a few moments ago I was *there*,
in my mind's eye, one foot in the grave of that Falls Road of thirty
years ago, inhaling its gritty smoggy air." This piece has come as
far from "Queen's Gambit" as that poem had come from "Dresden."
Having imagined himself, if only in fantasy, as a perpetrator of

escapades against British soldiers (there are parallels to Heaney's artful voyeurism), Carson now turns that sense of solidarity with the Falls against himself, representing himself as a victim of his own people. The incident is rich in irony. The very stance which Carson has cultivated most (the liberal *vir bonus*, amiable but lost) now puts him in grave peril at the hands of his own tribe. Having been a spectator of maps, he must become a map by reproducing as for a camera the very places he had grandiosely condemned to extinction when he played the avenging Archangel. Faced with the choice of becoming the map or perhaps dying, he finds that he must reproduce in his self the very extinction which he had wished upon the old place.

It came, no doubt, as a relief to this captive that the IRA men could say of him, as Marlow says of Jim, "he was one of us." Whereas Heaney, Mahon, Muldoon, and Paulin, in their different ways, all manage to unearth their unconscious belongings to some violent tribe (returning like a dog to its own boke, as Paulin would have it), Carson has made such belonging his conscious stock in trade—the crack, the songs, the local knowledge. In "Last Orders," "The Mouth," and now "Question Time," however, Carson has the violent tribe unearth *him*—he becomes the surveyed, caught, passive victim of his own people. Whereas in the narrative fantasy of "Queen's Gambit," the poet had permitted his grandiose mind to imagine a "cattle raid" on the Tomb Street Post Office, now he is forced to knuckle under, not just to use but to become his conformist self, turning his mind and body into the obsolete map of a dying culture.

Such a confrontation with his violent heritage, and therefore with his violent self, puts Carson, as it put the Heaney of *North*, in an impasse, a place where the double identities of liberal and traditionalist, cosmopolitan and tribesman, enlightened and enraged, can no longer be maintained. Carson has negotiated the impasse while remaining in Belfast. His continued career as an expert in musical culture, as his brilliant *Last Night's Fun* shows, provides him with the role of cultural diplomat—of bringing to consciousness the artistry and genius of a popular culture, a culture whose sordid activities are over-publicized. As a lyric poet, though, Carson has embraced the more serious and more interesting task of dealing with personal even more than cultural reality. Following *Belfast*

Confetti he has written from a place even further within a self whose violent ambience he now recognizes as a quality of his being.

Now, in his poetic investigation of self and society, Carson turns to language, that favorite topic of Irish cultural discourse. *First Language*, his next book of poems, whimsically associates Irish (the language spoken in Carson's home when he was a child) with the myth of innocence, a pre-verbal state: "English not being yet a language, I wrapped my lubber-lips around my thumb."[18] In a studied manner which calls to mind Rimbaud and Dylan Thomas, Carson elaborates a sensuous, beautiful-sounding world of pure impression (using a sophisticated vocabulary to do so). The Wordsworthian myth of primal innocence gives Carson a convenient way of indicting those who turn the city into a battlefield on which children are forced to grow up: shades of the no-go zone begin to close about the growing boy. To suppose, as Carson does in "Second Language," that one once "whooped and hollered in [an] unforked tongue," is to opt for an extreme romantic position. This position must be buttressed by a nostalgic style, compounded of sentimental diction, a legacy from Kavanagh, Montague and Heaney ("A single star blazed at my window. Crepuscular, its acoustic perfume dims / And swells like flowers on the stanzaic-papered wall"). In this Wordsworthian view, the good angel of the child's here-and-now gives way to the malevolent forces of time and society ("the future looms into the mouth incessantly . . . I glimpsed the noise of years").

Evidently aware that this myth is an exhausted one, Carson also adopts other, more self-critical views of human development and violence. At the opening of "Two to Tango," it is as though he is waging an inner debate on the issue of the free, self-determining will versus the inevitable passivities of social conditioning:

> Whether you want to change your face or not's up to yourself.
>   But the bunk of history
> They'll make up for you. Someone else's shoes. They can put
>   you anywhere. Where's a mystery.
> (*First Language*, 18)

"Anywhere"—environmental conditioning being no greater or less in Ireland than anywhere else.

The point of "Two to Tango" is that the code language for terrorism resembles the code language of gendered sexual development. In a voice whose speech acts of direct address sometimes sound like any older man's advice to any younger man and sometimes like instructions to a novice terrorist, the poem issues a code of conduct which could be equally well applied to a secret mission or to manipulating a woman in a relationship: "You'll find ways around it, yawning, getting up to 'go out for a couple of hours' . . . Tell no one, I mean no one, what you're up to." Is such a code of conduct already written in to the male gender? "Use body language tags, especially for men: / *He punctuated his words with repeated clicks of his Mont Blanc ball-point pen.*" Sexuality is the nemesis of the male terrorist because it makes him let down his guard: "For when you stop saying *never*, that's when you'll get dead. You'll put your sweet lips / A little too close to the phone and talk of *always* in a fatal momentary lapse." Mutually discordant clichés ("It takes two to tango," "Keep your head down. Know yourself") play off against each other. Carson dismantles his myth of the primally pure person by showing how all aspects of human development, from intimacies of sexuality to rules for public behavior, are written in clichés common the world over, clichés which inscribe violence into human experience.

Although one must always beware of sex, says the poem in its advice to the male operative, one should also use it to one's advantage, and here the advice contains a strange item:

And contrast is important, between male and female dialogue.
   Then there's changes of identity;
But be careful of the cliché where the protagonist is torn
   between identical

Twins.
(*First Language*, 20)

Identical twins, like Muldoon's Castor and Pollux, call to mind the two sides in Northern Ireland, indistinguishable from each other in everything except religion (which cannot be "told" merely by looking). Change of identity—one person as two—is opposed to twinning—two persons as one. Furthermore the twins (according to this particular cliché) constitute opposing love objects for the imagined protagonist, the young man listening to the poet's advice. If young men are warriors, sex is always dangerous, unless it is understood as a cliché, as insignificant. The one thing to beware of, however, is the trap of allowing sexuality to lead one into a state of equal benevolence or love for two equals (Ulster's identical twins). For in choosing a single twin, one will be vulnerable to the other twin's violence—the unforgivable error if you are a male warrior. The fact that violence is written or encoded into the psyche (violent isolation over against vulnerable relatedness) makes us ask whence that writing comes; but Carson dissolves such questions by his use of clichés. No perception of original nature is free from the tawdry mediation of cultural bromides, he seems to say. This too—the imposition of inherited notions on whatever is born—is another form of violence.

Violent inscription extends itself to Carson's favorite trope of the city map, now a brain map. In "On Not Remembering Some Lines of a Song," he imagines some tourists who have gotten lost while watching a Protestant celebration such as the twelfth of July; he also imagines his own feeling of being lost, for very different reasons, during the same celebrations ("I came from the wrong side of the tracks"). He finally imagines the center of consciousness, lost in the process of trying to retrieve what has been forgotten, trying to find the on/off switch, "the split chink / Through which you peer with half an eye / And glimpse the other, time-drenched world."[19] Topographical, sociological and psychological confusions are presented together, so that it is impossible to adjudicate as to the causality or influence of any one on any other. The next poem continues the conceit with the appearance of a mechanical brain, a "robot bomb-disposal expert," and is followed by "The Brain of Edward Carson," a poem written in three five-line stanzas with uncharacteristically strict aabba rhyme scheme, which permits the poem to represent the brain as a closed circuit, self-determining and self-destroying.

One wondered when Carson would explore the irony implicit in a name which he shares with Edward Carson, the symbol of Ulster opposition to Catholicism in the early twentieth century (the poet's great-grandfather was a Protestant who converted after marrying a Catholic). He imagines what happens when the brain of Edward Carson is opened, revealing an inner topography of the violent world that his namesake represented: "Barbaric instruments inserted there, like hook and razor, iron picks. . . . The map of Ulster opened up, hexagonal and intricate, tectonic." Nothing could be farther from the idea of the psyche being written on by a violent world than this image of the brain as an inner, violent world. Whose brain does not work in such "bronze circuitry," with such a "rivetted, internal gaze," until the moment of disintegration? In this latest version of the identical twins, Castor and Pollux, Ciarán forces himself to stand together with Edward. If the brain is a binary mechanism, operating in the split chink betweeen *on* and *off*, *yes* and *no* (but what is the Irish for no?), then gentle, confused Ciarán and violent, insistent Edward must share a single space.

Violence has the last word of *First Language* in "The Ballad of HMS *Belfast*," the poem which contains Carson's famous joke about "Catestants and Protholics." This fanciful sea-adventure narrative, written in rhyming couplets and perpetuating the hallucinated aura of Rimbaud's "Drunken Boat" (translated elsewhere in the volume), has a purpose as simple as its style is complex, a purpose manifest in the last four couplets:

> The atmosphere dripped heavy with the oil of anchovies,
> tobacco-smoke, and chaw;
> We grew languorous with grass and opium and *kif*, the very
> best of draw,
>
> And sprawled in urinous piazzas; slept until the fog-horn trump
> of Gabriel.
> We woke, and rubbed our eyes, half-gargled still with
> braggadoccio and garble.
>
> And then the smell of docks and ropeworks. Horse-dung. The
> tolling of the Albert clock.
> Its Pisan slant. The whirring of its ratchets. Then everything
> began to click:
>
> I lay bound in iron chains, alone, my *aisling* gone, my sentence
> passed.
> Grey Belfast dawn illuminated me, on board the prison ship
> *Belfast*.
> (*First Language*, 74)

Like Muldoon in "7, Middagh Street" and like Mahon before him,
Carson represents himself as trying to flee from the sordid violence
of Belfast. Since Carson never has fled, however, he cares little for
the geography of Mahon and Muldoon, whose ships shuttle back
and forth over oceans. Carson's alternative, symbolist voyage, that
of the dream, takes him back again to the Keats of "Ode to a Night-
ingale," whose escape from grim actuality can only be imagined, a
dream from which, in whatever last stanza one chooses, there must
always be an awakening. Even Carson's prison ship, though, is
imagined or dreamed, so that when he awakes it is to the whirring
ratchets of his mind. "On Not Remembering Some Lines of a Song"
begins with a similar characterization of the mind's workings: "It's
the pawl-and-ratchet mechanism / Of one of those antique, whirli-
gig-type wooden rattles, only / Some of the teeth are missing." If
the titanic, machine-like brain of Edward Carson ends by decom-
posing into a sphinx-like, catatonic slumber, the brain of his twin—
Ciarán Carson the wandering boat—ends by restarting itself, a
clumsy, unstoppable machine. Keats awoke to the dull brain that
perplexes and retards, and to the diseased body that dies. Muldoon
fled to New York, only to find himself back in Belfast. Carson boards
the *Belfast* to escape from Belfast, but reawakening on the *Belfast*
(a prison ship) in Belfast, he discovers that he has never been any-
where but inside his own consciousness, where he still is—not a
dull brain but a violent one, a set of twins always at war with each
other.

Carson has presented a further version of Ulster violence, one
inspired by an invitation from Michael Hofmann and James Lasdun
to contribute to their collection of modern versions of Ovid.[20] Remi-
niscent of Heaney's *North*, which Carson so disliked when it ap-
peared, this is a version of violence as ur-myth. In his three
translations from the *Metamorphoses*, Carson gives a succinct but
comprehensive anatomy of violence during the Troubles. First in
the story of Ascalaphus (who revealed that Proserpine had eaten a
pomegranate in Pluto's kingdom), Carson deals with informers and
hunger-strikers. Next in the story of Hecuba (the wife of Priam and
mother of Paris who, seeing her daughter sacrificed on Achilles'
grave and her son murdered by drowning, savagely killed her son's
murderer and was herself transformed into a savage dog), he pre-
sents bereaved mothers and the overarching topics of revenge and

savagery. Finally, in the story of the Memnonides (the birds which
emerged from Memnon's funeral pyre, splitting into two rival forces
and returning each year to re-enact their ritual of strife), Carson
emblematizes the fundamental Ulster phenomenon of division into
two.

In this last narration, the changes Carson makes in his trans-
lation of Ovid are worth considering. The Loeb prose translation
runs thus:

> Dark ashes whirled aloft and there, packed and con-
> densed, they seemed to take on form, drew heat and vi-
> tality from the fire. (Its own lightness gave it wings.) At
> first, 'twas like a bird; but soon, a real bird, it flew about
> on whirring pinions. And along with it were countless
> sisters . . . and all were sprung from the same source.
> Thrice round the pyre they flew, and thrice their united
> clamor rose into the air. At the fourth flight the flock
> divided and in two warring bands the fierce contestants
> fought together, plying beak and hooked talons in their
> rage, wearing wing and breast in the struggle. At last
> these shapes kin to the buried ashes fell down as funeral
> offerings and remembered that they were sprung from
> that brave hero.[21]

Here is Carson's version of the same lines:

> Soot and cinders flocked together in a bird-shaped aura
> That becomes a bird. Like an opening fist, it creaks its wings.
> Squawks and flutters.
>
> And then the squab engendered other birds innumerable. They
> wheeled
> In pyrotechnics round the pyre. The Stukas, on the third ap-
> proach, split
> In two like Prods and Taigs. Scrabbed and pecked at one an-
> other. Sootflecks. Whirl-
> Wind. Celtic loops and spirals chawed each other, fell down
> dead and splayed.
> (*First Language*, 59)

Carson's pyrotechnics generate a rich symbolism of violence, presenting two points for consideration. First concerning the origin of the violent birds: from the funeral pyre of a violently murdered man Jupiter causes a bird to arise, and then to divide endlessly into warring factions. Violence, then, does not come from factions, but factions from violence. Second, while Carson shortens Ovid's verse, he also opens it up by adding a small section of his own invention: "Sootflecks. Whirlwind. Celtic loops and spirals." Ovid is content to observe that the birds mutually destroy each other; Carson insists on the *shapes* of this mutual destruction. *First Language* begins with a love poem in Irish, printed with the other poems and reproduced in Irish script inside the front cover; the programmatic "Second Language" rhapsodizes generously on the arabesques of letters as elements in the pure consciousness of a child. Given this presentation of an original language—a linguistic myth of innocence—the Celtic loops and spirals of the "Remember Memnon birds" appear as horribly sinister, suggesting that the earliest letters to appear in consciousness are but characters of the urmyth's text of original violence.

In "Latitude 38° S" Carson concludes his mythology of violence in *First Language* by recounting Apollo's flaying of Marsyas. The poem's title is curious, since the 38th parallel north traverses Athens, whereas its southern counterpart traverses southern Australia. We may infer that the modern bards of mythological violence are like those familiar members of "the Falls Road Club which meets on the first Thursday of every month in the Woolongong Bar in Adelaide" to reconstruct all the grafitti in the Slate Street School.[22] In its story "of the cruelty of gods and words and music," this poem not only expunges the Wordsworthian myth of primal purity, but also the Keatsian myth of escape from horror through art ("They gaze into the stream's cold pastoral, seeing / Fossil ribs and saws embedded there, the fluteplayer's outstretched fingers").[23] Carson opposes the instruments of writing (they are sharp, like pincers and saws) to Marsyas' flute; he opposes the library's "security requirements, conduits, wiring, laminates and ducts" to the books themselves. The cruelty of the gods generates an original writing, whether of words or music, written on the body and the mind.

It is fascinating to compare Carson's thoughts on violence,

culminating here in the ironic development of an ur-myth, with his negative review of Heaney's *North* when that volume first appeared in 1975. Writing harshly of the last two stanzas of "Punishment," Carson says, "It is as if he is saying, suffering like this is natural; these things have always happened; they happened then, they happen now, and that is sufficient ground for understanding and absolution. It is as if there never were and never will be any political consequences of such acts; they have been removed to the realm of sex, death and inevitability."[24] Whether or not Carson was correct in his reading of Heaney is less at issue here than what Carson says about inevitability. In this passage written at the age of twenty-four, Carson clearly believes it perverse to say or think that history repeats itself, or that political suffering is inevitable, for to say this is to excuse it. As he was to discover, however, in working through violent identities in poetry, not to say this is to generate an equally embarrassing set of assumptions: that there is always some innocent or pure base in human nature which is invaded by some bad, but changeable social situation. If we could only reform society a bit more, all would be well, or at least less bad.

In his poetic explorations of languages and maps, Carson has been led to acknowledge an original writing upon the body and the mind, a writing by the gods which speaks of violence. To find this writing, as both Heaney and Carson do, to read and translate it, is not to excuse or absolve what the writing speaks of; it is only to be drawn to a deeper level of irony than before one read the writing, when one imagined oneself innocently standing over against the perpetrators of violence. It is now possible to understand why Northern Irish poetry, when it best characterizes Northern Irish violence, most successfully eludes the label of "political poetry." It is not possible, finally, both to show the experience of violence as an experience of identity and at the same time to write politically, in support or condemnation of some action. The language of lyric poetry implicitly explains why so little social discourse ever effects the changes for which it calls. If the kind of consciousness which poetry manifests and requires—its awareness of the self—were to be a precondition for political action, what might not be the results? Such a destruction of mental walls might bring about, for the first time, the realization of those goals for which political assertions call out in vain.

Published after the first cease-fire of 1994, Carson's more recent collection of poems, *Opera et Cetera* (1996), provides dazzling verbal entertainment. Although the book does little to extend or deepen the poet's sense of a self, the little it does do is significant. Apart from a set of adaptations (from Stefan Augustin Doinas), these short poems (each in five rhymed couplets) are set in arrangements (two alphabets, with a poem for each letter, and one series on Latin proverbs) which allow Carson once again to conceal any personal center behind, or within, an exuberance of sound. Letters represent things, either as they do in a child's ABC's ("F stands for forceps"), or as a sound ("The train slowed to a halt with a sigh like *Schweppes*"), or as an ideogram, so that C represents "the moon, the fingernail, the scimitar," and Y a slingshot.[25] Carson continues to portray Belfast, although choosing letters rather than maps for his signposts. Rimbaud again makes his influence felt, (a translation of his "Bateau ivre" appeared in *First Language*) as when Carson sets a Rimbaudian cornucopia of words and hallucinatory sensations next to a military horn of plenty (that other obsession of his), spewing out its dots, flashes, flares, and buzzes of surveillance and terrorism. This *mélange* of the ludic and horrific persists: as the "gnats, gads, gargle-flies and gall-flies" of "G" "[lay] their eggs in gigabits in data-banks and files of lies," someone's hand has been "clamped in a G-clamp to the Black & Decker work-bench" as a preparation for unspeakable torture.[26]

    Here as elsewhere Carson allies himself with Muldoon's *horror vacui*, his loading every vein with verbal play. Muldoon's O, imprinted on a victim's forehead by the pressure of a gun barrel, reappears in Carson's alphabet. As for the allusion to cross-gartered Malvolio (Muldoon's ampersand, Carson's zig-zag), both of which appear in books of the same year, one can imagine the two poets sharing the joke and retiring to their respective *escritoires*.[27] In both "O" and "Z," verbal artifice acts as a mask. The O of terrorism matches the teacup stain left on a white tablecloth—can be laid over it, like the cup itself. Z is the route followed by the poet's father, a postman, as he delivers his letters, and by the postman's son the poet, as he delivers his literary letters, from *A* to *Z*. Both the stains of violence and the dark territories of memory and destiny awake feelings, one supposes, but Carson vigilantly prevents this awakening, instead transposing emotions into figures.

When the figures permit, the self appears, least surprisingly in "I," but only to contradict and cancel itself: "*I* is the vertical, the virtual reality. I tell it slant. / I am leaning into you to nudge you. I am Immanuel, and you are Kant" (*Opera*, 19). The icon-letter, italicized and leaning (as it admits), contradicts its own claim to verticality, but then contradicts the contradiction by asserting that it is the *I* of Immanuel, not the "leaning" *K* of Kant. These contradictions ("You are cocaine, I am the nose. You walk straight and narrow. I am deviant"), piled one on another, tell it slant that there is no self as center, but say it so often that one wonders why the poet insists so much on his non-self.

Other occurrences of downward and slanting strokes provide Carson with further signs—but only signs—for a self: *N* ("Nemo is not a nobody"), *W* ("I call you Double You. You, you wouldn't know your *yin* from *yang*"), and *V*, the symbol of hostility ("To gouge out, as the eye with the thumb. To signal *Victory*, or *Up yours*") which becomes a symbol of identity: "I end up embodied in the glacier: my frozen outstretched *I* / Stared out at me, like the *v* in *Balaklava*, all wool and mouth and eyes" (*Opera*, 32). If *K* was a joke, one *I* leaning against another, *V* is the inverse of that joke, a gruesome presentation of the *I* and its self-reflection as the hooded face of a terrorist. Like the opening words ("to gouge . . . to signal"), the poem is composed of infinitives, actions lacking a personal agent, finding resolution only at the end with the subject and verb of "I ended." Such infinitive actions, the poem implies, engage the speaker in an impersonal, inevitable process of actions, as though the actions were carrying him through time ("to puff through the valley") or even sending him recessively back to his origins as he struggles to advance ("to listen to the murmuring inversion of its stream / In mill-wheels"). Infinitive actions finally engulf the one who both is and is not their source: "like an avalanche, infinitive comes into it and buries me," so that the speaker ends up in his glacier, confronting his double-I (to be followed by his double-you). This almost hysterical moment, a classic instance of violent twinning, belies the self-concealing artifices of this poem and discloses a self more closely engaged with the effects of violence on the mind than at any time in Carson's previous work. This unexpected split within the speaking self, a split into a rational I and a violent I, partly explains the poet's preoccupation with figures of the self and his need to trivialize that anxiety ("I think you understand my cant"[28]). The poet cannot confront his endless fear that he and the terrorist are "Twin and Twin at each other's throats"[29]; therefore the fear breaks out, as though unconsciously, when the person is least in control of his actions, as in the string of infinitive actions in "V." As a poem of unsuccessful denial, "Letters from the Alphabet" achieves immense success.

Like some last movement or aria, Carson's concluding alphabet (appropriately titled "Opera"), is written extravagantly, *con brio*. A, B, C . . . have become *Alpha, Bravo, Charlie*. . . . Once more in alliance with Muldoon (one thinks of "The More a Man Has, the More a Man Wants"), Carson presents a postmodern montage of Northern Irish surveillance mechanisms, scenes from NPR's (or RTE's) "Mystery," pop music and pub music, golf and Shakespeare, celebrities and paparazzi, another send-up of Heaney (in "Romeo"). All this is largely lacquered over with the language of drugs (many of the poems read like a lexicon of substances; the men of stout Cortez were silent because stoned, etc.). Always entertaining, Carson's extravaganza also fuels inevitable reflections on postmodern Ireland and the replacement of traditional values by new money and all the things new money can buy.

Neither the pyrotechnics of verbal excitement nor the generalities of cultural studies, however, constitute the real work of lyric poetry. In "Opera," as in "Letters from the Alphabet" and so much of Carson's other work, the significant particulars of some speaker's mind and feelings remain hidden behind the barrage of words and images. Yet here again the poet's persona does momentarily appear, as a rare bird might, all the more dramatically for being so rarely seen. With a loud and brilliant coda, Carson returns in the last four pages of "Opera" to some of his major "themes" (mind-altering substances, urban warfare, ethnic music, and childhood memory), but does so now in a way which allows him to question, and finally assert, the existence of a speaking self.

In "Whisky" the entire ten lines of the poem constitute one sentence, arranged in a syntactical series "Of how x is y," and ending, "thereof I meant to speak." Carson places traditional drunkenness together with traditional violence: "how the water of / The Liffey becomes Guinness; how explosive cocktails take the name of Molotov," finally rendering all metamorphosis as a brutal process whereby substances violently produce altered states ("you turn into an insect overnight . . . from eating magic / Mushrooms"). Even the basic alteration which occurs when a name is added to a thing is imagined as a violence wrought upon the named thing by the namer, a tactic employed by the Greeks to keep foreigners in place: "How the tongue gets twisted, how 'barbarian' is everyone who is not Greek; / How things are named by any other name except themselves, thereof I meant to speak" (*Opera et Cetera*, 89). "I meant to" implies "but I did not," a final admission of helplessness. Under the rubric "Whisky," the fundamental act of achieving identity through naming, of adding some predicate to some subject, appears as an act of violence, placed in tandem with terrorist explosives and the violence wrought upon the mind by intoxicants.

In "X-Ray" Carson scans the detritus of Belfast, the remnants of violence ("The razor-wire; the Confidential telephone; the walls that talk of *Fuck the Pope*"). This rubbish and the surveillance systems which scrutinize them, "are nothing to the blinks and blanks of night's inscrutable eternity, which stars / The Northern sky with campfire palimpsests of ancient wars." Northern Irish traditional violence is nothing to traditions of violence as old as the stars, and these stars "are nothing to the cerebral activity of any one of us who sets in train / These zig-zags, or the brain-cells decomposing in some rebel brain." Daily urban violence and surveillance, then, are subsumed to the cosmic order (seen as no less violent) and this order is subsumed in turn to the human brain, the ultimate repository of violent chaos.

In "Yankee" the poet tells of doodling on his flute, marching and playing incognito in a twelfth of July parade, possibly recreating the same childhood scene as "On Not Remembering Some Lines of a Song." He wears dark glasses to avoid detection: "I kept my mouth shut, so to speak; / I feared my syllables of shibboleth would be interpreted as Greek." Here is the artist as flute player—Marsyas about to be flayed by Apollo—moving cautiously among his persecutors, abject victim of the violence which will ensue if he is identified. "I became a pocket of an absolute nonidentity. . . ." As in "V" of "Letters from the Alphabet," the poet allows some abstract self to appear (a calligraphic figure, a named self, a pocket of negated but absolute identity) in conditions of extreme distress. It would be convenient for poet and reader to agree here that the wages of sin is postmodernism, that the culture of violence—the only culture Carson has ever lived in—makes self-realization impossible. Let us pile word upon word, and image upon image, we might all agree, because that is all we have left: violence is written in the stars, and even the naming of a person, even that person's uttering of a name, is a violent act—like taking a drink.

So it seems: or has this whole sequence of poems, like "Queen's Gambit," only been an elaborate set-up, a ruse to make us send our thought-pawns too far into self-denial, to commit ourselves heedlessly to acts of bad faith? Finally (so the poem's "at last"), in "Zulu," Carson looks back to his childhood and (can it be?) denies the loss of center he had seemed to affirm, or, rather, affirms that self which he had seemed to deny:

> At last, I remember the half-broomstick assegai with which I used to kill
> Imaginary soldiers. I danced around them like a hound of Baskerville.
>
> I faced the typecast phalanxes of English, shielded only by a dustbin-
> Lid; sometimes, I'd *sotto voce* whistle 'The Dragoons of Inniskillin,'
>
> Till an Agincourt of arrows overwhelm'd me, shot by Milton, Keats and Shakespeare,
> And I became a redskin, foraging behind the alphabetic frontier.
>
> Pale boldface wagons drew themselves into a hurried O of barricade;
> Mounted on my hobby-horse, I whooped so much, I had to take a slug of orangeade.
>
> I loved its cold-jolt glug and fizz, tilted bottle upheld like a trumpet
> To the sun; or so it might be, in the gargled doggerel of this dumb poet.
> (*Opera et Cetera*, 92)

252 • Tongue of Water, Teeth of Stones

The final image of bottle upheld like trumpet had already appeared in "Juliet," where trumpets are upheld like bottles, and where Carson is indulging in a complicated code-discourse concerning literary affiliations (playing Juliet to Heaney's Romeo). In the earlier poem, trumpets become coke-bottles and coke becomes dope, so that the proclamations of art ("the grand piazza [of Verona] was pizzaz") are dissolved in "skywriting smoke." Carson, like Muldoon, imagines the professional literary world as another aspect of that violence which overarches, as do the stars, all experience and does violence to the self, subsuming the self into its hostile universe. "At last," however, the poet confronts his *writing* self, his boyhood self, as it emerged from wars with imaginary soldiers and entered into battle with literary armies. The literary noble savage, confronting the paleface, boldface soldiers of English type and overwhelmed by the arrows of canonical authors, insists on his primitive, savage qualities, and finally claims the right to be heard as a voice in the wilderness, an alternative poet.

Carson's brash, anti-canonical moves and his "gargled doggerel" (a post-colonial version of Tony Harrison's "On Not Being Milton" but also, with the reference back to "Juliet," a subtler, all-Irish "On Not Being Heaney") do not here constitute a cultural statement about the rights of Irish poetry or language. What Carson is doing, I think, is more interesting than that. Over four books of poetry, spanning slightly less than a decade, he has pondered the problem of the artist in a violent society, and done so in a growing and full recognition that this violence emerges from within that society and even from within the minds of its inhabitants, including himself. He has also pondered artistic ways of solving that problem: writing the Wordsworthian escape poem, the Keatsian escape poem, the Rimbaudian escape poem, the cartography escape poem, the pub-talk escape poem, and finally the Ovidian escape poem. Again and again, however, his artistic solutions have been undermined by the fact that the poems' constructed self has been an uncertain one, the voice of a person lost in a familiar world, the man who knows a place like the back of his hand but who finds that his hand has been cut off.

"How did I end up like this?" asked Heaney at the end of *North*, and then closed that book and a whole chapter of his *oeuvre*, turning to other matters. I sense that, with his "at last" in "Zulu,"

Carson has reached a similar moment in his artistic development. Holding his bottle of orangeade up to the sun like a trumpet, he seems now to have the confidence of a Whitman or a Ginsberg or even a C.K. Williams, those ancestors of his in the long-line tradition. Here at last Carson may have found a violence from within to withstand the violence from without. Until now he has struggled to imagine himself as a self rather than as a brain, or a mouth, or a set of elements, letters, or perhaps a verse. As such he has imagined himself as a locus of violence, a map of destruction, a body on which the cruel gods have written. Like his contemporaries, Carson too has represented violence in a process of coming to consciousness.

One cannot forever write from within an impasse. The artistic solution to violence, as Eagleton says, is to work through an old identity and come to a new one. Yet how much credence can one put in a *deus ex machina* such as this, a suddenly appearing self, hoisting his bottle-turned-trumpet in the last three lines of the last poem of a collection in which the self has been hidden or something seen in a bad dream? What if this arrangement of letters, poems on letters, and kaleidoscopic images were but a lengthy gambit, lulling the listener into a sleep and a forgetting, so that, with a pop, the poet can "at last" hoist the bottle of orangeade, turn it into a trumpet, and declare the birth of a writing self? The self that Carson reveals is a self that has had to struggle just to believe in its own existence. The duress the cyclist endured when subjected to interrogation in the Falls Road now appears as only symbolic of the larger, never-ending duress of a speaker without personal coordinates, without an assured sense of identity. Whatever may be the ultimate sources of Carson's elusiveness, it has been his poetic achievement to represent this struggle in becoming a self as a struggle against social violence. Carson, in "Zulu," represents himself as having arrived at a moment of change in which a new poetic persona is emerging, a self which has overcome the violence from without which had hitherto suppressed it. Now, what lies after *Z*?

This chapter would have ended with that interrogatory flourish, had not Carson revealed what lies after *Z* by publishing new poetry, including *The Twelfth of Never,* a collection of seventy-seven sonnets.[30] Consolidating his move away from long-line narrative and choosing a poetic form designed, as it were, for the presentation of a self, Carson comes forth exuberantly as a poetic persona. Or rather, selves, personae.

Carson's heteroglossia, when it bursts on the ear, sounds like many voics talking at once, but as one listens further, a number of separate voices can be identified. I counted seven. First there is the singer—usually a singer of folk songs, old Irish ballads. This voice gives way to the ventriloquist, a more literary speaker who does impressions of Emily Dickinson and Peig Sayers, Coleridge and Keats. The poetic speaker now becomes a narrator, both in the first and third persons, of tales from the 1798 rebellion and the Napoleonic Wars. Next to this raconteur sits another, a first-person narrator named Carson who tells us about his travels in Japan. Working in tandem with this voice is a political satirist who gives fictive accounts of Japanese occasions of state. The applicability of these narratives to Ireland (they feature a female president) will not be lost on Carson's Irish readers. Sometimes, when it seems as if all these voices are speaking at once, they coalesce into a new, sixth voice, that of a citizen who is ordinary in every sense except that his tales always include alteration of consciousness, the effect of drink or drugs. This voice sometimes gives way, finally, to one whom we may call "the poet," a sober, even troubled self who, in the final sonnet, takes responsibility for all that has gone before.

The title of this collection, and its historical mise en scène, will require little explanation for anyone conversant with the events in Northern Ireland of 1998. As I write—to be precise, on the thirteenth of July in that year—the much-acclaimed political "peace agreement" of Good Friday has been followed by the extreme tribal violence now being enacted as accompaniment to the annual marches of the twelfth of July. By the time this book is printed, we will have discovered to what extent Carson's phrase achieved prophetic irony—one can only hope it was not full prophetic irony. All Carson's speakers agree in implying that the crux of Northern Ireland's problems is not to be found in politics, but rather in the pre-political, tribal darkness of human behavior.

As we listen to Carson's multiple voices, they organize themselves into five discourses, all converging, finally, on the one discourse of the poet. I will omit one of these, the doubled-voice narrative of the traveler in Japan and the political satirist, as it depends largely on topical reference for its effect, and least on the presentation of a poetic persona. Of the remaining voices, we turn first to the singer and the poetic ventriloquist. Carson, the expert in folk music, breaks into snatches of Irish music throughout the sonnets, only to interrupt those lilting fourteeners, jarringly, with the hexameters of his sonnet lines. Interruption is also the theme of the poetic ventriloquist, whose sonnet in the style of Dickinson collapses into a reprise of Carson's own "The Irish for No," itself a deconstruction of Keats. Keats's Hippocrene, in the poem of that name, becomes a Bloody Mary, whose tomato juice and vodka are transsubstantiated into the blood and snow covering the ground as Napoleon's troops slaughter horses during the retreat from Moscow. The fatal kiss of Keats's Belle Dame leaves warriors insatiable for violence, not sex ("The Arterial Route"). Now the folk singer takes over again, with a send-up of the commercialized Irish folksong. If you succumb to the endearing charms of Glockamorra, the singer implies, you too may "cohabit with the living dead." The bathos of the folksinger and the ventriloquist, their Laurel and Hardy act, is a long joke about belatedness: it's no go the viewless wings (as MacNeice would have put it), it's no go the narrow fellow in the grass, it's no go the charms of Mavourneen and Dark Rosaleen— but it's more than a joke. There is a plot in this act, one encapsulated in Carson's retelling of a dream made famous by the Blasket Island writers.[31] The speaker sees a butterfly emerge from the mouth of his sleeping friend, fly across a field, enter a horse's skull through one eye-socket and emerge through another, and then fly back into the mouth of the sleeping friend who, on awakening, tells of having dreamed that he entered a wondrous palace. Standing in for the speaker who sees the butterfly, Carson gives the standard interpretation of the dream (the butterfly is the visionary soul), with its implicit celebration of the simple but deep religiosity of the Blasket islanders. The poem concludes, however, with the grim observation that "many who've elaborated on this theme / Have never seen the inside of a horse's head."

This comment grows even darker when placed in the context of other sonnets, where the inside of a beast symbolizes the last confines of violence. In "Dancers," the poem immediately following the dream-sonnet, a sinister crew of pirates dances on a floor just over a horse's head, as the headless horse stands ready to be ridden at dawn. In "Wolf Hill," after the speaker has tracked down a Yeatsian beast and slit open its carcass, the body of "little Erin, like one of the undead," is found inside. We return to Napoleon's retreat from Moscow in "Picador," where a soldier and his horse find themselves abandoned without bullets or food, surrounded by wolves (who howl like Irish banshees). "I carved the horse's belly open and I crawled / Inside. I ate her flesh for weeks, expiring by degrees. / Some day you'll find us where a horse's bones and mine are sprawled"(68). Carson's modulation of the benign, religiously allegorical dream from the Blasket Islands into a narrative of horror rejoins his other re-tellings and re-singings; his beast is indeed descended from Yeats's beast, an expression of historical doom.

The Napoleonic soldier brings us to the next set of narratives, in which Carson offers a poetic commentary on Tom Paulin's view of the rebellion of 1798. Carson's carefree, deranged ruffian of that period, Captain Rock ("Wallop the Spot"), believes in "the future history / Of Ireland free, where beauties waited to be born." Last *seen,* the captain is hanging on a gallows. Next *heard,* "his skin was someone's drum, / His tibiae and humeri were Orange flutes." Like Paulin, Carson represents those early dreams of a free and equal republic (dreams as insubstantial, in Carson's view, as contemporary Keats's dreams of his nightingale) as tragically transformed into the mutual sectarian hatreds of today's Northern Ireland. Here, lest it be thought that Carson himself is indulging in partisanship, he pairs a voice from one side with a voice from the other, so that Captain Rock's tale is followed in "The Lily Rally" by that of the captain's counterpart, burned in a papist bonfire and whistling "The Protestant Boys" as he dies. Perhaps the most interesting sonnet of this group—the one most clearly turning in the direction of Carson's unified discourse—is "1798," ostensibly written as an aisling, the style of Irish allegory in which the poet meets a romantic female who symbolizes whatever version of ideal Ireland the writer wishes to espouse (in this case "her pallid lips were red with Papal Spanish wine"). This particular enchantress possesses the second sight and prophesies that the poet will abandon Ireland. Kissing him, she sucks broken English from his Gaelic tongue. In an Ovidian gesture, she then winds him "in her briary arms of Eglantine," an embrace in which he and she have remained for two centuries, abiding "like emblems of a rebel song no longer sung"(39). By ventriloquizing the voice of an Irish bard of 1798, the poet of 1998 divides his consciousness, raising an insoluble doubt as to who is guilty of abandoning Ireland, his ancestor or he. In "Manifest," a grimmer version of "1798," a ghostly captain cuts off the poet's head for being unable to answer "what I had thought or done or said / To make Old Ireland free, or had I fought at Waterloo?"(63). Captain Rock was last seen hanging in the early nineteenth century, and next heard as the material for Orange flutes and dreams. Carson's bard was last heard in 1798, and since then only seen and not heard, with his political interior paramour, as the emblem, not the refrain, of a rebel song. Carson's nostalgias, whether for Keatsian flight or bardic political song, now prompt new resonances, those of a troubled, yet strong voice, strong enough to utter his contemporary cynicism in the tones of ancient idealism.

Carson's purely contemporary speaker, that loose-living fellow, now provides us with an important new discourse. Like Keats, Carson uses the drowsy numbness brought on by opiates as a way of escaping from the present and (in Carson's case) of retreating into the past: "I plunged my head into the laudanum-black pall / And gazed into the crystal lens of yesteryear" ("Fairground Music"[21]). Over against the gathering stupor of the past lies the future, into which one enters suddenly and with total loss of consciousness, as from "alcohol and gauze" or "a condom time-bomb": "then everything was over in about a sec." One cannot but think of Muldoon when Carson uses alterations of consciousness as a double emblem, first of regressive escape from a hostile present into pleasure, but then of sudden entrapment in present and future violence. *The Twelfth of Never*, in this sense, is Carson's "The More A Man Has," or his "Madoc." "Drunk as a bee," in "Twelfth Day," the poet lies in a field listening to all the insects murmuring, as though he had a radio turned down to "insect decibel," but "someone turned the volume up in Portadown, / And then I heard the whole field pulsing like an Orange drum"(57). Given Portadown's notoriety as the focal point of Orange anger, especially in July 1997 and 1998, one suspects that "Twelfth Day" may acquire special distinction in the annals of political verse. (As "The Lily Rally" followed "Wallop the Spot," Carson follows this attack on the Orange Order with an equally strong attack on the Ancient Order of Hibernians.)

When we are tipsy, our reflections sometimes stare at us from the mirror as hostile others. Carson's drunk man—this latest version of his familiar *vir bonus,* confused and lost in his own city—now appears as lost in time, somewhere between past dream and present reality. Carson's intoxicated personae multiply within himself, staring back at him as he experiences the dividedness of historical change. As his Napoleonic narrator tells of those fallen in the Egyptian campaign, he adds, "We'd hear the footsteps of their walking mummied dead / Retreating into the shifting interior." The interior which shifts—it even shifts metrically, in the ambiguous scansion of a five-word hexameter—is that of a Jungian psyche experiencing previous historical moments as various aspects of the self. So the poem continues: "Murmuring the names of our selves, that they might be known, / We'd carve them with our bayonets on a Pharaoh's head. / Let you trace them in a future black as the Rosetta stone"(82). When Yeats, in "Easter, 1916," murmured name upon name, he was reciting the roll call of specific actors on a stage of history, the condemned rebels of the Easter Rising. In a significant mutation, Carson's soldiers murmur the different names of themselves, the various aspects of their shifting interiors; they warn that these murmurings may be unintelligible in the future. The following poem ("Legions of the Dead") continues this reflection, strongly equating historical violence with unintelligibility ("their armies were composed of hieroglyphic men"), but concluding with the belief that the hieroglyphs might be read, and the multiple personae reconciled, within the psyche: "Opposing soldiers are at one within our regimen." In "Heart of Oak," the penultimate poem of the book, the speaker (is he the old soldier or the modern drunk?) starts to come to, and in doing so he appropriates everything from the past which might be of use—"Only the guns and shot were completely useless. / I left them there to rust when I regained my liberty." These lines speak with allegorical plainness. Carson has superimposed multiple voices, multiple times, and multiple places, representing them phenomenologically as a state of inebriation, but a state from which one must *come to.* To what? To a unified consciousness, to a strong sense of self. Such a sense of self is nowhere given: yesterday's political dreams have become today's mutual antagonisms; yesterday's folk-songs have become today's commodified kitsch; yesterday's romantic discourse has become today's cliché. What can the poet do? He can, as Carson does, allow the chaos of history to reproduce itself as the stupor of a drugged self, and then proceed to work through the miasma, both playfully and courageously, as he comes to a unified, reconstructed consciousness.

Switch, then, to the last voice, one often muted and more often interrupted, the voice of the sober, troubled poet, who can write a whole sonnet about the things he fears. Well, not always sober. Taking on the voice of the Napoleonic soldier, the poet (in "Crack") confesses to a wild night in which his companions got him intoxicated, dressed him as a woman, and took him to the body of the dead captain (who "looked like William Blake"). "Come dawn, they asked me to fulfill my woman's role. / I breathed smoke into him, and said the Backwards Creed. / His eyes sprang open, and I saw his very soul"(54). As woman, not man, exhaling, not inhaling, and saying the creed backwards, not forwards, the poet (who has spent the night chasing Blake's burning tiger) becomes his culture's opponent for the express purpose of opening the eyes of the dead (beginning with himself), seeing into the very soul. Here Carson appropriates the Yeatsian esoteric figure of the poet, tracing him (and her) back to Blake, putting Yeats's spiritualist genie in a bottle of strong ale and claiming the right to gaze into souls for his "ordinary" drunkard. This claim is fueled by more than a democratic impulse to modulate from a lofty to a mundane voice. Carson also wishes to appropriate Yeats's prophetic role, the voice of "Leda" and "The Second Coming," but insists that this voice speak from within, not from above, the filthy modern tide. He unites transcendent vision and historical tragedy in "The Display Case," where the poet sees Hibernia in a vision and must write her words on his body with his blood ("I opened up a vein")—words which may now be read on a disembodied arm, salvaged from the scaffold where the poet-victim was quartered.

But sober, finally, in the last poem ("Envoy"), where the poet bids farewell to the reader who has finished the poems and reawakened, having "travelled through the Land of Nod and Wink [Ulster, Heaney's land of wink and nod], / And sucked the pap of *papaver somniferum* [poppy]." Having come to, we now realize that "everything is slightly out of synch." No ink is indelible; all news is unreliable. In his final sestet, the poet arranges all his creatures, everyone from maidens to headless men, on a "long ladder

propped against the gates of Heaven." The poet ironically repre-
sents this scene as a parable of service and reward: "They're queued
up to be rewarded for their grand endeavour, / To receive their
campaign haloes on the Twelfth of Never"(89). End of book. This
wonderful image, with its oxymoronic "campaign halo," first play-
fully reminds us of the most radical stimulus to violence in North-
ern Ireland, the religious conviction on both sides that *we* will be
rewarded with campaign haloes and *they* will not. Secondly, the
ladder on which angels ascend and descend may remind us of Jacob's
dream—a dream of the place where the terrestrial and celestial come
into contact. And what is that place, the rabbis of old used to ask,
if not the meeting place of body and soul, the human person? "Of
maidens, soldiers, presidents and plants I've sung; / Of fairies, fishes,
horses, and of headless men; / Of beings from the lowest to the
highest rung." Boldly, Carson takes his procession of personages
marching horizontally through time, joins them with an imaginary
world of fairies and fishes, and upends the lot, rearranging them
vertically on a ladder, so that the horizontal "never" becomes a
vertical "no/where." "Now/here" is in fact the ladder's accurate
location; the only place where maidens and soldiers, presidents and
plants may be reconciled is within an individual consciousness.
Carson's poet has entered into his stupor and reawakened, work-
ing through the violent historical chaos of Northern Ireland as a
phenomenon of inner dividedness and multiplicity. He has fulfilled
the trumpet-hoisting prediction of "Z;" his strong voice now
struggles to reconcile multiple conflicts in that first, indispensable
place of political confrontation, the poem, where the deepest men-
tal roots of violence are unearthed.

8

MEDBH MCGUCKIAN

Sperm names, ovum names, push inside
each other.
                              —*Captain Lavender*

"I began to write poetry so that nobody would read it," said Medbh
McGuckian to Nuala Ní Dhomhnaill in 1992, claiming full owner-
ship of the cryptic style which has set her apart from her Northern
Irish contemporaries, even Muldoon.[1] Until the publication of *Cap-
tain Lavender* in 1995, McGuckian's obdurately coded verse, pre-
occupied with a secret inner world, had resisted critics' efforts to
read her poetry in some public context. If Peggy O'Brien's advice to
"admire what we cannot understand" represented a widely shared
view of McGuckian, it was difficult to see what more could be said
about her.[2] With the publication of *Captain Lavender* in the mid-
nineties, however, McGuckian has offered more accessible poetry
while also touching down on the terrain of Northern Irish political
poetry, leaving on that landscape a print of her own making.
    Dwelling on the facts that McGuckian was female in gender,
private in subject matter, and idiosyncratic in style, many of the
critics dealing with her earlier work—*The Flower Master* (1982),
Venus and the Rain (1984), *On Ballycastle Beach* (1988), *Marconi's
Cottage* (1991)—enlisted McGuckian as a feminist, leftist and
postmodernist poet. Now that *Captain Lavender* has appeared, these
initial assessments may be seen as premature. Because McGuckian's
new book really does deal with Northern Irish politics, it imposes

262 • Tongue of Water, Teeth of Stones

on us a twofold task: first to see what she was and was not doing in her previous, nonpolitical poems, and then to see exactly what she is doing here. Full justice can scarcely be done to both tasks in one chapter (a full-length study of McGuckian is needed), but since the topic of this book calls for a consideration of *Captain Lavender*, I must give a sense of McGuckian's earlier style and my reasons for thinking that it is not political.

Most predictably, critics writing in the late eighties read McGuckian as a writer of sexual politics, inscribing female experience into the patriarchal canon of Irish poetry.[3] That could be: if one thinks of the specifically masculine character of Northern Irish violence, an aspect emphasized in the work of McGuckian's contemporaries Paulin and Muldoon, one can easily conceive of a Northern Irish female poet taking up arms against the patriarchy in which she lives. The difficulty is that, although her work is undeniably feminine—many poems in the first four volumes deal with pregnancy and childbirth—it resists alignment with feminist discourse. "I'm for feminism," McGuckian candidly admits, "as long as it doesn't destroy in the woman what is the most precious to her, which is her ability to relate and soften and make a loving environment for others as well as herself. . . . I find feminism attractive in theory but in practice I think it ends up influenced by lesbians and— very lonely and embittered and stressed and full of hatred."[4] To an unblinking feminist, these adjectives appear to chain McGuckian more tightly than ever to traditional male-dominated Irish society. It remains for individual exegesis to determine whether or not McGuckian's verse strikes out for a brave new female world; in the first four books her cryptic style discouraged such efforts.

A second approach, making a virtue of McGuckian's obscurity, characterizes her as postmodern in her fracturing of the self, the lyrical "I."[5] Rejecting readings of McGuckian as narcissistic or self-obsessed, Wills sees her style as overturning that "stable and secure centre, a grounding for the authenticity of personal experience,"[6] the self which she and David Lloyd have identified as a hallmark of colonialist oppression. The theoretical issue of the self, amply discussed elsewhere in this book, may be left aside here in favor of a factual question of style: does McGuckian in fact fracture the lyric self within her poems? I doubt it, since she says, "My work is almost totally autobiographic."[7] I doubt it further when, commenting on a translation of Ní Dhomhnaill in which she replaces an impersonal pronoun with a personal one, she says, "Whereas [Nuala] is trusting the quietness, and can do without the personal, I can't."[8]

It is time for an example. The title poem of McGuckian's second major collection, "Venus and the Rain," deals with the circumstances surrounding the birth of McGuckian's first child:

White on white, I can never be viewed
Against a heavy sky—my gibbous voice
Passes from leaf to leaf, retelling the story
Of its own provocative fractures, till
Their facing coasts might almost fill each other
And they ask me in reply if I've
Decided to stop trying to make diamonds.

On one occasion, I rang like a bell
For a whole month, promising their torn edges
The birth of a new ocean (as all of us
Who have hollow bodies tend to do at times):
What clues to distance could they have,
So self-excited by my sagging sea,
Widening ten times faster than it really did?

Whatever rivers sawed their present lairs
Through my lightest, still-warm rocks,
I told them they were only giving up
A sun for sun, that cruising moonships find
Those icy domes relaxing, when they take her
Rind to pieces, and a waterfall
Unstitching itself down the front stairs.
(*Venus and the Rain*, 31)

Clair Wills, who has interviewed McGuckian on several occasions, omits the autobiographical implications of this work from her analysis, preferring instead to treat it as a puzzle poem or enigma.[9] For Wills, as perhaps for any reader, this poem presents two views of a woman: Venus, the ideal figure of love, and Venus in the rain, the woman subject to the manifold consequences of

264 • Tongue of Water, Teeth of Stones

sexual processes. Commenting on stanza 1 ("provocative fractures"), Wills hears the poetic voice "seducing or provoking the reader by fractures or gaps, promises of future significance." In her close reading Wills discusses each obscurity and ambiguity as a continuation of the riddle, the postponement of meaning, and concludes: "The 'truth' of woman is that, although she can be charted (as the planet Venus has been), she cannot be 'known' and thereby appropriated. The alternative narrative in McGuckian's poems is not perhaps a way of expressing female experience, but a way of resisting invasion." Wills, of course, means invasion of the female by the male, and so, via Barthes' hermeneutics and Irigaray's feminism, she is able to enlist this poem as part of a sexually political discourse.

"Venus and the Rain," like its companion pieces "Venus and the Sun" and the later "Venus and the Sea," places the sexual speaker in touch with elemental male forces.[10] Playing with images taken from sciences of sky and earth, as does Adrienne Rich in "Planetarium," McGuckian allows her speaker both to imagine such forces as overpowering but then to internalize them, to appropriate them to her own inner space. In doing so she imaginatively repeats the processes of conception and birth. Venus gets pregnant, and therefore she loses her distinctive character as Venus: "white on white," she can barely be seen against a sky full of the rain which fills her body. It doesn't take a long stretch of the imagination to sense that her "gibbous voice" refers to two mouths: the vocal orifice and the sexual orifice, the latter with its gibbous changes of shape, its provocative fractures, its sagging sea, and its widening to ten times its normal size. At first the sexual mouth, proud at having put forth a child, taunts the narrative mouth, asking when it will stop trying to make diamond-like poems and start acting more like a mother. After speaking of the exciting sexual events leading up to birth ("rang like a bell"), Venus retreats within her body, imagining it as a physiological Xanadu where (as they say) the sun doesn't shine, and where sacred rivers flow in as an erosive trickle from a sexual partner and flow out as the waterfall of birth. In each stanza Venus ("I") remembers conversing with her body: she hears a troublesome question from her sexual mouth (will you still write poems?); she replies with a promise ("birth of a new ocean"). Finally—most daringly—she addresses the sperm within

her, the alien "cruising moonships" in her body, welcoming them
to their new home and predicting their life to come. Venus, whose
separate existence appears first as compromised against the back-
ground of male sexuality (white on white), succeeds in creating
beautiful spaces *within* her body, so that she can emerge as faithful
both to her individuality (Venus) and to the sexual processes which
form her destiny (rain, rivers, moonships). Not that Venus really
achieves a conclusion to her dialogue: while speaking to the
moonships, she allows these alien guests to take over her discourse
in the final three lines, converting her to an object in the third per-
son, one which is being taken to pieces (peeled, flooded, unstitched,
thrown downstairs), overwhelmed again.

Here as elsewhere, McGuckian wages an inward debate with
her immediate environment—domestic, emotional, biological. One
can comb her poems for points of contact with a public world, but
the task is an ungrateful one. Wills, to be sure, acknowledges
McGuckian's privacy in this poem, the "tension . . . between her
wish to represent the self . . . and her wariness of opening herself up
in public," but insists that the poet uses this tension to "[restruc-
ture] the relationship between public and private narratives. The
personal narrative becomes a metaphor for a public and political
one." Where is the evidence for this move to public discourse? By
maintaining the privacy of her subject matter, McGuckian locates
her poems within a long tradition of non-political lyric poetry. By
maintaining the privacy of her style, she intensifies that inward-
ness, as if her choice to withdraw from the political were her own
way of responding to the Northern Irish *Zeitgeist*, the literary world
of responsible writing. So far from fracturing the lyric self, then,
the earlier McGuckian uses her "I" to absorb the surrounding world
into her commanding, inward self.

Calvin Bedient, writing in 1990, comes closest to an accurate
estimate of the early McGuckian when he writes, "No, she's not
Catholic Ireland's daughter, after all . . . she's the heir, however
captious, of the Romantics."[11] Erotic, domestic, sensitive to detail,
and private, McGuckian uses changes of perspective and incoher-
ence as a way of protecting her lyric self from public scrutiny while
offering it for public admiration (so that we can admire what we
cannot understand).

Attempts to draft McGuckian into the Troubles have proved

no less difficult than efforts to coopt her into the sexual and cultural wars. In 1990, when asked, "So . . . you choose not to deal with the Irish Troubles or with war?" McGuckian lost no time in replying, "Oh God no. Oh, no, I couldn't. I mean, how could I? I can't even sit through the films of that."[12] Other *obiter dicta* give further credence to Bedient's judgment, such as her rejection of the grim tones of post-war political poetry from Eastern Europe in favor of an unreflective artistic optimism: "I don't want to hear [the "negative" poetry of Piotr Sommers]. I just want to begin again and have a new romanticist view, the friends of the earth and all that. OK, that's phony, but it's so very important, the conservation thing."[13] Her forays into the "language question," that obligatory conversation piece for Irish writers, quickly involve her in contradictions. After complaining that "my son is growing up speaking English, whereas his soul is Irish, so that's a pity," McGuckian in almost the same breath declares that "the Irish language isn't strong enough to *hold* what I want to say, or what a lot of people want to say. It hasn't evolved. It's a dead language."[14] There is not much here to suggest that McGuckian has any strong interest in extending or deepening the political dimensions of her poetry, that we should try to see her as other than, in O'Brien's happy phrase, "a literalist of the feelings."[15] While it is true, as Ann Beer maintains, that McGuckian's poetic emphasis on maternal values constitutes an implicit argument against the masculine and the bellicose, the argument thus far remains implicit, formulated by critics far more than by the poems themselves.[16] To be born a poet in Ulster, as Heaney long ago pointed out, does not require that one have a microphone at one's lips. When McGuckian talks about responsibility, she means motherhood.[17]

Bedient, who in 1990 recognized that McGuckian was a very private person, wrote that "should [she] splash cold water on her face and write about the torn civil war around her, the results might be flat. (Or they might be astonishing.)"[18] In 1995, by publishing *Captain Lavender*, Medbh McGuckian did indeed splash cold water on her face. Whereas the focal points of her previous works, her pregnancies and the births of her children, were expressed in hermetic metaphors, regressive techniques of merging her identity with that of her erotic and maternal worlds,[19] the two parts of *Captain Lav-*

ender are organized around two events resistant to regression. The death of her father and her experiences of teaching both Roman Catholic and Protestant political prisoners in Northern Ireland's Maze Prison now force her to clarify, for herself and for us, her separateness from the objective world.[20]

So great a step is this demarcation of self from world in defining the style of her most recent poems that McGuckian devotes the first poem of the collection, "Lines for Thanksgiving," to its establishment. The two floors of her house and the staircase joining them may, she reflects, be seen as a means of establishing togetherness (the two floors are "interwoven like the materials for a nest") or, conversely, as a form of separation: the staircase is "crouching muscularly," as if to push, keeping the floors "as gracefully apart / as a calvary from a crib." Whereas the world of the crib is an unconscious one, the adult world of calvary is, or should be, one of conscious and difficult choice. Only through choice can one realize a higher destiny—make one's road a saint's calvary (so "the stranger me . . . is satisfied / by any street with the solemn name of a saint"). This poem's thanksgiving celebrates, as though it had been won only after a long struggle, the separation of calvary from crib, of consciously chosen adult experience from unconscious submission to natural forces: "If I had just won a victory / it was over everything that was not / myself, by the water's edge" (*Captain Lavender* [CL], 13). Giving thanks for the achievement of objectivity, the poet also celebrates the end of regressive metaphor, the secret code-language used both to hide her self from public scrutiny and to refuse conscious separateness from an objective world.

McGuckian prefaces *Captain Lavender*, her fifth major collection, with an epigraph, words from a letter Picasso wrote during World War II: "I have not painted the war . . . but I have no doubt that the war is in . . . these paintings I have done." *Captain Lavender*, then, will somehow deal with the Troubles. Since social violence may be traced to fundamental difficulties of individuals in establishing separate personal identities, "Lines for Thanksgiving," where she speaks of the war between self and object, or between self as infant and self as adult, may be read as McGuckian's poetic entry into the Troubles.[21] It would be a salutary exercise—although the work of another day—to reread McGuckian's first four works in the light of her new-found objectivity, and to realize that Venus's submission to the rain, her ultimate coming undone beneath the paring knife and the unstitched waterfall, do indeed (as Beer argued) betoken female submission to a process which the poet imagines as inherently violent. A work such as Muldoon's "Anseo," published just four years earlier than "Venus and the Rain," sketches the male child's unconscious submission to violence, but does so with the sardonic acuity of a sober observer. Muldoon's rod of hazel, Heaney's shovel, Mahon's mushrooms, and Carson's maps symbolize scenes of violence which, by being held at arm's length, help to bring their lyric observer to consciousness. In her own poems of the war, McGuckian acknowledges that, until now, she has been unable to objectify violence, that her consciousness of violence has been confined to her body and to its immediate selfobjects (lover, ex-lover, husband, children). The very fact that she can now declare that the war is in her poems constitutes ample material for giving thanks—thanks for the gift of objectivity.

In her published conversation with Nuala Ní Dhomhnaill, undertaken in December, 1992, McGuckian speaks in detail about her father's wake and so provides a necessary background for Part 1 of *Captain Lavender*. The day before the funeral she approached the open coffin of her father, whom she had adored, and kissed him "for the first time ever. I decided I'd kiss his lips, and it was the strangest thing, you know, to kiss your father's lips, and no one else there and I felt as if it was a rape of him and in some way that he didn't mind. I felt that some part of me was taking advantage of him because we never would have done that, or I never would have done it." Here McGuckian enacts the role of her father's true lover, since Irish custom requires that, at the closing of the coffin, the wife give her spouse a public farewell kiss. When that moment occurred, McGuckian tells us, she judged her mother's kiss to have been an awkward one. Understanding "how numb she must have felt at that time and how difficult warmth of that kind, after such inhibition, would have been," the daughter attempted to give her own mother a kiss, but

> she just pushed me away in front of everyone. My kiss to her was refused, and she did it again in the chapel. And when that kind of thing happens to me, I think, "Thanks be to God, I can deal with it, because of my poetry." I

can deal with the Troubles and I can deal with that and I
can deal with my father's death. I imagine I can deal with
everything, but the poetry is the dealing, and without the
poetry it would be a bullet in the head or the mental
home.[22]

Three moments emerge here, each one essential to understand-
ing the poems which follow. First, in kissing her father as she does
(and telling the world about it), McGuckian imagines herself to be
redressing a lifetime of love refused. Second, in being rebuffed by
her mother (and telling the world about that too), she imagines the
reign of refusal to be continuing. Third, McGuckian equates such
refusal of love with the Troubles, and tells us that she deals with
both matters in her poetry. Such are the touchstones of intimacy
which mark McGuckian's points of entry into the discourse of the
Troubles.
   So it is that, before considering her feelings for her father,
McGuckian takes up her mother's refusals of love in "Porcelain
Bells," the second poem of the collection.[23] In this painfully resent-
ful work, after cryptically recounting the incidents surrounding the
wake and unflinchingly portraying her unloving mother as a hos-
tile civic space ("You are walled round, a too-well-laid-out path"),
McGuckian takes the step of fully equating her mother's spiritual
condition with that of her city, Belfast: ". . . even as you refuse to
be understood, / like your city in which nothing / is ever forgiven."
In the poem's conclusion, McGuckian imagines herself as a quasi-
divine being—here she looks back at Carson's avenging angel and
forward to *Captain Lavender*'s ending—able to bring some saving
rebirth both to her mother and to the soil which produced her: "I
would hold like a resurrection / to my breath . . . I will dive you
back to earth / and pull it up with you."
   Among all Northern Irish poetry concerned with social vio-
lence, "Porcelain Bells" may be the unique case of a poem dealing
with female violence—violence in the Girardian sense of internecine
hostility between members of a community unable to find a scape-
goat as receptor for their hostile impulses. Whereas in poems by
Ulster males the warring citizens are typically trapped in a space
created by England, here we have women trapped in a space cre-
ated by men—a familiar enough theme in literature, but nonethe-

less a remarkable one in this political context. Leading us away from the personal foci of psychoanalysis and biographical detail, McGuckian objectively symbolizes the refusal of kisses, the positioning of "chairs in faraway countries," and the city where nothing is forgiven. To deal with such suffering is to deal with the Troubles, she says, making it clear that she and her mother both suffer as victims of a loveless world in which the divisive object of desire is the simultaneously longed-for lover and father, himself the archetypal author of love's prohibition. Having long been dominated in mind and body by the sexual male and by the children gotten on her, McGuckian can show the hostility dividing mothers from daughters as a further legacy of the male, who wills hostility precisely by being the object of desire. If there is to be a solution to such hostility, the poem implicitly argues, it must be sought in new erotic creations.

McGuckian's subsequent poem to her dead father begins, then, with the same event of the kiss ("You give me your mouth uncluttered / by ordinary corrupt human love") and quickly puts on incorruption, as her father begins his "astral journey" (so this section of the poem is appropriately titled "Faith"): "You are giving the name of islands / to the wave of onrushing clouds."[24] But this pilgrimage to the sky only represents the hostile male-female scenario once again (think of Heaney's sky-born Hercules and mould-hugging Antaeus as man and woman), giving the daughter yet another grievance against her love-refusing father. McGuckian speaks of all this in her conversation with Nuala Ní Dhomhnaill:

> Recently at Annaghmakerrig, two weeks after my father's death, I showed Derek Mahon a poem I'd written. The theme of the poem was me and my father and what had happened to him and how I was left here abandoned and he's gone off on his space journey, and he says, "Where do the rows end?" ["rows" to rhyme with "cows" = arguments] So then I began to feel, well, I can pay tribute to my father best by adopting his maleness, by ending my rows in a male way, and maybe that would be one way of embedding my father, it would be one way of . . . because he was a man, let's face it.[25]

McGuckian's way of answering Mahon (to whom she dedicates

the poem) and of ending the row with her father is indeed to be-
come male. Deciding to accompany her father on his journey by
playing Icarus to his Daedalus, she uses her Joycean stance (enti-
tling part 2 of the poem "Et animum dimittit" and part 4 "ignotas
in artes") to transform female abjection into artistic rather than
specifically male power. Even on this astral flight, however, her
father cannot easily escape the hostility of his culture, which pur-
sues him like a lethal weapon, a knife hurled at his back:

> as if he could forget so soon
> the finer taste, the finer terror,
> of that mute province we call home,
> in the sense that we know home.
> ("The Appropriate Moment," CL, 22)

Instead of perpetuating the quarrel of daughter with father, the
poet erases the terms of the quarrel by joining her father on his
journey and revisions the father-daughter quarrel as "the finer ter-
ror of that mute province." By dealing with her father's death, she
is dealing with the Troubles.

Paradoxically such a metamorphosis of the self requires a
strong sense of original identity. It does not escape the poet's notice
that, in her previous state of subjection, she wrote and thought in
regressive metaphors which merged her with the objects around
her, obliterating her sense of self. Now, however, that she has won
her victory "over everything that was not myself," she can success-
fully fuse herself with other being and talk about it . "They say that
I am not I, / but some kind of we, that I do not know / where I
end," she wryly writes in this poem, at just the moment when she
can objectively consider boundaries and how they are crossed ("I
feel my body poured into all the seasons"). No less wryly, she inter-
rogates her father about such crossings ("Do you see an action in
that, in your general thirsting after death?"), recognizing this im-
pulse as a wish for death and transmuting it into a consciously
expressed call for artistic and erotic self-transformation: "I still have
to grow into your face." As Icarus and Daedalus climb the sky "in
long spirals, / sitting square, talking / with immense satisfaction of
death," the poet realizes the true, greater dimensions of meaning to
which this individual death ("death on the small scale / of a marine

insect") is bringing her: ". . . this body-breaking journey / was the leap of a torn-out heart / decaying, locked and magical, / into untenanted, uninhabitable space." As decaying, the heart refuses love, refuses kisses; as locked, it remains trapped within the confines of the loveless Province; as magical, it can yet be transformed by the power of art and transported into a new space, one in which no one has yet taken up residence (and we know what happened to Icarus).

When Mahon (whom Heaney once called "the Stephen Dedalus of Belfast") asks where the rows—the cycles of familial lovelessness and provincial hostility—end, McGuckian responds by "adopting . . . maleness," adopting Joyce's version of sonship and artistic self-transformation. In so doing she incorporates more of Joyce's vision into this poem than Heaney does in his more famous encounter with the dead poet in "Station Island 12."[26] There Joyce's message was merely one to an individual poet—to forget "that subject people stuff" and to write for the love of writing. McGuckian, twenty years later, embraces a vaster idea of "ignotas artes"—arts which are unknown, not just because the poet has never practiced them, but because no one has ever practiced them. McGuckian here represents herself as aspiring, in a way which Heaney avoided, to Stephen's vocation as bard to the race and its uncreated conscience. Having grown up and written in an atmosphere where every line was examined for political correctness, Heaney felt an insistent need to escape from the merely political and to search for inwardness. McGuckian, having previously marked out for herself an inner, obscure territory where objective points of reference could only be guessed at, now escapes from mere inwardness into an attempt at synthesizing private and public worlds, derived from the early Joyce.

The myth of Daedalus and Icarus cannot, however, long sustain McGuckian in her post-death flight with her father, since Daedalus lives and Icarus dies. Feeling, as filial artist, the need to help her dead parent, McGuckian turns to the Christian story of Dives and Lazarus:

If I had dipped the tip of my finger
in water to cool your tongue,
you would have tasted salt off trees

forty miles from the sea.
("Field Heart," *CL*, 37)

Anyone who dies is like Dives, needing comfort from others; anyone alive is like Lazarus, removed from the dead by a great space, a space here envisioned as geographical. In the story, it is only distance which separates Dives from Lazarus; in McGuckian's text, it is also the fact that, in Ulster, the living have nothing but salt to place on the tongues of the dead. Who will help whom? In further myths about death, those of the "tunnel experience" and of the liberated soul coming to the aid of the living, McGuckian again reimagines her father, now coming to her aid and that of all the Irelands:

You were now inside a lift
rising between two floors, no longer noticeable,
being whipped like the cork of a champagne bottle
out through a dark and narrow shaft
or rushing valley, into a higher frequency,
a faster vibration—into all the Irelands!

Bring your loosened soul near,
look through,
meet my day-consciousness
in the lawfulness of what is living:
return a different June to me—
once only, slide
until the union holds.
(CL 38)

Here it is as if the poet is Dives and her dead father Lazarus, sent to comfort the tortured souls of the province, to meet their "day-consciousness" and to give them a "union" with each other, one considerably different from what the Northern Irish commonly understand that word to mean. McGuckian extends this romantic vision in "Black Note Study," where memories of playing four-hand piano music with her father are turned to idealistic allusions to Ireland's four green fields, an imagined music of the spheres, as it were, coming to occupy the everyday space of Irish life.[27]

McGuckian concludes Part 1 of *Captain Lavender* with a new kind of seriousness, different in tone from the personal struggles of "Porcelain Bells" and "The Appropriate Moment" or the fanciful flights of "Field Heart" and "Black Note Study." In "Elegy for an Irish Speaker" and "The Aisling Hat," she turns to formal literary modes—elegy, aisling, and also keen—which fully enshrine her father's death and her own grief within a public space. The opening lines of the elegy (the first two together comprise one line of iambic pentameter, the next two a drawn-out fourteener) resonate with pure sonorities unlike anything that one accustomed to McGuckian's arhythmic images would expect:

> Numbered day,
> night only just beginning,
> be born very slowly, stay
> with me, impossible to name.
> (*CL*, 42)

To characterize her father as an Irish speaker, admits McGuckian, "is completely crazy because he never spoke Irish, but he should have."[28] On her account the poem is all about redeeming her father from his name Albert and from the apparent shame of his having had to die in the Royal Victoria Hospital and be buried on Prince Charles Way. McGuckian, however, does not always do full justice to her work: her elegy presents a more complex and intriguing answer to the question, why an Irish speaker? In Plathian accents the poet apostrophizes "Miss Death" as the new heroine who will mate with her own hero. Challenging Miss Death, she writes,

> Are you waiting to be fertilized,
> dynamic death, by his dark company?
> To be warmed in your wretched
> overnight lodgings
> by his kind words and small talk
> and powerful movements?
> He breaks away from your womb
> to talk to me,
> he speaks so with my consciousness

and not with words, he's in danger
of becoming a poetess.
(CL, 42)

Who is Miss Death, waiting for someone to fertilize her, shiv-
ering in her wretched lodgings? One thinks of that famous Irish
lady, the Shan Van Vocht or poor old woman, waiting for her lover
to come and turn her into the fair damsel she once was. (Prolong-
ing the nationalist frame of reference, she has her father emerge
from death's tunnel into "all the Irelands.") Father is an Irish speaker
because he embraces Miss Death, the representative of Irish women
or of Ireland itself—longing for the male who will never fulfill her
needs, suffering under the male who binds her with chains.
    This particular Cathleen, though, must compete with the poet
herself, and so replaces McGuckian's mother as the hated rival for
her father's love. The Irish that he will now speak is not, in fact, a
Hibernian tongue but one whose words are feelings, not sounds, a
means of uniting selves to supplant the "knitting together of your
two spines," which father and Miss Death were enacting. Nor should
we suppose that the daughter-poet makes this gift of speech to her
father (that would be the Joycean fancy); it is his silent language
which she craves from him. Nor again should we imagine this as a
trivial Oedipal wish: what the poet really wants from the dead fa-
ther is that he be her ideal reader: "Most foreign and cherished
reader, / I cannot live without / your trans-sense language." Fulfill-
ing the ideal parental role, father will be the one who always un-
derstands, and in doing so he will give life and meaning to his
daughter's poetry. Father can only exercise his role as ideal reader
when dead and therefore schooled in "trans-sense language." Fi-
nally, then, the poet herself is Miss Death, celebrating the death of
her father (a Plathian daddy) and *her* consequent liberation into all
the Irelands—into public, objective and effective speech. In order
for the male both to fulfill the daughter-poet and to free her, he
must free his spirit from its "frozen body" by dying and at last
listen to her unspoken thoughts in his trans-sense language. By lis-
tening he will rejuvenate her and she will save him. As a hag, Miss
Death is Ireland; if the male is to rejuvenate Miss Death, he must
first die.
    Whereas, in "Elegy for an Irish Speaker," McGuckian aspires

to the grave density of Kinsella's elegies for O'Riada, the longer "Aisling Hat" echoes rather the desperate lyricism of Muldoon's "Incantata." In a poem of forty-seven three-line stanzas (the Dantean formal sign for a journey to the other world), the speaker is largely preoccupied with lament and praise, praise and lament, as she remembers father's beauty even at the moment of death: "Your golden hands like hills / of tired rags stirred up the dust, / flushed horseman, streaked feldspar" (CL, 46).

Her keen is an aisling because, as in "Elegy," she anticipates receiving a gift from the beloved whose loss she bemoans: "I search for a lost, unknown song / in a street as long as a night, / stamped with my own surname" (CL, 44). We recall from "Lines for Thanksgiving" that "stranger me that is satisfied / by any street with the solemn name of saint" and we can now recognize that street, named for the poet's beatific self, as the long passage of her father's death, leading to erotic and artistic freedom, to empowerment for speech to all the Irelands. The keen, accordingly, changes to aisling toward the poem's end, when "I felt a shiver of novelty / as if someone had summoned you / by name, to the most beautiful applause" (CL, 47). Father is no longer in danger of becoming a poetess; rather "he controls my hair, my fingernails, / he swallows my saliva." Now, however, this assimilation of one person to another is a conscious one, so that the poet can say, "I need to get to know his bones" (as she had earlier said, "I still have to grow into your face").[29] More than these personal learnings, though, the poet will acquire from her dead lover-father a new script, a new writing of her life. Ending the poem she says she will learn

How cancelled benevolence gains a script

from a departure so in keeping
with its own structure—his denial
of history's death, by the birth of his storm.
(CL, 49)

With "his denial," followed by three prepositional phrases forming a dactylic line of pentameter (the traditional effect of "horses' hooves"), McGuckian concludes the first part of her journey in Captain Lavender. Although, as a moment in her own artistic development, these poems mark a transition from private to public speech, their thrust does not move from the inner to the outer. Rather McGuckian reaches out to exterior spaces, surrounding them with her personal concerns and drawing them in to the center of her imagination. The forty miles which separate her from the sea become the space dividing the living Lazarus from the dead Dives. When father rushes out of his narrow shaft into all the Irelands, the Irelands have been moved into his astral space, not he into theirs. McGuckian's imagination in these poems is consistently transformative, modulating Ulster's discords into her four-hand harmony. History's death, the long, drawn-out life of the hag, is denied "by the birth of his storm," when he and Miss Death make the beast with two backs, or when he becomes the "most foreign and cherished reader" of his daughter's poems.

Writing of McGuckian's earlier poetry, Bedient describes her style as "pseudo-hysterical," meaning that her female sensibility, with "its color, fragrance, and music—all flights from the father's stout book of rules," acts in such a way as to dissolve the boundaries between the sexes, denying the father's existence and reducing it to a magical, female world.[30] Now, in poems that "celebrate" the death of her beloved father, McGuckian finally succeeds in freeing herself from him and can thereby use her "pseudo-hysterical" energies not to dissolve real boundaries into some magic "symbiosis," but rather to reimagine the public space occupied by the father in new, erotic terms. The male lover's rejuvenation of Miss Death, whether she be seen as the Irish hag or the poet herself, becomes the joyful event, the *hieros gamos*, which enables the poet to imagine herself as a new Daedalus, a new shaper of Ireland's soul. It remains, in the second part of *Captain Lavender*, to see whether McGuckian can find any "real space" in which to incarnate this exhilarating but as yet abstract vision.

Whatever noble impulses may have moved McGuckian to undertake teaching political prisoners, her decision to do so constituted an admirable poetic choice. Symbolically the internees mirror her father in contradictory ways. In one sense they continue to enact the father's role: she can love them and flirt with them, but cannot touch them, since they are separated from her by bullet-proof glass ("In the sealed hotel men are handled / as if they were furniture, and passion / exhausts itself at the mouth"[31]). In another, more important sense, her relationship with the prisoners alters her relationship with her father. He gave to her; she gives to them. She desired him; they (she imagines) desire her. Playing "Reverse Cinderella," she is the princess bestowing visitations on abject men. As the poem of this title makes clear, the poet's erotic relationship with both father and prisoners is based on the fact that both are dead, the prisoners no less than the father: "my cleverly dead and vertical audience."[32] "Like him I kissed you once," she says to a prisoner, "but you didn't know."[33] Father didn't know because he was dead; the prisoner didn't know because the kiss was imagined. As the prison replaces the father's coffin, social violence emerges as the Northern Irish state of death, the hag's wretched lodgings. The poet herself, however, no longer plays Miss Death, awaiting the lover's kiss. Already liberated from that death by the father's death, it is she who now flies to the dead, awakening them with kisses of her own.

It is not surprising that, in Part 2, her father buried at last, McGuckian is ready to play, exhibiting new-found powers. How strange that she chooses to play with such serious matter as the culture of terrorism! Resembling Muldoon in her refusal to honor violence with gravity, she differs from him in the precise quality of her own "whimfulness," preferring image-play to wordplay, the fantastic to the sardonic. The title of the opening poem in this section, "Flirting with Saviours," sets the exact tone. Invoking the heavy, pseudo-religious mythology of religious sacrifice and acts of terror, McGuckian suggests a pleasant kind of blasphemy in the thought of flirtation with self-styled messiahs ("worse than saints"). Implicit in her conceit is the idea that it is really she, by flirting, who will do the saving, who will humanize these dogged murderers, teaching them lessons in sensitivity and love. Imagining the draughty prison as a place of extreme sexual tension ("Folded world of fierce under-winds that cried / eye-catching kisses most speakingly"), she represents herself as a sexual good angel, introducing sweetness into a place of deadly fixity:

> In our gentle meetings wrath did not seize them,
> but the elements paused, without greatly moving air,
> a kind of false or treasonable sunlight,

where something frightening that happened was fixed forever.
(*CL*, 53)

No act of charity, one supposes, is without some self-interest, least of all acts of charitable flirtation. In "The Colour Shop," McGuckian gladly acknowledges the solace she found after her father's death in receiving letters from these men ("I was half-dead until the end of April, unable to make sense of my mail . . . I needed your vital transfusions through the post") and visiting them ("For two months I have been permanently / drunk on your orchards . . . I lean / back into you as into a gale"). No small part of her satisfaction comes from the pleasure she imagines herself transmitting to her new-found friends. Expressing with prosaic bluntness this sense of herself as meeting their needs ("You do not possess / what you need to be productive, / but my tenderness that isn't tender / enough floods in by every other post"), McGuckian senses her own sexual pleasure increasing to the extent that she can convert the prisoners from the ice of terrorist dogma to the bloom of her own brand of sensitivity:

Upholding dogma, bringing an ice-axe
to yourself, you made my heart hot . . .

How did you, rough-barked men,
break into flower, with Death behind you
shaking his head, as behind a young couple?
(*CL*, 59)

Playing this ambiguous Victorian role of the lady with the lamp ("as if I had boarded a nineteenth-century / train at a quarter after midnight"), the poet's self appears in two new, eye-catching guises. First as a kind of female Bluebeard, she makes it clear that the men, "men utterly outside themselves, with the taint of women," are her prisoners too.[34] "I still have your head, body, arms, legs, / all in my keeping," she declares with voracity, " . . . I stick to you against your will," suggesting that the way in which she haunts them (as she believes) puts them squarely in her erotic, that is, in her artistic power.[35]
Secondly and in a more complex fashion, McGuckian here

presents herself in a way not unlike Heaney's self-presentation in the bog poems, as a fascinated observer of strangely attractive, lifeless victims of violence. Her enamoured inventories descend from "The Tollund Man" ("bold-breasted and full of seeds"), "The Bog Queen" (you lay entombed in dark cells"), "The Grauballe Man" ("the lilac-black of your furrows, / your ever-rotting heather"), "Punishment" ("you are helpless to advance into the world"), and even "Strange Fruit" ("your deep-set eyes / say no"). Here McGuckian is writing her own *North*. "You retrieve the betrayed North of my soul," she declares to the prisoners, leaving us to ask how it was betrayed and how they retrieved it.[36] The simple answer would be that they themselves, as terrorists, represent the betrayers, but that they retrieve what they had betrayed by their new role as her love-prisoners. One senses here that the North, for a woman whose name and its spelling identify her with an ancient, powerful and sexually active Northern queen, represents an ideal kingdom which she is trying to revive by making love and art. In one of the poems to her dead father, she says, "Now you are my Northerner, / more first than first love," suggesting a prior, erotic state of affairs which precedes one's own earliest erotic history.[37] Her prisoners, like her father, have entered into her North because they "have clearly left the human world, / the bankruptcy of worm-eaten states." Because of their confinement, they have become sexual monks in an ascetic novitiate, "the tiny lung-particles / of the world's virginity," ready for the renewal which she will bring. As the queen, she wages her erotic power in dialectical opposition to the old hostilities of the North:

> You are being painted out,
> but still you choose your side,
> till I arrive almost smiling,
> like a southern death.
> ("The Colour-Shop," [*CL*,] 63)

Whereas in the North of political fact these men are being painted out, rendered invisible, the poet in her color-shop is rediscovering their reds, yellows, and blues. Gazing at his Windeby girl and guardedly declaring, "I almost love you," Heaney attempts to understand his own complicity in a male world of violence. Gazing at her prisoners and unabashedly making verbal love to them, McGuckian offers to save the saviors through the erotic adventure of a southern death, and so to restore the betrayed North to its rightful ruler, Queen Medbh.

The title poem of *Captain Lavender* presents McGuckian's erotic perspective on politics in sharp focus:

> Night-hours. The edge of a fuller moon
> waits among the interlocking patterns
> of a flier's sky.
>
> Sperm names, ovum names, push inside
> each other. We are half-taught
> our real names, from other lives.
>
> Emphasise your eyes. Be my flare-
> path, my uncold begetter,
> my air-minded bird-sense.
> (*CL,* 76)

Sperm is to ovum as captain to lavender, a male and female principle—joined so that the prisoner is feminized and the poet rendered male. Since, in all the erotic poems of this collection, no sexual narrative can be literally accomplished, the sexual union between captain and lavender must be a symbolic one, a symbiosis of names. (One is not quite sure why names are so sexually significant for McGuckian; she diagnoses her frigid mother as suffering from a "mysteriously-suppressed / name-sickness.")[38] "Symbiosis" is the accurate term, since the sperm name exercises no activity upon the ovum name which the ovum name does not also exercise upon the sperm name: they "push inside each other." These are the interlocking patterns of a sky in which the flier, the sexual adventurer, seeks the fuller moon, the new kingdom. While stanza 2 deals with the interlocking patterns (including the classic idea that we are only a half-self until completed by sexual union with our other half),[39] stanza 3 ascends into the sky, imagining the prisoner both as a muse in flight and, as "uncold begetter," a descendant of Shakespeare's only begetter, the muse of his sonnets. (By turning "only" into "uncold," McGuckian reminds herself that her muses are many in number and that they are at once dead—because prisoners—and not dead—because hers.) As "air-minded bird-sense," the prisoner-lover takes on the dead father's role as ideal reader, the speaker of a "trans-sense language."

Perhaps it is no coincidence that McGuckian, having written back to Heaney, now writes back to Muldoon, drawing from her shop of colors the same hue which appears in "Meeting the British." Muldoon's mirroring of lavender in the winter sky and the general's handkerchief, like the meeting of waters under the ice, symbolizes the encounter between native Americans and invading Europeans, a tragic encounter expressed in Muldoon's ironic language. As female, McGuckian replaces the native American speaker. She has the lavender all to herself, but successfully unites this "ovum name" with the "sperm name" of Captain; they push inside each other. This emphasizing, pushing, interlocking, flying, and (best of all) begetting are meant to replace Muldoon's helplessly tragic mirroring. Who ever dreamed that prisons could be such bowers of inspiration?

McGuckian's concluding poem, "Dividing the Political Temperature," confidently replays the major themes of her book, like a symphony's last movement. The three verse paragraphs which appear to be sonnets (but are fourteen, fifteen, and twelve lines long) once more represent love, death and poetic inspiration. In paragraph one, McGuckian images herself and her prison lovers redeeming Yeats's evil stones in the river's bed ("Like two stones in Tuscan water, we intersect / without meeting, without the water breaking") by their erotic, deep-water encounters: "Stars twinkle as if in my womb, / their endless ribbon brushes the weak erection / of dreamlets" (thus the male's sexuality, as well as the female's is evoked as fantasy alone). McGuckian's use of the words "Tuscan" and "Mediterranean" in this poem, and the "Promethean head" of "The Aisling Hat," suggest a striving for classical serenity, the kind of objectivity whose acquisition she celebrated as a victory in "Lines for Thanksgiving." There the two floors of unconscious childhood and conscious maturity are kept separate as the condition for acquiring objectivity. Now objectivity in its turn provides the basis for a new, imagined symbiosis with men from whom the poet is separated by stone walls and iron bars.

Turning from *eros* to *thanatos* in the second paragraph, the poet reflects again on the death-in-life of prison and of the erotic contact of mouths (in speech—her only form of love) which then becomes an erotic form of death ("the wafer of your mouth, the body of / your mouth, your body's mouth, your mouth's / body. So we become a double tomb"). This morbid sexuality leads, in the last stanza, to a reprise of McGuckian's "bog" style, in which the beloved (dead) body is examined with almost febrile curiosity:

> I explore your seabed like a knife embedded
> in a table, you are fragile as paper or fossilised
> seaweed, the tree of your veins like lilies
> caked in silver. One bell produces the effect
> of four.
> (CL, 82–83)

In their paper-like fragility, the prisoners take their place beside the poet's dead father ("I could almost tear your voice, / such a dry, old-paper feel to it / like thawing ice or dry straw")[40] and echo the poet's desire for all-Ireland, one-in-four harmonies. The moon is enlarged and the prisoner-muse provides words which the poet can "finger into [the] small rooms" of poetic stanzas. "Nothing," she concludes, "will now disturb our night."

Confident as this poetry is in its imaginative synthesis, it leaves behind it a trail of questions. Granted that the war is in this book, what exactly does the book do with the war? As one of the most widely acclaimed female poets in Northern Ireland, McGuckian will have realized that mention of the war would focus attention on these poems as a new artistic treatment of the Troubles. What, then, is to be said?

On the face of it, McGuckian appears solidly convinced of her female role as erotic ambassador from the republic of peace to the hard men of the province of violence. "Make love not war," a simplistic creed, is one to which she evidently assents, even though, when she deals with the only two women in Captain Lavender, her mother and Miss Death, the atmosphere brims with hostility. McGuckian is aware of these feelings, although perhaps not sure what to do with them. "I'm finding evil no longer just to be a military thing," she said to Rand Brandes in the context of discussing

Captain Lavender, "but part of myself and to be cleansed only with tremendous help and effort."[41] In her self-representation as a woman, McGuckian implicitly raises autobiographical issues which only a more complete study of her works and life could illuminate. Such a study would clarify her ambiguous passion for her father over against the personal victory over oppression which his death permits her to obtain, her desire to exclude other women from contact with her love-objects (in Part 2, it never occurs to her that the prisoners may be sexually interested in other women than her), and her exclusive preoccupation with men who are unavailable to her as real lovers.

Were McGuckian a male, writing about visits to female prisoners—if "reverse Cinderella" were reversed once again—one wonders how her politically correct readers would welcome such lines as, "I still have your head, body, arms, legs, / all in my keeping." McGuckian enjoys manipulating the objects of her poetic consideration in a way which occasionally borders on the tasteless. As prisoners of a brutally repressive system, these men enjoy none of that victory over the object-world which the poet celebrates in "Lines for Thanksgiving." Although she represents her visits to them as bringing solace and a sense of self-worth, one might ask what more she is doing than enjoying a captive audience, playing with the feelings, as she imagines them, of men whose ability to build their own erotic lives she underestimates. Care for the fate of prisoners and inclusion of them in sensitive writing constitute an important step in redressing the evil done in Ulster. Yet McGuckian's treatment of them, prescinding from their separate identities and subsuming them to her own sexual imperatives, does little to exemplify the humanistic concerns for individual people—as opposed to members of categorized groups—which are so clearly needed today in such violent cultures as Northern Ireland and the United States.

To say this may be to misrepresent McGuckian by taking her too seriously. At the end of Part 1, McGuckian moves Ireland into her own astral space; in Part 2, although she goes to Long Kesh, her fundamental movement of interiorizing the external remains unchanged. Even though she does in fact visit prisoners, McGuckian continues to subsume objective space into the world of her imagination, to treat real selves as "a mirror-script of loanwords I can finger / into small rooms," as she writes in her closing lines. All poets, of course, transform the objective world imaginatively; it is McGuckian's lack of compromise with the realities she chooses to confront—a dead father, jailed terrorists—which constitutes her lapses in taste but also, perhaps, her genius. Kissing her dead father on the lips (an act she compares to a rape) and imaginatively prolonging that rape with bodies in the bondage of the state, McGuckian aggressively challenges the conventional sensibilities of the state's citizens. In her favor one could claim, as she herself does while talking with Ní Dhomhnaill, that loveless families and hateful terrorism contribute to the same weight of evil, and that it is this that she must address in her poetry. If McGuckian's imaginative forms of making love are at all shocking, that may be to emphasize how shocking is the domestic and political war that is in her poems, the war against which she wages her uncompromising resistance of erotic power.

Beyond these possible judgments of political appropriateness or inappropriateness lie the questions of *Captain Lavender*'s success as a work of art. Possibly altering her style to satisfy a demand that all major Northern Irish poets have their say about the Troubles, McGuckian has engaged in a measure of parody, notably of Heaney's bog poems but even of Muldoon, himself a parodist of political poetry. Debunking the high seriousness of the seventies has become a stock in trade for the younger poets writing at mid-life in the eighties and nineties; possibly this too has been McGuckian's fun.

The note she sounds most deeply, though—the passion she paints most vividly—is anger, anger against the men who have denied love, removing themselves in one way or another from commerce with women. Part 2 of *Captain Lavender* is not only McGuckian's *North*; it is also her *Midnight Court*, as she calls up men *already* in custody, already judged, and metes out their punishment, taking them as her sexual slaves. In so doing, she brings a whole male culture to the bar of female, erotic, domestic consciousness. The women of *Lysistrata* thought to end war by refusing to sleep with their warrior-husbands; McGuckian now writes back even to Aristophanes, offering to end war by imaginatively forcing Ireland's warriors to sleep with her. "Let them all sleep with me," we sense her demanding, "let me finger them all into my little rooms." For McGuckian the time for cautious taste and poetical correctness has passed. Let the interlocked sperm and ovum push and push into each other, she declares. Long live Captain Lavender!

9

CONCLUSION

"I confess," says Dillon Johnston, "a partiality toward difficult poetry, poetry written, and required to be read, at the forward edge of language." Writing in the Preface to the second edition of his *Irish Poetry after Joyce*, Johnston continues: "Complexity of thought and our inevitably partial and tentative understanding of the sources of emotion and, even, of consciousness—an understanding that evolves or perhaps just changes with our historical moment—justifies difficult poetry."[1] For my part I confess that I do not share Johnston's partiality so much as his sense of requirement. Reading Northern Irish poets, I often long for more transparent utterance; I would willingly relinquish my seat on the forward edge of language for one that was slightly more comfortable. That is not to be: Northern Irish poets have required me to remain on that edge, and for exactly the reasons which Johnston notes. Their formal and conceptual complexities, and especially their search for the sources of emotion and consciousness, require readers to respond with negative capability, the power of dwelling "in uncertainties, mysteries, doubts, without any irritable reaching after fact and reason."[2] What oft was thought, poets once believed, could always be said better. For the modern poet what has once been felt can only be said by the indirections of lyric art, as it points to some feeling or thought which was unique. "Gleaning the unsaid off the palpable,"[3] the poet requires of the reader some art of touch similar to his own.

Both the writer's and the reader's arts are something other than what much of contemporary critical practice represents them to be, at least in the case of Northern Irish poetry: the encoding and decoding of political statement. Political discourse is by nature partisan; its genre is debate. In the dialectical struggle of thesis against antithesis, one side is always prevailing against another. As political animals we love to take sides. The difficulty about this approach to poetry, at least in the context of Ulster, lies in the futility of side-taking—and here an important characteristic of Northern Irish poetry emerges in stark characters. It is easier to write a political poem when one side is clearly right and the other wrong, than it is to write such a poem when either side is as good or bad as the other. If one thinks of the great "engaged" poets of the century—Mandelstam, Lorca, Celan, Milosz, Neruda, Lowell—it is immediately apparent that they all can lay claim to the rightness of their cause. Sartre maintained that there *could not* be a good Nazi poet, and in fact, there was none. We admire great art that celebrates the unimpeachable rights of human decency over ruthless power, and while we allow and even welcome depictions of the contrary claims, we withhold approval from art which espouses them as its own.

It takes little thought for any impartial observer of Northern Irish politics to realize that whatever the answer to the Troubles may be, it does not lie in the victory of one side over the other. In this dispute over rival cultural and religious claims, there is nothing intrinsically better or worse about either position; no overwhelming majority of population to give anyone a mandate; no longer any glaring injustice to vindicate one morally superior side over another; no side whose vocal extremists do not incessantly demand outcomes utterly abhorrent to their hostile counterparts. If Northern Irish poetry were fundamentally partisan, it would *a priori* be essentially flawed in both style and content. Not surprisingly Northern Irish poetry thus differs fundamentally from much of the great political poetry of this century, even from the Eastern European poetry which has had such a great effect on Seamus Heaney. Whereas the poets of Poland and Russia wrote from high moral ground (ground upon which Heaney would dearly love to stand), Northern Irish poets occupy only that soft terrain "whose wet centre is bottomless."

I do not mean to suggest that criticism of Irish poetry is no better than political rhetoric—although it is ironic that Heaney has so often been taken to task, on the one hand, for not writing more for his "side," and on the other hand (by those of the other side), for doing so in excess. Too much "theoretical narrative," as McDonald calls it, engulfs the subtle details of poetry in ideological masterplots whose driving ideas (viz., violence as an understandable response to the iniquities of colonialism) tend to function as expressions of a political side.

One alternative to such critical writing, for many, lies in ignoring politics altogether and concentrating on felicities of style—always a rewarding task. To do this exclusively, though, is to polarize criticism into opposing camps, only one of which concerns itself with what is indeed the focal point of so much great Northern Irish poetry—politics and social violence. The truth of the matter, as I have tried to show in these pages, is that good lyric poetry does politics, not by making statements—whether openly or cryptically—but by representing a persona struggling with itself in the context of political struggle. In psychoanalytic terms, the lyric poem works through political issues as personal issues.

If the poetry of Seamus Heaney has occupied so many of these pages, it is because Heaney has labored so extensively in this field of self-making, and because he has so often returned to the task of understanding violence as a fact about the self. The tension between Heaney's own literary criticism, which has tended to be Parnassian in its emphasis on art as an alternative to violence, and his poetic practice, which has shown the self implicated in the violence it would overcome, suggests that the imperative of self-knowledge sometimes competes with the imperative of artistic choice as his driving force. It is because of this tension that Heaney's acts of faith, such as that of "Mycenae Lookout" in the purity of poetry's spring, even as it flows up out of blood and dirt, have the power to move and to convince.

As urban Protestants, Longley and Mahon initially exhibit personal impulses different from that of rural Catholic Heaney. Whereas Heaney, in his earliest poetry, celebrates his roots—in every sense of that word—Longley and Mahon wish to distance themselves from what they perceive as a narrow, stultifying milieu. Heaney, like his two contemporaries, will have to distance himself from "home" because it is a violent place, but he will try to do so while maintaining his rootedness—a matter of endless complexities. Longley—in this sense Heaney's opposite—will have nothing to do with any kind of rootedness in a tribal culture; indeed, he does not really belong to such a culture. Only in the latter part of his career, with his masterful versions of Homer, has Longley overcome his tendency to assume the generically innocent stance implicit in a domestic narrative while writing of politics, and has instead employed lyric to embrace and even enfold the violence of epic into a poetic milieu all his own. By successfully imagining himself as vindictive Odysseus, futile Phemios, and (best of all) as Priam, consciously choosing passionate resignation to what must be, Longley has achieved some of the finest working-through of Northern Irish poetry.

Mahon, the adolescent rebel (more so, even, than Muldoon), shakes the dust of Glengormley from his feet as soon as he can leave the place, declaring his emancipation not only from the Belfast suburb, but also from history. Yet Mahon's itinerary, too, is one in which he will retrace his steps, not just to Glengormley (where he will "learn what is meant by home") but beyond, to the very sources of violent emotion and consciousness. Perhaps the most introspective of the poets studied here, the most uncompromisingly critical of himself, Mahon tears away the veils from his liberal humanism, moving backwards and inwards until, in "The Hunt by Night,"he comes as close as any of his contemporaries to the original nightmare of social violence.

Heading the second generation of post-war Northern Irish poets (in a poetic population as dense as this, a generation lasts only a decade or so), Muldoon uses the greatest wit, the most extravagant stratagems, to disengage his self from violence—to be, that is, a nonviolent self. This is because, like Heaney (whom he most resembles in his rural background) and the other Catholic poets, Muldoon's sense of rootedness in tribalism is a deeper one than those of Longley, Mahon, or Paulin. The trajectory of Muldoon's poetry through *Meeting the British* and even *Madoc* is one of disengagement through wit. By disintegrating structures of discourse and continuities of voice, Muldoon withdraws from his Irish milieu (including his professional literary milieu) while exercising on himself a kind of violence, that of self-irony. As the early Muldoon writes out longer and longer narratives of violence, he increases the need for an ever more dramatic escape of the self from that violence—an escape achieved, or so it would seem, by fracturing or even exploding the self into little bits. In Muldoon's recent elegiac writing, however, and in the domestic lyrics considered in this study, the poet, now in his forties, turns from self-irony to self-confrontation.

While the early Muldoon mocks one form of Irish tribalism, the early Paulin inveighs against another. Paulin is the one poet in this group who has seriously studied and written about traditional Irish Protestantism (primarily Presbyterianism), a religion and a culture he both admires and despises. This ambivalence and its attendant rage heighten the interest of Paulin's earlier poetry while weakening its credibility. With "The Caravans on Lüneburg Heath," however, in a movement not unlike Heaney's in *North*, Paulin succeeds in widening his gaze geographically and deepening it historically. Like Heaney he succeeds in coming to greater consciousness of a self which must now confront its own immersions in violence—immersions that, in Paulin's case, take the form of accepting citizenship in a corrupt state. By imagining himself as Simplex, the wise fool with the unbuttoned tongue, Paulin achieves new perspectives, both personal and political: by finding a way to see himself as part of a warring society, he finds a means to stand outside of it.

Carson, not unlike Muldoon, uses an arsenal of verbal dodges to write out the tale of Ulster violence without writing himself into it. Unlike Muldoon, Carson does so on location, never leaving Belfast. In his most recent poetry, though, Carson has begun to work through these dodges. First acknowledging the self as the origin of violence, and then finding a more self-proclaiming voice, he has begun a new process of self-definition.

Like Longley, McGuckian initially deals with violence by having nothing to do with it, surpassing his aloofness by rejecting the topic altogether. Yet with the recent *Captain Lavender*, McGuckian enacts a ritual of liberation from patriarchy, first by writing elegies for her father, and then almost literally embracing violence by constructing herself as the imaginative lover of the terrorists whom she visits in prison.

What one thing can be said about all seven of these poets? Very little, except that each one has had to establish a self defined within the context of a violent world, and therefore to define that self as both belonging to the violence and yet free from it.

One further element has appeared in the work of all seven poets: they have all reconsidered in their recent poetry—their poetic selves. In each case—Heaney's "Mycenae Lookout," Longley's poems from Homer, Mahon's "Hudson Letter," Muldoon's *Prince of the Quotidian*, Paulin's "L," Carson's sonnets, and McGuckian's *Captain Lavender*—we see brilliant attempts at rediscovery. Heaney's new source of water for the blood-stained warrior, Longley's embrace of Achilles' feet, Mahon's expatriate persona, Muldoon's resolutions for the Feast of Saint Brigid, Paulin's unbuttoned tongue, Carson's captains, and McGuckian's sperm names and ovum names—all these constitute ways in which writers are working through violence, not by writing out rhetorical versions of theory, but by writing through dilemmas of the poetic self.

All of these poets have grown up with the Troubles; for those who live in Belfast (Longley, Carson, McGuckian) the conflict endures with depressing immediacy. Fewer violent deaths occur, and the Anglo-Irish accord of 1998 has raised new expectations for Northern Ireland's political future. Yet that disposition can do little to dispel the hostility and rancor which continue to obstruct any true realization of peace. Is there anything to be learned about violence or peace from these poems, anything which could contribute to mutual understanding and the cessation of hostility? For those who think that the conflict is primarily an English-Irish one or who believe that it all depends on what politicians do and say, the answer is of course no; the only thing anyone can do, in that case, is continue to read the newspapers and curse the stupidity of others. For those, on the other hand, who are willing to admit that part of the problem lies in mutual Irish hostilities, there is much to be learned in poems whose single most important lesson is that they have no "lesson"; they embody no masterplot of social thinking, no overarching theory. Poems resist generalizations and in doing so they force us to examine particulars, ultimately ourselves.

It is no doubt dangerously naive to speak or even think of massive changes of heart; we identify such sentiments with the platitudes of weekly collects, to which the faithful reply "Amen" before resuming lives of mutual distrust. "Change of heart" is a pious cliché, we think, and even if religion is not the ultimate cause of the conflict in Ulster (as some maintain), it is hard to see how it could be the ultimate solution. Not all Ulster Protestants hate the Catholic Church, but many fear it, and the ever-dwindling number of Ulster Protestants does nothing to allay those fears. One solution to Northern Irish problems, for better or for worse, may occur with the demise of religion, with an Americanization similar to that already underway in the Republic. As the short-term benefits of a capitalist culture make themselves more and more felt, and as the influence of Christianity is progressively replaced by a tolerant but bland secularity, people may care less and less about the issues that once divided them. Change of heart? Change of income, of living conditions, of neighborhoods, of opportunities—these might be the forces that persuade the Northern Irish to forget (rather than consciously forsake) their old animosities, although perhaps only to acquire new ones.

The term "animosity" derives from the word for soul, and it is with the soul that lyric poetry concerns itself. The best poems of social violence, again and again, return to examination of the soul. Heaney's sentry keeping watch, Longley's Odysseus seeking sleep, Mahon's sensitive child hidden somewhere in a courtyard at Delft, Muldoon's Joe Ward with his hazel whip, Paulin's wee Tommy with his collection of aesthetic trash, Carson's cyclist under interrogation, McGuckian's erotic internee—all are souls, awakening to discover their confinement in a mode of being they recognize as violent. The artistic ways in which these souls work through their identities—ways proper only to lyric poetry—constitute lyric's political action. To work through such a poem is to work through being-in-violence. One does not expect a universal change of heart in Ulster and certainly not one to be brought about by teaching people in the millions to read Heaney and Muldoon, Longley and McGuckian. Not even the most fantastic of collects ever prayed for that. Those who do read these poets, though, may profitably do so by avoiding doctrinaire generalizations and engaging instead in the labor to which poems call us, the understanding of one particular soul's being. The work of reading poetry, carried out in this way, constitutes a model for the more general work of understanding personal being which is in turn the necessary prelude to any authentic process of peace. A good poem, as Mahon once said, is a paradigm of good politics.[4]

This book has not been about politics or peace processes; it has been about poems. In reading these poems, I have tried to break down the wall between so-called aesthetic and political approaches to poetic art. I have assumed that the fullest emphasis on poetry as poetry would lead to the deepest and most accurate estimate of poetry's political value. Lyric poetry presents selves outside of a social context; politics represents selves within a community. It is the tension between the personal and the social which constitutes the particular interest of political lyric poetry. The Northern Irish poem of social violence succeeds as poetry when it becomes the poem of consciousness, the poem of the soul. Over the last thirty years, the still unending crisis has exercised an increasingly urgent pressure on poets to write of self-understanding, a pressure to which they have responded with a deepening power of art. Those who read and study these poems arrive, sooner or later, at the point of sharing with the poems that sense of urgency, that need for a personal response. As Picasso said, the war is in them. Readers who engage in that war—poetry's quarrel with itself—will have encountered great lyric art.

NOTES

Introduction

1. "Clonfeacle," *Mules and Early Poems*, 20.

2. "Easter, 1916," Yeats, *Collected Poems*, 181.

3. McDonald, *Mistaken Identities*, 64.

4. Heaney, *The Government of the Tongue*, xxi, adapted from *Place and Displacement*, 5–6. Interestingly Heaney has dropped the sentence cited second ("The idea of poetry . . .") from his reworking of the Grasmere Lecture in *The Government of the Tongue*.

5. I take this view of the political value of form to be that adopted by Edna Longley in her book appropriately entitled *The Living Stream* (although she certainly does not derive this view from Heaney).

6. *Place and Displacement*, 7.

7. Vendler, *The Breaking of Style*, 1.

8. Bew and Gillespie, *Northern Ireland*, 57. In 1969 in Northern Ireland there were 13 deaths arising from the Troubles; in 1970, 25; in 1971, 174. The only year to exceed the 1972 level of carnage was 1980, with 760 deaths.

9. "A Trifle," *Quoof*, 30. (The Tannoy: P.A. system.) McDonald offers a good reading of this poem in *Mistaken Identities*, 68–69.

10. "Afterwords: Poetry, Schools and Belfast Revisited," *Fortnight* (spring 1986); reprinted in *How's the Poetry Going?*, 93.

11. By making a strategic allusion to Girard in the context of discussing Seamus Deane, Michael Allen (*Seamus Heaney: New Casebooks*, 5) gives the misleading impression that Deane is a proponent of Girard. I look upon Girardian thought as an antidote to Deane's politicization of violence.

12. Girard, *Violence and the Sacred*, 82.

13. Ibid., 146.

14. Ibid., 159.
15. Ibid., 18.
16. 2 Samuel 11.1.
17. Girard, 53.
18. Yeats, "Remorse for Intemperate Speech," *Collected Poems*, 255.
19. Heaney, "Whatever You Say, Say Nothing," *North*, 51–54; *Opened Ground: Selected Poems (SP)*, 124.
20. Girard, 143.
21. Samuel Beckett, *Waiting for Godot*, 49.
22. Cairns, *Caught in Crossfire*, 117.
23. Heaney, "Summer 1969," *North*, 63–64; *SP*, 132.
24. Cairns, 111.
25. Terry Eagleton, *Heathcliff and the Great Hunger*, 19 f.
26. Fionnuala O Connor, *In Search of a State*, 47.
27. Bernstein, *Bitter Carnival*, 108.
28. Judt, "The New Old Nationalism," and Ignatieff, *Blood and Belonging*, 213–49 (where Ignatieff considers Protestant traditions of hostility in Northern Ireland).
29. Kee, *The Green Flag*, 23–27, 41–45.
30. Ibid., 456.
31. Smyth, "Weasels in a Hole," 149–50.
32. Terry Eagleton, *Nationalism, Colonialism, and Literature*, 37.
33. Jim Smyth, "Weasels in a Hole." For an extended treatment see Herr, "A State o' Chassis."
34. Heinz Kohut, *Self Psychology and the Humanities*, 9.
35. Kohut, 10; Layton and Schapiro, *Narcissism and the Text*, 6.
36. Kohut, 63 f.
37. Ibid., 91 f.
38. Ibid., 19 f.
39. Cairns, 121; O'Connor, 195.
40. Heaney, dedicatory verse to *Wintering Out*, 5; reprinted with alterations as part of "Whatever You Say, Say Nothing" in *North*, 54 and *SP*, 125.
41. Heaney, *Crediting Poetry*, 53.

2. Seamus Heaney

1. Heaney, *Crediting Poetry*, 30–31; *SP*, 423.
2. Heaney, *The Government of the Tongue*, 107.
3. Heaney, *North*, 31; *SP*, 112-13.
4. *The Government of the Tongue*, 110, 113, 116.
5. Heaney, *Preoccupations*, 56.

6. Ibid., 30.

7. Feldman, *Formations of Violence,* 53.

8. Brandes, "The Dismembering Muse," 183–86, provides a detailed analysis of the metonymic substitution of finger and thumb for working body in "Digging."

9. *Death of a Naturalist,* 4, 44; *SP,* 5, 14.

10. "Feeling into Words," *Preoccupations,* 41–60.

11. The complete text of *Stations* (see bibliography) remains in pamphlet form. For a useful overview of this little-known work, see Hart, "Crossing Divisions and Differences."

12. "Punishment," *North,* 31; *SP,* 113.

13. Cairns, *Caught in Crossfire,* 165.

14. Kinahan, "Artists on Art," 411: "I felt that I'd come through something at the end of *North;* there was some kind of appeasement in me."

15. Hufstader, "Coming to Consciousness."

16. See above, ch. 2, n. 5.

17. Glob, *The Bog People.*

18. "Coming to Consciousness," 62 f. So Corcoran (*Seamus Heaney*): "[T]he connection which actually supplies [the poem's] emotional sustenance is not that between Ireland and Jutland, but that between the Tollund man and Heaney himself."

19. Longley, "'North': 'Inner Emigré' or 'Artful Voyeur'?" 66, 74 f.

20. Frazer, *The Golden Bough,* 309, 340, 440.

21. Freud, *Totem and Taboo,* ch. 4.

22. Girard, *Violence and the Sacred,* 18.

23. Jung, *Symbols of Transformation,* 306, 389, 408–35.

24. Carson, "Escaped from the Massacre?" 184; O'Brien, "A slow north-east wind," 404; Longley "'North,'" 77; Lloyd, *Anomalous States,* 31–33.

25. O'Malley, *The Uncivil Wars,* 313.

26. See Hart, *Seamus Heaney,* 96.

27. Haffenden, *Viewpoints,* 67.

28. Longley, "'North,'" 79.

29. Deane (*Celtic Revivals,* 180) also notices Heaney's "uneasiness" in surrounding the woman of the Roum fen with myth.

30. Heaney, *Preoccupations,* 56–57.

31. Eagleton, *Nationalism, Colonialism and Literature,* 27.

32. *North,* 56; *SP,* 126.

33. McDiarmid, "Heaney and the Politics of the Classroom."

34. *North,* 66–67; *SP,* 135-36.

35. *Stations,* 14.

36. Heaney, *The Redress of Poetry*, 203.

37. Heaney's remarks, see Walsh, "Bard of Hope and Harp."

38. Kinahan, 411. See also O'Donoghue (*Seamus Heaney*, 3, 6, with notes 6, 15, 16) for further references to this much-noted change in style and voice.

39. Stevenson, "The Recognition of the Savage God," 320–21.

40. Deane, *Celtic Revivals*, 182.

41. McDonald (*Mistaken Identities*, 52–58) further analyzes the complexities of "The Toome Road."

42. "The Strand at Lough Beg," *Field Work*, 17–18; *SP*, 145-46. "Station Island 8," *Station Island*, 83; *SP*, 239.

43. *The Redress of Poetry*, 187.

44. Interview with June Beisch, *Literary Review*, 168.

45. Vendler, *The Given and the Made*, 17.

46. Deane, *Celtic Revivals*, 183.

47. Goldensohn ("The Recantation of Beauty") believes that McCartney's view of "The Strand at Lough Beg" is also Heaney's.

48. "Whatever You Say Say Nothing," *North*, 52; lines omitted from *SP*.

49. Heaney, "Envies and Identifications," 19.

50. "Feeling into Words," *Preoccupations*, 56.

51. Vendler, "On Three Poems," 66.

52. "Alphabets," *The Haw Lantern*, 1–3; *SP*, 269-71. Desmond ("Allegories of Dual Citizenship") points out how "Alphabets" traces the poet's evolution from a pre-conscious to a distantly intellectual frame of mind while also, in characteristic Heaneyan fashion, reversing that direction with "a movement downward into the pre-reflective world of intuition."

53. In July, 1995, after ten months of calm, intense rioting broke out in West Belfast when John Major released Lee Clegg, a British army officer serving a life sentence for the murder in 1990 of Karen Reilly, one of several teenagers riding in a stolen car. The youths had apparently decided to run the army roadblock; the driver and this one passenger were killed. Many British saw Clegg as a good soldier doing his duty in a dangerous situation; Irish nationalists, as their actions showed, had a different opinion.

54. "From the Frontier of Writing," *Haw Lantern*, 6; *SP*, 274. When Joyce has finished his admonitions to Heaney the pilgrim, "The shower broke in a cloudburst, the tarmac / fumed and sizzled. As he moved off quickly / the downpour loosed its screens round his straight walk." *Station Island*, 94; *SP*, 246.

55. "Clearances," *The Haw Lantern*, 30–31; *SP*, 289-90.

56. "From the Canton of Expectation," *The Haw Lantern*, 46–47; *SP*, 295-96. See Vendler,"On Three Poems," 67–68.

57. "The Impact of Translation," *The Government of the Tongue*, 39: "For these poets, the mood of writing is the indicative mood and for that reason they constitute a shadow-challenge to poets who dwell in the conditional, the indeterminate mood."

58. "Squarings," viii, *Seeing Things*, 62; *SP*, 338; see above, ch. 2, n. 36.

59. As Desmond ("Allegories of Dual Citizenship") points out, allegory is the right mode in which to examine ideologies, as opposed to events or patterns of behavior.

60. "Fosterling," *Seeing Things*, 52; *SP*, 331.

61. "So walk on air against your better judgment" ("The Gravel Walks," *The Spirit Level*, 49; *SP*, 396), cited in *Crediting Poetry*, 9–10; *SP*, 416-17. See Jenkins, "Walking on Air."

62. *Crediting Poetry*, 9; *SP*, 417.

63. "Keeping Going," *The Spirit Level*, 13–16; *SP*, 375-77.

64. Heaney. "The Flight Path," *P-N Review*, 31.

65. Fennell, *Whatever You Say*.

66. Aeschylus, *Agamemnon*, 6.

67. "Personal Helicon," *Death of a Naturalist*, 44; *SP*, 14; "Mossbawn: Omphalos," *Preoccupations*, 17–21.

68. Camus, *The Fall*, 145.

69. Bernard-Donals, "Governing the Tongue," 75. A dissenting and therefore welcome voice is that of Anne Stevenson ("The Peace Within Understanding," 133), when she speaks of Heaney's "personality and self-conflicts [as] . . . central to his perceptions," including his perceptions of culture and politics.

3. Michael Longley

1. Longley, *Tupenny Stung*, 72.
2. Healy, "Interview," 559.
3. *Tupenny Stung*, 25.
4. Ibid.
5. Healy, "Interview," 560.
6. McDonald, *Mistaken Identities*, 133.
7. Mahon, "Afterlives," *Selected Poems*, 51.
8. Healy, "Interview," 559.
9. Longley, "Letter to Seamus Heaney," *Poems*, 84.
10. "The Neolithic Light," 103.
11. *Tupenny Stung*, 15–29.
12. Healy, "Interview," 560.
13. *Tupenny Stung*, 18.

14. Ibid.
15. "Master of Ceremonies," *Poems*, 133.
16. "The Third Light," *Poems*, 200.
17. *Poems*, 148.
18. "The Ice-cream Man," *Gorse Fires*, 49 (see McDiarmid, "Packing for the Rest of Your Life").
19. Bayley, "Irishness," 16.
20. *Tupenny Stung*, 73.
21. "To Derek Mahon," "Letters," *Poems*, 82.
22. "Letters," *Poems*, 76.
23. "The War Poets," *Poems*, 168. For children as victims of war, see "Kindertotenlieder," *Poems*, 87.
24. Epigraph to "An Exploded View (1968–1972)," *Poems*, 59.
25. *Wintering Out*; see the altered version in *North*, 54, Heaney, *SP*, 125.
26. See McDiarmid, "Packing for the Rest of Your Life."
27. "The Tollund Man," Heaney, *SP* 62; "Tollund," *SP*, 410. See above, pp. 83-84.
28. "Homecoming," *Gorse Fires*, 13; *Poems*, 30 f; cf. Healey, "Interview," 560: "a cheeky retelling of the myth."
29. Thus the translation of Fitzgerald, *Odyssey*, 244.
30. "Eurycleia," *Gorse Fires*, 31.
31. Fitzgerald, *Odyssey*, 380.
32. *Gorse Fires*, 35.
33. "Argos," *Gorse Fires*, 45; cf. Fitzgerald, *Odyssey*, 331–32.
34. "The Butchers," *Gorse Fires*, 51; cf. Fitzgerald, *Odyssey*, 434–37, 457; McDiarmid, "Packing for the Rest of Your Life."
35. Ricks, *The Force of Poetry*, 55.
36. "The Camp-fires," *The Ghost Orchid*, 37; cf. Fitzgerald, *Iliad*, 198–99.
37. "The Helmet," "The Parting," *The Ghost Orchid*, 38; cf. Fitzgerald, *Iliad*, 157.
38. "Ceasefire," *The Ghost Orchid*, 39; cf. Fitzgerald, *Iliad*, 584 (stanza 1), 587 (stanza 2), 588 (stanza 3), 583 (stanza 4).
39. "The Scales," *The Ghost Orchid*, 43 (after *Iliad*, bk. 8); cf. Fitzgerald, *Iliad*, 183–84.
40. "Phemios & Medon," *The Ghost Orchid*, 44 (after *Odyssey*, bk. 22); cf. Fitzgerald, *Odyssey*, 431–33.
41. "A Bed of Leaves," *The Ghost Orchid*, 33 (after *Odyssey*, bk. 5); cf. Fitzgerald, *Odyssey*, 106-7.
42. "The Oar," *The Ghost Orchid*, 58 (after *Odyssey*, bks. 11 and 23); cf. Fitzgerald, *Odyssey*, 201, 449–50.
43. "Detour," "Ghetto," *Gorse Fires*, 7, 40–43.

4. Derek Mahon

1. "The Small Rain," *The Hudson Letter*, 59. "The Last of the Fire Kings," *The Snow Party*; *Selected Poems* (*SP*), 58.
2. This conflict is clearly conceptualized in Dawe, "'Icon and Lares'" 218–19.
3. Seamus Heaney, *The Place of Writing*, 48.
4. Kathleen Shields, "Derek Mahon's Poetry of Belonging," 68.
5. "Glengormley," *Night Crossing*; *SP*, 12.
6. "An Unborn Child," *Night Crossing*; *SP*, 22 f.
7. "Homecoming," *Lives*, 1; *SP*, 26.
8. "Lives," *Lives*, 14–16; *SP*, 36–38.
9. MacNeice, "Autumn Journal 16," in *Selected Poems*, 61–64. See my "MacNeice's Critic Jailed in the Mind."
10. "Beyond Howth Head," *Lives*, 33–38; *SP*, 44–49.
11. "Afterlives," *The Snow Party*, 1; *SP*, 50–51. In *SP*, Mahon has removed the word "cunts" and substituted for it the word "twits." For more on this move, see below, n. 14.
12. René Girard, *Violence and the Sacred*, 253, 255.
13. "Rathlin," *The Hunt by Night*, 16; *SP*, 122.
14. In an interview, Mahon explains the revision as having been made when he realized that the word was offensive to women: "I discussed it with friends, and it became apparent that it was an unacceptable use of the word" (McDiarmid, "Q. and A. with Derek Mahon," 28).
15. Bernstein, *Bitter Carnival*.
16. Paulin ("A Terminal Ironist: Derek Mahon," *Writing to the Moment*, 83) provocatively suggests that "perhaps [Mahon's] aestheticism has parallels with the dedicated fanaticism of a hunger-striker whose absolute personal pride must also involve a complete rejection of personal identity."
17. Heaney, *Place and Displacement*, 9.
18. MacDiarmid, "Q. and A. with Derek Mahon," 28. "A Garage in Co. Cork," *The Hunt by Night*, 55; *SP*, 150–51.
19. "The Hunt by Night," *The Hunt by Night*, 30–31; *SP*, 174–75.
20. See Kohut's counter-arguments to the theory of violence as a drive in "Thoughts on Narcissism and Narcissistic Rage," *Self Psychology and the Humanities*, 124–60.
21. *The Hudson Letter*, 59.
22. Ibid., 28
23. Ibid., 27, 33, 37.
24. *The Yellow Book*, 27.
25. Ibid.
26. *The Hudson Letter*, 61.

27. Ibid., 55.
28. *The Yellow Book*, 51.

5. Paul Muldoon

1. Burt, "Paul Muldoon's Binocular Vision," 95.
2. E. Longley, *The Living Stream*, 263, 200.
3. Ibid., 226.
4. Wills, *Improprieties*, ch. 1, 6 ("Paul Muldoon: Dubious Origins"), esp. pp. 194–97. Wills's sympathetic account of Muldoon resonates with Lloyd's unsympathetic account of Heaney, whom Lloyd charges with adherence to doctrines of origins and identity.
5. For example, Patrick Williams, "Spare that Tree."
6. *The Living Stream*, 52.
7. Ibid., 54–55: "If Paul Muldoon . . . postpones statement, this deferral dramatises epistemological scruple rather than psychic irresolution or ever-ramifying narratives."
8. Keller, "Interview," 12: "Because that's the way to read: if you just start, and you go and you don't worry too much about what Nietzsche has to do with that damn horse, or whatever."
9. McDonald, "Paul Muldoon and the Windlass-Men," in *Mistaken Identities*, 145–88.
10. "The Centaurs," *Mules*, 44. The *OED*, uncertain about the etymology of this familiar word, sends us back to Liddell and Scott, who derive it from *kenteo*, the verb to prick, goad, or spur. "Centaur" originally referred to a warlike race in Thessaly, and only later acquired its more poetic meaning. Might Spenser's gentle knight, because he was pricking, be imagined as a centaur, a human whose agency is dehumanized or divided between his horse and his lance?
11. "Vaquero," "Mules," *Mules*, 55, 82; *SP*, 34.
12. Shakespeare, Sonnet 65; Heaney, *Preoccupations*, 57.
13. "Truce," *Why Brownlee Left*, 26; *SP*, 55. So the first line of "History" (*Why Brownlee Left*, 27): "Where and when exactly did we first have sex?"
14. "Something of a Departure," *Why Brownlee Left*, 30; cf. Caesar, *Taking It Like a Man*.
15. Haffenden, *Viewpoints*, 136.
16. Stokes, *Revue Celtique*, 10:91.
17. Ricks, 3.62–66; Muldoon "dreadful" in Haffenden, 139.
18. Bernstein, 100.
19. *Quoof*, 6.
20. Tell, "Paul Muldoon's America," 71.

21. "Gathering Mushrooms," *Quoof*, 7–9; *SP*, 71–73.
22. Kendall, *Paul Muldoon*, 102.
23. To take but one instance, the lines "A pony fouled the hard-packed snow / with her glib cairn" ("Yggdrasill," *Quoof*, 26–27; *SP*, 80–81) satirize Heaney's preoccupation with the events of 1798 ("glib") and with poetic archaeology ("cairn") in *North* (and that title is itself satirized by Muldoon's monosyllabic *Quoof—his North*).
24. McCurry, 95–97.
25. See McCurry, 99, for further allusions to Frost.
26. "The Sightseers," *Quoof*, 15; *SP*, 76.
27. "Ontario," "The Coney," "The Toe-Tag," "7, Middagh Street," *Meeting the British*, 9, 11–12, 37, 44; *SP*, 113, 115–16, 132 ("The Toe-Tag" is omitted from *SP*).
28. "Christo's," *Meeting the British*, 28; *SP*, 122. Conversely, in "7, Middagh Street," Muldoon imagines all Ireland covered with a strip of linen—this one starting in Ulster, of course, and extending all the way to the south.
29. O'Toole, "Island of Saints and Silicon."
30. Fiacc's *The Wearing of the Black* is a well-known collection of Northern Irish protest poetry.
31. "The Lass of Aughrim," *Meeting the British*, 23; "The Wishbone," *Meeting the British*, 22; *SP*, 120. Hofmann, "The Recent Generations at Their Song."
32. "7, Middagh Street," *Meeting the British*, 43–62; *SP*, 131–53. Muldoon's source for this poem is Carpenter, *W. H. Auden*, an account which should be corrected by the more sober version of Davenport-Hines, *Auden* ch. 7. Stanfield gives invaluable added context in "Another Side of Paul Muldoon."
33. Yet see Muldoon's claim in an interview of 1994 that "poetry must make something happen" (Kendall, 125).
34. Cited in Stallworthy, *Louis MacNeice*, 288.
35. *The Living Stream*, 51.
36. *Madoc*, 257.
37. Wills, "*The Annals of Chile*," 137.
38. *The Prince of the Quotidian*, 16, 17. Liturgically curious readers may wonder how it is that the Twelfth Night poem is the sixth in the sequence and the Epiphany poem the seventh, since those two occasions fall on January 5th and 6th. The first of the pair is about "last night's fun," and the next one is about "today." Hence, one slight interruption in the illusion of "dailiness."
39. Lowell, *Selected Poems*, 89–90.
40. Wills, "Paul Muldoon," 119.

41. See Wills, "Paul Muldoon," 121–24 for an analysis of "Brazil" (*The Annals of Chile*, 6–7), in which O'Higgins appears with his Annals of Chile.

42. McDonald, "Paul Muldoon and the Windlass Men," 156–57 and 187–88, where he concludes, "for an artist like Muldoon, identity is just one of the available certainties (or determinisms) which originality has to understand and get beyond and which, in the inevitable embraces of poetic form, real poetry steels itself against."

6. Tom Paulin

1. "Donegal Diary." For a good introduction both to Paulin's politics and his poetry, see Andrews, "Tom Paulin."

2. "Northern Protestant Oratory."

3. *Ireland and the English Crisis*, 13.

4. "Presbyterian Study," *Liberty Tree*, 49; *Selected Poems*, (*SP*), 62.

5. *Ireland and the English Crisis*, 192.

6. "Inishkeel Parish Church," "Ballywaire," *State of Justice*, 15, 32 ("Ballywaire," *SP*, 14).

7. O'Malley, *The Uncivil Wars*, 146. Paulin attacks Conor Cruise O'Brien's argument (in *States of Ireland*) that Sophocles' Creon represents sensible politics over against Antigone's fanaticism (*Ireland and the English Crisis*; reprinted in *Writing to the Moment*, 1–17).

8. See below, p. 226.

9. Auden, *Selected Poems*, 86–89.

10. "Disaffection and Defection: W. H. Auden," *Ireland and the English Crisis*, 85–91.

11. Ibid., 94.

12. *The Strange Museum*, 42–47.

13. *Liberty Tree*, 21–27; *SP*, 46–51.

14. See, for instance, Paulin's essay on Elizabeth Bishop in *Minotaur*, 190–204.

15. So Paulin's reflections on the word "jack" in *Minotaur*, 117–20.

16. Andrews, ("Tom Paulin," 337) aptly characterizes Paulin's ambivalent criticisms of the Protestant mentality, although from a somewhat different point of view.

17. *Liberty Tree*, 32.

18. "Paisley's Progress," *Writing to the Moment*, 48–50.

19. Hughes, "Q. and A. with Tom Paulin."

20. Dawe, review of *Liberty Tree*.

21. "Northern Protestant Oratory," 314, 318.

22. See Bruce, *The Red Hand*, esp. the final chapter 11, which con-

cludes by focusing on the ultimate Protestant nightmare, expulsion from the United Kingdom (p. 290). Michael Ignatieff's more journalistic account of such fears in *Blood and Belonging* is not inconsistent with Bruce's.

23. "Images": "Manichean Geography II" *Liberty Tree*, 44; "can't pray": "'What Kind of Formation are B Specials?,'" *Liberty Tree*, 15.

24. *Fivemiletown*, 46 f.; *SP*, 97 f.

25. Ibid., 67.

26. "Loyal as Ever," *Walking a Line*, 75 f.

27. *Fivemiletown*, 6–8, 30 f., 48 f.; *SP*, 76–78, 90 f., 99 f.

28. *Walking a Line*, 71, 72.

29. *Fivemiletown*, 55–66; *SP*, 102–13, where the spelling of the German place-name has been corrected.

30. See Paulin's notes (*Fivemiletown*, 67; *SP*, 120) and Clair Wills's amplifications in *Improprieties*, 148–55.

31. Heaney, "The Seed Cutters," *North* xi; *SP*, 94.

32. See above, p. 146.

33. Bruce, *The Red Hand*, 288.

7. Ciarán Carson

1. "Belfast Confetti," *The Irish for No*, 31.

2. "Zulu," *Opera et Cetera*, 92.

3. For such a list of pubs, see Carson, *Last Night's Fun*, 101, 138 f.

4. Carson, "Against Oblivion," 115 f.

5. Williams, *Selected Poems*, 84.

6. "Against Oblivion," 116.

7. Williams, *Selected Poems*, 108; *The Irish for No*, 11.

8. Interview with Rand Brandes, 79, 83.

9. On Carson's version of the sonnet, see interview with Rand Brandes, 84.

10. *The Irish for No*, 34, 36, 37.

11. Ibid., 39.

12. Corcoran, "One Step Forward," 224 f.

13. *The Irish for No*, 49–50.

14. Interview with Rand Brandes, 87.

15. "Ambition" and "Jawbox," *Belfast Confetti*, 27–31, 90–94.

16. Interview with Rand Brandes, 88.

17. Ibid., 87.

18. "Second Language," *First Language*, 10–13.

19. *First Language*, 27 f. When he was a child, Carson's father would take him every twelfth of July to watch the Orangemen's parade (*Last Night's Fun*, 182).

20. Hofmann and Lasdun, *After Ovid.*
21. Ovid, *Metamorphoses*, 13:604–16. Here is the original:

> atra favilla volat glomerataque corpus in unum
> densetur faciemque capit sumitque calorem
> atque animam ex igni (levitas sua praebuit alas)
> et primo similis volucri, mox vera volucris
> insonuit pennis, pariter sonuere sorores
> innumerae, quibus est eadem natalis origo,
> terque rogum lustrant, et consonus exit in auras
> ter plangor, quarto seducunt castra volatu;
> tum duo diversa populi de parte feroces
> bella gerunt rostrisque et aduncis unguibus iras
> exercent alasque adversaque pectora lassant,
> inferiaeque cadunt cineri cognata sepulto
> corpora seque viro forti meminere creatas.
> (Loeb 2.270–72)

22. "Schoolboys and Idlers of Pompeii," *Belfast Confetti*, 53; cf. "The Exiles' Club," *The Irish for No*, 45.
23. *First Language*, 69.
24. Carson, "Escaped from the Massacre?" Corcoran gives a helpful account of Carson's position in "One Step Forward," 213–16. My analysis of "Punishment" (ch. 2) implicitly opposes Carson's reading.
25. "Letters from the Alphabet," *Opera et Cetera*, 11–36.
26. *Opera et Cetera*, 17.
27. O: *Opera et Cetera*, 25 and Muldoon, "The Sightseers," *Quoof*, 15 (*SP*, 76); "the Twelfth" and zigzags: *Opera et Cetera*, 36 and Muldoon, *The Prince of the Quotidian*, 16.
28. "I," *Opera et Cetera*, 19.
29. Muldoon, "Armageddon, Armageddon," *Mules and Early Poems*, 87 (*SP*, 39).
30. Dillon Johnston of the Wake Forest University Press was most kind to let me read *The Twelfth of Never* in manuscript.
31. "Sayers, or, Both Saw Wonders," *Twelfth of Never*, 49. Although Carson attributes the dream to Peig Sayers, the best-known version may be found in O'Sullivan, *Twenty Years A-Growing*, 13–15. Thanks to Joseph Lennon for sharing his knowledge of the Blasket Island library.

8. Medbh McGuckian

1. McGuckian, "Comhra," 590.

2. Peggy O'Brien, "Reading Medbh McGuckian," 239.

3. Haberstroh, *Women Creating Women*, 157; Wills, *Improprieties*, 163; McCurry, "'Our Lady dispossessed.'"

4. Sailer, "An Interview," 121.

5. Docherty "Initiations," Haberstroh, 125; Wills, 187.

6. Wills, 191.

7. Sailer, 113.

8. "Comhra," 600.

9. Wills, 162–66.

10. "Venus and the Sun," *Venus and the Rain*, 9; "Venus and the Sea," *Marconi's Cottage*, 81.

11. Bedient, "The Crabbed Genius of Belfast," 196.

12. Sailer, 117.

13. Ibid., 116.

14. Ibid., 123 f; cf. "Comhra," 589, and McCracken, "An Attitude of Compassion," 21: "Irish was imposed on me in such a patriarchial way I still have a horror of it, like the chill I feel in the Gaeltacht areas."

15. O'Brien, 241.

16. Beer, "Medbh McGuckian's Poetry," 197.

17. Cf. Sailer, 115: "[Heaney's] poetry is full of tension and responsibility . . . and that's the way I am too. I must not let my mother down or my children down."

18. Bedient, 201.

19. Bedient, 202–5; note his interesting comparison of McGuckian to Gertrude Stein.

20. For details concerning McGuckian's prison teaching, see Brandes, "An Interview," and McDiarmid, "Ritual Encounters," 11.

21. See Kohut's theory of the self in ch. 1.

22. "Comhra," 584 f.

23. "Porcelain Bells," *Captain Lavender (CL)*, 14–19.

24. "The Appropriate Moment," *CL*, 20–25.

25. "Comhra," 605.

26. See my discussion of *Station Island*, ch. 2.

27. *CL*, 39 f.

28. "Comhra," 608.

29. "The Appropriate Moment," *CL*, 23.

30. Bedient, 207, using Kristeva's theory of "The True-Real."

31. "The Over Mother," *CL*, 64.

32. Ibid., 64.

33. "Reverse Cinderella," *CL*, 54 f.

34. "Flirting with Saviours," *CL*, 53.

35. "The Colour Shop," *CL*, 58–63.

36. "The Colour Shop."
37. "Black Note Study," *CL*, 39.
38. "Porcelain Bells," *CL*, 16.
39. So Aristophanes' speech in Plato's *Symposium*.
40. "The Appropriate Moment," *CL*, 20.
41. Brandes, "An Interview," 56.

Conclusion

1. Johnston, *Irish Poetry*, xvii.
2. John Keats to George and Tom Keats, December 1817.
3. Heaney, "The Harvest Bow," *Field Work*, 58; *SP*, 170.
4. Mahon, "Poetry in Northern Ireland."

BIBLIOGRAPHY

Aeschylus. *Agamemnon.* Trans. Richard Lattimore. Vol. 1 of *Greek Tragedies,* ed. David Grene and Richard Lattimore. Chicago and London: Univ. of Chicago Press, 1960.

Allen, Michael, ed. *Seamus Heaney: New Casebooks.* New York: St. Martin's Press, 1997.

Andrews, Elmer. "Tom Paulin: Underground Resistance Fighter." In *Poetry in Contemporary Irish Literature,* ed. Michael Kenneally, 329–43. Gerrards Cross, England: Colin Smythe, 1995.

Auden, W. H. *Selected Poems.* Ed. Edward Mendelson. New York: Vintage International, 1989.

Batten, Guinn. "Ciarán Carson's Parturient Partition: The 'Crack' in MacNeice's 'More than Glass.'" *The Southern Review* 31, no. 3 (summer 1995): 436–56.

Bayley, John. "Irishness." Review of *Gorse Fires,* by Michael Longley. *New York Review of Books* 39 (25 June 1992): 14–16.

Beckett, Samuel. *Waiting for Godot.* 1954. Reprint. New York: Grove Press, 1982.

Bedient, Calvin. "The Crabbed Genius of Belfast." *Parnassus* 16 no. 1 (1990): 195–216.

Beer, Ann. "Medbh McGuckian's Poetry: Maternal Thinking and a Politics of Peace." *Canadian Journal of Irish Studies* 18 no. 1 (July 1992): 192–203.

Bernard-Donals, Michael. "Governing the Tongue: Seamus Heaney's (A)Political Aesthetic." *Canadian Journal of Irish Studies* 20 no. 2 (December 1994): 75–88.

Bernstein, Michael André. *Bitter Carnival: Ressentiment and the Abject Hero.* Princeton: Princeton Univ. Press, 1992.

Bew, Paul, and Gordon Gillespie. *Northern Ireland: A Chronology of the Troubles 1968–1993.* Dublin: Gill and Macmillan, 1993.

Brandes, Rand. "The Dismembering Muse: Seamus Heaney, Ciarán Carson, and Kenneth Burke's 'Four Master Tropes.'" In *Irishness and (Post)Modernism*, ed. John Rickard (Lewisburg, Pa.: Bucknell Univ. Press, 1994), 177–94.

———. "An Interview with Medbh McGuckian." *The Chattahoochee Review* 16, no. 3 (spring 1996): 56–65.

Bruce, Steve. *The Red Hand: Protestant Paramilitaries in Northern Ireland*, Oxford and New York: Oxford Univ. Press, 1992.

Burt, Stephen. "Paul Muldoon's Binocular Vision." *Harvard Review* 7 (fall 1994): 95–107.

Caesar, Adrian. *Taking It Like a Man: Suffering, Sexuality and the War Poets: Brooke, Sassoon, Owen, Graves*. Manchester and New York: Manchester Univ. Press, 1993.

Cairns, Ed. *Caught in Crossfire: Children and the Northern Ireland Conflict*. Syracuse, N.Y.: Syracuse Univ. Press, 1987.

Camus, Albert. *The Fall*. 1957. Trans. Justin O'Brien. Reprint, New York: Alfred A. Knopf, 1982.

Carson, Ciarán. "Escaped From the Massacre?" *The Honest Ulsterman* 50 (winter 1975): 184–85.

———. *The New Estate*. Winston-Salem, N.C.: Wake Forest Univ. Press, 1976.

———. *The Irish for No*. Winston-Salem, N.C.: Wake Forest Univ. Press, 1987.

———. *Belfast Confetti*. Winston-Salem, N.C.: Wake Forest Univ. Press, 1989.

———. "Against Oblivion." Review of *Selected Poems*, by C.K. Williams. *The Irish Review* 6 (spring 1989): 113–16.

———. "Ciarán Carson Interviewed by Rand Brandes.." *The Irish Review* 8 (spring 1990): 77–90.

———. *First Language*. Winston-Salem, N.C.: Wake Forest Univ. Press, 1994.

———. *Opera et Cetera*, Oldcastle, Ireland: Gallery Press, 1996.

———. *Last Night's Fun: A Book About Irish Traditional Music*. London: Jonathan Cape, 1996.

———. *The Twelfth of Never*. Winston-Salem, N.C.: Wake Forest Univ. Press, 1998.

Chandler, Raymond. *The Big Sleep*. 1939. Reprint, New York: Ballantine, 1975.

Corcoran, Neil. *Seamus Heaney*. London and Boston: Faber and Faber, 1986.

———. "One Step Forward, Two Steps Back: Ciaran Carson's *The Irish for No*." In *The Chosen Ground: Essays on the Contemporary Po-*

etry of Northern Ireland, ed. Neil Corcoran, 213–36. Chester Springs, Pa.: Dufour, 1992.

Curtis, Tony, ed. *The Art of Seamus Heaney*. 1985. Reprint, Chester Springs, Pa.: Dufour, 1994.

Dawe, Gerald. Review of *Liberty Tree*, by Tom Paulin. *Irish Literary Supplement* 3, no. 1 (summer 1984): 29.

———. "'Icon and Lares': Derek Mahon and Michael Longley." In *Across a Roaring Hill: The Protestant Imagination in Modern Ireland*, ed. Gerald Dawe and Edna Longley, 218–35. Belfast and Dover, N.H.: Blackstaff Press, 1985.

———. *How's the Poetry Going? Literary Politics and Ireland Today*. Belfast: Lagan Press, 1991.

Deane, Seamus. *Celtic Revivals: Essays in Modern Irish Literature*. London and Boston: Faber and Faber, 1985.

Desmond, John F. "Allegories of Dual Citizenship: Seamus Heaney's *The Haw Lantern*." *Eire-Ireland* 27, no. 2 (1992): 60–75.

Docherty, Thomas. "Initiations, Tempers, Seductions: Postmodern McGuckian." In *The Chosen Ground*, ed. Neil Corcoran, 191–210. Chester Springs, Pa.: Dufour, 1992.

Dunn, Douglas, ed. *Two Decades of Irish Writing*. Chester Springs, Pa.: Dufour, 1975.

Eagleton, Terry. *Heathcliff and the Great Hunger: Studies in Irish Culture*. London and New York: Verso, 1995.

Eagleton, Terry, et al. *Nationalism, Colonialism, and Literature*. 1988. Reprint, Minneapolis: Univ. of Minnesota Press, 1990.

Farrell, J.G., *Troubles*. New York: Knopf, 1971.

Feldman, Allen. *Formations of Violence: The Narrative of the Body and Political Terror in Northern Ireland*. Chicago and London: Univ. of Chicago Press, 1991.

Fennell, Desmond. *Whatever You Say, Say Nothing: Why Seamus Heaney is No. 1*. Dublin: ELO Publications, 1991.

Fiacc, Padraic, ed. *The Wearing of the Black: An Anthology of Contemporary Ulster Poetry*. Belfast: Blackstaff Press, 1974.

Fitzgerald, Robert, ed. and trans. *The Odyssey*, by Homer. Garden City, NY: Anchor Press, 1961.

———. *The Iliad*, by Homer. Garden City, NY: Anchor Press, 1974.

Frazer, James. *The Golden Bough*. Abridged edition. New York: Macmillan, 1953.

Freud, Sigmund. *Totem and Taboo*. London: Routledge and Kegan Paul, 1950.

Friel, Brian. *Translations*. Boston: Faber and Faber, 1981.

Girard, René. *Violence and the Sacred.* Baltimore MD: Johns Hopkins Univ. Press, 1972.

Glob, P.V. *The Bog People: Iron Age Man Preserved.* London: Faber and Faber, 1969.

Goldensohn, Barry. "The Recantation of Beauty." *Salmagundi* 80 (fall 1988): 76–82.

Grass, Günter. *The Meeting at Telgte.* Trans. Ralph Mannheim. London: Secker and Warburg, 1981.

Haberstroh, Patricia Boyle. *Women Creating Women: Contemporary Irish Women Poets.* Syracuse, NY: Syracuse Univ. Press, 1996.

Haffenden, John. *Viewpoints: Poets in Conversation.* London: Faber and Faber, 1981.

Hart, Henry. "Crossing Divisions and Differences: Seamus Heaney's Prose Poems." *The Southern Review* 25 (1989): 803–21.

———. *Seamus Heaney: Poet of Contrary Progressions.* Syracuse, NY: Syracuse Univ. Press, 1992.

Heaney, Seamus. *Death of a Naturalist.* London and Boston: Faber and Faber, 1966.

———. *Door into the Dark.* London and Boston: Faber and Faber, 1969.

———. *Wintering Out.* New York: Oxford Univ. Press, 1973.

———. *North.* London and Boston: Faber and Faber, 1975.

———. *Stations.* Belfast: Ulsterman Publications, 1975.

———. *Preoccupations: Selected Prose 1968–1978.* New York: Farrar, Straus and Giroux, 1980.

———. "Artists on Art: An Interview with Seamus Heaney." By Frank Kinahan. *Critical Inquiry* 8, no. 3 (1982).

———. *Place and Displacement: Recent Poetry of Northern Ireland.* Pete Laver Memorial Lecture. Delivered at Grasmere (2 August 1984). Grasmere: Trustees of Dove Cottage, 1985.

———. *Station Island.* New York: Farrar, Straus and Giroux, 1985.

———. "Envies and Identifications: Dante and the Modern Poet." *Irish University. Review* 15, no. 1 (1985): 5–19.

———. *The Haw Lantern.* New York: Farrar, Straus and Giroux, 1987.

———. *The Government of the Tongue: Selected Prose 1978–1987.* New York: Farrar, Straus and Giroux, 1988.

———. *Field Work.* New York: Farrar, Straus and Giroux, 1979.

———. *The Place of Writing,* Atlanta: Scholars Press, 1989.

———. *Seeing Things.* New York: Farrar, Straus and Giroux, 1991.

———. "The Flight Path." *P-N Review* 19 no. 2 (November/December 1992): 31–32.

———. *The Redress of Poetry.* New York: Farrar, Straus and Giroux, 1995.

————. *Crediting Poetry: The Nobel Lecture*. New York: Farrar, Straus and Giroux, 1995.

————. *The Spirit Level*. New York: Farrar, Straus and Giroux, 1996.

————. *Opened Ground: Selected Poems 1966-1996*. New York: Farrar, Straus and Giroux, 1998.

Herr, Cheryl. "A State o' Chassis: Mobile Capital, Ireland, and the Question of Postmodernity." In *Irishness and (Post)Modernism*, ed. John S. Rickard, 195–229. Lewisburg, Pa.: Bucknell Univ. Press, 1994.

Hofmann, Michael. "The Recent Generations at Their Song." *Times Literary Supplement* (30 May 1986): 585–86.

Hofmann, Michael, and James Lasdun, ed.. *After Ovid: New Metamorphoses*. New York: Noonday Press, 1994.

Hufstader, Jonathan. "MacNeice's Critic Jailed in the Mind." *Essays in Criticism* 44, no. 3 (July 1994): 190–212.

————. "Coming to Consciousness by Jumping in Graves: Heaney's Bog Poems and the Politics of *North*." *Irish University Review* 26, no.1 (1996): 61–74.

Ignatieff, Michael. "Northern Ireland." In *Blood and Belonging: Journeys into the New Nationalism*, 213–49. New York: Farrar, Straus and Giroux, 1993.

Jenkins, Nicholas. "Walking on Air." Review of *The Spirit Level*, by Seamus Heaney. *Times Literary Supplement* (5 July 1996): 10–12.

Johnston, Dillon. *Irish Poetry After Joyce*. 2d. ed. Syracuse, N.Y.: Syracuse Univ. Press, 1997.

Judt, Tony. "The New Old Nationalism." *New York Review of Books* 41, no.10 (26 May 1994): 44–51.

Jung, C. G. *Symbols of Transformation*. London: Routledge and Kegan Paul, 1956.

Kee, Robert. *The Green Flag: The Turbulent History of the Irish National Movement*. New York: Delacorte Press, 1972.

Kendall, Tim. *Paul Muldoon*. Chester Springs, Pa.: Dufour, 1996.

Kohut, Heinz. *Self Psychology and the Humanities: Reflections on a New Psychoanalytic Approach*. Ed. by Charles B. Strozier. New York: W.W. Norton, 1985.

Layton, Lynne, and Barbara Ann Schapiro, ed. *Narcissism and the Text: Studies in Literature and the Psychology of the Self*. New York and London: New York Univ. Press, 1986.

Lloyd, David. "'Pap for the Dispossessed': Seamus Heaney and the Poetics of Identity." In *Anomalous States*, 13–40. Durham, N.C.: Duke Univ. Press, 1993.

Longley, Edna. "'North': 'Inner Emigré' or 'Artful Voyeur'?" In Curtis, 65–95.

———. *The Living Stream: Literature and Revisionism in Ireland.* Newcastle-upon-Tyne: Bloodaxe Books, 1994.

Longley, Michael. "The Neolithic Light: A Note on the Irishness of Louis MacNeice." In Dunn, 98–104.

———. *Poems 1963–1983.* Winston-Salem, N.C.: Wake Forest Univ. Press, 1987.

———. *Gorse Fires.* Winston-Salem, N.C.: Wake Forest Univ. Press, 1991.

———. *Tupenny Stung: Autobiographical Chapters.* Belfast: Lagan Press, 1994.

———. "An Interview with Michael Longley." By Dermot Healy. *The Southern Review* 31, no. 3 (summer 1995): 557–61.

———. *The Ghost Orchid.* Winston-Salem, N.C.: Wake Forest Univ. Press, 1996.

Lowell, Robert. *Selected Poems.* 1976. New York: Noonday Press, 1991.

MacNeice, Louis. *Selected Poems of Louis MacNeice.* Winston-Salem, N.C.: Wake Forest Univ. Press, 1990.

Mahon, Derek. *Night Crossing.* Oxford: Oxford Univ. Press, 1968.

———. "Poetry in Northern Ireland." *Twentieth-Century Studies* 4 (November 1970): 89–93.

———. *Lives.* London: Oxford Univ. Press, 1972.

———. *The Snow Party.* London: Oxford Univ. Press, 1975.

———. *Poems 1962–1978.* Oxford: Oxford Univ. Press, 1979.

———. *The Hunt by Night.* Winston-Salem, N.C.: Wake Forest Univ. Press, 1983.

———. "Q and A with Derik Mahon." By Lucy McDiarmid. *Irish Literary Supplement* 10, no. 2 (fall 1991): 27–28.

———. *Selected Poems.* New York: Penguin, 1992.

———. *The Hudson Letter.* Winston-Salem, N.C.: Wake Forest Univ. Press. 1996.

———. *The Yellow Book.* Winston-Salem, N.C.: Wake Forest Univ. Press, 1998.

McCurry, Jacqueline. "'Our Lady, dispossessed': Female Ulster Poets and Sexual Politics." *Colby Quarterly* 27, no.1 (1991): 4–8.

———. "'S'crap': Colonialism Indicted in the Poetry of Paul Muldoon." *Eire-Ireland* 27, no. 3 (1992): 92–109.

McDiarmid, Lucy. "Joyce, Heaney, and 'the subject people stuff.'" In *James Joyce and His Contemporaries*, ed. Diana A. Ben-Merre and Maureen Murphy, 131–39. Westport, Conn.: Greenwood Press, 1989.

———. "Packing for the Rest of Your Life." Review of *Gorse Fires*, by Michael Longley. *New York Times Book Review* (2 August 1992): 12.

———. "Heaney and the Politics of the Classroom." In *Critical Essays on*

Seamus Heaney, ed. Robert F. Garratt, 110–20. New York: G.K. Hall, 1995.

————. "Ritual Encounters" Review of *Captain Lavender,* by Medbh McGuckian. *New York Times Book Review* (14 April 1996): 11.

McDonald, Peter. *Mistaken Identities: Poetry and Northern Ireland.* Oxford: Clarendon Press, 1997.

McGuckian, Medbh. *Venus and the Rain.* Oxford: Oxford Univ. Press, 1984.

————. "The Light of the Penurious Moon." Review of *Goddess on the Mervue Bus,* by Rita Ann Higgins. *The Honest Ulsterman* 85 (1988): 60–62.

————. "An Attitude of Compassion: Q. and A. with Medbh McGuckian." By Kathleen McCracken. *Irish Literary Supplement* 9, no. 2 (fall 1990): 20–21.

————. *Marconi's Cottage.* 1991. Winston-Salem, N.C.: Wake Forest Univ. Press, 1992.

————. "An Interview with Medbh McGuckian." By Susan Shaw Sailer. *Michigan Quarterly Review* 32 (winter 1993): 111–27.

————. *Captain Lavender.* 1994. Winston-Salem, N.C.: Wake Forest Univ. Press, 1995

————. "An Interview with Medbh McGuckian." By Rand Brandes. *The Chattahoochee Review* 16, no. 3 (spring 1996): 56–65.

McGuckian, Medbh, with Nuala Ní Dhomhnaill and Laura O'Connor. "Comhra." *The Southern Review* 31, no. 3 (summer 1995): 581–614.

Muldoon, Paul. *Mules and Early Poems.* 1977. Winston-Salem, N.C.: Wake Forest Univ. Press, 1985.

————. *Why Brownlee Left.* Winston-Salem, N.C.: Wake Forest Univ. Press, 1980.

————. *Quoof.* Winston-Salem, N.C.: Wake Forest Univ. Press, 1983.

————. *Meeting the British.* Winston-Salem, N.C.: Wake Forest Univ. Press, 1987.

————. *Madoc: A Mystery.* 1990. New York: Farrar, Straus and Giroux, 1991.

————. *Selected Poems 1968–1986.* New York: Noonday Press, 1993.

————. *The Annals of Chile.* New York: Farrar, Straus and Giroux, 1994.

————. "An Interview with Paul Muldoon." By Lynn Keller. *Contemporary Literature* 35, no. 1 (1994): 1–29.

————. *The Prince of the Quotidian.* Winston-Salem, N.C.: Wake Forest Univ. Press, 1994.

————. *New Selected Poems 1968–1994.* London and Boston: Faber and Faber, 1996.

O'Brien, Conor Cruise. *States of Ireland*. 1972. New York: Pantheon Books, 1974.

———. "A slow north-east wind." *The Listener* (25 September 1975): 404.

O'Brien, Peggy. "Reading Medbh McGuckian: Admiring What We Cannot Understand." *Colby Quarterly* 28, no. 4 (1992): 239–50.

O'Connor, Fionnuala. *In Search of a State: Catholics in Northern Ireland*. Belfast: Blackstaff Press, 1993.

O'Donoghue, Bernard. *Seamus Heaney and the Language of Poetry*. New York and London: Harvester Wheatsheaf, 1994.

O'Malley, Padraig. *The Uncivil Wars: Ireland Today*. Boston: Beacon Press, 1983.

O'Sullivan, Maurice. *Twenty Years A-Growing*. Trans. Moya Llewlyn Davis and George Thomson. Oxford: Oxford Univ. Press, 1953.

O'Toole, Fintan. "Island of Saints and Silicon: Literature and Social Change in Contemporary Ireland." In *Cultural Contexts and Literary Idioms in Contemporary Irish Literature*, ed. Michael Kenneally, 11–35. Gerrards Cross, England: Colin Smythe, 1988.

Ovid. *Metapmorphoses*. Trans. Frank Justus Miller. Loeb Classical Library. 2 vols. Cambridge: Harvard Univ. Press, 1916.

Paulin, Tom. *A State of Justice*. London: Faber and Faber, 1977.

———. *The Strange Museum*. London and Boston: Faber and Faber, 1980

———. *Liberty Tree*. London and Boston: Faber and Faber, 1983.

———. *Ireland and the English Crisis*. Newcastle-upon-Tyne: Bloodaxe Books, 1984.

———. *Fivemiletown.* London and Boston: Faber and Faber, 1987.

———. "Q. and A. with Tom Paulin." By Eamonn Hughes. *Irish Literary Supplement* 7, no. 2 (fall 1988): 31–32.

———. "Northern Protestant Oratory and Writing." In *The Field Day Anthology of Irish Writing 3*, ed. Seamus Deane. Derry: Field Day Publications, 1991: 314-18.

———. *Minotaur*. Cambridge: Harvard Univ. Press, 1992.

———. "Donegal Diary." *London Review of Books* 14 (8 October 1992): 21.

———. *Selected Poems 1972-1990*. London and Boston: Faber and Faber, 1993.

———. *Walking a Line*. London and Boston: Faber and Faber, 1994.

———. *Writing to the Moment: Selected Critical Essays 1980-1996*. London: Faber and Faber, 1996.

———, ed. *The Faber Book of Political Verse*. London and Boston: Faber and Faber: 1986.

Ricks, Christopher. *The Poems of Tennyson*. Vol. 3. Berkeley and Los Angeles: Univ. of California Press, 1987.

———. *The Force of Poetry*. Oxford: Clarendon Press, 1984
Schnitzler, Arthur. *La Ronde*. Trans. F. and J. Marcus. London: Methuen, 1982.
Shields, Kathleen. "Derek Mahon's Poetry of Belonging." *Irish University Review* 24, no.1 (spring/summer 1994): 67–79.
Smyth, Jim. "Weasels in a Hole: Ideologies of the Irish Conflict." In *The Irish Terrorism Experience*, by Yonah Alexander and Alan O'Day, 135–53. Aldershot, England and Brookfield, Vt.: Dartmouth, 1991.
Stallworthy, Jon. *Louis MacNeice*. New York and London: W.W. Norton, 1995.
Stanfield, Paul. "Another Side of Paul Muldoon." *North Dakota Quarterly* 57, no. 1 (1989): 129–43.
Stevens, Wallace. *The Necessary Angel: Essays on Reality and the Imagination*. New York: Random House, 1951.
Stevenson, Anne. "The Recognition of the Savage God: Poetry in Britain Today." *New England Review* 2 (1979): 315–26.
———. "The Peace Within Understanding: Looking at *Preoccupations*." in Curtis, 132–37.
Stokes, Whitley. "The Voyage of Mael Duin." In *Revue Celtique*, 9 (1888): 447–95, 10 (1889): 50–95. Paris: F. Vieweg, 1888–89.
Tell, Carol. "Utopia in the New World: Paul Muldoon's America." *Bullán: An Irish Studies Journal* 2, no.2 (winter/spring 1996): 67–82.
Vendler, Helen. "On Three Poems by Seamus Heaney." *Salmagundi* 80 (fall 1988): 66–70.
———. *The Breaking of Style*. Cambridge and London: Harvard Univ. Press, 1995.
———. *The Given and the Made: Strategies of Poetic Redefinition*. Cambridge: Harvard Univ. Press, 1995.
Walsh, John. "Bard of Hope and Harp." *The Sunday Times* (London: 7 October 1990): sect. 7, pp. 2–4.
Williams, C.K. *Selected Poems*. New York: Farrar, Straus and Giroux, 1994.
Williams, Patrick. "Spare That Tree." *The Honest Ulsterman* 86 (1989): 49–52.
Wills, Clair. *Improprieties: Politics and Sexuality in Northern Irish Poetry*. Oxford: Clarendon Press, 1993.
———. "Paul Muldoon: *The Annals of Chile*." In *Poetry and Politics*, ed. Kate Flint, 111–39. *Essays and Studies*, n.s., 49. Cambridge, UK: D.S. Brewer, 1996.
Wilson, Willam A. "Paul Muldoon and the Politics of Sexual Difference." *Contemporary Literature* 28, no. 3 (fall 1987): 317–31.
Yeats, William Butler. *The Collected Poems of W. B. Yeats*. Ed. Richard J. Finneran. New York: Macmillan, 1983.

INDEX

www.ingramcontent.com/pod-product-compliance
Lightning Source LLC
Chambersburg PA
CBHW020406100426
42812CB00001B/215